Drama from Ibsen to Brecht

Criticism
Culture and Society
Towards 2000
Communications
Television: Technology and Cultural Form
Drama in Performance
Modern Tragedy
The English Novel from Dickens to Lawrence
Orwell
The Long Revolution
Politics and Letters (interviews)
Problems in Materialism and Culture
(selected essays)
The Country and the City

Fiction
Border Country
Second Generation
The Fight for Manod
The Volunteers
Loyalties
People of the Black Mountains I The Beginning
People of the Black Mountains II The Eggs of the Eagle

Drama from Ibsen to Brecht

RAYMOND WILLIAMS

The Hogarth Press
LONDON

Published in 1993 by
The Hogarth Press
20 Vauxhall Bridge Road
London SW1V 2SA

First published by
Chatto & Windus Ltd 1952

Third Impression 1996

A CIP catalogue record for this book is
available from the British Library.

ISBN 0 7012 1028 1

Printed and bound in Great Britain by
Mackays of Chatham PLC, Chatham, Kent

Cover design and illustration by Jeff Fisher

Foreword

THIS book began as a revision and extension of *Drama from Ibsen to Eliot*, which was written between eighteen and twenty years ago. It can now more properly be described as based on that earlier book, since about half of it is new, either in new essays or in revision of sections of earlier chapters. It is also substantially rearranged, to give a different though still related critical emphasis. I have drawn on essays published at intervals between 1947 and 1961, in *Politics and Letters, Essays in Criticism, The Highway, The Critical Quarterly, Encore, World Theatre, The Twentieth Century* and in *Preface to Film* and *Drama in Performance,* but these also have been revised, in a developing general view. New essays in the present volume include those on Lorca, Büchner, O'Casey and Recent Drama, and the Conclusion. The main argument of the book was given in lectures in Cambridge between 1965 and 1967.

As it now stands, *Drama from Ibsen to Brecht* can be read as one of a set of three books on drama: a critical study which goes with the analysis of ideas in *Modern Tragedy* (1966) and with the special study of the relations between the written and the acted play in *Drama in Performance* (revised edition, 1968).

R. W.

Acknowledgements

Thanks are due to the copyright owners and publishers of the following works for permission to quote from them in this volume: W. H. Auden and Christopher Isherwood, *The Dog Beneath the Skin*, *Ascent of F.6* and *On the Frontier:* the authors and Faber and Faber Ltd., London; Random House Inc., New York. T. S. Eliot, *Collected Plays* and *Collected Poems:* Mrs. Valerie Eliot and Faber and Faber Ltd., London. From *Collected Poems 1909—1962*, copyright, 1936, by Harcourt, Brace & World Inc.; copyright © 1963, 1964, by T. S. Eliot. From *Murder in the Cathedral*, copyright 1935 by Harcourt, Brace & World, Inc.; renewed copyright 1963, by T. S. Eliot. From *The Family Reunion*, copyright 1939 by T. S. Eliot; renewed 1967 by Esme Valerie Eliot. From *The Cocktail Party*, copyright 1950 by T. S. Eliot. Reprinted by permission of the publishers. Christopher Fry, *Venus Observed* and *The Lady's Not For Burning:* the author and Oxford University Press, London and New York. The Plays and Prefaces of George Bernard Shaw: the Public Trustee and the Society of Authors. W. B. Yeats, *Collected Plays:* M. B. Yeats and Macmillan & Co. Ltd., London; copyright 1934 by The Macmillan Company of New York; renewed 1952 by The Macmillan Company.

Contents

FOREWORD

INTRODUCTION · · · · · 11

1. A GENERATION OF MASTERS:
   1. Henrik Ibsen · · · · 33
   2. August Strindberg · · · 75
   3. Anton Chekhov · · · · 101

2. THE IRISH DRAMATISTS:
   1. W. B. Yeats · · · · · 115
   2. J. M. Synge · · · · · 129
   3. Joyce's *Exiles* · · · · 141
   4. Sean O'Casey · · · · 147

3. ALTERNATIVE ACTIONS,
   ALTERNATIVE CONVENTIONS:
   1. Luigi Pirandello · · · 157
   2. Federico Garcia Lorca · · 167
   3. T. S. Eliot · · · · · 174
   4. Poets and Plays, 1935-1955:
      (*a*) Auden and Isherwood · 199
      (*b*) Christopher Fry · · 206
      (*c*) Dylan Thomas's Play for Voices · 211
   5. Plays and Myths:
      (*a*) O'Neill: *Mourning Becomes Electra* · 222
      (*b*) Giraudoux: *Electre* · 223
      (*c*) Sartre: *The Flies* · 225
      (*d*) Anouilh: *Antigone* · 227

4. SOCIAL AND POLITICAL DRAMA:
   1. Georg Büchner: a retrospect · 233
   2. Hauptmann: *The Weavers* · 240
   3. Bernard Shaw · · · · 244
   4. D. H. Lawrence: *The Widowing of Mrs Holroyd* · 257
   5. Toller: *Hoppla!* · · · 261
   6. Arthur Miller · · · · 267
   7. Bertolt Brecht · · · · 277

CONTENTS

5. RECENT DRAMA:
   1. Six Plays:
      Long Day's Journey into Night: O'Neill   293
      The Lesson: Ionesco   296
      Waiting for Godot: Beckett   299
      The Balcony: Genet   305
      The Fire Raisers: Frisch   308
      The Physicists: Dürrenmatt   312
   2. Four Plays:
      Marching Song: John Whiting   316
      Look Back in Anger: John Osborne   318
      The Birthday Party: Harold Pinter   322
      Serjeant Musgrave's Dance: John Arden   325

CONCLUSION   331

NOTES   348

INDEX   349

INTRODUCTION

(i)

IT is now just over a hundred years since Ibsen published *Brand* and *Peer Gynt*. The drama written and performed in the intervening century is by any standards a major achievement. There has never been, in any comparable period, so much innovation and experiment, and this has been related, throughout, to a growth and crisis of civilization which the drama has embodied, in some remarkable ways. For much of the century, and especially for its first seventy-five years, the play was overshadowed by the novel, as a major form. Yet it is still impossible to understand modern literature without the work of at least eight or ten dramatists, or, in another way of putting it, without a critical understanding of dramatic naturalism, dramatic expressionism, and certain related movements. At the same time, since Ibsen published *Brand* and *Peer Gynt* rather than submitting them for performance, there has been a very complicated and difficult relationship between literature and the theatre: a relationship which at times obscures and always affects the achievement of this drama. The crisis of performance, and of the theatre as an institution, itself affected by new means of dramatic performance in the cinema, in radio and in television, has made the continuing problem of dramatic form especially acute. Certain orthodoxies have hardened, and many damaging gaps have appeared and continued to appear. But also, through and within these difficulties, the energy and power of dramatic imagination have continued to create some of the essential consciousness of our world. Without this drama, we would all lack a dimension, and to study and understand it is then a major critical challenge.

When I came back from the army in Germany in 1945, I began to read Ibsen and went on until, for a few necessary weeks, I had in effect to be stopped, to complete the rest of a university course. I went back to the plays as soon as I could, and have been reading and seeing them performed, with the many hundreds of plays that succeeded them, as a central interest ever since. The studies in this book come mainly from that experience: I was moved by the plays before I even saw the critical problems. Yet as the experience continued, and as I read accounts of it, I began to see problems which are still, I think, of the utmost difficulty: problems which eventually resolve themselves as theoretical, and which raise many radical questions in fields other than drama. I have gone on working on these, and in fact almost continuously redefining them and changing the emphasis of my conclusions. I suppose and hope that this will go on, but in the last few years a phase, at least, of that original impulse has seemed to complete itself, and I have felt able to get back again to trying to draw together, in a general account, its particular experiences.

The studies of plays and dramatists which make up most of this book have been written and revised over some twenty years. They stand, in that sense, on their own: as direct and considered responses. But as I have become more aware of the theoretical problems, and of their changing definitions, I have used certain ideas and a certain vocabulary which run through the particular studies. It is then necessary, in this brief introduction, to describe these directly, for the convenience of the reader, though the general critical position to which, in the end, they relate is best reserved for the conclusion, in which there are the many readings of plays to draw on. What I need mainly to explain here, in relation to a critical question of dramatic form, is what I mean by "convention" and by a "structure of feeling".

(ii)

In a period as various, as experimental and innovating, as modern drama, the problem of conventions is necessarily central. Indeed the idea of convention is basic to any understanding of drama as a form. Yet it is always a difficult idea, and especially so in a period in which certain basic conventions are changing. It is worth, then, looking at the idea of convention directly.

The ordinary dictionary senses provide a useful starting point. Thus, *convention* is the act of coming together; an assembly; union; coalition, specially of representatives for some definite purpose; an agreement previous to a definitive treaty; a custom. *Conventional*, similarly, is: settled by stipulation or by tacit consent; as sanctioned and currently accepted by tacit agreement; agreeable to accepted standards; agreeable to contract. As we go through these senses, and through those of the various derived words, we see an ambiguity which is important both because it indicates a possible source of confusion, which requires discussion, and because it indicates an important point of entry for an analysis of the place of conventions in drama.

INTRODUCTION

The possible source of confusion is the fact that convention covers both *tacit consent* and *accepted standards*, and it is easy to see that the latter has often been understood as a set of formal rules. Thus it is common in adverse comment to say that a work is just *conventional; a familiar routine; old stuff; the mixture as before.* We use the word in the same way in adverse comment on people and actions that we find dull, or narrow, or old-fashioned, or unoriginal, or unreceptive to new ideas. To explain the development of *conventional* as an adverse term in criticism would take us a long way into cultural history. Briefly, it is the result of the controversy that was part of the Romantic Movement, in which emphasis fell heavily on the right of the artist to disregard, where he saw fit, the rules that had been laid down by others for the practice of his art. This was an essential emphasis, from which we have all gained. But it is then unfortunate that *convention* and *conventional* should have been so heavily compromised. For an artist only leaves one convention to follow or create another; this is the whole basis of his communication. Yet when *conventional* carries the implications of old fas' ned, o narrow, and when it is used, a   is now ofter used, as an easy and adverse contrast with *realistic*, it is difficult to use the word at all without being misunderstood. Yet it is possible to think of the ambiguity as the means of an important insight; and it is this that must now be discussed.

Convention, as we have seen, covers *tacit agreement* as well as *accepted standards*. In the actual practice of drama, the convention, in any particular case, is simply the terms upon which author, performers and audience agree to meet, so that the performance may be carried on. *Agree to meet*, of course, is by no means always a formal or definite process; much more usually, in any art, the consent is largely customary, and often indeed it is virtually unconscious.

This can be seen most readily in the conventions of our own period. In a naturalist play, for example, the convention is that the speech and action should as closely as possible appear to be those of everyday life; but few who watch such a play realize that this is a convention: to the majority it is merely "what a play is like", "the sort of thing a play tries to do". Yet it is, in fact, a very remarkable convention that actors should represent people behaving naturally, and usually privately, before a large audience, while all the time maintaining the illusion that, as characters, these persons are unaware of the audience's presence. The most desperate private confession, or the most dangerous conspiracy, can be played out on the stage, in full view and hearing of a thousand people; yet it will not occur to either actors or audience that thi' is in any way strange, because all, by the tacit consent of custom, have accepted this procedure as a convention.

Not long ago, and perhaps still in some places, it was, however, thought very strange if a character spoke in soliloquy, whether this was thought of as "thinking aloud" or "directly addressing the audience". The complaint would be that this was "artificial", or "not true to life", or even "undramatic"; yet it is surely as natural, and as "true to life", when one is on a stage before a thousand people, to address them, as to pretend to carry on as if they were not there. As for the soliloquy being "undramatic", this is the kind of conditional statement, elevated into a "law", which continually confuses dramatic criticism, since it is well known that the soliloquy, in many periods, has been a normally accepted part of dramatic method.

The various conventions which have been used in drama are too numerous to list. A two-day battle between considerable armies may be represented by the passage of a few soldiers in a few brief scenes, lasting no more than a few minutes. The last hour of a man's life may be played out on a stage, with deliberate emphasis on the tension of waiting, and yet the dramatic "hour" may be no more than five minutes. A man may walk on to a bare stage, hung only by curtains, and from what he says we will agree that he is in Gloucestershire, or Illyria, or on a mythical island. He can be a Roman general, speaking to us in English blank verse from a wooden step that we take to be a rostrum in the Forum of Rome. He can be a ghost or a devil or a god, and yet drink, answer the telephone, or be wound off the stage by a crane. He can put on a grey cloak, and we will agree that he is invisible, though we continue to see him. He can speak to us, acknowledging his most private thoughts, and we will agree that while we hear him from the back of the gallery, he cannot be heard by a man a few feet away from him, or waiting in the wings. With the slightest of indications, we will accept that the events we watch are occurring four thousand years before Christ, or in the Middle Ages, or in a flat in Paris on the same night as we are in a theatre in Manchester. The men whom we see as inspector and criminal we recognize as having seen last week as criminal and inspector, or as butler and peer, but we do not challenge them. We accept; we agree; these are the conventions.

Since the use of conventions of this kind is inherent in the process of drama, it is at first surprising that when the basic convention, that of acted performance, has been accepted, there should be any difficulty in particular instances. Yet it is obvious that such difficulties are acute and recurrent. We will agree that the person on the stage is a spirit, and that, quite unaware of our intent presence, he is talking privately to his widow, in the year 1827; but if the widow attempts to address us in an aside, we can become uneasy. We will agree that a murderer may hide behind a door (where we can still see him), and that he may look down, with an expression of agony, at his hands (which we at once agree are stained with innocent blood); but if he should come forward to the front of the stage, and in twenty lines of verse, or in recitative or song, or in dance, express (if more fully and more intensely) the same emotion, we at once, or many of us, feel uneasy, and are likely to say afterwards that it was "unreal". We may even, if we accept the phrases of the journeymen, conclude that the play was highbrow, or surrealist, or pretentious (an increasingly common word among those whose professional and doubtful pretension is normality). And while we may be able to reject this kind of simplification, we shall not be able, merely by taking thought, to create an alternative convention.

This, indeed, is the central difficulty; for while it is true that the average audience is more open-minded than the average entrepreneur, so that the basis for change and development in convention always potentially exists, it is only academically true that a dramatist may use any convention that suits his material and intention. A convention, in the simplest sense, is only a method, a technical piece of machinery, which facilitates the performance. But methods change, and techniques change, and while, say, a chorus of dancers, or the cloak of invisibility, or a sung soliloquy, are known dramatic methods, they cannot be satisfactorily used unless, at the time of a performance, they are more than methods; unless, in fact, they are conventions. Dramatist, actors and audience must be able to agree that the particular method to be employed is acceptable; and, in the nature of the case, an important part of this agreement must usually *precede* the performance, so that what is to be done may be accepted without damaging friction.

Ultimately, however, we judge a convention, not by its abstract usefulness, and not by referring it to some ultimate criterion of probability, but rather by what it manages, in an actual work of art, to get done. If in fact it were not historically true that certain works have been able, by their own strength, to modify old conventions and to introduce new ones, we should have had no change at all, short of some absolutist decree. We accept, with a common and easy sentiment, such triumphs of the past. We read, sympathetically, the biographies of an Ibsen or a Stanislavsky. But the sympathy is merely sentimental unless it can be made active, and creative, at our own point in time.

Ibsen and Stanislavsky have won, as Æschylus won when he introduced the second actor, or Shakespeare when he transformed the tragedy of blood. Yet the history of art is not one of continual evolution into higher and better forms; there is debasement as well as refinement, and a novelty, even a transformation, may be bad as well as good. It would be absurd to imagine that our own contemporary segment from the great arc of dramatic possibility is, because the latest, necessarily the best. Yet, because of the nature of convention, because of the dependence of any dramatic method upon this particular type of agreement, it is not possible, in any age, to go very far from the segment which is that age's living tradition, or to begin from anywhere but within or on its borders.

Thus we have the necessity of tradition—convention as tacit consent—and at times the equal necessity of experiment, from the development of new modes of feeling, and from the perception of new or rediscovered technical means—convention as dramatic method. It is to the interplay of these two senses of convention that we must now turn.

If we think of a dramatic convention as a technical means in an acted performance, it is clear that there is no absolute reason why any means should not be employed, and judged by its dramatic result. But we have seen that, in practice, this absolute freedom of choice is not available: a dramatist must win the consent of his audience to any particular means that he wishes to employ, and while he may often be able to do this in the course of a work itself, by the power of the effect which the method makes possible, he cannot entirely rely on this, for even if the audience is sympathetic, too great a consciousness of the novelty or strangeness of the means may as effectively hamper the full communication of a play as would open hostility. It seems probable, when we look back into the history of drama, that the effective changes took place when there was already a latent willingness to accept them, at least among certain groups in society, from whom the artist drew his support. But while it is possible to see this in retrospect, it could never have been easy, and it is not easy now, to see such a situation, with sufficient clarity, in the flux of present experience. It is here that we find ourselves considering the very difficult relations between conventions and structures of feeling.

(iii)

All serious thinking about art must begin from the recognition of two apparently contradictory facts: that an important work is always, in an irreducible sense, individual; and yet that there are authentic communities of works of art, in kinds, periods and styles. In everyday discussion, we succeed in maintaining both ideas at the same time, without real consideration of the relations between them. We see a particular play, and say, often genuinely, that in this speech, this character, this action, a particular dramatist makes himself known; it is for this specific achievement that we value his work. But then, sometimes in the next breath, we look at the speech, the character or the action and say: this is characteristic of a particular kind of drama, in a particular period. Each kind of observation is important; each helps us, every day, to understand drama better. But the difficulty raised by their apparent contradiction—here pointing to a single hand, there to a group or period—must in the end be faced. For the contradiction cannot be resolved by saying that we are in each case pointing at a different kind of fact. It is true that in some works it is possible to separate out different elements, and to say: here the dramatist is simply following the conventions of his genre or period, but here he is contributing something entirely his own. Yet in many important works it is not possible to do this: the individual genius and the particular conventions through which it is expressed are or seem inseparable. In pointing to what a particular man has done, in a particular style, we are often in the position of learning what that style is, what it is capable of doing. The individual dramatist has done this, yet what he has done is part of what we then know about a general period or style.

It is to explore this essential relationship that I use the term "structure of feeling". What I am seeking to describe is the continuity of experience from a particular work, through its particular form, to its recognition as a general form, and then the relation of this general form to a period. We can look at this continuity, first, in the most general way. All that is lived and made, by a given community in a given period, is, we now commonly believe, essentially related, although in practice, and in detail, this is not always easy to see. In the study of a period, we may be able to reconstruct, with more or less accuracy, the material life, the general social organization, and, to a large extent, the dominant ideas. It is often difficult to decide which, if any, of these aspects is, in the whole complex, determining; their separation is, in a way, arbitrary, and an important institution like the drama will, in all probability, take its colour in varying degrees from them all. But while we may, in the study of a past period, separate out particular aspects of life, and treat them as if they were self-contained, it is obvious that this is only how they may be studied, not how they were experienced. We examine each element as a precipitate, but in the living experience of the time every element was in solution, an inseparable part of a complex whole. And it seems to be true, from the nature of art, that it is from such a totality that the artist draws; it is in art, primarily, that the effect of a whole lived experience is expressed and embodied. To relate a work of art to any part of that whole may, in varying degrees, be useful; but it is a common experience, in analysis, to realize that when one has measured the work against the separable parts, there yet remains some element for which there is no external counterpart. It is this, in the first instance, that I mean by the structure of feeling. It is as firm and definite as "structure" suggests, yet it is based in the deepest and often least tangible elements of our experience. It is a way of responding to a particular world which in practice is not felt as one way among others—a conscious "way"—but is, in experience, the only way possible. Its means, its elements, are not propositions or techniques; they are embodied, related feelings. In the same sense, it is accessible to others—not by formal argument or by professional skills, on their own, but by direct experience— a form and a meaning, a feeling and a rhythm—in the work of art, the play, as a whole.

We can often see this structure in the drama of the past. But then it follows, from the whole emphasis of the term, that it is precisely the structure of feeling which is most difficult to distinguish while it is still being lived. Just because it has then not passed, or wholly passed, into distinguishable formations and beliefs and institutions, it is known primarily as a deep *personal* feeling; indeed it often seems, to a particular writer, unique, almost incommunicable, and lonely. We can see this most clearly in the art and thought of past periods, when, while it was being made, its creators seemed often, to themselves and others, isolated, cut off, difficult to understand. Yet again and again, when that structure of feeling has been absorbed, it is the connections, the correspondences, even the period similarities, which spring most readily to the eye. What was then a living structure, not yet known to be shared, is now a recorded structure, which can be examined and identified and even generalized. In one's own time, before this has happened, it is probable that those to whom the new structure is most accessible, in whom indeed it is most clearly forming, will know their experience primarily as their own: as what cuts them off from other men, though what they are actually cut off from is the set of received formations and conventions and institutions which no longer express or satisfy their own most essential life. When such a man speaks, in his work, often against what is felt to be the grain of the time, it is surprising to him and to others that there can be recognition of what had seemed this most difficult, inaccessible, unshared life. Established formations will criticize or reject him, but to an increasing number of people he will seem to be speaking for them, for their own deepest sense of life, just because he was speaking for himself. A new structure of feeling is then becoming articulate. It is even possible, though very difficult even by comparison with the analysis of past structures, to begin to see this contemporary structure directly, rather than only in the power of particular works. Many such expositions are too early, too superficial or too rigid, but it remains true that discovery of actual contemporary structures of feeling (usually masked by their immediate and better recognized predecessors) is the most important kind of attention to the art and society of one's own time.

The artist's importance, in relation to the structure of feeling, has to do above all with the fact that it is a *structure*: not an unformed flux of new responses, interests and perceptions, but a formation of these into a new way of seeing ourselves and our world. Such a formation is the purpose of all authentic contemporary activity, and its successes occur in fields other than art. But the artist, by the character of his work, is directly involved with just this process, from the beginning. He can only work at all as such formations become available, usually as a personal discovery and then a scatter of personal discoveries and then the manner of work of a generation. What this means, in practice, is the making of new conventions, new forms.

It is in this respect, finally, that I see the usefulness of "structure of feeling" as a critical term. For it directs our attention, in practical ways, to a kind of analysis which is at once concerned with particular forms and the elements of general forms. We can begin, quite locally, in what is still called practical criticism, with direct analysis: to discover the structure of feeling of a particular play. This structure, always, is an experience, to which we can directly respond. But it is also an experience communicated in a particular form, through particular conventions. There is indeed always a critical relation between the form and the experience: an identity, a tension, at times, in effect, a disintegration. It is not at all a question of applying an external form, and its rules, to a particular play; it is how the experience and its means of communication relate, by a primarily internal criterion. The first study of a structure of feeling is then always local, particular, unique. But what is being drawn on, in the means of communication, is already wider than the particular work: in a language, in methods, in conventions. As we collect our experience of particular plays, we see the structure of feeling at once extending and changing: important elements in common, as experience and as method, between particular plays and dramatists; important elements changing, as the experience and the conventions change together, or as the experience is found to be in tension with existing conventions, and either succeeds or fails in altering them. Slowly, what emerges is much wider than particular work: it is a problem of form, but also, crucially, a problem of experience, for many dramatists, and in effect for a period and for successive periods. In any real analysis, the relationships are usually very difficult to sustain; but there is the possibility, which I am especially testing in this study of modern drama, of substantial connections between the most particular and the most general forms. What the analysis often shows is a change in dramatic method, but the point of my argument, through the relation of conventions and structures of feeling, is that we can look at dramatic methods with a clear technical definition, and yet know, in detail, that what is being defined is more than technique: is indeed the practical way of describing those changes in experience—the responses and their communication; the "subjects" and the "forms" —which make the drama in itself and as a history important.

(iv)

The most persistent difficulty, in the analysis of structures of feeling, is the complexity of historical change and in particular, as is very evident in modern drama, the coexistence, even within a period and a society, of alternative structures. These facts determine the arrangement of the essays in this book, though the arrangement does not point to any simple conclusion. It is a fact that there is a general historical development, from Ibsen to Brecht, from dramatic naturalism to dramatic expressionism. This indicates a general chronological arrangement, so that, for example, I start with Ibsen and end with plays of the 1950s and 1960s. But then it is not only that we have to get beyond the descriptions of naturalism and expressionism to their often more significant crossings and variants. It is also that, throughout the period, certain forms are in effect rediscovered, or go through a particular development in some intense local situation. Following the real experience through, yet at the same time trying to present it in a critically significant way, I have, within the overall historical development, followed

INTRODUCTION

particular kinds and areas of work through to their own conclusions, before resuming their order in time. I begin, in my first
part, with the three major dramatists who seem to me to establish
the importance of this period: Ibsen, Strindberg and Chekhov.
They were not actual contemporaries—Ibsen was born twenty-one
years before Strindberg, and thirty-two years before Chekhov—
but they were all writing in the 1880s and 1890s, and it is in the
substance and range of their work that modern drama, essentially,
came into existence. I turn then, in my second part, to one remarkable national tradition: that of the Irish dramatists, from Yeats
in the 1890s through Synge and Joyce to O'Casey in the 1940s.
This tradition, as it happens, includes most of the major modern
dramatic forms, but in a particular national and historical situation,
which requires emphasis. In my third part, I turn to an area of
experiment which has been of major importance: the dramatic
uses of illusion, as in Pirandello, and of myth, as in several dramatists
from O'Neill to Giraudoux, Anouilh and Sartre; and I have considered, alongside these, the contrasting experiments in poetic
drama, as in Lorca and Eliot, and in a range of British dramatists.
In my fourth part, I have brought together, for particular emphasis,
a range of writers and methods in social and political drama:
beginning with a retrospect to Büchner, and his relation to
Hauptmann, and going on through the contrasting figures of Shaw
and Lawrence, Toller and Miller, to Brecht. In my fifth part, I
discuss ten recent plays: by O'Neill, Ionesco, Beckett, Genet,
Frisch and Dürrenmatt; and, among British dramatists, by
Whiting, Osborne, Pinter and Arden. There are problems in
this arrangement, and I have been very conscious of them. But
since, finally, all the studies are related, the arrangement may be
acceptable; it has certainly enabled me, while staying close to
particular work, to follow certain themes and kinds through. What
I then attempt, in my conclusion, is a more general statement,
based on the particular studies, of the history and significance of
the main dramatic forms—the conventions and structures of
feeling—of this remarkable hundred years.

PART I

A Generation of Masters

I

HENRIK IBSEN

I

"FAME", said Rilke, "is the sum of misunderstanding which gathers about a new name." The English, indeed the European, fame of Ibsen is perhaps a case in point. It is still widely believed that his main concern was to write plays about the social problems of his day, and that his typical dramatic manner is that of the conversational play, in which every character is provided with a family, and every room with heavy furniture, a certain stuffiness in the air, and a Secret mouldering in the corner cupboard. These ideas spring from a mistake of emphasis, which, in England, began with the London performance of *A Doll's House* in 1889, and of *Ghosts* and *Hedda Gabler* in 1891. These plays—*Ghosts* in particular— were hysterically abused by a "compact majority" of the reviewers and right-thinking men of the day.

> This new favourite of a foolish school [wrote Clement Scott, in a *Daily Telegraph* leading article drawing attention to his own review of *Ghosts*] . . . this so-called master . . . who is to teach the hitherto fairly decent genius of the modern English stage a better and a darker way, seems, to our judgement, to resemble one of his own Norwegian ravens emerging from the rocks with an insatiable appetite for decayed flesh.

Ghosts was compared to "an open drain; a loathsome sore unbandaged; a dirty act done publicly; a lazar-house with all its doors and windows open". Scott's outbursts are distinguished from others only by the lack of restraint encouraged by a fluent pen and a waiting press.

It is best, in such cases, if no attempt is made at defence. Since the attacks are irrelevant, defence will only give away the artist's case. For Ibsen, unfortunately, there were too many defenders. Ibsen*ism* and Ibsen*ites* sprang up everywhere. Bernard Shaw wrote *The Quintessence of Ibsenism*, having, it seems, decided quite firmly in advance what the plays ought to mean. What Shaw expounded in his book was hardly what Ibsen had written in his plays. But the Ibsenite emphasis on subject, as something which could be considered apart from the words of the plays, was characteristic, and it was very welcome to those many people who looked, not for a dramatist, but for a moral leader. The effect of this emphasis was to centre attention on elements in Ibsen which were in fact incidental: on the Emancipation of Women, and the Freedom of Youth; on the "whited sepulchres" of Christian fathers and gentlemen; on the slam of Nora Helmer's front door, which "brought down behind it in dust the whole Victorian family gallery". These things made the scandal, and, in the way of scandals, they made the success; they made Ibsen. When the pages were turned back to his earlier productions, it was shocks of this order which were sought, but which were not found. So it was assumed that his plays had become valuable only when he discarded verse for prose, and legend for observation. Similarly, when later productions appeared, and were found to be neither "shocking" nor "enlightened", it was whispered that Ibsen was, after all, an old man, and that his powers might well be failing.

The orthodox account of Ibsen as dramatist proposes four major periods: first, the "apprenticeship", ending with *The Pretenders*; secondly, the major non-theatrical plays, *Brand*, *Peer Gynt*, *Emperor and Galilean*: thirdly, the prose plays, sometimes called the domestic plays, beginning with *The League of Youth* and passing through *A Doll's House* and *Ghosts* to *Hedda Gabler*; and fourthly, the "visionary" plays, from *The Masterbuilder* to *When We Dead Awaken*. As a mnemonic this account has its uses; but, too often, on the naïve assumption that the development of an artist can be described in terms of the maturing and decay of an organism, it is used as a kind of graph of value. The graph, of course, is drawn on Ibsenite assumptions. Since the domestic plays were taken as the high point, the works before them must be represented as mere preparation for maturity. Similarly, since after maturity comes decline, the last works are the mere product of failing powers. What this account amounts to is a fragmentation; the Ibsenites have been the disintegrators of Ibsen. The re-valuation that I propose rests on the essential unity of the work of Ibsen, a unity, incidentally, on which he always himself insisted. The fact that he was writing in a period of great experiment in the drama is important, and I hope to be able to add something to the understanding of his innovations. But it is with the unity of his work that I am mainly concerned.

2

The part of Ibsen's work which is normally neglected, but which is essential to a critical understanding of his development, is the product of the difficult years between 1851 and 1864, during which he worked as dramatist, producer, and stage-manager in small, struggling theatres at Bergen and then at Oslo: years of apprenticeship, in one sense, but of frustration also. While Ibsen was at Bergen, one hundred and forty-five plays were produced, and seventy-five of them were French. The typical production was the play of dramatic intrigue, which depended on a complicated plot, moving at high speed around certain stock scenes: the confidential document dropped in public; the abducted baby identified by a secret talisman or birthmark; the poisoned goblet passing from hand to hand, and being drunk in the end by anyone but the intended victim. Characters were similarly conventional: "heavy father, innocence distressed, rough diamond, jealous husband, faithful friend". The plays, that is to say, did not deal in nuances. Character and action were drawn in bold, theatrical lines: action was varied, complicated, and continuous in order to provide excitement and surprise and suspense in the theatre; characters were set in a single, simple, colourful mould, in order to provoke theatrical recognition.

A familiar case can be made against that kind of play: that life is not like that; that the stock situations and characters are stagey and theatrical; that the total effect is not drama but melodrama. Yet this is too simple. All these devices can be found, as effective dramatic conventions, in the major drama of the past. Many of them, indeed, go back to the recognition scenes and the catastrophes based on misunderstanding in Greek tragedy. They are again extensively used in Renaissance drama: the most famous scene of the passing of the poisoned cup is, after all, in *Hamlet*, and Shakespeare and his contemporaries repeatedly used fatal documents and falsely compromising objects, as well as identifying talismans and birthmarks. Life was no more like that then than now; the critical case cannot be made in those terms. What we have really to understand is that very complicated process in which a particular structure of feeling, finding its effective form in particular dramatic conventions, breaks down in the course of historical development, but for a time—often a long time—survives in its external characteristics. The conventions, that is to say, are still there; are indeed well understood and locally effective; but their survival is mainly at a technical level, while the controlling structure of feeling, and the range of serious interests held and expressed in it, have effectively gone. What was worked through in the Greek scenes of recognition and misunderstanding was that most serious contemporary experience: the essential difficulty of understanding, at any point, the real character of the forces which were believed to determine men's history, in the actions of fate and of the gods. The actions at the basis of the conventions were then instances of this general experience. In the Renaissance scenes, elements of this supernatural and fatal design are still present: there is a working through, by sign, coincidence and what seems chance, of a wider and providential order: now normally less directly presented, but coming through in the intricacies of action. There is also the new and specific interest in inheritance, with all its connotations of lawful and false authority, which was crucial in feudal and post-feudal society, and the recognition scenes are often directly related to this. Within both Greek and Renaissance drama, there are cases, certainly, in which the conventions originating in an important structure of feeling become, within the period, no more than theatrical devices, in the ordinary run of familiarity and expectation. Yet while the central cases hold, the conventional dramatic form is still deeply related to serious experience.

By the time of the intrigue theatre, this relation had gone. It is exactly the movement we now recognise, from historical to costume drama. The plots, and the stock characters, devices and situations within them, no longer express the awareness of a determining external order, with its critical problems of understanding and recognition, nor the general importance of inheritance, in its public bearings on innocence and authority. Deprived of these determining experiences, as was inevitable and should have been welcomed in the course of historical development, the methods of the older drama declined to devices; the colour and excitement, always locally effective, were there for their own sake. The polished shell was still present, but the body had died. New conceptions of destiny and responsibility, new feelings of relationship and personality, new attitudes to psychology and motivation, needed new conventions to emerge as drama, and were merely compromising and sentimentalising when applied, externally, to the conventions still running in the theatre. This is a recurring situation in dramatic history.

Behind the mechanics of the "well-made" play, and the gaslit experiments in new kinds of archaeologically accurate or locally convincing reproduction of costume and scene, any and every device was used, for what was called (and is still called) in an abstract way, effect. We can trace this complicated development through Ibsen's own early work. Take first what has always been a problem, involving fundamental attitudes to dramatic experience and the nature of dramatic action, in the use of what can be technically isolated as "aside" and "soliloquy". Here are some examples:

(a)

L: My lords, with all the humbleness I may,
I greet your honours from Andronicus.
[*Aside*] And pray the Roman gods confound you both.

D: Grammercy, lovely Lucius, what's the news?

B: [*aside*]: That you are both deciphered, that's the news,
For villains marked with rape.

(b)

L: Ah, right, right; the papers from Peter Kanzler.

S: See, here they all are.

L [*aside*]: Letters for Olaf Skaktavl. [*To Stensson*] The packet is
open, I see. You know what it contains?

(c)

T: I know how, step by step, you've led him on, reluctant and
unwilling, from crime to crime, to this last horrid act. . . .

M [*aside*]: Ha! Lucy has got the advantage and accused me first.
Unless I can turn the accusation and fix it upon her and Blunt,
I am lost.

(d)

B: You were a fair maiden, and nobly born: but your dowry
would have tempted no wooer.

M [*aside*]: Yet was I then so rich.

(e)

M: I thank you, gentlemen.
[*Aside*] This supernatural soliciting
Cannot be ill; cannot be good:—if ill,
Why hath it given me earnest of success,
Commencing in a truth? I am thane of Cawdor.
If good, why do I yield to that suggestion
Whose horrid image doth unfix my hair,
And make my seated heart knock at my ribs,
Against the use of nature? Present fears
Are less than horrible imaginings:
My thought, whose murder yet is but fantastical,
Shakes so my single state of man, that function
Is smother'd in surmise; and nothing is
But what is not.

B: Look how our partner's rapt.

M [*aside*]: If chance will have me king,
Why, chance may crown me,
Without my stir.

(f)

L [*alone*]: At last then I am at Ostraat—the ancient hall of which
a child, two years past, told me so much. Lucia. Ay, two years

ago she was still a child. And now, now, she is dead. Ostraat. It's as though I had seen it all before, as though I were at home here. In there is the Banquet Hall. And underneath is— the grave vault. It must be there that Lucia lies. . . . In there— somewhere in there is sister Elina's chamber. Elina? Ay, Elina is her name.

The first of these examples (*a*) is a structural device, rather than a dramatic convention in the full sense. It is, like (*b*), simply a way of keeping the audience informed of the progress of the action. In (*c*) this device is developed somewhat further; its function is still to explain the action, but it has a new self-consciousness: the dramatist is using the device not only to explain, but also to create excitement. In (*d*) we have a fairly primitive use of the aside to provide a comment of character, a method which is developed and transcended in (*e*) where the soliloquy, prolonged from the aside, not only throws light on character, but communicates a level of experience to which both character and action are subsidiary—a part of the essential pattern of the whole play. In (*f*) again, how- ever, the soliloquy is no more than a structural device, for the explanation of the action and its setting.

The first and fifth of these examples are from Elizabethan drama; that from *Titus Andronicus* is still at the level of subterfuge, but the same device, in *Macbeth*, is developed to great dramatic power. The third example is from George Lillo's *The London Merchant* (1731), where the decline into theatricality is clear: Millwood is not only conscious of herself, but of the audience, to whom she is deliberately "playing". The remaining three examples, where aside and soliloquy are used mainly as devices to keep the action going, or for the crudest purposes of characterization, are from a dramatist writing in the intrigue manner: the young Henrik Ibsen.

Ibsen, writing in 1851 in the periodical *Andhrimmer* (*Manden*), had severely criticized the whole tendency of French drama to place too great a reliance on "situation", at the expense of "psycho- logy". But his subsequent experience in the theatre changed him, for some years. The theatrical effectiveness of the intrigue play was unquestionable, and Ibsen set to work, quite consciously, according to its methods. *Lady Inger of Ostraat* (1855) is a typical specimen of the form:

LADY INGER: Drink, noble knights. Pledge me to the last drop. . . . But now I must tell you. One goblet held a welcome for my friend; the other death for my enemy.

NILS LYKKE: Ah, I am poisoned.

OLAF SKAKTAVL: Death and hell, have you murdered me?

LADY INGER: You see, Olaf Skaktavl, the confidence of the Danes in Inger Gyldenlove. And you, Nils Lykke, can see how much my own countrymen trust me. Yet each of you would have me place myself in your power. Gently, noble sirs, gently.

This characteristic piece of business is the intrigue drama at its most normal; in the whole play Ibsen makes no significant departure from its deliberately theatrical conventions. And *Lady Inger of Ostraat* is only one example of the method of his drama at this period. In *The Feast at Solhoug* the same essential method may be everywhere observed. Here, for example, is a very favourite trick, the entry heightened by coincidence:

MARGIT: He is far from here. Gudmund cannot be coming.
BENGT [*entering, calls loudly*]: An unlooked-for guest, wife.
MARGIT: A guest? Who?
BENGT: Your kinsman, Gudmund.

This device may be seen at its most extensive in another of these early plays, *The Vikings at Helgeland*. Gunnar, believing his son Egil to have been abducted and killed by Ornulf, himself kills Thorolf, son of Ornulf. Gunnar comments:

My vengeance is poor beside Ornulf's crime. He has lost Thorolf, but he has six sons left. But I have none, none.

At this point the return of Ornulf is announced, and Gunnar calls his men to arms, crying:

Vengeance for the death of Egil.

Ornulf enters on the cry, carrying Egil in his arms. And the six sons of Ornulf have been killed in rescuing Egil from the actual abductors. Further, the killing of Thorolf was based on a *deliberate* misunderstanding: Thorolf himself allows a threat of the actual abductor to be taken as the words of his own father, even although he knows that they are not. He is, as a result, killed, but he makes no attempt at explanation. It is possible to put his death down to the Viking conception of honour; it is more to the point to ascribe it to the French conception of "situation".

Any drama must be judged in the context of its own conventions, and it is no good complaining against these plays of Ibsen's on the ground of their lack of realism. The plays could have proceeded on these lines, and still have been great plays, if the dramatic experience to be communicated had been of such a kind that the conventions could have expressed it, rather than manipulated it. In plays like *Lady Inger of Ostraat*, as in so many of the intrigue plays, the purpose of the drama is the communication of the devices.

This is a fair enough definition of theatricality in any period and in any form.

A skilled theatrical craftsman might well remain satisfied with such a situation, and go on writing plays for stock. But Ibsen was always an artist, for whom the communication of significant experience must be the primary concern. Already, in these early plays, elements of the curiously consistent pattern of experience which Ibsen wished to communicate may be discerned, struggling for expression in an uncongenial form. *The Vikings of Helgeland*, for example, is built on the austere pattern of Viking law and conduct, which, with its bare unquestioned conventions of fate and retribution, is very near in spirit to Ibsen's reading of experience. Its hard, bitter consistency, and its neglect of the romantic conceptions of personality, might well have seemed to Ibsen a satisfactory convention for the expression of his own emotional pattern. It falls short of this, however, in the form in which the play is cast, because of the intrigue habit of coincidence, which reduces the tragedy from the causal to the casual.

Ibsen's next play, written after an interval of four years, which had included a profound personal crisis, is set in a different mould. He had written an earlier version, *Svanhild*, but it eventually appeared as his first play of modern life—*Love's Comedy*. It is a play of considerable incidental talent, but it shows more clearly than ever the false position into which Ibsen had been driven by his acceptance of contemporary theatrical techniques.

There is a certain thematic element of "vocation", an experience to which Ibsen was to return again and again:

> the essence of freedom is to fulfil our call absolutely.

There is a certain amount of reasoning about "the contrast between the actual and the ideal": another persistent Ibsen theme. Indeed, the "discussion", which Shaw acclaimed as a new element in *A Doll's House*, is similarly present here:

> It's time we squared accounts. It's time we three talked out for once together from the heart.

But these elements cannot be adequately expressed in the dramatic form which Ibsen has chosen. The contrast between the actual and the ideal is seriously blurred by the fact that the central relationship—that between Falk and Svanhild—is a type situation of the romantic drama. Similarly, the beginning and end of the play are written in a kind of operetta manner: Falk sings a love-song, and a chorus of gentlemen support him. Again, there is a considerable element of caricature, which, though often incidentally successful, proceeds from an essentially different level of experience. Ibsen's intention is the expression of a theme, but the uncertainty of form is so great that the result is no more than a hybrid entertainment.

The final demonstration of the incompatibility of Ibsen's art with the theatre to which he had become apprenticed is *Kongsemnerne* (*The Pretenders*). It is a play based on a passage of Norwegian history, and its action is the rivalry of certain pretenders to the crown. There are obvious elements of contemporary nationalist politics in it, but it cannot be read as a "politico-historical" play. *The Pretenders* is in fact the first full embodiment of the most persistent single theme in Ibsen's whole work: the idea of vocation. The analysis of the relationship between the two main rivals—Hakon and Skule—is centred almost entirely on the definition of this experience. Skule is moved only by the prestige of the crown, and he knows his disadvantages against Hakon, who has the actual vocation of kingship:

> While he himself believes in his kingship, that is the heart of his fortune, the girdle of his strength.

Skule, for the purposes of faction, can assume such a vocation, and deceive even his son. But since the assumption is false, it leads only to crime, leads directly to desecration of the shrine of kingship, which his son drags from the Cathedral. Skule repents and submits to death:

> Can one man take God's calling from another? Can a Pretender clothe himself in a king's life-task as he can put on the king's robes? . . . Greet royal Hakon from me. Tell him that even in my last hour I do not know whether his birth was royal. But this I surely know—it is he whom God has chosen.

To anyone who has read *Brand* or *Peer Gynt*, *The Masterbuilder* or *When We Dead Awaken*, it will need no further demonstration that Ibsen is concerned here with one of his profound and lasting preoccupations: the nature of "calling" and its realization. The rivalry for the crown is used as "a situation, a chain of events, which shall be the formula of that *particular* emotion". But *The Pretenders*, as a whole, is still cast in the form of the intrigue play. The required complication of action, so that the expected "situations" may be prepared, hampers and almost obscures the genuine expression which is achieved in the relationship of Hakon and Skule. The theatrical form, that is to say, is inadequate for the expression of the dramatic experience.

Ibsen seems to have realized this fact quite clearly. He abandoned the attempt at compromise; left Norway, left the theatre, and left off writing for the stage. The intrigue drama was his inescapable inheritance, and for the rest of his writing life he was to be profoundly affected by it. But for the moment he would turn his back on the theatre which was dedicated to its service; he would seek, without reference to the theatre, a dramatic form adequate for the expression of his significant experience.

3

Ibsen had had thirteen years' practical experience of the theatre; but he only began to produce work that is now considered important when he left it. The first of these mature works was *Brand*, which was never intended for the stage, although it has once or twice been performed in its entirety, and more frequently in abridged versions. Unfortunately, Shaw's interpretation of the play as Ibsen's "exposure" of the harm caused by a fanatical idealist has so impressed itself in England that most of our versions are cut to fit that very dubious pattern. *Brand*, following *The Pretenders*, is essentially a statement on the claims of vocation; and its significant conclusion is the impossibility of fulfilling the vocation of the ideal under "the load of inherited spiritual debt". In this main theme there is no sign of satire, although one can understand why Shaw thought that there ought to have been.

The design of *Brand* is abstract, in the sense that the play is arranged, not so much to study a particular character, as to state a theme of which that character is the central element. For example, in the first act Brand defines his life in terms of vocation:

> A great one gave me charge. I *must*.

And there follow, as if in a scheme of characters, objections to any absolute response: the fear of injury and death, as stated by the peasant; the devotion to happiness, as stated by Einar and Agnes; the refusal of order, in a pagan adoration of nature, as stated by the gipsy-girl Gerd. Brand reviews these three temptations to refusal, and re-affirms his faith:

> War with this triple-handed foe;
> I see my Call.

This form of embodiment of a theme is the general method of the play. Its next aspect is the definition of Brand's mission, which is the restoration of wholeness. The present fault in man is seen, first, as the lack of wholeness:

Try every man in heart and soul,
You'll find he has no virtue whole,
But just a little grain of each . . .
. . . all fragments still,
His faults, his merits, fragments all . . .
But here's the grief, that worst or best,
Each fragment of him wrecks the rest.

It is in opposition to this kind of fragmentary living that Brand declares his consistent "All or Nothing". He declares it, at this stage, as the means of the achievement of the ideal, the way of bridging the gulf

Between the living world we see
And the world as it ought to be.

Now, at first sight, this seems like Shaw's definition of the play:

filling us with excited hopes of escape from idealistic tyrannies and with visions of intenser life in the future.

But this is to overlook the fact that it is the reforming element itself which comprises the ideal. The whole tragedy of *Brand* is that pursuit of the ideal is both necessary and fruitless. The call is absolute; so are the barriers. This tension is the whole action of the play; it is summarized, in a way very characteristic of Ibsen, in the significant lines:

Born to be tenants of the deep,
Born to be exiles from the sun . . .
Crying to heaven, in vain we pray
For air, and the glad flames of day.

This is the fundamental statement in *Brand*, and perhaps in the whole work of Ibsen. The action of *Brand*, as I have said, is the demonstration of this conflict, in which Brand himself is broken. The formal implications of "demonstration", incidentally, are completely appropriate.

In the beginning, most of Brand's speeches are in specifically social terms:

And now the *age* shall be made whole . . .
The sick *earth* shall grow sound again . . .
Nations, though poor and sparse, that live . . .

But it is part of the design of the play that this emphasis should change, that the vocation should come to be defined, not as social reform, but as the realization of the actual self; or rather, in the classic position of liberalism, that social reform is self-fulfilment—

the purpose of changing the world is to gain the conditions for being oneself:

> One thing is yours you may not spend,
> Your very inmost self of all.
> You may not bind it, may not bend,
> Nor stem the river of your call.
> To make for ocean is its end.
>
> Self completely to fulfil,
> That's a valid right of man,
> And no more than that I will.

This realization is not a matter of ideals. What happens is that the general aspirations come to be limited by the actual inheritance:

> To fulfil oneself, and yet
> With a heritage of debt?

By "debt" Ibsen means a guilt inherited both as a son and as a man. In Brand, the realization of debt comes through his meeting with his mother; he takes over both her sins and her responsibilities, and sees that the vocation must now be re-defined:

> As the morn, not so the night . . .
> Then I saw my way before me . . .
> Now my sabbath dream is dark.

Brand's mission can no longer be the reform of the world, but the actual, limited sphere of "daily duty, daily labour, hallowed to a Sabbath deed". Nevertheless, the command is still absolute, submission still necessary, even if this involves the sacrifice of life. Brand will not go to his dying mother; he will not save the life of his son. The conflict is a test of submission to the will of God, at whatever human cost. If the will to submission is strong enough, the conflict will be resolved.

> When will has conquered in that strife,
> Then comes at length the hour of Love.
> Then it descends like a white dove
> Bearing the olive-tree of life.

This, of course, is an exact prevision of the actual end of the play. It will be both love and death; when the avalanche descends ("he is white, see, as a dove") Brand cries that he has willed to his utmost strength. This, again, is the consummation which had been foreseen:

> I trust wholly in God's call . . .
> Mine is that Will and that strong trust
> That crumbles mountains into dust.

It is not, in the ordinary sense, a matter of choice. Once Brand has heard the call to wholeness, to the healing of "the fissured soul", his fate, and the fate of those connected with him, is determined. "All the generation" who have inherited sin "are doomed":

> Blood of children must be spilt
> To atone for parents' guilt.

This is a situation with which there can be no compromise; "the Devil is compromise". Brand refuses to compromise, but, in spite of this, he is, by his inheritance, compromised. It is not that he chooses wrongly, but that he could not choose at all; he could only accept his inheritance. The voice that cries through the avalanche— "He is the God of Love"—is not some kind of retrospective criticism of Brand's actions; it is the foreseen consummation, and the assurance of mercy. Brand is one of those who come to "stand in a tight place; he cannot go forward or backward". It is, as Ibsen sees it, the essential tragedy of the human situation.

One important element of the final dramatic realization is Ibsen's use of the figures of dove and falcon. These figures are closely interwoven throughout the play. The dove which will descend has been the ultimate love; when "will has conquered" the dove brings life. The falcon is its opposite and its counterpart. At the root of the particular sin which Brand is expiating, "a childish scene that lives in my mind like a festering scar", is his mother's robbery of the bed of his dead father, "sweeping down like a falcon on her prey". The falcon is also compromise, the mark of the devil. A great part of the effect of the climax of *Brand* depends upon these two figures. The phantom which appears to Brand in the mountains reveals itself as the falcon, and Gerd raises her gun to shoot it; "redemption", she says, "is at hand". She shoots into the mist, and the shot begins the avalanche:

> I have hit him . . .
> Plumes in thousands from his breast
> Flutter down the mountainside.
> See how large he looms, how white,
> He is white, see, *as a dove.*

It was the falcon, and it is the dove. The transformation is the whole resolution of the play.

In the last act of *Brand*, Ibsen reaches one of the heights of his dramatic power. And he achieves this mastery by concentrating on the central dramatic element of his conception, at the expense of both "representation" and "situation". *Brand* is one of the most dramatic works Ibsen ever wrote, but it is very far from what his contemporaries would have called a play.

The achievement is not, of course, without fault. The public elements in the play—the figures of Dean, Sexton, Schoolmaster, and Mayor—though necessary to the theme in that they define an aspect of fragmentariness—

> ... with the best will no one can
> Be an official and a man—

seem at times to be developed for their own sake, as caricatures. Again, it is true, as Ibsen wrote to Brandes, that the theme of the play is not necessarily religious; that he "could have made Brand's syllogism" equally in art, in love, or in politics. But the formula which he has chosen is religious; and it is a weakening of its objectivity—and hence its adequacy—when elements of the *original* emotion—(Ibsen's relation to Norway and to his work, as it seems almost certain to be)—enter the art form untransmuted. Ibsen's fondness of direct public address from the stage—which made Stockmann's meeting so congenial to him—is allowed, at a critical moment in *Brand*, to distract from the central theme with a sermon on weakness, freedom, and littleness (the speech on the mountains in Act Five). This surrender to "interestingness"—a surrender similar to the elaboration of the social caricatures—is a failure of discipline. And it is not merely an incidental failure. The desire for directness is part of the same failure as the tendency to dissociation.

Yet these elements, in their turn, relate to the essential structure of feeling. At first sight, *Brand* resembles a traditional morality play: a central figure faced by conflicting attitudes and choices, working out his destiny. But what is most interesting, on reflection, is its difference from that traditional form. Brand is not a representative but an exceptional figure: that is the key to the change. He is not Everyman, facing a common destiny, but a consciously separate and dedicated man, acting against the common condition of compromise. This makes him, in the usual phrase, an individual, and it is almost inevitable that we should feel that in this sense we do not know enough about him: that he is a theoretical creature —not because the experience which contains him is inorganic or insubstantial, but because it is, as manifested, rootless; it has been dug up and exhibited at the level of conscious debate. Yet this is then precisely a morality technique; it was just such abstraction which made the traditional form possible. The biggest change, evident both in change of convention and in direct description, between the morality tradition and that important body of Elizabethan drama which developed from it, is in just the recognition of process—of moment-by-moment experience—within the generalized values. It is this process which is again abstracted in *Brand*: but not as regression; rather as a new phase in a continuing development. For the paradox of Brand, the exceptional individual, is that he is seen, by his creator, as the essential spirit of man; it is for a general human liberation that this exceptional man struggles. And this is then, decisively, a modern consciousness: the classical position of a late, desperate liberalism. It is by acting against the common condition, and against even the process of detailed relationship which ties men to this, that this singular man (truly singular— the spirit of Man, as it was characteristically generalized in liberalism; singular in content, but plural and capital in form) expresses the ideal of humanity. It is Man against men; "the individual" against "Society": what is now liberal platitude but was then living faith: Man, exceptional man, the spirit of humanity, the liberator. The paradox so evident technically, in the construction and substance of *Brand*, is no simple failure; it is the structure of feeling of a particular and difficult phase. The vocation is liberation: the realization of what "man can become". The debt is received experience and received institutions: as embodied in others but active also in his own inevitable inheritance. At this point, Brand is torn but must go on; is certain to fail and die but will die climbing. This is the structure of feeling of liberal tragedy. And then what has really to be said, about the actual achievement of the play, is that Ibsen presented this structure in a consciously bare and explicit way. He did not, as so often happened later, evade its bleak consciousness, or cover it with an engaging personality and charm. What is here given straight—and is of course inhuman— has been given with sugar in a hundred subsequent plays. It is just that kind of limited paradoxical achievement: presenting bleakly and consciously what is preferred as hint and charm. It is what happens to a morality play in a straight liberal world (as we shall see again in the related cases of *Murder in the Cathedral* and *The Cocktail Party*).

As we have seen, to express this structure of feeling, in a consciously new dramatic form, Ibsen had to withdraw from the theatre. He is still withdrawn, still consciously independent from the available conventions, in his next play *Peer Gynt*. Here the will to liberation, by conscious opposition, struggle and statement, is replaced by a related but weakened desire: to fulfil oneself; to realize the "very inmost self of all", but not, now, in the name of humanity, and not by fighting but by dodging. With characteristic creative power, Ibsen took the opportunity, in this contrasting experience, to make more than a negative statement. For Brand's conscious opposition, statement had been the relevant method. Brand has, in effect, no unspoken experience, no hidden motivation (this is the essential difference from the handling of a similar experience of vocation in *Rosmersholm* and the later plays). For Peer Gynt's evasion, fantasy is the method: not the description of fantasy, but a lived fantasy—an action in fantasy. Drawing on the method and material of legend, Ibsen achieved—in a sense released —yet another new form. *Peer Gynt* is cast in the traditional form of the quest. But the quest of Peer is, in a real sense, itself a fantasy; in the illusion of self-sufficiency he is moving steadily away from that which he wishes to find; in seeking he is hiding; his straight road is the "round about" of the Bojg: his eye is "scratched" by the trolls, his vision is blindness. To the demonstration of fantasy of this order the tone of the play is particularly well suited; at the taken level, which is very uniform throughout, there is surprising richness. If not his most important, *Peer Gynt* is Ibsen's most consistently successful work.

> And of course one is glad to be quit of one's cares
> And try all one can to hold thinking aloof,
> Some take to brandy, and others to lies.
> And we? Why we took to fairy tales
> Of princes and trolls and of all sorts of beasts;
> And of bride-rapes as well. Ah, but who could have dreamed
> That those devils' yarns would have stuck in his head?

But in fact it is this inheritance which Peer will act out. It is the expression of fantasy which he understands as the expression of self. He is led by it, inevitably, to the trolls. In mating with the Green Woman, he is confirming this negative existence:

> GREEN WOMAN: Black it seems white, and ugly seems fair.
> PEER GYNT: Big it seems little, and dirty seems clean.
> GREEN WOMAN: Ay, Peer, now I see that we fit, you and I.

The fantasy of the troll-world is sufficient to itself:

> DOVRE-KING: Among men the saying goes: Man be thyself.
> At home here with us, in the tribe of the trolls
> The saying goes: Troll, to thyself be—*enough*.

For such self-sufficiency, however, as Peer quickly discovers, it is necessary to blind oneself, to mutilate one's senses:

> DOVRE-KING: In your left eye first.
> I'll scratch you a bit, till you see awry.
> But all that you see will seem fine and brave.

Peer refuses to be mutilated, and when the trolls attack him, he saves himself by calling on his mother; by calling, that is to say, on an actual relationship. The theme of self-mutilation is taken up again in the scene where Peer, in the forest, sees a youth cut off his thumb to avoid serving in the army. It is a determination which contrasts with his own impotence:

> Aye, think of it, wish it done, even will it,
> But do it! No, that's past my understanding.

The Bojg, that "familiar compound ghost", the amorphous creature which conquers but does not fight, is a similar temptation to fantasy. It is a kind of "reality" which Peer cannot enter, and in his failure he accepts its advice to "go round about".

Peer's protection, his only relation with reality after the death of his mother, is expressed in Solveig:

> If you dare dwell with the hunter here,
> I know the hut will be blessed from evil.

But he cannot stay with her, because of the debt which he has contracted: the child of the Green Woman. He can see the Green Woman as she is—a hag. But, as she reminds him:

> If you would see me fair as before
> You have only to turn yonder girl out of doors.

Solveig, in fact, is the guarantee of his actual sight, and hence of his actual existence. Yet he cannot stay with her; he cannot understand repentance. His only way is the "round about" of the Bojg.

The fourth act, which is looser and less integrated dramatically than those preceding, deals with his travels "round about". It is a history of fantasy and deception, the expression of his fantasy of self to the point where he is crowned by the madmen as the "Emperor of Selfhood". That is the consummation of the fantasy, and it is succeeded, in the fifth act, by the long way back to reality. As the Strange Passenger promises him:

> I'll have you laid open and brought to the light.
> What I specially seek is the centre of dreams.

When he is back in his own country, Peer sees the funeral of the man who had mutilated himself: "he followed his calling". It is a definition of his own life. There follows the auction of his own childhood possessions, and through these layers Peer seeks the centre of his own reality. But, as he strips the onion:

> To the innermost centre
> It's nothing but swathings, each smaller and smaller.

Peer has, in fact, no self. As the Button Moulder tells him:

> Now you were designed for a shining button
> On the coat of the world; but your loop gave way;
> So into the waste-box you must go,
> And then, as they say, be merged in the mass.

His failure (when his attachment to reality had "given way") is a failure to realize the nature of self. He has followed the troll maxim—"to thyself be *enough*". In other words, he has refused his vocation, "has set at defiance his life's design". "To be oneself", says the Button Moulder, "is to slay oneself." To respond to vocation is imperative, at whatever apparent cost. The actual self, rather than the fantasy of self, demands fulfilment, through response to "the design":

> To stand forth everywhere
> With the Master's intention clearly displayed.

Peer has chosen the negative way, is now simply a "negative print", in which "the light and shade are reversed". And now that he has been brought to see this, he can at last reverse the reversal:

> Round about, said the Bojg. No. This time at least
> Straight ahead, however narrow the path.

He returns to Solveig, in whom he has remained

> as myself, as the whole man, the true man.

Solveig is both wife and mother; is the guarantee of his existence.

PEER: My mother; my wife; thou innocent woman.

And the return is not only to Solveig, but to God:

SOLVEIG: Who is thy father?
> Surely He that forgives at the mother's prayer.

So, for the moment, Peer finds himself and his rest, while the Button Moulder waits for him at the last cross-roads.

Peer Gynt, clearly, springs from the same source in experience as most of Ibsen's major work. Indeed, by the time *Brand* and *Peer Gynt* were written, every major theme of his later work had been put into words. *Peer Gynt*'s success, and its difference from *Brand*, is that the mythological and legendary material which Ibsen uses provides a more completely objective formula for the central experience than any he found before or after. The fifth act, in particular, is magnificently *present* as drama. The images of the burned forest, of the auction, of the stripped wood-onion are part of a controlled pattern of realized experience, in which the images which function as characters—the Strange Passenger and the Button Moulder—are perfectly in place. The material is deliberately unrealistic—for the Act is an exposition of Peer's death and redemption; it is concerned, not with persons, but with a body of dramatic imagery "such that, when the external facts, which must terminate in sensory experience, are given, the emotion is immediately invoked". The sequence of dramatic imagery, embodied in language and character, of course put the play beyond the technical capacity of the nineteenth-century theatre. What had there been imagined became technically possible only in film. It is, in that full sense, a dramatic poem: the organization of language going beyond any available theatrical action, to create a new kind of dramatic action.

4

Brand and *Peer Gynt* had been written in Italy. In 1868, the year after *Peer Gynt* appeared, Ibsen went to Germany. He was then forty. In the next ten years he produced only three plays: the long *Emperor and Galilean*; *The League of Youth*; and *Pillars of Society*. He then returned to Rome. The whole of this period in Germany (the evidence is everywhere in the letters) was clearly a period of great crisis, in at least three important aspects of his life: his religion, his political philosophy, and his dramatic technique. But it is also one of those periods of personal crisis which are critical moments in the change of a civilization. Many forces were active, in Ibsen and in others, but in these years they were most significantly concentrated in this one mind, and from the decisions taken there came the modern prose play as we know it.

About the technical change Ibsen is explicit. Writing to his publisher about *The League of Youth*, he declares:

It will be in prose, and in every way adapted for the stage.

He has decided to abandon verse, and cultivate

the very much more difficult art of writing the genuine, plain language spoken in real life.

Of *Emperor and Galilean* he writes:

The illusion I wished to produce was that of reality. I wished to leave on the reader's mind the impression that what he had read had actually happened. By employing verse I should have counteracted my own intention. The many everyday insignificant characters, whom I have intentionally introduced, would have become indistinct and mixed up with each other had I made them all speak in rhythmic measure. We no longer live in the days of Shakespeare. . . . The style ought to conform to the degree of ideality imparted to the whole presentment. My play is no tragedy in the ancient acceptation. My desire was to depict human beings and therefore I would not make them speak the language of the gods.

The statements, and their root attitude, are self-explanatory; but certain of their implications deserve comment. Perhaps the key phrase is "in every way adapted for the stage". After the independence of *Brand* and *Peer Gynt*, Ibsen is returning to the contemporary theatre. It is indeed a return, rather than a new departure. The practices of the intrigue drama, which he seemed to have abandoned in despair, are to be accepted again. Ibsen will introduce new elements—prose dialogue and modern settings— but the fundamental dramatic practices of the old stage will remain his framework.

Of the three plays which he wrote in Germany, *Emperor and Galilean* is clearly the most ambitious: when he had finished it Ibsen regarded it as his masterpiece, and at the end of his writing life he retained this opinion. *Emperor and Galilean* is a poetic drama, cast in the form of a realistic historical play. That is its basic contradiction, and its importance as a transition in Ibsen's development. The contradiction is evident in Ibsen's own account of the work:

I am putting into this book a part of my own spiritual life; what I depict I have, under other forms, myself gone through, and the historic theme I have chosen has also a much closer relation to the movements of our own time than one might at first suppose . . . I have kept strictly to history. . . . And yet I have put much self-anatomy into the work.

In the central theme the most important elements are the relationship between Julian and Maximus, between Julian and Agathon, and between Julian and Makrina. Julian is the slave of vocation; he is born to be Achilles:

JULIAN: Why was I born?
VOICE: To serve the spirit. . . .
JULIAN: What is my mission?
VOICE: To establish the empire.
JULIAN: What Empire?
VOICE: The empire. . . .
JULIAN: By what power?
VOICE: By *willing*.
JULIAN: What shall I will?
VOICE: What thou must.

44

This vocation is reinforced by other auguries. The conflict to which he is called is at one level that between Caesar and Galilean, in historical as well as in absolute terms; at another that between flesh and spirit; at another that between the old beauty and the new truth:

> JULIAN: All that is human has become unlawful since the day when the seer of Galilee became ruler of the world. Through him, life has become death. Love and hatred, both are sins. Has he, then, transformed man's flesh and blood? Has not earth-bound man remained what he ever was? Our inmost healthy spirit rebels against it all;—and yet we are to will in the teeth of our own will. Thou shalt, thou shalt, thou shalt.

It is so with "all who are under the terror of the revelation". But:

> JULIAN: There must come a new revelation. Or a revelation of something new. It *must* come, I say, because the time is ripe. . . . The old beauty is no longer beautiful, and the new truth is no longer true.

To his doubts—

> Was I the chosen one? The "heir to the empire", it said. And what empire—? That matter is beset with a thousand uncertainties.

—Maximus opposes his confident prophecy:

> JULIAN: Then tell me. Who shall conquer? Emperor or Galilean?
> MAXIMUS: Both the Emperor and the Galilean shall succumb. . . . Does not the child succumb in the youth, and the youth in the man? Yet neither child nor youth perishes. . . You have striven to make the youth a child again. The empire of the flesh is swallowed up in the empire of the spirit. But the empire of the spirit is not final. . . . Oh fool, who have drawn your sword against that which is to be—against the third empire in which the twin-natured shall reign.
> JULIAN: Neither Emperor nor Redeemer?
> MAXIMUS: Both in one, and one in both.
> JULIAN: Emperor-God. God-Emperor. Emperor in the kingdom of the spirit, and God in the kingdom of the flesh.
> MAXIMUS: That is the third empire, Julian.

This empire Julian will seek, as Agnes said of her life with Brand

Through darkness to light.

Julian becomes ambitious of world-conquest, and a violent persecutor of the Christians. At the climax he burns his fleet, and this is followed by silence. At the moment of believing himself the Messiah to whom both Emperor and Galilean shall succumb, Julian is conquered by the Galilean.

> JULIAN: What if that at Golgotha was but a wayside matter, a thing done, as it were, in passing, in a leisure hour? What if he goes on and on, and suffers and dies and conquers, again and again, from world to world?

Even while he seeks the "beautiful earth" (which Peer Gynt had betrayed), and the city of the sun, his mission is not forgotten.

> MAKRINA: In him dwells a greater than he. . . . In him will the Lord God smite us even to death.

As Brand was taken by Gerd for the Redeemer, so the death of Julian reminds us of the death on the cross:

> AGATHON: With Christ for Christ!
> [*He throws his spear; it grazes the Emperor's arm and plunges into his side*] . . .
> AGATHON: The Roman's spear from Golgotha.

As he had come from the sacrifice in the catacombs with the cry

It is finished

so now, as he dies, he speaks these deliberately reminiscent words:

> Beautiful earth, Beautiful life. . . . Oh, Helios,
> Helios, why hast thou betrayed me?

Over his body, Maximus declares:

> Led astray like Cain. Led astray like Judas. Your God is a spendthrift God, Galileans. He wears out many souls. Were you not then, this time either, the chosen one; you, a victim on the altar of necessity? . . . But the third empire shall come. The spirit of man shall re-enter on its heritage.

And the Christian Makrina makes the last judgement.

> MAKRINA: Here lies a noble, shattered instrument of God.
> BASIL: . . . Christ, Christ, how came it that thy people saw not thy manifest design? The Emperor Julian was a rod of chastisement, not unto death but unto resurrection.
> MAKRINA: *Terrible is the mystery of election.* . . . Erring soul of man—if thou wast indeed forced to err, it shall surely be accounted to thee for good on that great day when the Mighty One shall descend in the clouds to judge the living dead and the dead who are yet alive.

At its close, the play takes us back to the world of *Brand*, and forward to the world of *When We Dead Awaken*. Judged on these elements alone, Ibsen's opinion of the worth of the play might be substantiated. The real difficulty was to find a clear enough dramatic form to express a development of civilization beyond the historical possibilities of the period from which the action was taken. The general impulse was to a new world; the tendency of the historical action to an old. Here future and past, as Ibsen so often conceived them, met and confused each other, in form and content; the loose hold on the third empire, in imagination, becoming the looseness of method of the play; the history taken for itself and for more than itself, and coming clear as neither.

In the two other plays of this period, Ibsen presents us with intrigue drama in modern Norwegian dress. It is not necessary to examine them in detail, but simply to record their methods as a step in the evolution of the romantic melodrama into naturalism. *The League of Youth* is an entertaining account of local politics, with Peer Gynt degenerated to the social caricature of Stensgard. There are the expected representative characters—local printer, doctor, student, industrialist, land-owner, and widow. The mechanism of the plot rests on characteristic devices: deliberate misunderstandings, substituted letters, complicated intrigue, "the classic *quid pro quo* of the proposal by proxy mistaken for the proposal direct", forged bankbills, and a "set to partners" happy ending. It is the "well-made play" with a certain flatness, which "comes of the local situation". *Pillars of Society* is very similar. Its plot is extraordinarily complicated; it is, in both senses, intrigue, and the result is an overall satire (on a very slight scale, as I take it) of the kind represented by the ironic title. It is possible to admire the ingenuity of the plot, which has been compared to that of a detective story. But in spite of its skilful carpentry, *Pillars of Society* is crude. Everything in it is a simplification of the order of Lona's last cry:

The spirits of truth and freedom—these are the pillars of society.

The skill is the *result* of simplification; the flawless plot is designed to exclude any real complexity. For a man who had done such work as Ibsen, the play is extremely immature. But *Pillars of Society* is not prentice-work. By the Ibsenities, indeed, it is represented as his entrance on maturity. For all the while he had in his pocket the plans for *A Doll's House*.

To each succeeding generation, and equally to our own, Ibsen is above all the writer of *A Doll's House* and of *Ghosts*. The plays have been interpreted, paraphrased, acted, and rewritten into a numb and stale prestige. *A Doll's House* is now, as it has always been, a social rather than a literary phenomenon. Its excitement lay in its relation to feminism, and, although Ibsen rejected the ascription of support for feminism, in practical terms this hardly matters.

What was it that made *A Doll's House*, as drama, appear so strikingly original? That it dealt with "real people in real situations"? This is surely very questionable. The characters of the play differ very little from the usual types of romantic drama: the innocent, childlike woman, involved in a desperate deception; the heavy, insensitive husband; the faithful friend. Similarly, the main situations of the play are typical of the intrigue drama: the guilty secret, sealed lips, the complication of situation around Krogstad's fatal letter. The appearance of Krogstad at the children's party is a typical "situation": the villain against a background of idyllic happiness (all the best murders are committed in rose-gardens). None of this is at all new, and it is the major part of the play.

But the novelty, it is said again, is that these deliberate romantic puppets are suddenly jerked into life. This, I think, is true, in one definite sense. But one must be careful in defining the mechanism of change. According to Shaw, this mechanism is the "discussion"— the movement into a new kind of reality with Nora's famous words:.

> We must come to a final settlement, Torvald. During eight whole years . . . we have never exchanged one serious word about serious things.

Now this is certainly an important change of mood, but one doubts whether "discussion" is the right word for it. What, in any case, is *discussed* in *A Doll's House*? The final scene between Nora and Torvald is not so much a discussion as a *declaration*. It is this in two ways: first, in Nora's declaration that she will leave Torvald; and secondly, in that it is a stated moral of the play. Now Torvald attempts to dissuade Nora, but his objections do not seem to be made in any substantial personal way. They are more like cues for her declaration; stock objections which the play as a whole (and not necessarily Nora) must answer:

TORVALD: Are you not clear about your place in your own home? Have you not an infallible guide in questions like these? Have you not religion?
NORA: Oh, Torvald, I don't really know what religion is.
TORVALD: What do you mean?
NORA: I know nothing but what Pastor Hansen told me when I was confirmed. He explained that religion was this and that. When I get away from all this and stand alone, I will look into that matter too. I will see whether what he taught me is right, or, at any rate, whether it is right for me.

My own judgement of passages like these is that they do not represent a "living confrontation between actual people", but are rather straight, single declaration. Torvald's questions, that is to say, are devices of the argument. They are, in fact, rhetorical questions, and could, essentially, be all spoken by Nora herself:

> You may say, have I not an infallible guide in questions like these? Have I not religion? I can only answer that I know nothing but what Pastor Hansen told me. . . .

It is not that we get a dramatic presentation of more substantial experience than is common in the late romantic drama. The experience is of the same limited kind, and is presented according to the same conventions. Then, in the statement of the moral, we get an unusual conclusion. The play does not go deeper than the usual mechanism of intrigue; it does not undercut the assumptions of romantic drama, with its mechanical versions of experience; it merely provides a reversal within the romantic framework. It is not a new positive dramatic standard; it is simply *anti*-romantic, a negative within the same framework of experience. That the negative is justified, on moral grounds, is true; and the play is valuable as a rejection of the earlier morality. But it is only a rejection of conclusions; it is not a rejection of the limited kinds of experience. We have only to go forward to Strindberg's *The Father* or *The Dance of Death*, for all their differences of viewpoint, to realize how deeply this is true. This is why, in the end, the description "problem play" or "thesis play" is justified. The term suggests abstraction, and abstraction is what we have. There have always been problems in drama, but in the greatest drama these are set in a body of specific experience which is not limited by the conventions of "situation" and "type character". In Elizabethan drama, "situations" and "type characters" were often present; but the range of the play's language provided, in the best work, the essential body of immediate and compelling specific experience. When the range of dramatic language was limited, the situations and type characters became merely mechanical: devices of communication for which no substantial communication had been devised. Ibsen's rejection of the conventional moral ending was only a limited cure for this deficiency—a partial negative within an essential acceptance. Any full cure would have involved the restoration of total dramatic substance.

A Doll's House, then, is an anti-romantic play, in the sense of the limited negative which I have defined. Naturalism, as it has been widely practised, is anti-romantic in this same limited sense.

Strindberg, as we shall see, proposed that naturalism should attempt to restore the whole substance. But the naturalism which came to dominate the theatre was of the more limited kind. It is in this respect that one must emphasize that naturalism is a legitimate child of the romantic drama; a child which makes a limited rejection of its parent, but which remains essentially formed by its general inheritance. The anti-romantic drama, down to the *teatro grottesco* and the work of Pirandello, is to be essentially understood in this way. For Ibsen, who in *Brand* and *Peer Gynt* had attempted, with considerable success, to restore substance, the development which *A Doll's House* typifies must be seen as essentially regressive. The fact that Nora and Torvald and Krogstad and Rank can function *simultaneously* as the stock figures of romantic melodrama and of the problem play is only one local indication of this general fact.

Ghosts is a play of the same essential kind as *A Doll's House*, but it is of a very different temper. Its issues are more serious, and Ibsen is more concentrated on their resolution. The condensed power of the play, however we may finally judge it, is undeniable. The situation which Ibsen examines is more nearly isolated from the irrelevant concessions to theatrical intrigue than all but a few others of his plays in this genre. The mechanical logic of its resolution is clear and exact. From the moment that the intriguing Engstrand appears in the first few words of the play—

ENGSTRAND: It's the Lord's own rain, my girl.
REGINA: It's the devil's rain, *I* say.

—the movement to inevitable disaster is played out at top speed. The only modern plays comparable with it in theatrical terms are Strindberg's *Lady Julie* and Ibsen's own *Hedda Gabler*.

The theme of *Ghosts* is not a new one in Ibsen. The reduction of Osvald to a state of death in life, calling for the sun, is closely related to the last cry of Brand—

Blood of children must be spilt
To atone for parents' guilt

—and the last cry of Julian:

Oh, Helios, Helios, why hast thou betrayed me?

That the inherited debt is a physical disease is a powerful local instance. But it was not only the pity and suffering associated with hereditary syphilis which mattered to Ibsen; although for obvious reasons it was what mattered to his admiring or repelled audience. The essential experience of *Ghosts* is not disease, but inheritance.

There is a curious ambiguity in the play, one's sense of which is reinforced when it is considered in the context of Ibsen's work as a whole. The specific text for consideration of this is Mrs Alving's famous speech:

> Ghosts! . . . I almost believe we are all ghosts, Pastor Manders. It is not only what we have inherited from our fathers and mothers that walks in us. It is every kind of dead idea, lifeless old beliefs and so on. They are not alive, but they cling to us for all that, and we can never rid ourselves of them. Whenever I read a newspaper I seem to see ghosts stealing between the lines. There must be ghosts the whole country over, as thick as the sands of the sea. And then we are all of us so wretchedly afraid of the light.

Here is the element of protest against subscription to dead beliefs, and the cry for light. But it is not simply a banner of the enlightenment, in the manner of the declaration of Lona in the first act of *Pillars of Society*:

> I'm going to let in some fresh air.

For it is recognized that:

> *We can never rid ourselves of them.*

We are, Ibsen insists, the creatures of our past. From the moment of our birth we are inevitably haunted, by every inherited debt. In *Brand*, Ibsen had written:

> Born to be tenants of the deep,
> Born to be exiles from the sun . . .
> Crying to heaven, *in vain* we pray
> For air and the glad flames of day.

And in *Brand* and *Emperor and Galilean* the progress had been, inevitably, "through darkness to light". Osvald, in *Ghosts*, was born to be an exile from the sun: in the final resolution of his life he prays in vain for the "glad flames of day":

> Mother, give me the sun.

The parallel with Julian is very close. Osvald, like Julian, had sought Helios:

> Have you noticed that everything I have painted has turned upon the joy of life?—always, always upon the joy of life?—light and sunshine and glorious air.

Osvald is as clearly as Julian a "sacrifice to necessity". But in *Ghosts* there are two important differences, in Ibsen's treatment of this recurrent theme, from his earlier, and from his later, treatments of it. The assurance of mercy is lacking; the absolution which was pronounced over Brand and Julian, and which was to be pronounced again over Rubek, is not given to Osvald. He goes out in his madness, in a fumble for the physical alleviation of his pain. This significant omission is related to the other new element in the play, the suggestion that the way "through darkness to light" is a false way:

> OSVALD: In the great world people won't hear of such things. There, nobody really believes such doctrines any longer.

It is the tone of liberal enlightenment, on which the Ibsenities seized.

There are hints, it is true, that Ibsen had not really changed his position. The idea of absolution had in many of his plays been bound up with the idea of a woman: it is Solveig who absolves Peer Gynt, Makrina who absolves Julian; each is described as "the pure woman". In *Ghosts* Osvald expects the act of mercy (although a different kind of mercy) from Regina. It is her refusal to act for him that denies him his peace. Again, the pursuit of "the joy of life", which is elsewhere shown as a strength, is hinted at as responsible for the sins of Captain Alving which begin the cycle of destruction. And the *uninsured* orphanage, to which Osvald is explicitly related, may suggest the very lack of the assurance of mercy which is caused by Mrs. Alving's absence of faith.

It is again a problem of convention, at that deepest level in which the relation between a belief and a method must be negotiated. Is *Ghosts*, that is to say, a human action, in which certain specific relationships are destructive, or is it a manifesting and generalizing action, in which the relationships *stand for* a design of forces beyond themselves? No simple answer can be given, for whereas elements of the dramatic design, in imagery and in what is called symbolism, suggest the latter, the immediate substance of the action, with its plotting of motivation, its insights into a private psychology, suggest the former, and this is powerfully reinforced by the local realism of speech and place. It is a compromise we have often subsequently seen: an apparent acceptance of naturalist attitudes to suffering, accompanied by a definite commitment to naturalist versions of observable reality, yet with a reserved, uneasy dimension in which the attitudes and observations are qualified, by hints of a different order of reality. But then what is interesting and permanent in *Ghosts* is the creative tension, so evident in its power to penetrate if not to connect, in which the nature of suffering is persistently explored, as a lived question. The form does not hold, as the many imitations have proved. It flies apart into the separate actions of an observed relationship, still essentially incomplete, and a revealed design, limited to hint and suggestion. In the end that choice must be made; its evasion is the history of orthodox naturalist drama. But here, in this powerful early example, the tension is active everywhere, and the achievement is exactly what we have described, in an essentially transitional writer: not that it controls or connects, but that it disturbs and penetrates.

5

In *Pillars of Society*, the leaky ship "The Indian Girl" becomes, in a sense, the play. The fortunes of all the persons are involved with it, and it would be possible to take it as an overall judgement on the dramatic situation. In *A Doll's House* the *tarantella* which Nora dances sums up the total situation of the play in a form which does not depend on words. In *Ghosts* the orphanage built in memory of Captain Alving, which is uninsured and which is burned down (it is a "whited sepulchre") is a similar statement of the total situation of the drama. In *An Enemy of the People* moral turpitude seems to find its material equivalent in the infected baths. In *The Wild Duck* the title-phrase, and the strange attic, summarize the total situation. In *Rosmersholm* the white horses seem to embody the past which gives meaning to the play. *Hedda Gabler* has a clear relation to the famous pistols.

All these elements, and some others in the last plays, comprise what is called Ibsen's "symbolism". The following abstract of certain statements about this method may form a basis for discussion. Consider:

Ibsen has no symbolism—GEORG BRANDES.

In Ibsen's case realism and symbolism have thriven very well together for more than a score of years. The contrasts in his nature incline him at once to fidelity to fact, and to mysticism.
—GEORG BRANDES.

Ibsen makes use of symbolism. . . . I should like to know the meaning of the house of a hundred stories built by Solness, from which he falls and breaks his neck—ÉMILE FAGUET.

The play [*A Doll's House*] is life itself. It has its symbol and it lays hold on the sympathy of the reader. But again it fails of artistic completeness. The symbol does not fit at all points.
—JEANNETTE LEE.

DRAMA FROM IBSEN TO BRECHT

In [*The Wild Duck*] and in *Rosmersholm* Ibsen perfected his own special power: the power to infuse the particular, drab, limited fact with a halo and a glory. . . . Ibsen had suppressed the poet in himself but this suppressed power lights up all his writing, giving it not only the rich concentration of *A Doll's House*, but the unifying cohesion of the symbolic.

—M. C. BRADBROOK.

The rationalist students of Ibsen tried to pin a single meaning on to his symbols: was the wild duck symbolic of Hedvig or of Hjalmar or of Gregers? Was Gregers a portrait of Ibsen or was he not? No one is likely to react in that way now.

—M. C. BRADBROOK.

Take for instance the history of Rubek's statue and its development into a group. In actual sculpture this development is a grotesque impossibility. In conceiving it we are deserting the domain of reality and plunging into some fourth dimension where the properties of matter are other than those we know. This is an abandonment of the fundamental principle which Ibsen over and over again emphatically expressed—namely, that any symbolism his work might be found to contain was entirely incidental, and subordinate to the truth and consistency of his picture of life—WILLIAM ARCHER.

Though Ibsen always strenuously denied that he used symbols, he fooled no one except William Archer—EVERT SPRINCHORN.

That the play is full of symbolism would be futile to deny; and the symbolism is mainly autobiographic. The churches which Solness sets out by building doubtless represent Ibsen's early romantic plays; the homes for human beings his social dramas; while the houses with high towers merging into castles in the air, stand for those spiritual dramas on which he was henceforth to be engaged—WILLIAM ARCHER.

Hedda Gabler *is* the pistol—JEANNETTE LEE.

Of course symbolism, at any time, is a difficult term. It indicates a permanent aspect of the creative process, in which meaning is concentrated into a unique image of action. At the same time, it has become a vogue word, and in one popular use is essentially presumptive of all normal methods of communication. Objects, as in modern literary idealism, are then regularly reduced to symbols, and the intensification of direct experience is seen as its transformation, into an alienated "symbolic" world. Now that it has been used so often, it is necessary to define, in the drama, the elements to which the term "symbolism" has been applied. To begin with, certain distinctions in Ibsen's practice must be noted.

In *Pillars of Society* the unseaworthy ship is not a dramatic device; it is nowhere shown. It is an external element and its main purpose is that of a precipitant in the action. Beyond this purpose, applied to the total situation of the play, it is merely a suggestive analogy. In *A Doll's House* the *tarantella* is a distinctly theatrical device; it adds nothing to the meaning of the play, but serves, in performance, to heighten a situation of which the audience has already, in direct terms, been made aware. It is the kind of device which Strindberg developed in the mimes of *Lady Julie*, a re-introduction of the elements of dance. In *Ghosts* the device is similar to that of "The Indian Girl". The situation is described in direct terms, but it is reinforced theatrically by the fire. The device, that is to say, comes very near to the provision of "stage atmosphere", referring back to the snowstorms in which the heroines of melodrama went out into the cruel world, and forward to the wind-machines of the contemporary playhouse. The orphanage in *Ghosts* is rather more particular than that; (and particularity is an important test of this device; when it is not particular it is simply "atmosphere").

In *An Enemy of the People* the infected baths are a non-visual element of the plot, giving Ibsen the opportunity to launch the crusading Stockmann. It is true, as with "The Indian Girl" that the infected baths may serve as an analogy for a corrupt society. But we do not need to ask ourselves anxiously whether they are symbolic. The analogy is expressly made, by Stockmann, in his speech at the public meeting. The play is not offered as anything more than a polemic (in reply to the vituperation which had greeted *Ghosts*) and as such it is still alive. The rhetoric against the compact, complacent liberal majority; the attack on sentimental devotion to "the masses"—"the masses are only the raw material from which a *people* is made"; the emphasis on the aristocratic principle (as opposed to the mediocrities who win popular applause); the declaration of the function of the conscious minority: all these still make lively liberal listening. Ibsen's desire to let loose some direct speech-making found its promised land in the famous scene at the public meeting. The play has been used as a banner by almost everyone, from anarchists to conservatives. In general terms, of course, they are all quite right. And this is the point about the analogy of the baths: in all political speeches analogy is a safe substitute for particularity. "The Indian Girl" is owned by the same company as the ubiquitous Ship of State. Dr. Stockmann's polluted baths have become the "swamp of mysticism and pornography" of M. Zhdanov.

But perhaps for those who make a case for Ibsen's use of symbolism in his prose plays, none of the works mentioned would be a main text. Such a text would almost certainly be *The Wild Duck*. This play, written in 1884, when Ibsen was fifty-six, is singled out by many critics as his greatest work.

Ibsen wrote of it to his publisher:

> The characters, in this play, despite their many frailties, have, in the course of our long daily association, endeared themselves to me. However, I hope they will also find good and kind friends among the great reading-public, and not least among the player-folk, to whom they all, without exception, offer problems worth the solving.

The play does as much as the fully naturalist play could ever do. It presents a richly assorted selection of characters, an interesting plot, and a high strain of emotion. The play is very skilful, and shows the elaboration of Ibsen's methods at this period at its most successful.

Clearly the central point for analysis is the wild duck, and its function. It may be right to rebuke the "rationalists" for trying to "pin the symbol" on to one or other of the characters; but the quarrel one makes in this respect is not really with William Archer and his men, but with Ibsen. What is the point which Ibsen makes about the bird?

> HJALMAR: She has lived in there so long now that she has forgotten her natural wild life; and it all depends on that.

The wild duck is an explicit figure for broken and frustrated lives. It is related to Hedvig:

> My wild duck; it belongs to me;

the child who, when urged to sacrifice the wild duck to prove that she loves her father, shoots herself. Gregers tells the father, Hjalmar:

> You have much of the wild duck in you.

Hjalmar thinks of the duck as his wife, Gina, the damaged present (the seduced maid) of the elder Wehrle:

> Mr Wehrle's wing-broken victim.

The damaged bird is also related to the elder Ekdal, who had been ruined by Wehrle:

> HJALMAR: Are you alluding to the well-nigh fatal shot that has broken my father's wing?

It is to Wehrle that all the damage goes back:

EKDAL: He was shooting from a boat, you see, and he brought her down. . . .

HEDVIG: She was hit under the wing so that she couldn't fly.

GREGERS: And I suppose she dived to the bottom.

EKDAL: Of course. Always do that, wild ducks do. They shoot to the bottom as deep as they can get, sir, and bury themselves fast in the tangle and seaweed, and all the devil's own mess that grows down there. And they never come up again.

GREGERS: But your wild duck came up again. Lieutenant Ekdal.

EKDAL: He had such an amazingly clever dog, your father had. And that dog—he dived in after the duck and fetched her up again.

GREGERS: [*turning to Hjalmar*]: And then she was sent to you here.

Gregers, Wehrle's son, becomes conscious of the debt, and sets out to pay it, in service to "the claim of the ideal". All he does is to finish off the work which his father had begun.

Ibsen speak of *The Wild Duck* as occupying

a place apart among my dramatic productions; its method of progress is in many respects divergent from that of its predecessors.

This has never been satisfactorily explained; but it would seem that the change is that the device, the "symbol", is used at every point in the presentation. It sets the total atmosphere of the broken, frustrated people who have forgotten "their natural life", and is the embodiment of the debt which Gregers so fatally pays. It thus covers the whole of the situation and action. In this respect it resembles the orphanage of Captain Alving or the infected baths or the unseaworthy ship. But it also does more: it is a means of definition of the main characters, who are all explicitly "revealed" in its terms. And it is this preoccupation with "character-revelation" that is the really new element of the play.

The problem in *The Wild Duck* is again one of convention, at an important and influential point in Ibsen's development. We shall find the same problem in Chekhov's *The Seagull*. The basic difficulty is to express the experience of a group through the "revelation" of individuals. To the extent that this is done through the action—the disturbance, by intrusion, of the settlement in which these people have come to terms with each other—*The Wild Duck* succeeds. But, just because the original disturbance is obscured, within the given relationships, and because it is also seen as general —a condition of mutual damage and lying which in the end takes the most innocent life—Ibsen needed a form which was more than the sum of the expressed relationships, and also more than the action, since the lost—the alienated—quality, the life that might have been possible and is still deeply desired, is by definition not available as action. The figure of the wild duck is his solution to both these problems. For the second, it is exact: it is an alienated, imprisoned life, which yet still has its defining identity. But for the first problem—the expression of more than the sum of the relationships, the expression of a group—it is less effective; it involves a constant reference, by individuals, to just that quality which is in their *relationships*, and yet which is pushed off-stage. In this difficulty, the references outward, to this defining but unseen quality, become in practice, often, a sentimental self-interpretation, for there is no other available general voice. It is true that this is an open form, in the special sense that it leaves elements of this inter-pretation to the actors; the play has always been popular in just that way. But the balance of the work is then exceptionally delicate: what is written as an outward process—the direction of separated people towards the element that connects them—can become a series of inward, self-conscious and self-regarding gestures: not, in fact, the revelation of character, in any general sense, but the demonstration, very consciously shown to an audience, of a kind of mirror-privacy: gestures made, not to understand oneself, but to show oneself to others, in some negotiable form. This procedure is now, of course, a whole method of acting; it is theatrical orthodoxy at its most practised and confident. What is called an acting skill (and it is of course skilful) is in so much contemporary theatre a craft to express a very particular structure of feeling: the "hidden" personality, the inner life that is not communicable but is yet continually drawn attention to, the awkwardness with others as each plays his separate part in this collective game. *The Wild Duck*, more than any other play, stands at the head of this theatrical tradition; Ibsen's genius embodied just that mode. But then the irony is that the penetration of an illusion, which is the theme of the play—a dangerous penetration, which ends in a death—can be effectively contradicted by just this self-conscious, self-revealing, self-acting tone. The real emotional disturbance gets into the convention which is meant to express it, and the result, though interesting, is very deeply insecure.

Rosmersholm, the next play, is a more substantial work than anything Ibsen had written since *Peer Gynt*. It realizes the tension which had lain behind *Brand*—the inevitable conflict between response to vocation and inherited debt. Ibsen examines this experience in a double aspect, through Rosmer and Rebekke, but it is a single experience, just as, in the play, Rosmer and Rebekke come to realize:

> We are one.

Rosmer is a creature of his past, the "death in life" of Rosmersholm. To fight his way out to life, to bring light

> where the Rosmer family has from generation to generation been a centre of darkness

his own strength is insufficient. While he has faith in Rebekke he can act; but the dead voice of Beata, revealed in her letter to Mortensgaard, ends his illusions. He has no choice. Against a past which was dark, Rebekke opposes ideas of emancipation. But the ideas "have not passed into her blood". She becomes simply predatory, and the ideal of a "pure" partnership with Rosmer in his crusade for nobility—a crusade to which she persuades him— becomes an "uncontrollable" physical passion which drives her to destroy his wife. From this guilt there is no living absolution. From this guilt Rosmer himself is not free; the very fantasy of his purposed nobility, his inherited inability to live, is her silent abettor. The freedom which might have been expected when Beata is gone is simply illusory. Guilt, the inheritance of Rosmersholm, has "infected her will".

> I have lost the power of action, Rosmer.

With both, in the words of *When We Dead Awaken*, it is

> a place where you stick fast, you cannot go forward or backward.

The crusade for nobility, like the "brief mountain-vision" of Brand, is nothing more than an "immature idea":

> We cannot be ennobled from without.

By whatever system their position is judged, the reality is the same:

> REBEKKE: I am under the dominion of the Rosmersholm way of life, now. What I have sinned—it is fit that I should expiate.
> ROSMER: Is *that* your point of view?
> REBEKKE: Yes.
> ROSMER: Well then, *I* stand firm in our emancipated view of life, Rebekke. There is no judge over us; and therefore we must do justice upon ourselves. . . . If you go, I go with you.

They die in the millrace, the stream of the old Rosmersholm:

> The dead woman has taken them.

Rosmersholm is an impressive play, with its finely worked texture, and its authentic particularity. The problem it raises most sharply, as again and again in this continually creative dramatist, is one of general form: here the difficult relation between the modern play and the modern novel. Rosmer and Rebekke are studied, as characters, in much greater detail (and in a different kind of detail) than the characters in earlier plays. This refinement, essentially, is fictional: a degree of attention to motive and development, seen as slow and partly unconscious processes, which had become actual in the European novel in the second half of the nineteenth century. At the same time, as characters in the play, in word, action and gesture, Rosmer and Rebekke must function as explicit figures: the characters are separated from the enclosing work, by the essential dramatic convention, to a degree well beyond that of the novel. The separation is an emphasis—the strength of the dramatic convention —and also a loss of dimension, when that kind of analysis of motive and development is in question. For what a novel has, and this kind of play has not, is the faculty of commentary and analysis. Even where the action and characters of a novel are presented in a generally naturalistic way, the novelist can at any moment use a different voice, introduce different kinds of evidence, bring in facts other than those communicable in direct or probable speech. In reaching out, in *Rosmersholm*, to that kind of substance—not simply the presented characters, but the characters developing and reflecting on their development, which they yet do not, in their simple capacity as characters, wholly understand—Ibsen drew on all his powers, and went as far as the method could take him; but still, inevitably, not really far enough. At the point where elements of the experience can not, by internal logic, be spoken, he intro- duces, in a development from *The Wild Duck*, the figure of the white horses (which was his first title for the play). Moreover, he develops, to a new degree, a structure of dialogue which, in its essential originality, is an important development, though it is also questionable. This is, within the imitation of speech, a form of persons talking past each other, at what is really an element out- side: the white horses, the Rosmersholm way of life, the mill-stream. It is not the series of self-revelations of *The Wild Duck*; it is a pattern of voices, controlled by something that is not a voice; it is "we two", but speaking to and in the shadow of the external result of their unspoken actions and experiences. The method corresponds, as so consistently in Ibsen, to the theme; it is this creative precision and development which is always impressive. But it is still a very diffi- cult form, in that the characters are at the same time explicit figures of the drama and as it were displaced summaries of the slowly realized figures of the novel:

ROSMER: There is no judge over us; and therefore we must do justice upon ourselves.

REBECCA (*misunderstanding him*): Yes, that is true, that too.

Or again:

ROSMER: The husband shall go with his wife, as the wife with her husband.

REBECCA: Yes, but first tell me this: is it you who follow me? Or is it I who follow you?

ROSMER: We shall never think that question out.

REBECCA: But I should like to know.

ROSMER: We go with each other, Rebecca—I with you and you with me.

REBECCA: I almost think that is the truth.

ROSMER: For now we two are one.

REBECCA: Yes. We are one. Come! We go gladly.

It follows exactly from this structure of dialogue, of the two talking past each other to a pattern and a consequence, that what they then do is seen by a shift of viewpoint, now differently external, as the housekeeper sees them fall to the millrace and concludes the play not with her voice but with the general voice of the determining structure:

HELSETH: . . . The dead wife has taken them.

There is one other aspect of the play to which attention must be drawn, as part of the exposition of Ibsen's essential attitude to experience. *Rosmersholm* has been spoken of as a play of the enlightenment; but it is in fact quite the opposite. When Rosmer speaks of atonement, Rebekke asks:

If you were deceiving yourself? If it were only a delusion? One of those white horses of Rosmersholm.

But Rosmer answers equivocally:

It may be so. We can never escape them, we of this house.

It is the cry of Mrs. Alving, faced by the ghosts:

We can never rid ourselves of them.

The command to attempt emancipation from the past is insistent; it is one aspect of "vocation". But the attempt, in Ibsen, is almost certain to fail. This is the persistent pattern. In *The Wild Duck*, we should not have heard so much of Ibsen's supposed repudiation of his former attitudes, if his actual work, and not merely Shaw's exposition of it, had been sufficiently known. For Ibsen recognized, in experience, both the command to emancipation, and its

61

consequences. Hedvig Ekdal is not the first casualty of a pursuit of truth; there were also Brand and the Emperor Julian.

Rosmersholm is the essential introduction to the last plays, but, before proceeding to them, Ibsen wrote two very individual works —*Lady from the Sea*, and *Hedda Gabler*. More justly than any other work of Ibsen, *Lady from the Sea* could be called a problem play. Ellida had been, in the words of Brand, "born to be a creature of the deep". This sense of origin, which is so crucial in Ibsen, seems here to be considered a mere obsession, susceptible to direct cure.

> WANGEL: I begin to understand you, by degrees. You think and conceive in images, in visible pictures. Your longing and yearning for the sea, the fascination that he, the stranger, possessed for you, must have been the expression of an awakening and growing need for freedom within you—nothing else. . . . But now you will come to me again, will you not, Ellida?
>
> ELLIDA: Yes, my dear, now I will come to you again. I can now, for now I come to you in freedom, of my own will, and of my own responsibility. . . . And we shall have all our memories in common.

And again:

> BALLESTED: Human beings can acclimatize themselves.
> ELLIDA: Yes, in freedom they can.
> WANGEL: And under full responsibility.
> ELLIDA: *That* is the secret.

This is the only positive example, in Ibsen's work, of the idea of acclimatization, of the past being overcome and absorbed into a living present. The Ellida theme in the play is powerful, and the tone of statement in its resolution is only unsatisfactory because the play as a whole is a hybrid of so many methods and achieves no compelling total form. The early acts are remarkable mainly for their observation of the local scene; in the development of the group of characters there is a looseness of technique which is surprising when one remembers the play's date. As a result, the Ellida theme is blurred, and does not achieve major emotional effect. It seems a half-felt *example*, and its resolution comes to appear didactic for this reason.

Hedda Gabler may also be taken as a psychological study, but it is a very much more powerful play. Ibsen wrote to Count Prozor:

> The title of the play is *Hedda Gabler*. My intention in giving it this name was to indicate that Hedda, as a personality, is to be regarded rather as her father's daughter than as her husband's wife.

For Hedda is still, fundamentally, a child, and a child of her particular past. She is the daughter of a General, with the narrow traditions of a military caste behind her; she has inherited the ethical nullity of her class. She cannot, like Ellida, find herself through freedom and responsibility. Freedom is inhibited by what she and Lovborg call cowardice, a dread of scandal. The dread is of adult responsibility, as here with the possibility of a child:

BRACK: A new responsibility, Fru Hedda?
HEDDA: Be quiet! Nothing of that sort will ever happen. . . . I have no turn for anything of the sort. . . . No responsibilities for me! . . . I often think there is only one thing in the world I have any turn for. . . . Boring myself to death.

Like Peer Gynt, and perhaps like Julian, her only outlet is the fantasy of self. Her desire to see Lovborg with "vine-leaves in his hair" recalls Peer's wish for the same adornment when he is with Anitra; or Julian's assumption of a wreath of vine-leaves when, at the moment of his apostasy, he impersonates Dionysus. But just as even Peer Gynt's myth of self-sufficiency could be sustained only by his inherited talent for romancing, so Hedda's is only thinkable while she retains "General Gabler's pistols". At every crisis, at every contact with a real situation, she has no equipment but her negative, and ultimately destructive, tradition; at every crisis she acts with the pistols. One might say that the only thing which explains and holds together the "overwhelming and incomprehensible" Hedda is the embodiment in General Gabler's pistols of her pre-adult amorality.

But this use of the pistols is not Ibsen's only resource. The situation is expounded in its own terms, explicitly. We see this in the passage quoted above, and in this characteristic question:

BRACK: Why should you not, also, find some vocation in life, Fru Hedda?
HEDDA: A vocation, that should attract me?
BRACK: If possible, of course.
HEDDA: Heaven knows what sort of vocation that could be.

The mechanical logic of Hedda's destruction is completely convincing, as well as being very exciting in the theatre. I find myself agreeing with Mr. Wolf Mankowitz when he writes:

In a sense *Hedda Gabler* is a farce.

It is indeed, the kind of savage farce which it is traditionally difficult to distinguish from melodrama: T. S. Eliot's example in this genre was Marlowe's *Jew of Malta;* from contemporary work one might add Canetti's *Auto-da-Fé*. Strindberg's *Lady Julie* is closely related, and Ibsen certainly seems to have been very conscious of Strindberg's work at this time. The plays form an interesting ground for comparison, and, although Strindberg's play was written three years earlier, the question of influence would not be a simple one to determine. For although there are many features in Ibsen's play which seem simply reminiscent, Ibsen was in fact, in *Hedda Gabler*, consolidating the features of much of his early work—work of which the younger Strindberg was well aware. *Hedda Gabler*, too, is thematically centred in Ibsen's major work, for, like so many others, Hedda is destroyed by her inherited debt. But there is no mercy; "merciless" indeed is the predominant mood.

6

Look!
When I left the country I sailed by here. . . .
In there, where the screes and the clefts lie blue,
Where the valleys, like trenches, gloom narrow and dark,
And lower, skirting the open fiords:
It's in places like *these* human beings abide.
They build far apart in this country. . . .

The speaker of these words is an old white-haired man, of a "somewhat hard expression", who leans on the rail of a ship from the South, approaching the coast of Norway at sunset. He is returning to the land of his birth, from which as a young man he had gone into exile. To his side, a minute later, comes a Strange Passenger, offering to buy and take possession of his dead body. What the passenger seeks, he explains, is the "centre of dreams".

The name of the old man is not Henrik Ibsen, but Peer Gynt. Ibsen had written *Peer Gynt* in the early years of his own exile, in 1867. In 1891, after twenty-seven years of exile, Ibsen made his own return to Norway. He was then sixty-three, and an acknowledged master of European drama. In the next eight years he wrote his four final plays.

"You are essentially right," Ibsen wrote to Count Prozor, "in assuming that the series which ends with the Epilogue [*When We Dead Awaken*] began with *The Masterbuilder*." The last plays have indeed long been recognized as a group; but it is less often realized that they are a group very much within Ibsen's work as a whole. The immediately preceding plays had foreshadowed something of their mood; and the return from exile is not only to Norway, but to the world of *The Pretenders*, *Brand*, and *Peer Gynt*.

The Masterbuilder resembles *Brand* and *When We Dead Awaken*
in the final climb to annihilation, but the fact that Solness falls by
his own act, whereas Brand and Rubek are overwhelmed by an
external force, the avalanche, marks an essential difference of
resolution. The use of fire as a crisis in development relates *The
Masterbuilder*, in a minor degree, to *Little Eyolf*, where the love of
Allmers and Rita is described as a "consuming fire", but it relates
even more to the burned forest of *Peer Gynt*, to the fire at the old
house in *On the Vidda*, to the burning of Julian's fleet in *Emperor and
Galilean*, to Hedda Gabler's crucial burning of Lovborg's manuscript, and to the fire in *Ghosts* which destroyed the memorial to
Captain Alving. The theme of the unborn children in *The Masterbuilder* relates back to *Hedda Gabler* as well as forward to *When We
Dead Awaken*. Similarly, in *Little Eyolf*, the figure of the Rat-Wife
relates, not to any of the last plays, but to the Strange Passenger in
Peer Gynt ("there went Death and I, like two good fellow-travellers")
and to the Stranger in *Lady from the Sea*. The drowning of Eyolf may
similarly be related to the incident in *The Wild Duck*, in which old
Wehrle shoots the wild duck, which falls "to the bottom of the sea,
as deep as it can get".

Further, the important experiences of vocation and of debt,
which appear directly in all the last plays, appear also, as we have
seen, in *The Pretenders*, *Brand*, *Peer Gynt*, *Emperor and Galilean*, *Ghosts*,
Rosmersholm, and *Hedda Gabler*. *Little Eyolf* ends in a resolution within
life, as had *Lady from the Sea*, and, equivocally, *Peer Gynt*. *The
Masterbuilder*, *John Gabriel Borkman*, and *When We Dead Awaken*,
like *Brand*, *Emperor and Galilean*, *Ghosts*, *Rosmersholm*, and *Hedda Gabler*,
have their only solution in death.

And, if the last plays cannot be set apart in theme, neither can
they in technique. *Little Eyolf* resembles *Rosmersholm* and, more
particularly, *Lady from the Sea* more than it resembles *John Gabriel
Borkman*. The method of *The Masterbuilder* is more that of *Rosmersholm* or of *Ghosts* than of *When We Dead Awaken*. *John Gabriel Borkman*
and *When We Dead Awaken* have important resemblances of theme,
but as plays they are as different as, say, *Rosmersholm* and *Brand*.

What I am arguing is that we should not let biography usurp
the functions of criticism. The Ibsenites, having placed Ibsen's
maturity somewhere between *Ghosts* and *Rosmersholm*, prolonged
their biological simile and dismissed the last plays as a decline.
"Down among the Dead Men," said Shaw, and Down, Down,
Down was the estimate of the last plays as they appeared. Mysticism,
hypnotism, symbolism, supernaturalism; these are the terms which
abound in the usual accounts. And it is true that these elements, or

elements resembling them, appear in the last plays. But they appear also almost everywhere in Ibsen's work. It is only in the sterilized figure of his dogmatic admirers and opponents that there is no room for these consistent and essential elements of his art.

The last plays, then, cannot be explained, or explained away, as a period. Our judgement of them is an integral part of our general judgement of Ibsen. The four plays demand consideration each as an individual work of art.

The Masterbuilder is in some ways the most interesting. It is a powerful realization of the experience of guilt and retribution; conscience is altogether the wrong word.

> All that I have succeeded in doing, building, creating . . . all this I have to make up for, to pay for. And not with my own happiness only, but with other people's too. That is the price which my position as an artist has cost me, and others. And every single day I have to look on while the price is paid for me anew. Over again, and over again, and over again for ever.

The foundation of Solness's career was the burning of the old house which he and his wife had inherited. The fire may not have been his fault; in practical terms, it clearly was not. Yet:

> . . . Suppose the fault was mine, in a certain sense. All of it, the whole thing. And yet perhaps—I may not have had anything to do with it.

When Hilde asks,

> But may it not come right, even yet?

Solness answers:

> Never in this world, never. That is another consequence of the fire.

Solness is the agent of his own fate; he climbs himself to the tower from which he falls. But

> . . . it is not one's self alone that can do such great things. Oh no, the helpers and servers, they must do their part too. But they never come of themselves. One has to call upon them very persistently; inwardly, you understand.

To this last scene of his life, Hilde, the "bird of prey", has been called, *by himself*. She is the "helper and server" of his final payment.

"What is the meaning," asked M. Émile Faguet, "of the house of a hundred storeys, built by Solness, from which he falls and breaks his neck?" It was not as high as all that, but the question, in one form or another, is a very frequent one. It is, of course, a question

that cannot be answered, except within the terms of the play. The
tower is not something else. It is a part of the play's landscape
which one has to accept, as were the mountains in *Brand*, the
shipwreck in *Peer Gynt*, or the ocean in *Lady from the Sea*. None of
these elements is a symbol, in dramatic terms, except in the sense
that everything in a work of literature—event, character, landscape
—is symbolic. It is of course true that certain elements in *The
Masterbuilder*—the tower itself, the crack in the chimney, the nine
dolls which Aline carried under her heart, the dreams of Solness
and Hilde that they are falling, with their "legs drawn up under"
them—are capable of an explanation in Freudian terms, in the
same way as are the pistols in *Hedda Gabler*, or the gallery of John
Gabriel Borkman. But one cannot abstract certain elements of a
work, and try to explain them outside its terms. It is a central
difficulty of *The Masterbuilder* that there are, as it were, alternative
schemes of dramatic imagery; or if not alternatives, a scatter of
images, at a point of creative tension, which in the end are not fully
integrated. It is not the method of the single dominant image, as
in *The Wild Duck*, but this is because the emphasis is shifting to a
more internal search. What comes through is not so much a
dramatic definition as a release of images, as in a dream. And then
the leading image, of the builder and the tower, is developed to the
point where it offers to assimilate the others, though in fact it
attracts them by tension rather than by composition and integration. The tower and the climb are of course powerful: it is the
movement of the end of *Brand* and *When We Dead Awaken*—that
essential moment in Ibsen when a man dies climbing. But such a
moment is simpler, in feeling, in the imagery of the mountains;
in *The Masterbuilder* it edges, on reflection, towards analogy. And
yet in the moment itself, in that triumphant terrible cry—"*my
masterbuilder*"—as the body is distantly seen falling, Ibsen actual-
ized a disturbing and persistent fear with what, even for him, is an
exceptional power.

The particular significance of *Little Eyolf*, the play which, after
the customary two-year interval, next appeared, is that it virtually
dispenses with "characters", in the sense in which Ibsen, and the
naturalist theatre after him, understood the term. The main
persons of the play are not so much independent portraits, as
aspects of a central dramatic concept. This concept is that of
Eyolf, the embodiment of remorse. Eyolf is not only the crippled
child whose "calling" is to be a soldier. Eyolf is Asta, the woman
with whom Allmers had lived in happiness, and also Allmers
himself. Rita, with her "gold, and green forests", comes to be

governed by Eyolf, first in her desire to be rid of the child's "evil eye", and later by the wide-open eyes of the drowned child staring up at her from the depths. The Rat-Wife is a "helper and server". Only Borgheim, the faithful roadbuilder, is part of the usual mechanism of character. The rest exist only as aspects of the specific consciousness of Eyolf.

The play is written in an even, restrained language, which bears the tone of analysis rather than declamation. It is the language to which Ibsen was to return in *When We Dead Awaken*. After parts of *The Wild Duck* and *The Masterbuilder* this cool, tempered style is particularly satisfying.

The child Eyolf is crippled as a direct result of Allmer's betrayal of himself for the "gold, and green forests", in the person of the beautiful Rita:

ALLMERS: You called, you, you, you—and drew me after you.
RITA: Admit it. You forgot the child and everything else.
ALLMERS: That is true. I forgot the child, in your arms.
RITA: This is intolerable of you.
ALLMERS: In that hour you condemned little Eyolf to death.
RITA: You also. You also, if it is as you say.
ALLMERS: Yes, call me also to account, if you wish. We both have sinned. There was, after all, retribution in Eyolf's death.
RITA: Retribution?
ALLMERS: Judgement. Upon you and me. Now, as we stand here, we have our deserts. While he lived, we let ourselves shrink from his sight, in secret, abject remorse. We could not bear to see it, the thing he must drag with him.
RITA: The crutch.

With Rita the impulse was passion, the desire for absolute possession of the man she had bought. With Allmers, the crippling of Eyolf is the result of an older debt. His love for Asta began as payment of a debt inherited from his father:

I had so much injustice to compensate.

And, farther back, the sin of Asta's mother cripples their life. For Asta was not the child of Allmers's father, but of another, and her mother had lied. The love of Allmers and Asta could never be consummated because of an assumed blood-relationship, which was, in fact, only the covering of this lie. So Allmers married Rita, and the cycle of retribution widened. For their "love" was only

a consuming fire.

It was Asta, "Little Eyolf" as Allmers had habitually called her, who forced them on each other under the crippling weight of her mother's lie.

And then the crippled child is drawn away by the Rat-Wife, the "sweetener of the earth", drawn away and drowned in the depths of the fiord:

ALLMERS: How merciless the fiord looks today, lying so heavy and drowsy, leaden-grey, with splashes of yellow, reflecting the rain-clouds.

ASTA: You must not sit staring over the fiord.

ALLMERS: Yes, over the surface. But in the depths—there sweeps the rushing undertow.

ASTA: For God's sake, do not think of the depths.

But from the depths the "little stranger-boy" stares up with wide-open eyes. And the crutch floats. These are the substance of remorse.

After Eyolf's death, Allmers dreams that he sees him whole and alive again, and thanks and blesses—whom? He will not name God; his faith has long been lost. In his trip to the mountains, however, in contact with "the loneliness and the great waste places", he had become conscious of death:

There went death and I, like two good fellow-travellers.

In the light of this consciousness, his life-effort had seemed insubstantial. And when his fellow-traveller took Eyolf, to whom he had turned for solace but whom he had never really known,

Then I felt the horror of it; of it all; of all that, in spite of everything, we dare not tear ourselves away from. So earthbound are we, both of us. . . . And yet, an empty void on all sides.

Allmers had reached, in Conrad's phrase, the "heart of darkness"; his cry is that of the dying Kurtz—"The horror, the horror." But Allmers attempts to fill the void, in caring for the children of the quayside, which Rita has undertaken

to make my peace with the great open eyes.

It is the resolve of Brand:

Daily duty, daily labour,
Hallowed to a Sabbath deed.

ALLMERS: We have a heavy day of work before us, Rita.

RITA: You will see—that now and then a Sabbath peace will descend on us.

ALLMERS: Then perhaps we shall know that the spirits are with us—those whom we have lost. . . .

RITA: Where shall we look for them?

ALLMERS: Upwards. Toward the peaks. Toward the stars. Toward the great silence.

This ending of the play should make it clear that what Ibsen has in mind is not an "acclimatization", although a summary of the action, showing Allmers and Rita filling their personal loss with "a heavy day of work" might indicate this. The word is *acceptance*, in its spiritual sense; the final acceptance of the concept of "Eyolf".

John Gabriel Borkman, like *Little Eyolf*, expresses a situation in which very little is possible. Its persons are essentially shadows; creatures of an inevitable Death, which they must learn to accept:

> Never dream of life again. Lie quiet where you are.

Borkman, Gunhild, and Ella can no more break out of their deadlock than could Allmers and Asta and Rita. They can move, but only into the death of Borkman.

Yet the method of the play is very different from that of *Little Eyolf*. It is not only John Gabriel Borkman who paces the long gallery, to the arranged playing of the *danse macabre*; it is the ghost of the romantic theatre. The end of the play is the conventional finale of the romantic tragedy, the joining of hands over the dead:

> We twin sisters, over him we have both loved.
> We two shadows, over the dead man.

The play as a whole is the last act of a romantic tragedy. The other acts are included, are assumed, by what is known as Ibsen's "retrospective technique". But one must not think of this technique in terms of a textbook "device" to provide economy. The manner is retrospective because the whole experience of the play is retrospect. Those critics of the play who "tell the story" of the ruined banker, starting at the beginning and leading up to the end, miss the essential point. It is not Borkman's past, his "story", which matters, but his attitude to the past. The tension of the play is between Borkman's retrospect, which is his life, and his actual condition, which is death.

In *When We Dead Awaken*, Ibsen made his last attempt: the dramatic epilogue to his whole response to "calling". *When We Dead Awaken* is an epilogue, but it is also a drama. To argue that it is "not really a play at all" is simply to argue that it is not a naturalist play. The work has always been curiously misunderstood.

The most notable single factor about the technique of *When We Dead Awaken*, for which there is a certain precedent in *Little Eyolf*, and a clear precedent in *Brand* and *Peer Gynt*, is Ibsen's rejection of the "individual personality" as the basis of the character-convention in drama. Rubek, Irene, Maia, Ulfheim, are "ultimately . . . not human at all, but purely symbols of a poetic vision". The "drama is enacted by symbolic creatures formed out of human consciousness; puppets if you like; but not human *individuals*".

Rubek and Irene conceived and formed, in their youth, a figure, the lovely image of

the Resurrection, a pure woman awakening to light and glory.

But Rubek, for his life-work, rejected the real Irene, under the command that had lain on Julian:

Kill the body that the soul may live.

He rejected his human destiny, his own and that of Irene. He was concerned only with his "vocation", with the statue that would bring him glory, that would be placed in museums— "grave-vaults" as Irene calls them. He says, much later:

RUBEK: All this talk about the artist's vocation and the artist's mission and so forth began to strike me as being very empty, and hollow, and ultimately meaningless.

MAIA: What would you put in its place, then?

RUBEK: Life. . . . Is not life in sunshine and beauty a hundred times better worth while than to hang about to the end of your days in a raw damp hole, wearing yourself out in a perpetual struggle with lumps of clay and blocks of stone?

Irene, too, has betrayed her destiny:

It was self-murder, a deadly sin against myself. And that sin I can never expiate. . . . I should have borne children into the world, many children, real children, not such children as are hidden away in grave-vaults.

With Rubek, the rejection of life affects his art also:

I learned worldly wisdom in the years that followed, Irene. "The Resurrection Day" became in my mind's eye something more and something—more complex. The little round plinth, on which your figure stood, erect and solitary, no longer afforded room for all the imagery I now wanted to add. . . . I imaged that which I saw with my eyes around me in the world. . . . I expanded the plinth, made it wide and spacious. And on it I placed a segment of the curving, bursting earth. And up from the fissures of the soil there now swarm men and women with dimly suggested animal faces. Women and men, as I knew them in real life. . . . I had, unfortunately, to move your figure a little back. For the sake of the general effect.

This was "the masterpiece that went round the world", which made Rubek famous.

MAIA: All the world knows it is a masterpiece.

RUBEK: "All the world" knows nothing. Understands nothing. . . .
What is the good of working oneself to death for the mob and
the masses, for "all the world"?

MAIA: Do you think it is better, that it is worthy of *you*, to do
nothing at all but a portrait bust now and then?

RUBEK: These are no mere portrait busts I can tell you. There is
something equivocal, something cryptic, lurking in and behind
those busts—a secret something that the people themselves
cannot see . . . I alone can see it. And it amuses me unspeakably.
On the surface I give them the "striking likeness", as they call
it, that they all stand and gape at in astonishment. But at
bottom they are . . . simply the dear domestic animals, Maia.
All the animals which men have bedevilled in their own image,
and which have bedevilled men in return. . . . It is these
equivocal works of art that our excellent plutocrats come and
order from me. And pay for in all good faith. . . .

The situation of Rubek and Irene can be summarized in the
words of Julian:

The old beauty is no longer beautiful, and the new truth is no
longer true.

Irene, the lovely and innocent woman, has become the naked
poseur at variety shows. The new truth, "the striking likeness", is
a simply zoological naturalism.
Irene has played out lust into madness.

They lowered me into a grave-vault, with iron bars before the
loop-hole, and with padded walls, so that no one of the earth
above could hear the grave-shrieks.

The vision of innocence is dead and crippled. And Rubek, the
"strong man who stands alone", has simply, like the scorpion,
emptied his poison into the soft flesh, and is incapable of a living
relationship. His marriage to Maia is simply

a tedious coasting-voyage to the north.

He is capable, indeed, of remorse:

Let me tell you how I have placed myself in the group. In
front, beside a fountain . . . sits a man weighed down with guilt,
who cannot quite free himself from the earth-crust. I call him
remorse for a forfeited life. He sits there and dips his fingers in
the stream—to wash them clean—and he is tortured by the
thought that never, never will he succeed.

But Irene tells him:

> You are nerveless and sluggish and full of forgiveness for all the sins of your life, in thought and in act. You have killed my soul, so you model yourself in remorse, and self-accusation, and penance—and with that you think your account is cleared.

All that is certain is:

IRENE: We see the irretrievable only when . . .
RUBEK: When? . . .
IRENE: When we dead awaken.
RUBEK: What do we really see then?
IRENE: We see that we have never lived.

But the "two clay-cold bodies, playing together by the Lake of Taunitz", make one last attempt: to spend

> a summer night on the uplands . . . for once live life to its uttermost, before we go down to our graves again.

Maia is happy with the hunter Ulfheim; Rubek and Irene believe they are free. But as they climb, they come, in Ulfheim's words,

> to a tight place where you stick fast. There is no going forward or backward.

While Maia sings triumphantly, from the depths below, of her freedom, Rubek and Irene, high up on the snowfield, are engulfed by the avalanche, and perish. Over them, the Sister of Mercy makes the sign of the cross before her in the air, and pronounces the blessing:

> Peace be with you.

It is the last absolution.

There is hardly any action in the play, and certainly no individual characters. The work is not a return to poetic drama, but it holds related intentions. In the technical sense, the interesting development is one that has become historical. Perhaps under the influence of Strindberg, and certainly under the weight of his ruthless self-analysis, Ibsen has here written what came to be called an expressionist play. The "speaking likeness" of naturalism is realized for what it is, and rejected. The statue which is central in the play is clearly a development of Ibsen's earlier attempts at "symbolism": an external framework for examination of a pattern of experience. But it is the characters which are new. The expressionist play has been described as a "manifestation of an inner, autobiographical drama, projected into characters which are posed in contrasted poles". This would be a just description of *When We Dead Awaken*. "The tight place, where you stick fast; there is no going forward or backward." When he had finished *When We Dead Awaken* Ibsen talked of "perhaps another attempt—in verse". But he had reached the end of his strength; he collapsed into physical and mental impotence, and passed his last years in a form of living death.

7

Ibsen's persistence of theme is important in itself, and because it is the answer to those, including his admirers, who have reduced his work to the dramatization of opinions and attitudes. As a whole experience it is still very powerful. It is still the crucial action of that movement of liberal tragedy which has been a central experience of modern Western civilization. It belongs to history now, but the actions are still valid, and still hold though they can no longer release the imagination. What we have also to recognize is the extraordinary creativeness in dramatic method: not only in the plays from *Ghosts* to *Rosmersholm*, in which he made a new major form with a precision and controlled power that are still, in that mode, unequalled; but in the other forms—in *Brand* and *Peer Gynt*; in *Hedda Gabler*; in the pale clear world of the last plays. There are still disturbing questions to put to his experience, and the precise success of this form and that has to be questioned, defined, often limited. But we have always to remember that in making any final valuation we are committed to valuing something of which we are still a part; something which, more than any other man, Ibsen created: the consciousness of modern European drama.

2

AUGUST STRINDBERG

I

"IBSEN", said Bjornson, "is not a man, but a pen." This unfortunate condition is not, of course, without its advantages. It serves at least to protect an artist from his biographers.

The velvet-coated Strindberg, his eyes fixed in "the diabolic expression", his hands burned by the crucibles of his experiments in alchemy; the rages, the passions, the renunciations; the series Siri von Essen, Harriet Bosse, Frieda Ulm; the pose at the window of the Blue Room in Stockholm above the triumphal torchlight procession; these phenomena, confronting us from scores of perfervid illustrated pages, suggest irresistibly the advantages of being remembered as a mere pen. "Nobody would ever have heard of a Lawrence who was not an artist," wrote Mr. Aldous Huxley, criticizing a similar beginning in hagiography. It is, after all, the pen for which we remember Strindberg.

Everyone who knows Strindberg knows that he drew directly on his personal experience in his writing. The biography can readily be used to gloss, but not to explain or judge, the literature. It is time to say, after fifteen wild Decembers, that criticism requires a different discipline. The present essay will be concerned solely with Strindberg as dramatist, and limitation of space is not pleaded as an apology.

2

Strindberg, in a writing life of nearly forty years, wrote more than sixty plays, as well as more than thirty works of fiction, autobiography, politics, and history. By any standard this is a very prolific output indeed, and it is understandable that most of us, in England, know only a part of it.

Mention of Strindberg, to the theatregoer, usually brings as narrowly defined a response as does mention of Ibsen. With Ibsen the association is feminism, heredity, and the fully-furnished family play—usually *A Doll's House* or *Ghosts*. With Strindberg it is anti-

feminism, hysteria, and the play of violent action or declaration—
The Father, say, or *Lady Julie*, or *The Dance of Death*.

These responses, like the public projections of most artists, contain an element of truth. But Strindberg, like Ibsen, cannot be easily typed; a study of his development shows a variety of dramatic method and purpose, and an immense range of technical experiment, which ought to be appreciated if we are to form anything like a just estimate of his status as a dramatist.

Strindberg was writing plays in his late teens and early twenties, and indeed from this period can be dated the very remarkable history play—*Master Olof*, which he went on revising and re-writing until he was twenty-eight, when it was at last produced in the form in which we now have it. During these years Strindberg had also been trying to become an actor, with very little success.

Master Olof shows in a remarkable degree that quality for which all Strindberg's historical plays may be valued: a freedom from abstraction and from what we may call historicism. Strindberg, like the maturing Shakespeare, took a series of historical events, not so much for their own sake, as for their potency to recreate the texture of a experience which the author might also have communicated directly. I mean that Strindberg took such stories as those of Olof, and in later years Gustav Vasa and Eric XIV, partly because they were the facts of his own history, but mainly because when communicated with his unique vigour and immediacy they became an embodiment of tangible contemporary qualities; fidelity, power, intrigue, ambition, and loyalty. The historical events provided an objective dramatic discipline.

His next important play is one of a group of three written in his early thirties: the fairy play *Lucky Peter's Travels* (1882). This play invites comparison with Ibsen's *Peer Gynt*, which had been written some fifteen years earlier. *Lucky Peter's Travels* is inferior, verbally, to *Peer Gynt*; but it shows that remarkable power of dramatic visualization which was to be so important in the later, more experimental, work of *The Road to Damascus*, *Dreamplay* and *Ghost Sonata*. Realism of scene is firmly set aside; the travels of Peter, the boy who achieves his manhood through a magical insight into the nature of power, are rendered with a virtuosity of scene that was quite beyond the theatre of Strindberg's own day. More clearly even than Ibsen, Strindberg was creating a kind of dramatic action—a sequence of images in language and visual composition—which became technically possible only in film. What was then only imagined is now familiar and—the stress is exact—conventional. Here is one characteristic scene movement:

Transformation. The landscape changes from winter to summer; the ice on the brook disappears and the water runs between the stones; the sun shines over all.

It is obvious that Strindberg was using the form of a play with little thought of immediate dramatic production. Like Ibsen, after an early attempt to come to terms with the ways of the contemporary theatre, and finding them at length only shackles on his genius. Strindberg drew strength from a more general dramatic imagination, and let the theatre, for a while, take care of itself. But the "demands of the new time" soon began to exert their pressure.

In the '80s the new time began to extend its demands for reform to the stage also. Zola declared war against the French comedy, with its Brussels carpets, its patent-leather shoes and patent-leather themes, and its dialogue reminding one of the questions and answers of the Catechism. In 1877 Antoine opened his Théâtre Libre in Paris, and *Thérèse Raquin*, although nothing but an adapted novel, became the dominant model. It was the powerful theme and the concentrated form that showed innovation, although the unity of time was not yet observed, and curtain falls were retained. It was then I wrote my dramas: *Lady Julie*, *The Father*, and *Creditors*.

Now Strindberg was, perhaps, in revolt against the same things as was Zola, against the "patent-leather themes" of the intrigue drama. But his own ideas for reform were different, and the experiments into which his ideas led him represent a unique and quite separate dramatic form. His position is more justly represented by the opening paragraph of his *Preface to Lady Julie* (1888).

Dramatic art, like almost all other art, has long seemed to me a kind of *Biblia Pauperum*—a bible in pictures for those who cannot read the written or printed work. And in the same way the dramatist has seemed to me a lay preacher, hawking about the ideas of his time in popular form—popular enough for the middle classes, who form the bulk of theatrical audiences, to grasp the nature of the subject, without troubling their brains too much. The theatre, for this reason, has always been a board school, for the young, for the half-educated, and for women, who still retain the inferior faculty of deceiving themselves and allowing themselves to be deceived: that is to say, of being susceptible to illusion and to the suggestions of the author. Consequently, in these days when the rudimentary and incompletely developed thought-process which operates through the imagination appears to be developing into reflection, investigation, and analysis, it has seemed to me that the theatre, like religion, may be on the verge of being abandoned as a form which is dying out, and for the enjoyment of which we lack the necessary conditions. This supposition is confirmed by the extensive theatrical decline which now prevails through the whole of Europe, and especially by the fact that in those civilized countries which have produced the greatest thinkers of the age—that is to say, England and Germany —the dramatic art, like most other fine arts, is dead. In some other countries, however, it has been thought possible to create a new drama by filling the old forms with the contents of the newer age; but, for one thing the new thoughts have not yet had time to become sufficiently popular for the public to be able to grasp the questions raised; moreover, party strife has so inflamed people's minds that pure, disinterested enjoyment is out of the question. One experiences a deep sense of contradiction when an applauding or hissing majority exercises its tyranny so openly as it can in the theatre. Lastly, we have not got the new form for the contents, and the new wine has burst the old bottles.

The Father (1887) and especially *Lady Julie* (1888) are attempts at such a new form. By this time, of course, Ibsen's prose plays were widely known. Although Strindberg was in many ways openly contemptuous of Ibsen—he called him "that famous Norwegian blue-stocking"—Ibsen's established practice was a definite part of Strindberg's new dramatic consciousness.

The substance of *The Father* is the conflict of man and woman in the specific instance of a battle for control of their child. The woman, Laura, drives her husband, the Captain, even to insanity, in order to gain absolute control of their daughter. Her main weapon, allied to interference with his work and talebearing of his growing madness, is an induced doubt as to whether the child is really his:

CAPTAIN: Have you never felt ridiculous in your role as father? I know nothing so ludicrous as to see a father leading his child by the hand along the street, or to hear him talking about his children. "My wife's children", he should say. . . . My child! A man has no children. It is women who get children, and that's why the future is theirs, while we die childless.

And the battle?

CAPTAIN: Laura, save me, save my reason. You don't seem to understand what I say. Unless the child is mine I have no control over her, and I wish for none. Isn't that the one thing you want? Isn't it? Or perhaps there's something else. Do you want to have sole power over the child and at the same time have me to maintain you both?

LAURA: The power, yes! What has all this life-and-death struggle been for, except the power?

CAPTAIN: For me, not believing in a life after death, the child was my idea of immortality, perhaps the only idea that has any real expression. Take that away and you cut off my life.

LAURA: Why didn't we separate in time?

CAPTAIN: Because the child linked us, but the link became a chain. . . .

LAURA: Do you remember that it was as your second mother I came into your life? . . . You were too big a child, or perhaps not wanted at all.

CAPTAIN: Yes, it was something like that. My father and mother didn't *want* me, and thus I was born without a will. So I thought I was completing myself when you and I became one, and that is why you got the upper hand. . . .

LAURA: . . . That is why I loved you as if you were my child. But whenever you showed yourself instead as my lover, you must have seen my shame. Your embraces were a delight followed by aches of conscience, as if my very blood felt shame. The mother became mistress! . . . That is where the mistake lay. The mother, you see, was your friend, but the woman was your enemy, and love between the sexes is strife. And don't imagine that I gave myself to you. I didn't give, I took—what I wanted. . . .

CAPTAIN: We, like the rest of mankind, lived our lives, unconscious as children, filled with fancies, ideals and illusions. And then we woke. Yes, but we woke with our feet on the pillow, and the man who woke us was himself a sleepwalker. When women grow old and cease to be women, they get beards on their chins. I wonder what men get when they grow old and cease to be men. Those who had crowed were no longer cocks but capons, and the pullets answered the call. So when sunrise should have come we found ourselves among ruins in full moonlight, just as in the good old days. It was nothing but a little morning sleep, with wild dreams; and there was no awakening. . . .

LAURA: . . . Now at last you have fulfilled your part as the—unfortunately—necessary father, and breadwinner. You are no longer needed, and you can go. You can go, now that you have realized that my brain is as strong as my will—since you won't stay and acknowledge it.

[*The Captain rises and throws the lighted lamp at Laura, who walks backwards through the door.*]

So this, some have said, is naturalism! It is necessary to look a little more closely at what Strindberg understood by the term:

Naturalism [he wrote] is not a dramatic method like that of

Becque, a simple photography which includes everything, even the speck of dust on the lens of the camera. That is realism; a method, lately exalted to art, a tiny art which cannot see the wood for the trees. That is the false naturalism, which believes that art consists simply of sketching a piece of nature in a natural manner; but it is not the true naturalism, which seeks out those points in life where the great conflicts occur, which rejoices in seeing what cannot be seen every day.

Strindberg's point is clearly relevant to *The Father*. The experience with which the play deals is intended as a "revealed truth"; it is obviously, in this form, not an "everyday experience". The principal distinction is the articulacy of the exposition. And this is not merely an articulation of the imperfect conversation of everyday people. The articulacy is not that of real persons' conversation made more explicit, but rather an articulation of the author's sense of certain facts about relationship.

But one must be concerned to distinguish between this method in a play like *The Father* and in a novel, say, like *The Rainbow*. In *The Rainbow*, the characters exist within a flow of description, of their experience, their actions, their speech and their world, from which they can never really be abstracted, separated out. It is otherwise in this kind of play. Although, essentially, Laura and the Captain are simply elements of the author's statement (so that it would be secondary to ask whether a woman like Laura would reveal herself as she does in speech) the framework of the conventions remains the simulation of a separated, self-presented existence. So that, in performance, bodied forth by naturalist actors, in the fully furnished atmosphere of an everyday home, the characters inevitably aspire to a different kind of personality, and are so communicated. This is the inescapable tension of such drama. The characters lose their elemental quality in the local particularity of the presented drama (the same process is evident in the filmed versions of *Wuthering Heights*). Strindberg, more definitely than Ibsen in his *The Doll's House—Wild Duck* period, assumes the conventional element in his characters. He rejects the formal carpentry of the well-made play which Ibsen so often retained. *The Father* is "formless" and is played out at a single level. But while this permits more adequate expression of the central experience (compare the speeches of Laura and the Captain with those of Nora and Torvald), the very formlessness, the absence of "theatricality", only reinforces the illusion that this is a claim to be direct observation. And this illusion limits the achievement of the essentially conventional literary expression.

Strindberg realized this, and in *Lady Julie* he attempted to fashion new conventions. The "new wine had burst the old bottles"; or, more precisely, the old bottles had soured the new wine.

> In the present drama I have not tried to do anything new—for that is impossible—but merely to modernize the form in accordance with what I imagined would be required of this art from the younger generation. . . . In regard to the character-drawing, I have made my figures rather characterless, for the following reasons:
>
> The word "character" has, in the course of the ages, assumed various meanings. Originally, I suppose, it signified the dominant characteristic of the soul-complex, and was confused with "temperament". Afterwards it became the middle-class expression for the automaton. An individual who had once for all become fixed in his natural disposition, or had adapted himself to some definite role in life—who, in fact, had ceased to grow—was called a "character". . . . The middle-class conception of the immobility of the soul was transferred to the stage, where the middle-class has always ruled. A "character" on the stage came to signify a gentleman who was fixed and finished: one who invariably came on the stage drunk, jesting, or mournful. For characterization nothing was required but some bodily defect—a club-foot, a wooden leg, a red nose; or the character in question was made to repeat some such phrase as "That's capital", "Barkis is willin' ", or the like. . . .

This analysis of characterization remains a central text for the study of naturalist drama. But we must carefully distinguish the two senses of "naturalism". What Strindberg meant by the term, as we saw earlier, is primarily an attitude to experience: in this period, critical, scientific, experimental (as would follow from a main use of "naturalism" in philosophy). What was later meant by "naturalism", almost everywhere, was a kind of photography: what Strindberg had attacked as passive, uncritical reproduction of a surface reality. It is an awkward confusion of terms, but we can take the point in Strindberg when we find him arguing that the naturalist writer, to express his new reading of experience, must find new dramatic styles: new conventions of reality. We can refer to this meaning as "critical naturalism".

> I do not believe in simple characters on the stage. And the summary judgements on men given by authors: this man is stupid, this one brutal, this one jealous, etc., should be challenged by naturalists, who know the richness of the soul-complex, and recognize that "vice" has a reverse side very much like virtue. . . .
> . . . My souls [characters] are conglomerations from past and

present stages of civilization; they are excerpts from books and newspapers, scraps of humanity, pieces torn from festive garments which have become rags—just as the soul itself is a piece of patchwork. Besides this, I have provided a little evolutionary history in making the weaker repeat phrases stolen from the stronger, and in making my souls borrow "ideas"—suggestions as they are called—from one another.

So far as this method of characterization is concerned, Strindberg's theory was at this time in advance of his practice. Julie and Jean are not "simple characters", it is true; one could define them in Strindberg's terminology as "souls", "elemental". Julie is the aristocratic girl, fixed in the conscience of inherited debt, consumed by romantic ideals of honour, and in practice a predatory "half-woman". Jean, the valet, by contrast, is "on the upgrade", "sexually, he is the aristocrat"; he is adaptable, has initiative, and hence will survive. When they meet, when they clash sexually, it is Julie who goes to pieces. Their love-act has no meaning:

> Love, I think, is like the hyacinth, which must strike root in the dark *before* it can produce a vigorous flower. In my play, it shoots up, blossoms, and runs to seed, all at the same time, and that is why the plant dies quickly.

The clash of Julie and Jean is, then, a convention to express a fact which Strindberg has perceived in relationship. And although the relationship is specific, it is hardly personal. The "drama is enacted by symbolic creatures formed out of human consciousness". But Strindberg's definition of his method of characterization hardly seems relevant to his practice in this play, although it is certainly relevant to his later, expressionist, pieces. It is true that Jean, as the stronger, imposes his ideas on Julie, the weaker, but this is rather the specific situation than an instance of the general method of the play.

> Finally, as to the dialogue: I have rather broken with tradition in not making my characters catechists who sit asking foolish questions in order to elicit a smart reply. I have avoided the mathematically symmetrical construction of French dialogue and let people's brains work irregularly, as they do in actual life, where no topic of conversation is drained to the dregs, but one brain receives haphazard from the other a cog to engage with. Consequently my dialogue too wanders about, providing itself in the earlier scenes with material which is afterwards worked up, admitted, repeated, developed, and built up, like the theme in a musical composition.

Strindberg was right, of course, as Ibsen was right, in rejecting the vapid artifice of well-made dialogue. But what he proposes to substitute is not necessarily a controlled literary medium, but, at first sight, simply haphazard conversation. (We shall see, later, in some mid twentieth-century drama, how the idea of haphazard conversation—indeed as of cogs engaging—was adopted as a style; but this is very different from anything in Strindberg, where the single psychological action is always dominant). The idea of a verbal theme—what came later to be called "contrapuntal dialogue" —is the creative point, and Strindberg's use of this method is important in such pieces as *Dreamplay* and *Ghost Sonata*. But it would be extravagant to see in the dialogue of *Lady Julie* an example of this method. In such passages as the following, phrases that have been used earlier are repeated, but only as a means of argument— the one casting the other's words back in a reversal of a previous situation:

JULIE: So that's the sort of man you are. . . .

JEAN: I had to invent something: it's always the pretty speeches that capture women.

JULIE: Scoundrel!

JEAN: Filth!

JULIE: And now you've seen the hawk's back.

JEAN: Not exactly its back.

JULIE: And I was to be the first branch. . . .

JEAN: But the branch was rotten.

JULIE: I was to be the signboard at the hotel. . . .

JEAN: And I the hotel.

JULIE: Sit inside your office, lure your customers, falsify the accounts.

JEAN: *I* was to do that.

JULIE: To think that a human soul could be so steeped in filth.

JEAN: Wash it then.

JULIE: You lackey, you menial, stand up when I'm speaking.

JEAN: You mistress of a menial, you lackey's wench, hold your jaw and get out. Are you the one to come and lecture me on my coarseness? No one in my class has ever behaved so coarsely as you have tonight. Do you think any servant girl attacks a man as you did? I have only seen that sort of thing among beasts and fallen women.

In this passage, at least, we are back to something very like the "catechism".

The prose of *Lady Julie* is effective, not so much by pattern, as by force. It has a vigour wholly consonant with the dramatic speed of the action. From the first words—

JEAN: Lady Julie's mad again tonight, absolutely mad.

—to the closing scene where Jean sends Julie out to suicide—

JULIE: I am asleep already—the whole room seems like smoke. And you look like an iron stove, a stove like a man in black clothes with a tall hat. And your eyes are like coals when the fire is going out, and your face is a white patch like the ashes . . . it's so warm and lovely . . . and so light—and so peaceful.

JEAN: [*putting the razor in her hands*]: There is the broom. Now go, while it's light—out to the barn—and . . . It's horrible. But there's no other possible end to it. Go!

—the language has the explicit, calculated violence of the whole dramatic method. But it is the rush of passionate statement rather than the patterned verbal theme which Strindberg, in the Preface, seemed to have in mind.

The whole virtue of *Lady Julie* is its speed. In this, Strindberg's new formal devices play their part:

In order to provide resting-points for the public and the performers without allowing the public to escape from the illusion, I have introduced three art-forms, all of which come under the heading of dramatic art, namely, the monologue, the mime, and the ballet: all of which, too, in their original forms, belonged to ancient tragedy, the monody now becoming the monologue and the chorus the ballet.

Most impressive is the "ballet" where the peasants sing a Midsummer Eve drinking song while Jean and Julie are alone in the bedroom. Kristin's mime is less successful; it has the air of simple defiance of normal theatrical practice, and serves little dramatic purpose. Strindberg, it seems, felt the need for formal devices of this kind, but felt it theoretically rather than practically. It is interesting to note that he considers the possibility of the actor working independently, being encouraged to improvise in these interludes. But in *Lady Julie*, where so much energy is concentrated for a clear single effect, it is vital that a single control should be retained.

Strindberg suggests other experiments in performance:

As regards the scenery I have borrowed from impressionist painting its symmetry and its abruptness . . . [backcloth and furniture are set diagonally].

Another perhaps not unnecessary novelty would be the abolition of footlights. . . . Would not the use of sufficiently powerful sidelights . . . afford the actor this new resource—the strengthening of his powers of mimicry by means of the face's chief asset—the play of the eyes?

He would like to "turn the stage into a room with the fourth wall missing", but thinks this might be premature.

Strindberg's Preface, and the partial exemplification of its theories in *Lady Julie*, offers very interesting evidence of the disturbance produced in the mind of an original and serious dramatist by the state of the stage of his day—where dramatic conventions had virtually disappeared under the weight of theatrical conventions, and where convention, as a result, conveyed only the idea of false artifice. If parts of the Preface now fall rather coldly, it is because we have seen "experimental drama" come to mean no more than theatrical experiment, and are as far as ever from significant *dramatic* conventions. But the Preface retains a genuine interest, and we need add only Strindberg's own later judgement (in *An Open Letter to the Intimate Theatre*—1909):

> As the Intimate Theatre counts its inception from the successful performance of *Lady Julie* in 1906, it was quite natural that the young director should feel the influence of the Preface, which recommended a search for actuality. But that was twenty years ago, and although I do not feel the need of attacking myself in this connexion, I cannot but regard all that pottering with stage properties as useless.

It was not the theatre, but the drama in the theatre, that really needed to be changed.

After *Lady Julie* Strindberg wrote a series of naturalist plays, which gained him considerable success in the new theatres of Paris and Berlin. There is *The Stronger*, played by two people, only one of whom speaks. There are *Creditors* and *Playing with Fire*. The dramatic aim is constant: to find the crisis, the moment of struggle, and to reveal normal experience in its light. The virtue of all these plays is the intensity of the revealed experience, the unforgettable power of a savage insight into motive and situation. The limitation, as in *The Father* and *Lady Julie*, is the occasional incongruity between the bared, elemental experience of crisis and the covering apparatus of seen and spoken normality. The reduction to elements foreshadowed in the proposed conventions for *Lady Julie* is never, on the surface of the plays, achieved. It is this limitation, a limitation of convention, which led to the critical error of dismissing Strindberg as wild and abnormal, and to the further error of a search for an explanation in his autobiography. The elemental characters of Heathcliff and Catherine in *Wuthering Heights* are acceptable, to those who will read the novel as it is, because of the strict conventional form on which the novel is built. But Strindberg's interpretation of naturalism as the moment of crisis was caught up in the incongruous naturalism of the general dramatic movement, and was communicated in the apparent texture of normality. It was necessary for Strindberg to try yet again; his attempt was the wholly new dramatic form of *The Road to Damascus* (1898).

3

In a note on a list of his works Strindberg writes of this new period:

> The great crisis at fifty: revolutions in my mental life, wanderings in the desert, devastation, Hells and Heavens of Swedenborg. Not influenced by Huysmans' *En Route*, still less by Pauldan, who was then unknown to the author . . . but based on personal experiences.

The Road to Damascus has already been extensively quarried, by Swedish critics, for its autobiographical deposits. Their yield is not impressive. One can relate the Lady, at various periods of the play, to Frieda Uhl or Harriet Bosse; the Woman to Siri von Essen; the first scene to Dorotheenstrasse, Berlin; the café to "Zum Schwarzen Ferkel", the mountain village to Klam. None of these discoveries advances comprehension of the work in any respect. But one can understand why critics should have been reluctant to write of the play itself, which is always strange, and at times bewildering.

The first critical point to be made may be indicated by an extract from Strindberg's prefatory note to *Dreamplay*:

> In this Dream Play, as in his earlier work, *Til Damaskus*, the Author has tried to imitate the disjointed but apparently logical form of a dream. Anything may happen: everything is possible and probable. Time and space do not exist: on an insignificant groundwork of reality imagination spins and weaves new patterns: a mixture of memories, experiences, unfettered fancies, absurdities, and improvisations. The characters are split, doubled, and multiplied: they evaporate and are condensed; are diffused and concentrated. But a single consciousness holds sway over them all —that of the dreamer.

The Road to Damascus will not be understood unless this method is realized. The whole construction is subject to the dream form which Strindberg has described, although the particular "method" of each dream is different in each of the three parts of the play. Each part of the work is as long as a normal play; and each part is a separate work in the sense that *Burnt Norton* or *East Coker* is a separate poem; although the full richness of the work, as in *Four Quartets*, only emerges from the series.

The Road to Damascus, as the title implies, is a drama of conversion. Each part ends with the Stranger's conversion but the Second and Third Parts begin again with his unbelief; the conversion at the end of each part increases in conviction until at the end of the play it is final. Thus the First Part ends with the Lady inviting the stranger to the church:

LADY: Come.
STRANGER: Very well. I'll go through that way. But I can't stay.
LADY: How can you tell? Come. In there you will hear new songs.
STRANGER: It may be.
LADY: Come.

The last words of the Second Part are:

STRANGER: Come, priest, before I change my mind.

At the end of the Third Part, the Stranger is buried so that his resurrection may come:

TEMPTER: Farewell.
CONFESSOR: Lord! Grant him eternal peace.
CHOIR: May he be illumined with everlasting light!
CONFESSOR: May he rest in peace!
CHOIR: Amen.

The way, the road to Damascus, is in each part a different way. In the highly formal pattern of the First Part, it is, in a sense, the "round about" of Ibsen's Peer Gynt.

It is played in seventeen scenes, of which the first eight represent a progression to the climax of the ninth, which is then succeeded by eight scenes which correspond, in reversed order, with the opening eight. Thus the play begins and ends at a street corner, and passes through and through again a Doctor's House, a hotel room, a beach, a road, a path in a ravine, a kitchen, and a room known as the "Rose Room". The climax is played in a convent, which the Stranger believes is an asylum, and in which appear shadowy likenesses of persons who have been encountered in the other scenes. At the beginning of the return journey, the Stranger speaks of his loss of consciousness in the convent:

I lay watching my past life unroll before me like a panorama, through childhood, youth. . . . And when the roll was finished it began again. All the time I heard a mill grinding.

In the beginning the Stranger is waiting outside the Post Office for a letter containing money with which he can pay his debts. He will not ask for it. Similarly, he will not enter the church:

> ... I feel I don't belong there ... That I'm an unhappy soul and that it's as impossible for me to re-enter as to become a child again.

He goes "round about"; the panorama is unrolled, stretching back to childhood. When he returns he goes in to ask for the letter. It had been awaiting him:

STRANGER: I feel ashamed of myself. It's the money.
LADY: You see. All these sufferings, all these tears, in vain.
STRANGER: Not in vain. It looks like spite, what happens here, but it's not that. I wronged the Invisible when I mistook ...
LADY: Enough! No accusations.
STRANGER: No. It was my own stupidity and wickedness. I didn't want to be made a fool of by life. That's why I was.

The whole exploration of identity, and the quest for knowledge, was fruitless, but inevitable. Salvation, or the money to pay his debts, was there at the starting-point; but the Stranger could not take it. He suggests a reason for this:

> It's whispered in the family that I'm a changeling. ... A child substituted by the elves for the baby that was born. ... Are these elves the souls of the unhappy, who still await redemption? If so, I am the child of an evil spirit. Once I believed I was near redemption, through a woman. But no mistake could have been greater. My tragedy is I cannot grow old; that's what happens to the children of the elves. ...

LADY: We must see if you can't become a child again.
STRANGER: We should have to start with the cradle; and this time with the right child.
LADY: Exactly.

It is, in fact, the elves ("that fairy story") who determine his "round-about" search for self-knowledge and redemption. They represent his unbelief, and press him on in an attempt to know. They even represent him to himself as a Liberator.

The Liberator goes out, creating the chimeras with which he will fight. He tries to rescue Ingeborg from the "Werewolf" who holds her prisoner: her husband, the Doctor. But the "Werewolf" is one of his own past victims: a schoolfellow whom he had allowed to be punished for one of his own misdeeds. In taking the punishment for the Stranger's sin, the Doctor has in a way become part of the Stranger himself. This is the type of the dream figure: the apparent person, of separate appearance, who is in fact only a mask for an aspect of the Dreamer's life. There are other masks: the Beggar, who like the Stranger bears the brand of Cain; the Housebreaker, a man with the Stranger's past, now being buried in a parody of celebration; and Caesar, the lunatic, who is in the Doctor's charge—the Stranger had been nicknamed Caesar at the school at which he betrayed the Doctor. The search is for identity. The central figure seeks to identify the Stranger who is himself.

The conventional nature of the drama should be clear; the characters are not persons, but symbolic figures enacted out of a single consciousness. Ingeborg, whom the Stranger will not see as a person ("I should prefer to think of you like that: Impersonal, nameless . . . Eve") is the essential context of this inward search for identity:

> STRANGER: You sit there like one of the Fates and draw the threads through your fingers. But go on. The most beautiful of sights is a woman bending over her work, or over her child. What are you making?
> LADY: Nothing. Crochet work.
> STRANGER: It looks like a network of nerves and knots on which you've fixed your thoughts. The brain must look like that—from inside.

When she has read his "terrible book", she tells him:

> My eyes are opened and I know what's good and evil, as I've never known before. And now I see how evil you are, and why I am to be called Eve. She was a mother and brought sin into the world. Another mother brought expiation. The curse of mankind was called down on us by the first, a blessing by the second. In me you shall not destroy my whole sex. Perhaps I have a different Mission in your life.

When the Stranger leaves Ingeborg, the central crisis is on him. In what he takes to be a convent (but which he suspects later is a hospital or an asylum) he confesses, and wakes to find himself cursed by the whole company of his relations: by the mourners, by the Beggar, by the madman Caesar, by the Werewolf, by the wife and children he has abandoned, by the Lady, by her parents, by his own parents, and by the Confessor. None of these main figures is exactly real; all that can be perceived is a resemblance. The "doom-session" is convened by the Stranger himself. He is sent, under the curse, back along his way.

At the opening of the second part the Stranger's sight, like that of Saul, remains blinded; his conviction of the powers which assailed him leads him only into an attempt to exorcise them by magic: to call down the lightning and to "upset the table of the money-changers" by the alchemist's gift of gold. There remains a hope of salvation in the child which Ingeborg bears, "the being . . . who can wipe out the darkness of the past and bring light".

But the child is threatened by the werewolf. Here again, the "Werewolf" Doctor, and the lunatic Caesar, are no more than aspects of the Stranger: the Doctor, in particular, is part of the Stranger through their succeeding relationships with Ingeborg, and more fundamentally, through their common past.

The climax of the second part is the banquet given in the Stranger's honour: given, as he thinks, by the Government in honour of his discovery of gold, but in fact given by the Drunkard's Society. The gold which promised salvation is merely dross, and the Stranger becomes convinced that he is finally damned. Even the birth of his child is too late to save him:

> Because I have slain my brother.

This phrase, and the reiteration of the Stranger's brand of Cain, a brand which the Beggar also bears, is to be understood in relation to the substitution by the elves. The Stranger—the child of the elves—has slain himself, the real child.

STRANGER: The crime I committed in this life was that I wanted to set men free.

BEGGAR: Set men free from their duties, and criminals from their guilt. . . . You're not the first and not the last to dabble in the Devil's work. . . . But when Reynard grows old, he turns monk—so wisely it is ordained—and then he's forced to split himself in two and drive out Beelzebub with his own penance. . . . You'll be forced to preach against yourself from the housetops. To unpick your fabric thread by thread.

The splitting-in-two, and the preaching against himself, are of course related, on this road to Damascus, to the dualism of Saul and Paul, and the preaching after conversion. But in the real psychological process, in which there is no scheme of faith, there is no simple action of "before" and "after". Indeed, the time-sense, appropriately enough in this structure of dream or nightmare, has yielded to a simultaneity of past and future. The unpicking of the fabric is already well under way. The Stranger goes for comfort to the Dominican who had cursed him. The Dominican is also the Beggar, and the first lover of Ingeborg. The Stranger can take no comfort:

> Over these only was spread a heavy night, an image of darkness which should afterward receive them; yet were they unto themselves more grievous than the darkness.

The third part opens with the Stranger being led by the Confessor "along this winding hilly path that never comes to an end". He seeks "death without the need to die—mortification of the flesh, of the old self. . . ."
Because:

> One knows nothing, hardly even that one knows nothing; that is why I have come so far as to believe.
> LADY: How do you know you can believe, if belief's a gift?
> STRANGER: You can receive a gift, if you ask for it.
> LADY: Oh yes, if you ask, but I've never been able to beg.
> STRANGER: I've had to learn to. Why can't you?
> LADY: Because one has to demean oneself first.
> STRANGER: Life does that for one very well.

When they cross the river towards the monastery, his debts begin to fall away. The Confessor tells Ingeborg:

> The evil in him was too strong; you had to draw it out of him into yourself to free him. Then, being evil, you had to suffer the worst pains of hell for his sake, to bring atonement.

It is the Stranger's ideal of redemption through a woman.
But at the last cross-roads the Tempter appears, with the Stranger's own phrases:

> Do you know why sin has been oppressing you for so long? Through renunciation and abstinence you've grown so weak that anyone can take your soul into possession. . . . You've so destroyed your personality that you see with strange eyes, hear with strange ears, and think strange thoughts. You've murdered your own soul.

At a village trial, the Tempter absolves all guilt by disputing as far as the final cause. But with the support of Ingeborg, the Stranger rejects this temptation, and reaches the Monastery. Here, in the picture-gallery, he meets a succession of "two-headed men": Boccaccio; Luther; Gustavus Adolphus; Schiller; Goethe; Voltaire; Napoleon; Kierkegaard; Victor Hugo; von Stollberg; Lafayette; Bismarck; Hegel.

> Hegel, with his own magic formula. Thesis: affirmation. Antithesis: negation. Synthesis: comprehension. . . . You began life by accepting everything, then went on denying everything on principle. Now end your life by comprehending everything. . . . Do not say: either—or. But: not only—but also. In a word, or two words rather: Humanity and Resignation.

With the last disputation,

STRANGER: What is loveliest, brightest? The first, the only, the last that ever gave life meaning. I too once sat in the sunlight on a veranda, in the spring—beneath the first tree to show new green, and a small crown crowned a head, and a white veil lay like morning mist over a face . . . that was not that of a human being. Then came darkness.

TEMPTER: Whence?

STRANGER: From the light itself. I know no more.

TEMPTER: It could only have been a shadow, for light is needed to throw shadows; but for darkness no light is needed.

STRANGER: Stop. Or we'll never come to an end.

the Confessor and the Chapter appear in procession, and wrapping him in the shroud, cry

> May he be illumined with everlasting light!
> May he rest in peace!
> Amen!

Even at the end, the idea of the changeling ("a face . . . that was not that of a human being") is intermittently retained. But the shadow came from the light; and the secret of identity will not be discovered by seeking among the images of darkness. The search is necessary because of the condition, but it brings only anguish: "they were unto themselves more grievous than the darkness". The search leads away from redemption, which awaits at the point of origin when one can "become as a little child". Yet—and this is the tragic paradox—to become as a little child seems to demand the search. In the end there is only submission, the absolute redemption by submission to the light.

I have traced the theme of *The Road to Damascus*, in this summary way, because it is necessary to assert that the play is a controlled realization of a theme. The orthodox "explanation" of it is in terms of Strindberg's recent insanity, and of his obsessions. But this is a failure of reading, rather than of the dramatist. The more closely one examines the work (having set aside prejudices about autonomous characters and representational form) the more one sees the firmness of its pattern, and its pervading relevance. In my account of the play I have, necessarily, omitted a mass of detail in order to isolate the main theme. But the whole substance of the work is controlled by this theme; and its strangeness, when the pattern is accepted, is seen, not as obsession, but as a powerfully original realization of deeply considered experience. That Strindberg has formulated his drama with elements of his personal experience is true; but these elements are placed so firmly in the larger scheme of the work that they are, in fact, transmuted; and so beyond the reach of biographical explanation.

The drama is enacted in scenes of strange power, achieved by Strindberg's new method: the breakdown of autonomous "characters"; the elaboration of a pattern of verbal themes; and complete rejection of the representational stage for a kaleidoscope of imaged expressionist scenes. If the scenic imagery is taken within the read work, the whole becomes a drama of rich and controlled complexity. But of course that was the problem: the practical integration of word and scene. What was available in the theatre was their *association*, but this is very different. It was the true sequence, the flow in one medium of scene and word, which Strindberg wanted and imagined, but which (as the record of the first production makes clear, with its breaks for scene-changing, its reduction of a sequence to Acts) he could not then get. Once again he was writing well ahead of his time, imagining a single word-and-scene medium—in effect the patterned control of film—which did not yet exist. A triumph of dramatic literature had to wait for new conventions of performance, and dramatic imagery had to be left as stage-directions.

4

The years at the turn of the century were a period of great production for Strindberg. In 1898 and 1899, as well as the first two parts of *Damascus*, he wrote *Advent, Crimes and Crimes*, and the historical plays *Saga of the Folkungs, Gustavus Vasa*, and *Eric XIV*.

Light after darkness [he writes at this time]. New production, with Faith, Hope, and Love regained—and absolute certainty.

Among five plays produced in 1900 and 1901 the most important are *Easter* and *The Dance of Death*. *The Dance of Death* has often been placed among the greatest of Strindberg's work. I think it is less than this. It is in a way a re-statement of the theme of *The Father*, and has moments of terrible power: the vampire scene between Kurt and Alice, for example, and the mime of the Captain's dissolution which precedes it. The sword-dance—the "dance of death"—is magnificent theatre. But the speed which sustained *The Father* is absent. In the first part, the merciless clarity of the conflict is convincing. It is the mood of savage farce; and the theme of the Captain's decay—"Cancel, and pass on"—is sustained by a verbal pattern which, superimposed on the representational language, removes the absolute limitations of the naturalism. But the second part is less acceptable. It resembles nothing so much as a middle-period "family-drama" of Ibsen, but then it lacks Ibsen's power of concentration. It is an attempt, doubtless, at objectivity; what Strindberg called "absolute certainty" seems to have driven him in this direction. But the effect of the dance of death on the younger generation has a curiously second-hand air which is very uncharacteristic of Strindberg. The new kind of well-made play which Ibsen had fashioned was ready to Strindberg's hand whenever his essential tension slackened; but he seems ill at ease in it.

Easter ("the school of suffering" Strindberg noted) is the nearest to Ibsen of any of his plays. Aspects of it remind us alternately of *The Wild Duck* and of *A Doll's House*. Eleonora is first cousin to Hedvig, although her experience in clearer and stronger. The bankrupt house, under the shadow of the father's ruin, is a formulation of collective guilt in the manner of *John Gabriel Borkman* or again of *The Wild Duck*. Ellis has a function similar to, if less equivocal than that of Hjalmar. Lindkvist, the "giant" who holds power over the family, is at first a villain in the recognizable dress of Krogstad. *Easter* has more plot, in the conventional sense, than any of Strindberg's plays. The action follows the habitual course: exposition; hint of danger; accumulation of danger; resolution. It begins in the shadows and goes out in sunlight. A morality of conduct is made explicit.

Easter is a play of fragmentary beauty and power. Eleonora, the strange child, is the Christ-agent in this singular passion and resurrection:

ELEONORA: We ought not to possess anything that binds us to earth. Out on the stony paths and wander with wounded feet, for the road leads upwards, that is why it is so toilsome. . . . If we are not to weep in the vale of sorrow where then shall we weep? . . . You would like to smile all day long, and that is why you've suffered. . . . Most of it will clear away as soon as Good Friday is over, but not everything. Today the birch, tomorrow Easter eggs. Today snow, tomorrow thaw. Today death, tomorrow resurrection. . . .

. . . Look at the full moon. It is the Easter moon. And the sun, you know, is still there, although the light comes from the moon.

The atmosphere of the play—the Easter birch, the stolen flower, the moonlight—is summed up in the scene as the play ends, where

Eleonora strips off the days of the calendar and throws them into the sunlight:

> See how the days pass. April, May, June. And the sun shines on all of them. . . . Now you must thank God, for he has helped us to get to the country. . . . You may say it without words, for now the clouds are gone and it will be heard above.

In theatrical terms—and *Easter* is a typical piece of the naturalist theatre—this is always effective. At times, the realization of the theme of resurrection through suffering—a constant subject with Strindberg at this period—seems adequate. But ultimately one cannot overlook the incongruity of such emotion with the neat social melodrama which is its framework. *Easter* remains constantly on the edge of a merely sentimental "soulfulness". The play is a contradiction of experience and convention.

Strindberg turned again to experiment, both in the style of the fantasy of *Lucky Peter's Travels* (see *The Nightingale in Wittenberg*) and in the remembered manner of *The Road to Damascus*. The most important work in this latter kind is *Dreamplay*, the technique of which Strindberg explicitly related to *The Road to Damascus*. At technique, I would say, the relation ends. In the earlier, larger play the dream-method is a means of serious analysis of the experience of "identity". Except for certain sections of the third part (which was written at a later period than the first two, and in the same period as *Dreamplay*) there is little or no discursiveness. But *Dreamplay* is abstract and discursive from the beginning. It is based on the familiar idea of the Goddess who descends to earth to discover the truth about the suffering of mankind. A fantasy in these terms, where the unifying consciousness of the dreamer is not so much the substance of the play as its machinery, is only rarely connecting and substantial. *Dreamplay* is an astonishing feat of virtuosity, and its substance consistently tends back to serious experience, even if it fails to realize it. But the power is primarily visual, in what is still the dissociated medium of word and scene: the Growing Castle; the fire which reveals a wall of sorrowing human faces; the trefoil door which holds the secret of life; the linden which marks the seasons and which on one occasion strips its leaves to become a coat-and-hat stand. The effects are continuous, but the consciousness of the dreamer remains dissociated: what should be an eye (in performance, a film camera) is an awkward, consciously arranged presence. The flow of images is a direct experience, but the persons of the drama belong to the different world of the fable. This limits any full realization. When Indra's daughter prepares to go back to the heavens, and asks:

Have I not learned the anguish of all being,
Learned what it is to be a mortal man?

one is bound to answer "No". Anguish, futility, martyrdom,
redemption: all are mentioned; none, in convincing terms, is shown:

POET: Tell me your sorrows.
DAUGHTER: Poet, could you tell me yours without a single
discordant word? Could your speech ever approach your
thought?

In *Dreamplay* clearly it could not. We can extract minor symbolic
patterns from the work—there are very many—but we cannot
relate them to the major pattern, for this—in real terms—is never
a dramatic action.

Hush, you must ask no more, and I must not answer. The
altar is already adorned for the sacrifice; the flowers are keeping
watch; the lights are kindled; white sheets before the windows;
fir-twigs in the porch.

With these last words, describing an experience which *Dreamplay*
is far from realizing, Strindberg sets the scene for one of his latest
and most interesting plays—*Ghost Sonata*. This work is one of the
Kammarspel, or chamber plays, which Strindberg produced for his
own Intimate Theatre in Stockholm. It was written in 1907.

Certain major aspects of the dream technique are fundamental
to the play: characters are not, or not all, flesh and blood—some
can be seen by only one person on the stage. The Ghost Supper,
and the cupboarded Mummy, are clearly conventional. The
unifying consciousness is that of the Student, although that is more
objectively conceived than in *The Road to Damascus*. There is also
a change of visual convention: instead of the flow and sequence
appropriate to a searching internal consciousness, the experiences
of a group are fixed in three scenes or images: the façade, the round
drawing-room, the Oriental Room. It is more than stage-setting,
and yet more practicable than a moving sequence. What Ibsen
had imagined and established through verbal reference, in the wild
duck and the white horses, is now, in Strindberg's terms, made
actual, on a differently conceived stage, in which states of mind are
visually built and presented: not as a modification of an imitated
reality, but as dramatic scenes in their own right. This, again, is
an important step forward.

Ghost Sonata is short, shorter than *Lady Julie*. The dominant person
of the first two scenes is the Old Man: Jacob Hummel. The strange
world to which he introduces the Student is summed up in the
House of the Dead. At the façade appear in turn: the Janitress;

the Dark Lady—daughter of the Janitress by the Dead Man, for whom fir is being strewn on the steps; the Colonel, head of the house; his daughter; the old white-haired woman, fiancée of Hummel; the nobleman, son-in-law of the Dead Man. This is the appearance which Hummel arranged; it is not, as we shall see later, entirely accurate. All are seen in the normal way, but the Dead Man who comes to the door in his shroud, and the Milkmaid, from whom Hummel shrinks in horror, are seen only by the Student, who is a "Sunday-child". On the whole façade the Student comments:

> STUDENT: I understand nothing of all this. It's just like a story...
> HUMMEL: My whole life has been like a collection of stories, sir. But though the stories are different, they hang together on a common thread and the dominant theme recurs regularly.

Within the façade, in the second scene, appearances change. First revealed is the Mummy, who sits in a cupboard behind a papered door "because her eyes cannot bear the light". She is the original of the statue of the lovely woman who dominates the scene, and mother of the girl whose father is assumed to be the Colonel. She sits babbling in her darkness, like a parrot:

Pretty Polly! Are you there, Jacob? Currrr!

The Old Man enters uninvited:

> BENGTSSON [*valet*]: He is a regular old devil, isn't he?
> JOHANNSON [*Hummel's attendant*]: Fully fledged.
> BENGTSSON: He looks like Old Harry.
> JOHANSSON: And he's a wizard, too, I think, because he passes through locked doors.

Left alone, the Old Man inspects the statue, and from behind him in the wall hears the cackle of its original. The Mummy enters the room, and it becomes clear that the Young Lady is not the daughter of the Colonel, but of the Colonel's wife (the statue, now the Mummy) and the Old Man. The Colonel in his turn had seduced the Old Man's fiancée, the White-haired Woman (who sits all day using the window as a mirror, seeing herself from two aspects —the reflection and the outside world, but forgetting that she herself can be seen from outside). Another lover of the Mummy has been the nobleman, who is to marry the Dark Lady, daughter of the Janitress (who had been seduced by the Dead Man, father-in-law of the nobleman, and whose husband had in consequence been made janitor):

OLD MAN: A pretty collection. . . .

MUMMY: Oh God, if we might die! *If* we might die!

OLD MAN: But why do you keep together then?

MUMMY: Crime and guilt bind us together. We have broken our
bonds and gone apart innumerable times, but we are always
drawn together again.

They are drawn, in Bengtsson's words, to

the usual Ghost Supper, as we call it. They drink tea, don't say a
single word, or else the Colonel does all the talking. And then
they crunch their biscuits, all at the same time, so that it sounds
like rats in an attic. . . . They have kept this up for twenty years,
always the same people saying the same things, or saying nothing
at all for fear of being found out.

Before the Supper begins, the Old Man strips the Colonel,
whose title and rank he shows to be impostures, who is merely
"XYZ, a lackey . . . once a cupboard lover in a certain kitchen".
The Supper party assembles.

COLONEL: Shall we talk then?

OLD MAN: Talk of the weather which we know all about; ask one
another's state of health, which we know just as well; I prefer
silence, for then thoughts become audible and we can see the
past; silence can hide nothing, but words can. . . . My mission
in this house is to pull out the weeds, to expose the crimes, to
settle all accounts, so that the young people can start afresh
in the house which I give to them. . . . Do you hear the ticking
of the clock like a deathwatch in the wall? Can you hear what
it says—"It's time", "It's time", "It's time"? When it strikes
shortly your time will be up. . . .

But the Mummy interferes; she stops the clock:

I can stop the course of time. I wipe out the past and undo what
is done. Not with bribes, nor with threats, but with suffering and
repentance.

She challenges Hummel's right to judge, and, with Bengtsson's
aid, exposes his own past, and all his crimes. She reduces him to the
cackling of the parrot which had come from her own lips, and then,
as the Death Screen is drawn across, sends him to her cupboard to
hang himself:

MUMMY: It is finished. God have mercy on his soul.

ALL: Amen.

In the final scene we look for the resurrection. The Student and the Young Lady sit under the cluster of starlike flowers held by the Buddha image in the Oriental room:

> LADY: This room is named the Room of Ordeal. It is beautiful to look at, but it is only full of imperfections.

Over the prospect of their marriage broods the immense Cook, who diverts to herself all the vitality of the household, for she is "one of the Hummel family of vampires".

In this house of stagnation and decay, the Student, like Hummel, wishes to lay bare all secrets. But "it is only in a madhouse you say all you think".

There is only one liberator, the Sleep of Death: as the black screen is drawn in front of the girl—

> STUDENT: The liberator is coming. Welcome, thou pale and gentle one. Sleep, lovely, unhappy, innocent creature, whose sufferings are undeserved. . . . Sleep without dreaming. . . . You poor little child, you child of this world of illusion, guilt, suffering, and death, this world of eternal change, disappointment and pain. May the Lord of Heaven have mercy on you in your journey.

This is Strindberg's consistent conclusion in his later years. In *Ghost Sonata* he realizes the persistent pattern in a powerfully concentrated and eminently dramatic form.

5

The revaluation of Strindberg which I have proposed rests, essentially, on a realization of the nature of the experience which he wished to communicate, and on the incongruity with this material of the available dramatic forms. It involves a rejection of pseudo-biographical explanations of madness and obsession; the experience must be accepted for what it is, both in its strangeness and in its power. Strindberg's genius as a dramatist was that he found, against the grain of the dramatic methods of his time, forms of expression which were adequate at least for himself. His influence, of course, has been immense: both from the conflict plays (as directly to O'Neill) and from the experiments in dramatic sequence and imagery in the later work (as notably in expressionism and in the work of many experimental directors). What has then to be said, just because of this influence, is that he worked, always, from the experience to the method; the new conventions relate, directly, to a structure of feeling, and can not be abstracted from it, as in a simple "modernism". Strindberg's view of relationships, for all its strangeness, has become characteristic, in a particular phase of society, and in some places is now even orthodox. It is a view to question, certainly, in its abstracted forms, and we have seen both the structure and the methods become mechanical. But we could never say this of Strindberg himself. There the power, the creation, the astonishing invention, are authentic and lasting: an achieved and unforgettable dramatic world.

3

ANTON CHEKHOV

I regard the stage of today as mere routine and prejudice. When the curtain goes up and the gifted beings, the high priests of the sacred art, appear by electric light, in a room with three sides to it, representing how people eat, drink, love, walk, and wear their jackets; when they strive to squeeze out a moral from the flat vulgar pictures and the flat vulgar phrases, a little tiny moral, easy to comprehend and handy for home consumption; when in a thousand variations they offer me always the same thing over and over again—then I take to my heels and run, as Maupassant ran from the Eiffel Tower, which crushed his brain by its overwhelming vulgarity. . . . We must have new formulas. That's what we want. And if there are none, then it's better to have nothing at all.

THIS striking indictment of the naturalist theatre, an indictment which in seventy years has lost none of its force, is not, one had better begin by emphasizing, Chekhov's own. It is a speech which he gives to the young writer Constantine Treplef in *The Seagull*. Chekhov perhaps felt very much in this way (although from external evidence his literary position would seem to be more represented in *The Seagull* by Trigorin than by Treplef), but I do not wish to play the dangerous and tiresome game of identifications. The outburst, which has a characteristic late nineteenth-century ring, is better worth quoting as a first step in the analysis of some of Chekhov's plays, and as a preface to some remarks on the relation of the naturalist drama to fiction, and on the "symbolism" which naturalist dramatists have developed.

"Ibsen, you know," Chekhov wrote to A. S. Vishnevsky, "is my favourite author". And this affiliation is a point which the critic can no longer doubt. It is true that in England the public projections of Ibsen and Chekhov are very dissimilar. So acute an Ibsenite as William Archer could see nothing in *The Cherry Orchard* but empty and formless time-wasting. The devotees of Chekhov in the theatres of England, on the other hand, acclaim his work as "really lifelike and free from any tiresome moralizing". Taken over, as he has been, by a sentimental sect, he has even been welcomed, astonishingly, as "naturalism without politics". In this connection, one might hazard a supplementary remark to the sentence quoted from

Chekhov's letter: "*The Wild Duck*, you know, is my favourite play";
and imagine Chekhov saying, as Ibsen said of *The Wild Duck*:

> The characters, I hope, will find good and kind friends . . .
> not least among the player-folk, to whom they all, without
> exception, offer problems worth the solving.

For the buttress of Chekhov's popularity in England has been
his popularity with that kind of actor and atmosphere, with "the
high priests of the sacred art".

In Ibsen's *The Wild Duck* the crucial point for an evaluation of
the play is a study of the function of the title-symbol. The same is
true of *The Seagull*, where the "symbol", indeed, has passed even
beyond the confines of the work to become the emblem of a new
movement in the theatre. Chekhov introduces the seagull in the
second act, at a point where Treplef's play has failed, and where
his beloved Nina is about to pass from his influence to that of the
more famous Trigorin:

> [*Enter* TREPLEF *hatless, with a gun and a dead seagull.*]
> TREPLEF: Are you alone?
> NINA: Yes.
> [TREPLEF *lays the bird at her feet.*]
> NINA: What does that mean?
> TREPLEF: I have been brute enough to shoot this seagull. I
> lay it at your feet.
> [*She takes up the seagull and looks at it.*]
> TREPLEF: I shall soon kill myself in the same way. . . .
> NINA: You have grown nervous and irritable lately. You express
> yourself incomprehensibly in what seem to be symbols. This
> seagull seems to be another symbol, but I'm afraid I don't
> understand. I am too simple to understand you.

It is an incapacity—this failure to understand the symbol—
which, it becomes clear, the author does not intend the audience
to share. Trigorin makes the next point:

> A subject for a short story. A girl—like yourself, say—lives
> from her childhood on the shores of a lake. She loves the lake like
> a seagull, and is happy and free like a seagull. But a man comes
> along by chance and sees her and ruins her, like this seagull, just
> to amuse himself.

Since this is exactly what Trigorin is going to do to Nina—we
are often reminded of this prophecy—the point will doubtless be
regarded as subtle. It is a subtlety which stops perhaps a little
short of the diabolic—at the deadly.

When Nina has been seduced and abandoned by Trigorin she
writes regularly to Treplef:

TREPLEF: Her imagination was a little disordered. She signed herself "Seagull". In Pushkin's "Rusalka" the miller says he is a raven, so she said in her letters that she was a seagull.

And when Trigorin comes on a visit:

SHAMRAYEF: We've still got that thing of yours, Boris.
TRIGORIN: What thing?
SHAMRAYEF: Constantine shot a seagull one day, and you asked me to have it stuffed for you.
TRIGORIN: Did I? I don't remember.

Immediately afterwards Nina returns to see Treplef:

NINA: . . . I am a seagull . . . no, that's wrong. I am an actress. Yes, yes . . . I am a seagull. No, that's wrong. . . . Do you remember you shot a seagull? "A man comes along by chance and sees her, and, just to amuse himself, ruins her. . . . A subject for a short story." . . .

As she leaves, the stuffed seagull is brought in and placed on the table, with Trigorin still murmuring:

I don't remember. No. I don't remember.

At this moment Treplef shoots himself. ("I am still adrift in a welter of images and dreams. . . . I have been brute enough to shoot this seagull")

Now in Ibsen's *The Wild Duck* Hedvig, when told to shoot the wild duck, shoots herself. She identifies herself with the bird. In *The Seagull* the story of Nina's seduction and ruin is similarly identified with the bird. In *The Wild Duck* the bird is also used to define other characters and the whole atmosphere of the play. Similarly, in *The Seagull*, the bird and its death, and its stuffed resurrection, are used to indicate something about Treplef, and the general death of freedom which pervades the play. In this comparison, I am not attempting to prove plagiarism. All authors steal (it is only, it seems, in an industrial society, that this has been reckoned as wrong), and a good trick is always worth playing twice. I am trying, rather, to assess the function and validity of the device. The function is surely clear. The seagull emphasizes, as a visual symbol—a piece of stage property—the action and the atmosphere. It is a device for emotional pressure, for inflating the significance of the related representational incidents. After *Ivanov* (1887) and *The Wood Spirit* (1888), which had both failed, Chekhov, we are told by Princess Nina Andronikova Toumanova,

for seven long years gave up the stage, although the search for a new dramatic form unceasingly occupied his mind. He meditated upon a realistic play in which he could introduce a symbol as a means of communicating to the audience his deeper and inner thoughts.

This is the frank orthodox description of the form. The symbol, as we now know, came to hand biographically, and Chekhov commented on the seagull which his friend Levitan had shot:

> Another beautiful living creature is gone, but two dumb-bells returned home and had supper.

In the play the symbol is illustrative, and the centre of emotional pressure. I have described it as "inflating the significance of the incidents", which may seem to beg the question. But this very characteristic naturalist device is clearly a substitute for adequate expression of the central experience of the play in language. It is a *hint* at profundity. At a simple illustrative level it is precise. The correspondences, as we have seen, are established explicitly and with great care. At any other level, and at the symbolic level at which it is commonly assumed to operate, it is essentially imprecise; any serious analysis must put it down as mainly a lyrical gesture.

The Seagull is a very good example of the problem with which the talented dramatist, in a predominantly naturalist period, is faced. The substance of his play is settled as a representation of everyday life; and the qualities which Chekhov saw in everyday life were frustration, futility, delusion, apathy. This weary atmosphere, moreover, was characterized by an inability to speak out—an inability of which almost every notable writer in the last seventy years has complained. Major human crises are resolved in silence, or are indicated by the slightest of commonplace gestures.

> Let us [Chekhov wrote to Suvorin] just be as complex and as simple as life is. People dine and at the same time their happiness is made or their lives are broken.

Fidelity to the representational method, therefore, compels the author to show people dining, to depict their conversation in minor commonplaces. But if he is seriously concerned with experience, he cannot leave it at this. Either one or more of his characters may— for some reason—have an ability to speak out, to indicate the underlying pattern. In *The Seagull*, Trigorin, particularly, and Treplef, who are both writers, possess this faculty. Even then the author may not be satisfied; a total pattern has to be indicated, for since the characters are conceived as absolute, as "real persons", their statements may be merely personal and idiosyncratic. Here, in the final attempt to resolve the difficulty, is introduced such a device as that of the seagull.

That is an early play, and Chekhov was to go beyond it. But in one respect, this relation between what is felt and what can be said is decisive in all his work. There is no modern dramatist whose characters are more persistently concerned with explicit self-revelation: the desire and the need to tell the truth about oneself are overpowering. Yet this self-revelation can be very different in purpose and effect, as the following examples show:

TREPLEF: Who am I? What am I? Sent down from the University without a degree through circumstances for which the editor cannot hold himself responsible, as they say; with no talents, without a farthing, and according to my passport a Kiev artisan; for my father was officially reckoned a Kiev artisan although he was a famous actor. So that when these actors and writers in my mother's drawing-room graciously bestowed their attention on me, it seemed to me that they were merely taking the measure of my insignificance; I guessed their thoughts and felt the humiliation. (*The Seagull*)

UNCLE VANYA: I am intelligent, brave, and strong. If I had lived normally I might have become another Schopenhauer, or Dostoyevsky. (*Uncle Vanya*)

OLGA: I'm always having headaches from having to go to the High School every day and then teach till evening. Strange thoughts come to me, as if I were already an old woman. And really, during these four years that I have been working here, I have been feeling as if every day my strength and youth have been squeezed out of me, drop by drop. And only one desire grows and grows in strength. . . . To Moscow, as soon as possible. (*The Three Sisters*)

SHIPUCHIN: As I was saying, at home I can live like a tradesman, a *parvenu*, and be up to any games I like, but here everything must be *en grand*. This is a Bank. Here every detail must *imponiren*, so to speak, and have a majestic appearance. (*The Anniversary*)

GAYEF: I'm a good Liberal, a man of the eighties. People abuse the eighties, but I think I may say that I've suffered for my convictions in my time. It's not for nothing that the peasants love me. We ought to know the peasants, we ought to know with what . . .

ANYA: You're at it again, Uncle. (*The Cherry Orchard*)

Treplef and Olga are outlining their explicit situation; their speeches are devices of the author's exposition, which, because of the large number of characters he handles, is frequently awkward, as in *The Three Sisters*. There is also, with Olga and Treplef, a sentimental vein (with real persons it would be called self-pity) which depends on their explicitness. While retaining the manner of conversation, they are doing more, or attempting more, than conversation can ever do. In Uncle Vanya, this has become the full sentimentality, as it is also in Gayef. But in Gayef, the device is satiric. We are evidently *not* "intended to accept the character's sentimental interpretation of himself". Shipuchin is a more un-equivocal comic figure, but then *The Anniversary*—a short piece—is a less equivocal play: it is farce without strings. One's doubts about even the best of Chekhov's plays are doubts about the strings.

But then, as this response becomes clear, we have to put the critical question in a different way. We have to discover the rela-tion between this particular convention—of an explicit self-revela-tion, at times awkward and sentimental, at other times negotiated as satire or farce—and Chekhov's actual structure of feeling. And what we then see is an important change, from both Ibsen and Strindberg. It is not the passionate overt conflict of early Strindberg, nor the savage internal inquiry, the fixed distortions of an alienated group, of Strindberg's later world. Again, in the comparison with Ibsen, there is a crucial difference, beyond the surface similarities. Chekhov saw, as clearly as Ibsen, the frustration and stagnation of the available forms of social life; his difference, in his mature work, is that he does not set against these, even in defeat and failure, an actively liberating individual. In *Ivanov* this liberal structure is still present: an isolated, struggling man, against the habits of his group; breaking, and breaking others in his fall. For that structure, the dramatic methods of Ibsen were still relevant, and in *The Seagull*, where again a break is being attempted, by Treplev, they are still partly relevant. But in *The Three Sisters* and *The Cherry Orchard* something new has happened: it is not the liberating indi-vidual against the complacent group; it is that the desire for libera-tion has passed into the group as a whole, but at the same time has become hopeless, inward-looking—in effect a defeat before the struggle has even begun. Chekhov, that is to say, is not writing about a generation of liberal struggle against false social forms, but about a generation whose whole energy is consumed in the very process of becoming conscious of their own inadequacy and impotence. The dramatic conventions of liberal struggle had been clear: the isolation of the individual; his contrast with his group; and then an action which took this forward—not to the point of change, which Ibsen could not see happening, but to the point where the effort and the resistance, the vocation and the debt, reached deadlock: the hero died still climbing and struggling, but with the odds against him. As we have seen, this deadlock was never merely external: the limiting consciousness of the false society—"we are all ghosts . . . all of us so wretchedly afraid of the light"—was seen, by Ibsen, as inevitably entering the consciousness of the man who was struggling: the deadlock with a false society was re-enacted as a deadlock within the self. The methods of Ibsen's last plays, particularly, are related to this internal deadlock.

It was from this point that Chekhov began. He attempted the same action, and made it end in suicide. But he came to see this as "theatrical": a significant description of one of those crucial moments when a structure of feeling is changing, and when the conventions appropriate to it come suddenly to seem empty. As Chekhov explores his world, he finds not deadlock—the active struggle in which no outcome is possible—but stalemate—the collective recognition, as it were before the struggle, that this is so. Virtually everyone wants change; virtually no-one believes it is possible. It is the sensibility of a generation which sits up all night talking about the need for revolution, and is then too tired next morning to do anything at all, even about its own immediate problems.

This world, this new structure of feeling, is very powerfully created in *The Three Sisters* and in *The Cherry Orchard*. In *The Three Sisters* it is the longing to make sense of life, to have a sense of a future, in a stagnant and boring military-provincial society. In *The Cherry Orchard* it is an attempt to come to terms with the past: to live without owning the orchard and its servants. In neither situation is any real success possible: what happens is not to change the situation, but to reveal it. The counter-movement, against what would be simple fantasy (the desire to be in Moscow, although they would be the same people there) or simple nostalgia (the desire to have the orchard and yet to be free to go away), is an emphasis on redemption, effort, work. Characteristically, these cannot materialize as events; they can only be spoken about:

> They will forget our faces, voices, and even how many there were of us, but our sufferings will turn into joy for those who will live after us. . . . Your orchard frightens me. When I walk through it in the evening or at night, the rugged bark on the trees glows with a dim light, and the cherry-trees seem to see all that happened a hundred and two hundred years ago in painful and oppressive dreams. Well, we have fallen at least two hundred years behind the times. We have achieved nothing at all as yet; we have not made up our minds how we stand with the past; we only philosophise, complain of boredom, or drink

vodka. It is so plain that before we can live in the present, we must first redeem the past, and have done with it; and it is only by suffering that we can redeem it, only by strenuous unremitting toil.

Characteristically, this last speech is by Trophimov, who does practically no work. This does not mean that he is wrong, or that what he says can be disregarded: it is the dominant emotion of the play. But there is this precise paradox, in Trophimov and in the others, between what can be said and what can be done; what is believed and what is lived.

Inevitably, such a man, such a situation, such a generation can seem comic; it is easy to laugh at them and at what Chekhov calls their "neurotic whining". At the same time, to get even the strength to see what is wrong, to sit up talking to try to get it clear, can be, in such a time, a major effort. In its inadequacy and yet its persistence it is heroism of a kind, an ambivalent kind. It is then this feeling—this structure of feeling—that Chekhov sets himself to dramatize.

The consequences in method are important. First, there will be no isolated, contrasting characters; the crucial emotion is that of a group. Second, there will, so far as possible, be no action: things will happen, but as it were from outside: what happens within the group is mainly gesture and muddle. Third, the contradictory character, of the group and its feelings, has to be conveyed in the tone: a kind of nobility, and a kind of farce, have to co-exist. (This is not, by the way, a cue for the usual question: are we supposed to laugh or cry at such people and such situations? That is a servile question: we have to decide our response for ourselves. The point is, always, that the characters and situations can be seen, are written to be seen, in both ways; to decide on one part of the response or the other is to miss what is being said).

As we come to see that this is what Chekhov is doing, we are faced with very difficult critical problems. He is attempting to dramatize a stagnant group, in which consciousness has turned inward and become, if not wholly inarticulate, at least unconnecting. He is attempting to dramatize a social consequence—a common loss—in private and self-regarding feeling. It is, inevitably, a very difficult balance, a very difficult method, to achieve.

Now certainly, Chekhov's representation of living action is impressive. The structure is more finely and more delicately constructed than that of any of his contemporaries. The same method achieves, in his fiction, very valuable results. But the method, I would say, is ultimately fictional. In the bare, economical, and inescapably explicit framework of drama the finest structure of incident and phrase, left to itself, appears crude. The convention of general description, which in the novel is essentially a whole structure of feeling, is very difficult to achieve, in this kind of play. And then the miniatures are left suspended; there is a sense, as in Ibsen's *The Wild Duck*, of disintegration, which springs directly from this absence. A gap must be filled, and to the rescue, as before, comes the unifying pressure of a device of atmosphere. It is a poor compromise. The characters, which in fiction are more than their separated selves, now dissociate, outline themselves, by the conditions of dramatic presentation. Delineation degenerates to slogan and catchphrase, to the mumbled "and all the rest of it" with which old Sorin ends his every speech in *The Seagull*. For of such is a "character" built. The just comment is Strindberg's, in the Preface to *Lady Julie:*

> A character on the stage came to signify a gentleman who was fixed and finished; nothing was required, but some bodily defect—a club-foot, a wooden leg, a red nose; or the character in question was made to repeat some such phrase as "That's capital", "Barkis is willin' ", or the like.

Nothing is more surprising, in the genuine detail of experience which Chekhov so finely achieves, than the appearance—the repeated appearance—of that kind of fixed, external device of personality. Moreover, that separable "personality" is the more contradictory in that what Chekhov is essentially expressing is a *common* condition. It is this that is missed or weakened when personality declines to an idosyncrasy or a "human vignette".

On the other hand, Chekhov attempted to develop a new kind of dialogue which, paradoxically, would express disintegration without weakening the sense of a common condition. Such dialogue is very hard to read and to play, and it is, I think, only intermittently successful. But where it does succeed, something very original and in its own way powerful has come into modern drama. An unfamiliar rhythm is developed, in which what is being said, essentially, is not said by any one of the characters, but, as it were, inadvertently, by the group. This is not easy to illustrate, since the printed convention, separating and assigning the speeches, usually breaks it up. The major example, I think, is the second act of *The Cherry Orchard*, which as a theme for voices, a condition and an atmosphere created by hesitation, implication, unconnected confession, is more complete and powerful than anything else Chekhov wrote. A briefer example, from *The Three Sisters*, may allow the method to be seen more clearly (I omit the names of the speakers so that the form of a connected dialogue—connected, paradoxically, to show disconnection—can be followed):

We do not seem to understand each other. How can I convince you? Yes, laugh. Not only after two or three centuries, but in a million years, life will still be as it was; life does not change, it remains for ever, following its own laws which do not concern us, or which, at any rate, you will never find out. Migrant birds, cranes for example, fly and fly, and whatever thoughts, high or low, enter their heads, they will still fly and not know why or where. They fly and will continue to fly, whatever philosophers come to life among them; they may philsophise as much as they like, only they will fly . . .

Still, is there a meaning?

A meaning? Now the snow is falling. What meaning?

It seems to me that a man must have faith, or must search for a faith, or his life will be empty, empty. To live and not to know why the cranes fly, why babies are born, why there are stars in the sky. Either you must know why you live, or everything is trivial, not worth a straw.

Still, I am sorry that my youth has gone.

Gogol says: life in this world is a dull matter, my masters.

And I say it's difficult to argue with you, my masters. Hang it all.

Balzac was married at Berdichev. That's worth making a note of. Balzac was married at Berdichev.

Balzac was married at Berdichev.

The die is cast. I've handed in my resignation.

As we listen to this, it is obvious that what is being expressed is not a dealing between persons, or a series of self-definitions; it is a common, inadvertent mood—questioning, desiring, defeated. To the degree that we separate the speeches out, and see them as revealing this or that particular character, the continuing rhythm, at once tentative and self-conscious, superficially miscellaneous and yet deeply preoccupied, is quickly lost. And of course, in perform-ance, such continuity, such timing, is very difficult to sustain, if each actor sees himself as acting a separate part. It is the final paradox, in Chekhov's work, that the local identifying features, of the members of his dramatic group, are truly superficial, yet are the constant cues. What comes through or can come through is a very different voice—the human voice within and beyond the immediate negotiation and self-presentation. But within his conven-tions, and this is usually accentuated in performance, this human voice is intermittent and inadvertent; an unusual silence has to be imposed, if it is ever to be properly heard.

ANTON CHEKHOV

What Chekhov does then, in effect, is to invent a dramatic form which contradicts most of the available conventions of dramatic production. To perform him with any success at all, as we know from the record, Stanislavsky and Nemirovich-Danchenko had to find new methods of acting and design: to substitute an altered internal, suggestive method for what had been explicit, presented, articulate. It was a major development in the theatre, and is still, after seventy years, influential. But it is no surprise to find Chekhov dissatisfied, when he saw what was being done. In his persistent honesty, his scrupulous fineness of detail, he was presenting problems which could only ever be partially solved. The inherited conventions were either crude and loud, or, where they were refined to express individuality, were only partly relevant to his purposes. What happened in the theatre was that another kind of talent—a producer's talent—took over his work and found a way of presenting it, but, as can be seen from Stanislavsky's notes on his production of *The Seagull*, by adding and altering, to achieve a stageable effect. It is a significant moment, in the history of modern drama, for it shows a writer of genius beginning to create a new dramatic form, but in ways so original and so tentative that it is in constant danger of breaking down, and another kind of art has to be invented to sustain it. It is now seen as the triumph, but must also be seen as the crisis, of the naturalist drama and theatre.

PART II

The Irish Dramatists

W. B. YEATS

IN 1919, after some twenty years experience of the Abbey Theatre in Dublin which he had done so much to create, Yeats wrote:

> We have been the first to create a true *People's Theatre* and we have succeeded because it is not an exploitation of local colour, or of a limited form of drama possessing a temporary novelty, but the first doing of something for which the world is ripe, something that will be done all over the world and done more and more perfectly: the making articulate of all the dumb classes each with its own knowledge of the world.

The importance of the Abbey Theatre, and of the Irish dramatic movement which found a home there, deserves this emphasis. It was a response to an authentic national feeling, at a critical period of oppression and liberation, and it was given a particular quality by Yeats's emphasis, as a poet, on speech as history, and on an available popular speech from which inspiration could be drawn. He had written earlier:

> That idiom of the Irish-thinking people of the West . . . is the only good English spoken by any large number of Irish people today, and we must found good literature on a living speech, seeing "the difference between dead and living words, between words that meant something years ago and words that have the only thing that gives literary quality—personality, the breath of men's mouths". Falstaff gives one the sensation of reality, and when one remembers *the abundant vocabulary of a time when all but everything present to the mind was present to the senses*, one imagines that his words were but little magnified from the words of such a man in real life.

The social bases of his work, was:

> that conversation of the people which is so full of riches because it is so full of leisure, or . . . those old stories of the folk which were made by men who believed so much in the soul, and so little in anything else, that they were never entirely certain that the earth was solid under the foot-sole.

Yeats was committed, as any artist must be, to the actual and the contemporary; but elements of continuity in a society with which he had contact extended the immediacy of his experience with the content of a living tradition. At the same time, such a tradition was an alternative to a particular form of consciousness: a version of the Irish tradition could be used as a way of defining a falsely self-conscious drama, and in particular the drama of understatement and of abstraction.

> Of all artistic forms that have had a large share of the world's attention, the worst is the play about modern educated people. Except where it is superficial or deliberately argumentative it fills one's soul with a sense of commonness as with dust. It has one mortal ailment. It cannot become impassioned, that is to say, vital, without making somebody gushing and sentimental.

This caused him explicitly to reject the new advanced drama:

> Put the man who has no knowledge of literature before a play of this kind and he will say as he has said in some form or other in every age at the first shock of naturalism: "Why should I leave my home to hear but the words I have used there when talking of the rates?"

He called Ibsen—the Ibsen he knew from *Ghosts* and *Rosmersholm* and *A Doll's House*—"the chosen author of very clever young journalists who, condemned to their treadmill of abstraction, hated music and style". Yeats's failure to understand the real history of Ibsen's dramatic development was a continuing drawback; it cut him off from a main tradition of dramatic experiment. At the same time, it was the methods rather than the intentions of the free theatres with which he disagreed. He could write in 1903:

> We have to write or find plays that will make the theatre a place of intellectual excitement—a place where the mind goes to be liberated as it was liberated by the theatres of Greece and England and France at certain great movements of their history, and as it is liberated in Scandinavia today.

It is a complicated, perhaps a confused, ambition. The intellectual excitement and yet the customary speech were both wanted. It is a characteristic difficulty of writers at just that time; it was already exercising novelists, such as George Eliot and Hardy. Yeats's choice was an interesting one: he sought to exclude from the drama all those elements and conventions which had resulted from its domination by the novel, which was increasingly the most serious literary form. On the question of character, for example:

> One dogma of the printed criticism is that if a play does not contain definite character, its constitution is not strong enough

for the stage, and that the dramatic moment is always the contest of character with character. . . . When we go back a few centuries and enter the great periods of drama, character grows less and sometimes disappears. . . .

Of his collaboration with George Moore, he wrote:

> Because Moore thought all drama should be about possible people set in their appropriate surroundings, because he was fundamentally a realist . . . he required many dull, numb words. . . .

and, more significantly:

> He would have been a master of construction but that his practice as a novelist made him long for descriptions and reminiscences.

Minutiae of surface personality, alleged detail of place and feature, the exposure of labels of "character", patient carpentry of the exterior illusion: all these Yeats wished to reject, from a standpoint which was a central position in all his work:

> We lose our freedom more and more as we get away from ourselves, and not merely because our minds are overthrown by abstract phrases and generalizations, reflections in a mirror that seem living, but because we have turned the table of value upside down, and believe that the root of reality is not in the centre but somewhere in that whirling circumference.

2

Poets throughout the century before Yeats had made attempts to combine poetry and drama, after the long separation between literature and the theatre. Ordinarily, what they succeeded in combining was a limited kind of verse with an established dramatic form: Tennyson's *Becket* is an appropriate example. And since dramatic form had become rigid, in an increasingly confident and orthodox theatre, no dramatic advance had been possible. Yeats saw, in the Irish situation, an opportunity to break the mould. He would not listen to producers and actors inviting the dramatic poet to come into the theatre to learn his trade from them. When actors and producers were required for the new plays, George Moore wanted to import a stock-company of English-trained artists, but Yeats would not agree. He had his own ideas about performance and he was not willing to surrender them to the dogmas of the contemporary professional theatre. He discovered, by chance, a company of spare-time, amateur actors, working-men and women, led by two amateur producers, the Fays. By joining to their society the forces of the Irish Literary Theatre, he produced the organization which was to become the Abbey Theatre. By experiment in service of a dramatic idea, rather than by imitation of past theatrical habits, a new method of presentation was evolved, much of which remains of permanent importance—though it has effected no wide change—today.

It was not that Yeats was opposed to the theatre; a dramatist could hardly be that. But he believed the first condition of significant achievement to be the restoration of the "ancient sovereignty" of words, and that required a theatre in which language should not be subordinate, as throughout the Victorian theatre it had been, to spectacle or the visual elements of acting. So we find him writing:

> I think the theatre must be reformed in its plays, its speaking, its acting, and its scenery. . . . There is nothing good about it at present.

With the Fays' company he found something of what he wanted:

> They showed plenty of inexperience . . . but it was the first performance I had seen since I understood these things in which the actors kept still enough to give poetical writing its full effect upon the stage. I had imagined such acting, though I had not seen it, and had once asked a dramatic company to let me rehearse them in barrels that they might forget gesture and have their minds free to think of speech for a while. The barrels, I thought, might be on castors, so that I could shove them about with a pole when the action required it.

The point is ironic, now, when we have seen the English verse-drama experiment blocked by its inability to conceive an action and a movement corresponding to the rhythms of the verse: standing still, for the intenser passages, is no longer training or a joke. But Yeats was trying to get rid of existing theatrical conventions, to give the drama a new start. He made a comparable and understandable point about nineteenth-century stage design:

> The poet cannot evoke a picture to the mind's eye if a second-rate painter has set his imagination of it before the bodily eye.

Starting from such rejections, he learned as he went along, and was always prepared to experiment, with his plays as with the presentation, for new dramatic effects. All the time he was seeking a realized drama which would have the status of poetry, a rich and penetrating form which would reveal, not character, but those deeper forces of which character is a lineament. Like Strindberg, he hated the large mechanical theatre, with its intricate apparatus of illusion. Of his *At the Hawk's Well* he wrote:

My play is made possible by a Japanese dancer whom I have seen dance in a studio and in a drawing-room and on a very small stage lit by an excellent stage-light. In the studio and in the drawing-room alone, where the lighting was the light we are most accustomed to, did I see him as the tragic image that has stirred my imagination. There, where no studied lighting, no stage-picture made an artificial world, he was able . . . to recede from us into some more powerful life. Because that separation was achieved by human means alone, he receded, but to inhabit as it were the deeps of the mind. One realized anew, at every separating strangeness, that the measure of all arts' greatness can be but in their intimacy. All imaginative art remains at a distance, and this distance once chosen must be firmly held against a pushing world. Verse, ritual, music and dance in association with action require that gesture, costume, facial expression, stage arrangement must help in keeping the door. Our unimaginative arts are content to set a piece of the world as we know it in a place by itself, to put their photographs, as it were, in a plush or plain frame, but the arts which interest me, while seeming to separate from the world and us a group of figures, images, symbols enable us to pass for a few moments into a deep of the mind that had hitherto been too subtle for our habitation. As a deep of the mind can only be approached through what is most human, most delicate, we should distrust bodily distance, mechanism, and loud noise.

3

The question which has then to be asked is the measure of Yeats's own distance from the "pushing world". One is concerned, that is to say, with the nature of his withdrawal. The issue is most clearly raised in a passage like this:

> If the real world is not altogether rejected, it is but touched here and there, and into the places we have left empty we summon rhythm, balance, pattern, images that remind us of vast passions, the vagueness of past times, all the chimeras that haunt the edge of trance. . . .

We can consider, in relation to this, his two earliest plays: *The Countess Cathleen* and *The Land of Heart's Desire*. From the latter we can pick up a characteristic line—

Her face is pale as water before dawn.

—and see that "images that remind us of vast passions, the vagueness" are all too easily summoned, in what is really a reversion to a convention of late-Victorian poetry; not a breakthrough to new images, with "the breath of men's mouths". *The Land of Heart's Desire* is concerned with the conflict between the love of man and the love of the "old Sidhe". This is reduced to the simple story of the spiriting away of Mary, the conflict for her soul between, on the one hand, priest and husband, on the other, the fairy child. It is not because it is undramatic that the play fails, nor because it attempts the realization of a spiritual theme. It fails for the general reason which Mr. Leavis has urged against the early Yeats, an inheritance of stock poetic objects and manners

> —the faeries dance in a place apart,
> Shaking their milk-white feet in a ring,
> Tossing their milk-white arms in the air . . .

That this element is characteristic of the early Yeats, and that it deprives *The Land of Heart's Desire* of the very qualities that he had proposed for the drama—the difference between dead and living words—is certain. But there was always more to Yeats than that. As early as 1904 he himself wrote the best criticism of the play in question:

> It has an exaggeration of sentiment and sentimental beauty which I have come to think unmanly. The popularity of *The Land of Heart's Desire* seems to me to come not from its merits but because of this weakness.

And with the earlier play, *The Countess Cathleen*, he had already achieved something beyond the tradition which he had inherited. The form of the play is the recreation of a legend, and this is a difficulty, in all his work, since, in a theatre of national revival, legends seem equally available for recreation and for nostalgia. But here the legend is used, in the full dramatic sense, for the direct realization of an actual and contemporary experience. Yeats's account of the play's genesis is relevant:

> At first, if it (the play) has psychological depth, there is a bundle of ideas, something that can be stated in philosophical terms. My *Countess Cathleen* for instance was once the moral question: may a soul sacrifice itself for a good end? But gradually philosophy is eliminated until at last the only philosophy audible, if there is even that, is the mere expression of one character or another. *When it is completely life it seems to the hasty reader a mere story.*

The play is not more than minor, but for its date it is a noteworthy achievement. The incantatory verse of *The Land of Heart's Desire* (which it is interesting to note Yeats cut severely for performance—one wishes the pruning had taken place even earlier) has little in common with the quite successful verse of *The Countess Cathleen:*

> CATHLEEN: There is a something, Merchant, in your voice
>   That makes me fear. When you were telling how
>   A man may lose his soul and lose his God
>   Your eyes were lighted up, and when you told
>   How my poor money serves the people, both—
>   Merchants, forgive me—seemed to smile.
> FIRST MERCHANT: I laugh
>   To think that all these people should be swung
>   As on a lady's shoe-string—under them
>   The glowing leagues of never-ending flame.

This is not verse of any great intensity, but it is specifically dramatic in kind.

Through almost all the plays which Yeats wrote up to the time when he adopted the form of the Play for Dancers run certain particular themes, and the greater part are centred on the communication of a particular insight or vision. In one aspect this takes the form of the poet-plays, where the act of poetry itself is the foreground of the drama. Thus in *The Shadowy Waters* the poet Forgael says:

> I can see nothing plain; all's mystery.
> Yet sometimes there's a torch inside my head
> That makes all clear, but when the light is gone
> I have but images, analogies,
> The mystic bread, the sacramental wine,
> The red rose where the two shafts of the cross,
> Body and soul, waking and sleep, death, life,
> Whatever meaning ancient allegorists
> Have settled on, are mixed into one joy.

Yeats was always seeking to cast these images into dramatic form. The effort would be difficult enough even within an achieved dramatic tradition. Yeats's measure of success very naturally varies. *The Shadowy Waters*, in both of its versions, has moments of achievement, and its ending is impressive:

> Beloved, having dragged the net about us,
> And knitted mesh to mesh, we grow immortal;
> And that old harp awakens of itself
> To cry aloud to the grey birds, and dreams,
> That have had dreams for father, live in us.

But the play as a whole has certain major defects. In a sense they are those of which Yeats spoke when he wrote:

> When I began to rehearse a play I had the defects of my early poetry: I insisted upon obvious all-pervading rhythm.

The rhythm of the action, particularly at the climax between Forgael and Dectora, is over-simple, almost naive; it is a bad guess at the rendering of dream. The similar celebration of the poet in *The King's Threshold* has an emotional uncertainty and stridency which suggests that the form is perhaps too near the experience to allow more than displacement, in its displaced convention. The story of the poet who will not eat until the ancient right of poets to sit at the council table has been restored contains too much— and too idealized a version—of that "pushing world" which is the self. One notes about the play's method an attempt at movement from dialogue to ritual incantation (a technical problem with which Yeats was to continue to grapple and which Eliot was to take up after him) in the chant of the mayor, the old servant, and the cripples; but the device serves little more than its own ends; it is not absorbed into the structure of the drama. Of more immediate promise was the evidence of a lively prose speech, Yeats's drawing on the source of vitality in Irish country speech from which Synge was drawing his comedies. The small prose plays *Cathleen ni Houlihan* and *The Pot of Broth* are little more than anecdotes, but the latter particularly has a freshness of contact with words which was one of the forces which modified and overcame Yeats's excesses of romantic gesture. In *Deirdre* there is considerable dramatic success, both in design and speech. One can work back from the brevity of *Deirdre* to a realization of one of Yeats's intentions in the drama at this time. From the legend, which Synge was to handle in traditional narrative form. Yeats isolated the climax, and from this even he excluded all that can be excluded of conflict and suspense. The play is a lament, a surprisingly consistent abstraction from the play of character and action. The musicians are a chorus; and within their narrative, which continually leaps forward to the known end with presage of disaster, the persons of Deirdre, Naoise, Cuchulain, and Fergus move as if to their appointed places for the final dramatic instant, the tableau which is the insight. When Naoise has been killed Deirdre prepares the climax:

> Now strike the wire and sing to it a while,
> Knowing that all is happy and that you know
> Within what bride-bed I shall lie this night,

And by what man, and lie close up to him,
For the bed's narrow, and there outsleep the cock-crow.

The musicians provide the choric commentary:

1ST M: They are gone, they are gone. The proud may lie by the
proud.
2ND M: Though we were bidden to sing cry nothing loud.
1ST M: They are gone, they are gone.
2ND M: Whispering were enough.
1ST M: Into the secret wilderness of their love.
2ND M: A high grey cairn. What more is to be said?
1ST M: Eagles have gone into their cloudy bed.

It is for these particular realizations that Yeats strives, a process
of continuing refinement of the normal material of drama until
the final moment of insight is physically reached. And by insight he
did not mean the discovery of anything which could be formulated
outside the terms of art. His search was for pattern. The meaning of
Deirdre can be found in the earlier song:

> Love is an immoderate thing
> And can never be content
> Till it dip an ageing wing
> Where some laughing element
> Leaps, and Time's old lanthorn dims.
> What's the merit in love-play,
> In the tumult of the limbs
> That dies out before 'tis day,
> Heart on heart or mouth on mouth,
> All that mingling of our breath,
> When love-longing is but drouth
> For the things come after death.

Here the theme is the traditional identity of love and death as a
moment outside time, a moment when the torch burns. Yeats works
continually to express this in words; but his parallel effort takes for
material the physical stage, and already he is using elements of formal
grouping (which were also prominent in *The King's Threshold*) as a
means of precise communication. This is an element which had
been suppressed in the drama for very many years, and Yeats was
to bring it back, in his later work, to intensity.

The most interesting and successful play of this middle period is
On Baile's Strand, where he finds a word-structure that he was to
use again and again. There are formal visual elements—the masks of
beggar and fool; but the important conventions are verbal, of
chorus and of dramatic metaphor. The outer circle of the play is
in the conversation of the Fool and the Blind Man, which is in

prose. This conversation accomplishes a skilful exposition, but Fool and Blind Man are more: their incapacities, their energy for deceit and restlessness and vexation, make them the proper setting for the restlessness among the kings which drives Cuchulain to the slaughter of his own son, and then to an insane fight with the sea. In this play Yeats achieves an interpenetration of different levels of reality in an integral and controlled structure. From the outer circle of Blind Man and Fool the play tightens to the verse in which the tragedy is prepared. Through the altercation moves a chorus of women, and as Cuchulain goes out to kill against his instinct, they speak:

> I have seen, I have seen.
>> What do you cry aloud?
> The Ever-Living have show me what's to come.
> How? Where?
>> In the ashes of the bowl.
> While you were holding it between your hands?
> Speak quickly!
>> I have seen Cuchulain's rooftree
> Leap into fire, and the walls split and blacken
> Cuchulain has gone out to die.
>> O! O!
> Who would have thought that one so great as he
> Should meet his end at this unnoted sword.
> Life drifts between a fool and a blind man
> To the end, and nobody can know his end.

And the play moves outward again to the fighting of Blind Man and Fool, with the noise of the fight to the death of Cuchulain and his son as background. Cuchulain re-enters and wipes the blood from his sword with the Fool's feathers; it is the Blind Man who reveals that the man he has killed is his son. As Cuchulain runs fighting into the sea, the beggars continue their thievery.

For its date, *On Baile's Strand* is a remarkable achievement, and one on which Yeats and others were to build. Among other facts, one notes the assurance of Yeats's handling of his legendary material: the outer and inner circles of the play might be described as the movement from the present and actual into the living past, and also as the movement from the lively speech of the poet's countrymen to an authentic poetry. There was to be very little more romanticism about the "dim far-off times": what was living from tradition was to be taken into the present to provide depth for present creation. It is a measure of Yeats's increased assurance that he was able in 1910 to write *The Green Helmet* and to use the material and manners of his serious drama as a basis for farce. He himself described the change:

> To me drama . . . has been the search for more of manful energy, more of cheerful acceptance of whatever arises out of the logic of events, and for clean outlines, instead of those outlines of lyric poetry that are blurred with desire and vague regret.

This was clearly related to changes in certain radical attitudes. One may observe these changes clearly in such a play as *The Unicorn from the Stars* (a later version of *Where there is Nothing*):

> MARTIN: I thought the battle was here, and that the joy was to be found here on earth, that all one had to do was to bring again the old wild earth of the stories—but no, it is not here; we shall not come to that joy, that battle, till we have put out the senses, everything that can be seen and handled, as I put out this candle. We must put out the whole world as I put out this candle. We must put out the light of the stars and the light of the sun and the light of the moon, till we have brought everything to nothing once again. I saw in a broken vision, but now all is clear to me. Where there is nothing, where there is nothing—there is God!

This effective theatrical speech loses much of its power in its actual context: *The Unicorn from the Stars* is the nearest thing Yeats wrote to the conventional prose play, with its solid material setting for the communication of a particular spiritual experience. More successful is *The Hour-Glass* (which exists in prose and verse texts) where the form is that of a morality or, more exactly, of an interlude. The Wise Man has taught:

> There is nothing we cannot see, nothing we cannot touch.

but in the moment before death he acknowledges God's will:

> We perish into God and sink away
> Into reality—the rest's a dream.

But he is saved from obliteration (as was Peer Gynt) by the faith of the Fool, the only person whose faith has not been destroyed by the Wise Man's rationalism.

The movement and development in these plays is the same experience as that which refined his verse and which made him a great poet. To assume that he ended where he began, a slave to sentimental poeticism, is to ignore the evidence. And the search for dramatic form was a particular refining agent: the discovery of a way to write drama in verse again.

Nor has any poet I have read of or heard of or met with been a sentimentalist. The other self, the antiself or antithetical self, as one may choose to name it, comes to those who are no longer deceived, whose passion is reality.

4

Yeats claimed that his Plays for Dancers were a new art form, and in one sense this is true. They represent an intensification of particular elements of drama which, in the development of naturalism, had been suppressed or minimized. These elements were present in Yeats's work before the particular form of the dancer-plays: isolation of particular moments from their total context; physical realization through verbal and visual design. The five plays are all short. The brevity depends, as Mr. Ronald Peacock has put it, on an "acute judgement of what the method will stand". Yeats's own description of *At the Hawk's Well*, quoted above, could not be bettered as a description of intention. In method, there is the formal design of such plays as *At The Hawk's Well*, *The Only Jealousy of Emer*, and *Calvary*. The masked musicians are a dramatic development: they serve, variously, the purposes of prologue, chorus, and orchestra. In *The Cat and the Moon* the first musician speaks for the invisible saint. But the design of the plays is not only visual. In each case the song, which accompanies the folding and unfolding of the cloth which mark the beginning and end of the play, provides an image which is at the centre of the revelation into which the play then moves. The most obvious example is that of the heron in *Calvary;* but there are the withered leaves choking the well in *At the Hawk's Well;* the "white fragile thing" of *The Only Jealousy of Emer;* the "fantastic dreams" in a "cup of jade" in *The Dreaming of the Bones;* implicitly the cat and the moon in the play of that name. The plays achieve, in miniature, intensity and dramatic pattern.

> Why does my heart beat so?
> Did not a shadow pass?
> It passed but a moment ago.
> Who can have trod in the grass?
> What rogue is night-wandering?
> Have not old writers said
> That dizzy dreams can spring
> From the dry bones of the dead?
> And many a night it seems
> That all the valley fills
> With those fantastic dreams,
> They overflow the hills,

> So passionate is a shade,
> Like wine that fills to the top
> A grey-green cup of jade,
> Or maybe an agate cup.

The verse is not uniformly successful, and is always of a higher quality in the songs. But Yeats was concerned with dramatic *recital* rather than with dramatic representation. There was much to be done before a verbal pattern could become, again, a whole action. The limitation, but also the achievement, of the dancer-plays, is their creation of scenes which are images: to be danced, spoken, and sung. What is there is a fixed point, a moment: an isolated structure of feeling.

5

Yeats's prodigious capacity for development is well known, and many of the experiments of his latest years retain great interest. *The Resurrection* is an expansion of the dancer-play in other interests; it retains much of the beauty of the form, but includes new elements of discussion and celebration. *The Herne's Egg* is an entertaining play with literary affinities to that aspect of Nō technique which Yeats had adopted in his dancer-plays; definition by a single metaphor—here by the herne's egg and the donkey.

Purgatory achieves the old end of physical realization of a moment of insight, but without obvious stylization: there is complete isolation of the moment against the scene of a ruined house and a bare tree. The verse has the fine power of Yeats's later years:

> They know at last
> The consequence of their transgressions
> Whether upon others or upon themselves;
> Upon others, others may bring help,
> For when the consequence is at an end
> The dream must end; upon themselves
> There is no help but in themselves
> And in the mercy of God.

The dancer-play is further varied in *The Death of Cuchulain*, written in 1939, the year of Yeats's death. The mockery of the prologue—spoken by a "very old man looking like something out of mythology"—is succeeded by the isolation of Aoife and Cuchulain, and by the blind man taking the king's head, and Emer dancing in the shadow of the Morrigu. It is "antiquated romantic stuff", but it is alive on the lips of a singer at a contemporary Irish fair, with Yeats's permanent question:

Are those things that men adore and loathe
Their sole reality? . . .
What comes out of the mountain
Where men first shed their blood
Who thought Cuchulain till it seemed
He stood where they had stood.

What he had done, in his theatre, and what he had encouraged others to do, was indeed just this: to think, to imagine, a dramatic figure, until it "stood where they had stood". And then it was not only Cuchulain (in the legends that remained, for the most part, "an exploitation of local colour") but a contemporary Irish world.

2

J. M. SYNGE

THE body of Synge's dramatic work is small. There are only three full-length plays: *The Well of the Saints*: *The Playboy of the Western World*: and *Deirdre of the Sorrows*: and of these the last is unrevised. *The Tinker's Wedding* is a middle-length piece; and then there are the two short plays, *Riders to the Sea* and *The Shadow of the Glen*. This work was concentrated into a period of only seven years—from 1903 to 1910.

The Preface to *The Tinker's Wedding*, written in 1907, is a convenient document of a part of Synge's attitude to the drama, and some of his intentions. It may be quoted in full:

> The drama is made serious—in the French sense of the word—not by the degree in which it is taken up with problems that are serious in themselves, but by the degree in which it gives the nourishment, not very easy to define, on which our imaginations live. We should not go to the theatre as we go to a chemist's or a dram-shop, but as we go to a dinner where the food we need is taken with pleasure and excitement. This was nearly always so in Spain and England and France when the drama was at its richest—the infancy and decay of the drama tend to be didactic—but in these days the playhouse is too often stocked with the drugs of many seedy problems or with the absinthe or vermouth of the last musical comedy.
>
> The drama, like the symphony, does not teach or prove anything. Analysts with their problems, and teachers with their systems, are soon as old-fashioned as the pharmacopoeia of Galen—look at Ibsen and the Germans—but the best plays of Ben Jonson and Molière can no more go out of fashion than the blackberries on the hedges.
>
> Of the things which nourish the imagination humour is one of the most needful and it is dangerous to limit or destroy it. Baudelaire calls laughter the greatest sign of the Satanic element in man; and where a country loses its humour, as some towns in Ireland are doing, there will be morbidity of mind, as Baudelaire's mind was morbid.
>
> In the greater part of Ireland, however, the whole people, from the tinkers to the clergy, have still a life, and view of life,

that are rich and genial and humorous. I do not think that these country people, who have so much humour themselves, will mind being laughed at without malice, as the people in every country have been laughed at in their own comedies.

And in the Preface to *The Playboy of the Western World* (written earlier in 1907) he makes these points about language:

All art is a collaboration, and there is little doubt that in the happy ages of literature, striking and beautiful phrases were as ready to the storyteller's or the playwright's hand, as the rich cloaks and dresses of his time. It is probable that when the Elizabethan dramatist took his ink-horn and sat down to his work he used many phrases that he had just heard, as he sat at dinner, from his mother or his children. In Ireland, those of us who know the people have the same privilege. When I was writing *The Shadow of the Glen*, some years ago, I got more aid than any learning could have given me from a chink in the floor of the old Wicklow house where I was staying, that let me hear what was being said by the servant-girls in the kitchen. This matter, I think, is of importance, for in countries where the imagination of the people, and the language they use, is rich and living, it is possible for a writer to be rich and copious in his words, and at the same time to give the reality, which is the root of all poetry, in a comprehensive and natural form. In the modern literature of towns, however, richness is found only in sonnets, or prose poems, or in one or two elaborate books that are far away from the profound and common interests of life. One has, on the one side, Mallarmé and Huysmans producing this literature; and on the other, Ibsen and Zola dealing with the reality of life in joyless and pallid words. On the stage one must have reality, and one must have joy, and that is why the intellectual modern drama has failed, and people have grown sick of the false joy of the musical comedy, that has been given them in place of the rich joy found only in what is superb and wild in reality. In a good play every speech should be as fully flavoured as a nut or apple, and such speeches cannot be written by anyone who works among people who have shut their lips on poetry.

These familiar and valuable passages are worth emphasis for two reasons; first, that they directly present an important issue which is highly relevant to the staple of Synge's plays and to the material of most modern drama; and second—a more weighty reason—because they raise, perhaps unconsciously, certain complex issues of dramatic literature and language on which the final evaluation of Synge must depend.

J. M. SYNGE

2

Synge's plays are sometimes grouped into comedies—*The Shadow of the Glen, The Tinker's Wedding, The Well of the Saints,* and *The Playboy of the Western World*; and tragedies—*Riders to the Sea* and *Deirdre of the Sorrows.* I cannot myself agree that this classification is adequate, even as a working guide. *The Shadow of the Glen* and *The Tinker's Wedding* are very similar plays, and they are both comedies of a particular kind: both plays are basically naturalist, and their substantial element is a kind of knockabout farce. *Deirdre* is a fully serious, non-naturalist tragedy; *Riders to the Sea* is a tragic fragment of which the basic element is documentary naturalism, isolated to what is in effect a chorus. *The Playboy* is "serious drama— in the French sense of the word"—a satiric comedy which is an important example of "critical naturalism". *The Well of the Saints*— to my mind the least successful of Synge's works—is in effect a naturalist fable, of a kind which has since been widely used in modern drama.

The diversity is considerable; but it is what one might expect from a writer striking out on new bearings within a very short period: Synge wrote his first play when he was thirty-two, and his last when he was thirty-eight.

The two simplest pieces belong to his early writing years: their particular quality is their language. *Shadow of the Glen* takes as its central incident the simulation of death by an elderly husband in order to trap his younger wife with her lover.

At its own level the play is successful, and very well done:

NORA BURKE [*pouring him out some whisky*]: Why would I marry you, Mike Dara? You'll be getting old and I'll be getting old, and in a little while, I'm telling you, you'll be sitting up in your bed—the way himself was sitting—with a shake in your face, and your teeth falling, and the white hair sticking out around you like an old bush where sheep do be leaping a gap.

[DAN BURKE *sits up noiselessly from under the sheet, with his hand to his face. His white hair is sticking out round his head.* NORA *goes on slowly without hearing him.*]

It's a pitiful thing to be getting old, but it's a queer thing surely. It's a queer thing to see an old man sitting up there in his bed with no teeth in him, and a rough word in his mouth, and his chin the way it would take the bark from the edge of an oak board you'd have building the door. . . .

[DAN *sneezes violently,* MICHAEL *tries to get to the door, but before he can do so* DAN *jumps out of the bed in queer white clothes, with the stick in his hand, and goes over and puts his back against it.*]

131

MICHAEL: Son of God deliver us!
   [*Crosses himself and goes backward across the room.*]

This kind of incident is not exceptional in naturalist comedy; what distinguishes it from sketches which would get their laugh and be forgotten is its language; Synge's farces are given an extra dimension by the verbal play. One might say that *Shadow of the Glen* is less a work of art than an entertainment; but it is the merit of Synge's basic attitude that the distinction is unreal and unnecessary.

Synge's language, as we have seen, is based on recorded Irish country speech; but it is a literary product, which has undergone the normal process of shaping. It is clearly a rich language; but it is in the variations of its dramatic use that the important distinctions have to be made. It is not the isolable quality of "richness"— which may often be only strangeness—that matters. It is the relation of the language to the action; and this can vary from simple decoration through an added dimension to new kinds of imaginative control. We shall find examples of each of these uses.

The Tinker's Wedding is a two-act play. The comedy between the thieving tinkers and the mercenary priests is lively, although it is less controlled and concentrated than that of *The Shadow of the Glen*. The Tinker girl's complicated desires for marriage and for a fine life with the "great lads" are of the same order as those of Nora Burke. What weakens the play is an occasional elaboration of external rhythm and colour—a self-conscious verbal decoration which as it were overflows and drowns the experience—as in this speech of Mary Byrne's:

> It's sick and sorry we are to tease you; but what did you want meddling with the like of us, when it's a long time we are going our own ways—father and son, and his son after him, or mother and daughter and her own daughter again; and it's little need we ever had of going up into a church and swearing—I'm told there's swearing with it—a word no man would believe, or with drawing rings on our fingers, would be cutting our skins maybe when we'd be taking the ass from the shafts, and pulling the straps the time they'd be slippy with going around beneath the heavens in rains falling.

Here the force and the clarity of the feeling are marked, in the language, until the rings are reached; and what then takes over is another kind of verbal play, drawing attention mainly to itself.

For Synge was not yet always using his language dramatically; he was sometimes using it, rather, to add "flavour": an interpretation which his own critical description includes.

3

Riders to the Sea is a tragic chorus which draws its strength from the quality of acceptance which Synge had discovered in the islanders among whom he had lived. It moves on a limited plane: the inevitability of the conflict between men and the sea, and the inevitability of the men's defeat. When the last of Maurya's sons has been drowned she speaks to herself:

> They're all gone now, and there isn't anything more the sea can do to me. . . . They're all together this time and the end is come. . . . May the Almighty God have mercy on Bartley's soul, and on Michael's soul, and on the souls of Seamus and Patch, and Stephen and Shawn; and may he have mercy on the soul of every one is left living in the world. . . . Michael has a clean burial in the far north, by the grace of the Almighty God. Bartley will have a fine coffin out of the white boards, and a deep grave surely. What more can we want than that? No man at all can be living for ever, and we must be satisfied.

It is a powerful rhythm, within a deliberately limited action. Its paradox is the depth of its language and the starved, almost passive experience. It is as if the fatalism were determined at one level and the lives of the islanders at another, and then the two are fused, but incompletely, in a dominant single rhythm. As such it is a dramatic fragment for reasons other than its brevity, but what is achieved in this fragment is an indication of that common action which the theory of language might be, at its most serious. What has been achieved, that is to say, is a chorus, but not yet the action on which the chorus depends.

With *The Well of the Saints* Synge returned to a subject which had been part of his plot, if not of his theme, in *The Shadow of the Glen* and *The Tinker's Wedding*: the double nature of the imagination—its capacity for simple deceptive fantasy, and its frequent role as a liberator. This was to be the action of the *Playboy of the Western World*. The blind beggars, Martin and Mary Doul, are sustained in joy and self-respect by the illusion of their own beauty and comeliness. When their sight is restored by the holy water of the Saint, their revealed ugliness comes near to destroying them. But when their sight fades once more, they achieve a new illusion: of their dignity in old age, the woman with her white hair, the man with his flowing beard. They fly in terror from a renewed offer to restore their sight of the real world; although their neighbours realize that their continued blindness, leading them along "a stony path, with the north wind blowing behind", will mean their death.

The issue is related to that which Ibsen handled in *The Wild Duck* and *John Gabriel Borkman:* and indeed in any of his plays where the choice between happiness in illusion, and courage in truth, is the substance of the work. Synge's play has moments of great power, especially in the third act, but it is very uneven. The handling of blindness provokes serious dangers of sentimentality; not all of which Synge avoids. The scenes of the beggars' realization of their actual state are painful, as might be expected, but they provoke an acute embarrassment which has less to do with the elements of the situation than with what seems to be a direct appeal to audience or reader. In this connexion Synge's stage directions, which are radically different from those of *The Shadow of the Glen*, are critically important. With so capable a language as he commands, this method of embellishment, which others had developed because of the inadequacy of spoken language, and under the influence of fictional rather than dramatic methods, seems curiously unnecessary; but its constant employment suggests an unwillingness to be fully committed dramatically, which confirms one's reaction to the general tone of the play.

> MOLLY BYRNE: If it was a queer time itself it was a great joy and pride I had the time I'd hear your voice speaking and you passing to Grianan [*beginning to speak with plaintive intensity*], for it's of many a fine thing your voice would put a poor dark fellow in mind, and the day I'd hear it it's of little else at all I would be thinking.
>
> MARTIN DOUL [*seizing the moment he has her attention*]: I'm thinking by the mercy of God it's few sees anything but them is blind for a space [*with excitement*]. It's few sees the old women rotting for the grave, and it's few sees the like of yourself. [*He bends over her.*] Though it's shining you are, like a high lamp would drag in the ships out of the sea.
>
> MOLLY BYRNE [*shrinking away from him*]: Keep off from me, Martin Doul.
>
> MARTIN DOUL [*quickly with low furious intensity*]: It's the truth I'm telling you.

It is difficult to define one's uneasiness at such passages. It might be argued that it is only the stage directions which involve the audience in a kind of pathetic vibration, and that since these would not be heard in performance the objection is only secondary. But it is the spoken language which determines the nature of the dramatist's comments: his language involves the same kind of appeal. For the emotion is not there in the spoken language, nor in the incident it creates; response depends on the invitation to inclusion; depends in practical terms on the gestures of voice and body which the actor is directed to undertake in order to register a comment. The emotion is not in the body of the drama; ultimately it is a kind of external pointing, using explicit and tacit statement, and subsequent proof by illustration. And that is the basic method of the whole play.

4

The Playboy of the Western World is a brilliantly successful comedy which at last succeeds in integrating the range of language with an action to which the range is relevant. T. S. Eliot's important essay on Jonson contains passages which are highly relevant to the method and substance of the play. We can say that the comedy is satiric. But

> Jonson's drama is only incidentally satire, because it is only incidentally a criticism upon the actual world. It is not satire in the way in which the work of Swift or the work of Molière may be called satire: that is, it does not find its source in any precise emotional attitude or precise intellectual criticism of the actual world. . . . The important thing is that if fiction can be divided into creative fiction and critical fiction, Jonson's is creative.

Eliot's definition can be applied as it stands to *The Playboy*.

Perhaps the most important way in which Synge's play is to be distinguished from the main stream of English comedy is its attitude to character. The lively gang in the shebeen do not form a gallery of individual portraits, displayed to us by the normal processes of revelation; neither is the record of the interplay the process of the comedy.

> Whereas in Shakespeare the effect is due to the way in which the characters *act upon* one another, in Jonson it is given by the way in which the characters *fit in* with each other.

For it is not simply the fantasy of Christy Mahon, trailing the awesome (and bogus) glory of "a man has killed his da", with which Synge is concerned; but with the fantasy of the whole community who are equal makers of his illusion. The characters are an individual world rather than a representative group; the individual existence of each is less important than the common emotional process within which their world is circumscribed. It is, of course, a small world, what Grattan Freyer called "the little world of J. M. Synge". Eliot again made the essential point.

But small worlds—the worlds which artists create—do not differ only in magnitude; if they are complete worlds, drawn to scale in every part, they differ in kind also. And Jonson's world has this scale. His type of personality found its relief in something falling under the category of burlesque or farce—though when you are dealing with a *unique* world, like his, these terms fail to appease the appetite for definition. It is not, at all events, the farce of Molière; the latter is more analytic, more an intellectual redistribution. It is not defined by the word "satire". Jonson poses as a satirist. But satire like Jonson's is great in the end not by hitting off its object, but by creating it; the satire is merely the means which leads to the aesthetic result, the impulse which projects a new world into a new orbit.

In modern drama, the point can be made again by reference to *Peer Gynt* with which Synge's play has several correspondences. Ibsen satirizes the folk-fantasy of the Norwegians in much the same mood as does Synge that of the Irish. And as in the case of Peer Gynt, Christy Mahon's illusion of greatness is nourished and raised to the heights by a community where the mythology of force (compare the tales they spin of Red Jack Smith and Bartley Fallon) is dominant; Christy—"a man did split his father's middle with a single clout"—is the familiar tale of a giant. But when the revengeful father comes on his trail, the collapsed hero is as quickly turned to sacrifice. And when the hero does the famous deed in apparent truth, his shocked spectators learn "that there's a great gap between gallous story and a dirty deed".

But again the deed is not completed:

> Are you coming to be killed a third time, or what is it ails you now?

Finally Christy realizes that it is not the deed which made him glorious, but the telling of the deed, that "poet's talking". And this he retains. He goes out from the community confident in his new strength, but acknowledges that it is the community which made him:

> Ten thousand blessings upon all that's here, for you've turned me a likely gaffer in the end of all, the way I'll go romancing through a romping lifetime from this hour to the dawning of the judgement day.

It is not only Christy who is transformed; the community itself has made something. Their "hero" may go from them, but he is their creation—"the only Playboy of the Western World". A starved community—and this is the irony but also, unconsciously, the cruelty of the action—has at once alienated and launched its destructive and confusing fantasy. The fantastic deception is separated from them; lost to them; gone out into romance. It is a bitter comment on the poverty, which required other experience and other actions. It is also a bitter comment, as we now look back, on the real relation between the Irish drama and the Irish people of this period. What the writers found, in their own medium, was "richness", but the richness was a function of a more pressing poverty, and this was at times idealized, at times compounded; in *The Playboy* faced but then confidently superseded: the poverty and the fantasy, always so closely related, seen now as bitterly nourishing each other; grasped and projected into an exiled orbit.

5

A powerful dramatic language is not, ultimately, to be judged in terms of "reality" or "joy", and it is more than a question of "flavour". The highest dramatic language is that which contains within itself the substance of the drama, which discovers and creates its emotional structure. Mr. Freyer has pointed out (in the essay already referred to) that the dominant characteristic of Synge's language is an abundance of simile and a complete absence of metaphor or verbal symbolism. The observation, with reference to the plays up to *Deirdre*, is generally accurate, and it is most revealing. Synge's enrichment of naturalist language is an important achievement; but, in general, he does not push through to the action (including the history as action) which the language essentially contains. This is why the stock comparison with the Elizabethans is superficial, although it is not so unjustified as the similar comparison of the work of later Irish dramatists. There is a basic difference of intention: Synge's similes give flavour to speeches which might otherwise be "joyless" or "pallid"; the absence of metaphor distinguishes his work from a more fully embodied and, in the wide sense, more questioning drama. Most of his language is parallel to the action: the recording, separated poet; the folk-writer who is visiting the folk. When the relation is closer—when the "poetry" and the action are involved with each other—there is a gain of power but also a deep disturbance, which outdates all the earlier formulas. That was the achievement of *The Playboy of the Western World*.

Deirdre of the Sorrows was left unrevised when Synge died; and this is a loss, because there are signs that in this play Synge was working towards a different dramatic method.

As it stands, the play is slight, and suffers from a disturbing singleness of level. Its stained-glass quality is perhaps related to its theme, on which an earlier comment by Synge himself is relevant:

> No personal originality is enough to make a rich work unique, unless it has also the characteristic of a particular life and locality and the life that is in it. For this reason all historical plays and novels and poems . . . are relatively worthless. Every healthy mind is more interested in *Titbits* than in *Idylls of the King*.

As a description of the source of the strength of his own early work this is obviously true. It describes the particular quality of his genius, and explains the artificiality in *Deirdre*. Yeats tells us that Synge was not interested in the Heroic Age until he wrote *Deirdre*. Perhaps the choice was wrong. But in depriving him of many of the sources of his earlier strength, *Deirdre* forced the exploration, as was indeed inevitable, of a different kind of drama, to which his direct experience was drawing him. It is not a colourful observation, but an exposure, a dark separation:

> LAVARCHAM: Deirdre is dead, and Naisi is dead; and if the oaks and stars could die for sorrow, it's a dark sky and a hard and naked earth we'd have this night in Emain.

The substance of the tragedy, the inevitability of the destruction wrought by beauty—

> LAVARCHAM: I'm in dread so they were right saying she'd bring destruction on the world—

is summed up, in closely related imagery, in the speech of Deirdre herself:

> Who'd fight the grave, Conchubor, and it opened on a dark night?

The play moves on these bearings of the "dark night" and the "grave".

> What we all need is a place safe and splendid

says Conchubor early in the play, attempting to persuade Deirdre to become his queen. But Deirdre rejects him for Naisi although she is conscious that it is "for a short space only", and she is able to say in the end:

> It was the choice of lives we had in the woods, and in the grave we're safe surely.

The speeches of Deirdre and Naisi at their first meeting—

DEIRDRE: It should be a sweet thing to have what is best and richest, if it's for a short space only.

NAISI: And we've a short space only to be triumphant and brave.

initiate the pattern which is completed near their death:

NAISI: There's nothing, surely, the like of a new grave of open earth for putting a great space between two friends that love.

DEIRDRE: If there isn't, it's that grave when it's closed will make us one for ever, and we two lovers have had great space without weariness or growing old or any sadness of the mind.

And the same pattern is the basis of the fears of the second act:

OWEN: Three weeks is a long space, and yet you're seven years spancelled with Naisi and the pair.

DEIRDRE: Three weeks of your days might be long, surely, yet seven years are a short space for the like of Naisi and myself.

OWEN: If they're a short space there aren't many the like of you. . . .

DEIRDRE: Am I well pleased seven years seeing the same sun throwing light across the branches at the dawn of day? It's a heartbreak to the wise that it's for a short space we have the same things only.

Deirdre's definition of wisdom is related to the persistent reference to "knowledge":

CONCHUBOR: Isn't it a strange thing you'd be talking of Naisi and his brothers, or figuring them either, when you know the things that are foretold about themselves and you? Yet you've little knowledge, and I'd do wrong taking it bad when it'll be my share from this out to keep you the way you'll have little call to trouble for knowledge, or its want either.

DEIRDRE: Yourself should be wise surely.

CONCHUBOR: The like of me has a store of knowledge that's a weight and terror.

It is against this bitter knowledge that the final affirmation is set, in the voice of Deirdre:

Draw a little back with the squabblings of fools when I am broken up with misery. I see the flames of Emain starting upward in the dark night; and because of me there will be weasels and wild cats crying on a lonely wall where there were queens and armies and red gold, the way there will be a story told of a ruined city and a raving king and a woman will be young for ever. . . . I have put away sorrow like a shoe that is worn out and muddy, for it is I have had a life that will be envied by great companies. . . . It was the choice of lives we had in the clear woods, and in the grave we're safe surely. . . . I have a little key to unlock the prison of Naisi you'd shut upon his youth for ever. . . . It was sorrows were foretold, but great joys were my share always; yet it is a cold place I must go to be with you, Naisi, and it's cold your arms will be this night that were warm about my neck so often. It's a pitiful thing to be talking out when your ears are shut to me. It's a pitiful thing, Conchubor, you have done this night in Emain; yet a thing will be a joy and triumph to the ends of life and time.

The seven years of Deirdre's vision and the seven years of Synge's writing are an unintended, bitter coincidence. The genius of delight, which Synge had so clearly, was cut across by a pain, a separation, which was always there in the life of which he offered to write. The liveliness of idiom, the boisterous or mourning collective action, the collected literary legends: each of these, for a time, seemed a sufficient relation, and the drama was made from them. It is an important achievement, but, given its power, it is tragically unfinished: a close exploration, a brave affirmation, cut off by a darkness and a silence.

3

THE "EXILES" OF JAMES JOYCE

RICHARD: Once I had it, Robert: a certitude as luminous as that of my own existence—or an illusion as luminous. (*Exiles*, Act Second.)

If one has the stomach to add the breakages, upheavals, distortions, inversions, of all this chambermade music one stands, given a grain of goodwill, a fair chance of actually seeing the whirling dervish, Tumult, son of Thunder, self exiled in upon his ego a nightlong a shaking betwixtween white or reddr hawrors, noondayterrorised to skin and bone by an ineluctable phantom (may the Shaper have mercery on him!) writing the mystery of himsel in furniture. (*Finnegans Wake, p.* 184.)

I

TO skim the pages of the dramatic piece *Exiles,* which Joyce wrote in 1914, is to register surprise that the author of this three-act play divided in drawing-rooms is the writer of *Ulysses* and of *Finnegans Wake.* For it has seemed impossible to begin the play without preconceptions. On the one hand it is assumed that if we find the Fabulous Artificer of ancient and transitional legend down upon his knees prescribing stained planking for the drawing-room floor and "in the wall at the left a window looking out on the road", we find him in aberration and should quickly turn away. While, on the other hand, if we know the man's definitive biography, the early critical salute to *When We Dead Awaken,* and the artist's record that "as he went by Baird's stone-cutting works in Talbot Place the spirit of Ibsen would blow through him like a keen wind", then the aberration is explained, we are in the familiar preserve of Literary Influences, and "Drama: Ibsen-Joyce" may be inked in on the graph.

To the support of such conclusions, a reading of *Exiles* adduces little evidence. The result of the words of the play is not an experience formally different in kind from that of Joyce's more famous work. Neither is the method of Joyce's play closer to the method of Ibsen than, say, the structure of *Finnegans Wake* to the structure of *When We Dead Awaken.* There are precise particular relationships and distinctions to be drawn between the little play and the massive fictions, and between the Norwegian dramatist and the Irish; but they are relationships and distinctions definable only if they spring upwards from the play and not downwards from the public projection. *Exiles* is a work; not a chapter.

2

The title is not only the fact that two of the characters of the play are geographical exiles—that Richard Rowan and Bertha, by whom he has had a child, have just returned from voluntary exile in Rome. Exile is a keyword throughout Joyce's work, and a main condition of this play is the revealed isolation of each character from the others; each, in fact, in differing ways is "self-exiled in upon his own ego". The play, in Joyce's well-known term, is an epiphany, a showing-forth, of this isolation. It is a note directly sounded by Beatrice early in the first act:

RICHARD: And so you have followed me with pride and scorn also in your heart.
BEATRICE: And loneliness.

The same cry comes from Bertha in the final sequence of the play:

I was alone.

It is the position of all four of Joyce's persons. The statement of aloneness defines not only Bertha and Beatrice, but in each case the person by whom they become conscious of their isolation, the central person Richard. When Bertha tells him

Don't touch me! You are a stranger to me . . .
A stranger! I am living with a stranger!

she is reaffirming this separateness. In distant but antithetical passages Richard and Bertha attempt to assign blame for their isolation:

BERTHA: . . . You try to turn everyone against me. All is to be for you. I am to appear false and cruel to everyone except you.

and

RICHARD: You have driven her away from me now, as you drove everyone else from my side—every friend I ever had, every human being that ever tried to approach me.

In one sense, destruction of this isolation is achieved through sexual union. When Robert rhapsodizes, in his florid fashion, on physical love as an acknowledgement of the beauty of women—

A kiss is an act of homage

Richard replies sharply

It is an act of union between man and woman.

But this involves, in Joyce's view, not only union, but loss, a synthesis by destruction of the units—

> a death of the spirit.

Yet the play is not only, nor even primarily, a statement on the isolation of the four characters. It is a statement of a deeper isolation within Richard. Robert is a clearer demonstration of the superficial aspects of exile than is Richard. When quotations are sought by commentators intent on illustrating from this play the ideas which they assumed to be the persistent attitude of Joyce, it is from Robert only that they can be found. It is Robert who echoes the words of the young Joyce of the period of *Stephen Hero*:

> If Ireland is to become a new Ireland she must first beome European.

It is Robert, in his article on Richard, who defines an exile which can be taken as equivalent to the personal exile of Joyce:

> There is an economic and there is a spiritual exile. There are those who left her (Ireland) to seek the bread by which men live and there are others, nay, her most favoured children, who left her to seek in other lands that food of the spirit by which a nation of human beings is sustained in life.

Not only in his attitude to exile, but in his general enthusiasm:

> A battle of both our souls, different as they are, against all that is false in them and in the world. . . . There was an eternity before we were born: another will come after we are dead. The blinding instant of passion alone—passion, free, unashamed, irresistible—that is the only gate by which we can escape from the misery of what slaves call life. Is not this the language of your own youth that I heard so often from you in this very place where we are sitting now? Have you changed?
>
> RICHARD (*passing his hand across his brow*): Yes. It is the language of my youth.

Richard remembers the first time he betrayed Bertha, his bride in exile.

> RICHARD: I came home. It was night. My house was silent. My little son was sleeping in his cot. She, too, was asleep. I wakened her from sleep and told her. I cried beside her bed; and I pierced her heart.

It is different now: on her intrigue with Robert, Bertha says:

> I could have hidden it all from you.
>
> RICHARD: Perhaps you are sorry now that you did not.
>
> BERTHA: Perhaps I am.

RICHARD: What a fool you were to tell me. It would have been so nice if you had kept it secret.

BERTHA: As you do, no?

RICHARD: As I do, yes.

To exile now are joined "silence and cunning".

As Robert is revealed to us as the creature of Richard's youth, so is Bertha as the creature of his exile:

ROBERT: She is yours, your work. And that is why I too was drawn to her. You are so strong that you attract me even through her. . . . She and I have only obeyed your will.

Bertha says herself:

I am simply a tool for you.

Or again:

RICHARD: I tried to give her a new life. . . . Listen. She is dead. She lies on my bed. I look at her body which I betrayed—grossly and many times. . . . I know that her body was always my loyal slave. To me, to me only she gave. . . .

ROBERT: . . . She is loyal to you, body and soul. Why do you fear?

RICHARD: Not that fear. But that I will reproach myself then for having taken all for myself because I would not suffer her to give to another what was hers and not mine to give. . . . That is my fear. That I stand between her and any moments of life that should be hers, between her and you, between her and anyone, between her and anything. I will not do it. I cannot and I will not. I dare not.

The whole movement of the play is turned towards the achievement of isolation, of exile, by Richard from Bertha.

RICHARD: It is not in the darkness of belief that I desire you. But in restless living wounding doubt. To hold you by no bonds, even of love, to be united with you in body and soul in utter nakedness—for this I longed. And now I am tired for a while, Bertha. My wound tires me.

To be united in utter nakedness: these are the words of Ibsen, the longing of Rubek and Irene in *When We Dead Awaken*. But with Joyce they have a different meaning. In Ibsen they represent the return from exile; in Joyce, its achievement.

3

As a play *Exiles* is slight. It is also unusually static. To explain this, it is to Joyce's own definition of the dramatic that we must turn:

144

... dramatic art is the art whereby the artist sets forth his image in immediate relations to others;

and

the dramatic form is reached when the vitality which has flowed and eddied around each person fills every person with such vital force that he or she assumes a proper and intangible esthetic life.

Each of these definitions is underlined by the purpose of *Exiles*. But what we must then look at is the relation between this "dramatic form" and the "epiphany".

This is the moment which I call epiphany. First we recognize that the object is one integral thing, then we recognize that it is an organized composite structure, a *thing* in fact: finally, when the relation of the parts is exquisite, when the parts are adjusted to the special point, we recognise that it is *that* thing which it is. Its soul, its whatness, leaps to us from the vestment of its appearance. The soul of the commonest object, the structure of which is so adjusted, seems to us radiant. The object achieves its epiphany.

And it is then interesting that the incident which Joyce records in *Stephen Hero* as the starting point of this theory is a fragment of related conversation:

Stephen as he passed on his quest heard the following fragment of colloquy out of which he received an impression keen enough to afflict his sensitiveness very severely.

The Young Lady (drawling discreetly) ... O, yes ... I was ... at the ... cha ... pel. ....

The Young Gentleman (inaudibly) ... I ... (again inaudibly)... I ...

The Young Lady (softly) ... O ... but you're ... ve ... ry wick ... ed ....

This triviality made him think of collecting many such moments together in a book of epiphanies. By an epiphany he meant a sudden spiritual manifestation, whether in the vulgarity of speech or of gesture or in a memorable phase of the mind itself. He believed that it was for the man of letters to record these epiphanies with extreme care, seeing that they themselves are the most delicate and evanescent of moments.

In one way, this is the central ambition of naturalism, though the example given reduces it. But there is then the paradox, as always in Joyce, of the neutral observer, recording the revealing moments, and the intensely self-conscious writer, "self exiled in upon his ego". The form he chose, following Ibsen, in *Exiles*, is based on the neutral observation of speech, but the essential action is self-absorbed and secret. Although the situation described is one of crisis, there is about it an air of willed inaction, a quality characteristic of the Joyce of *Dubliners* and even of *Ulysses*. The central incident of *The Dead* is even slighter than that of *Exiles* which in some ways it resembles. But there its meaning and value find full expression through the author's commentary. The failure of *Exiles* is that the incident is left to stand alone. The only accessible means of communication would have been through some kind of conventional language. But Joyce keeps strictly to the canons of representational speech. At one level, that of simple statement, this is pointed and adequate:

> ROBERT: No man ever yet lived on this earth who did not long to possess—I mean to possess in the flesh—the woman he loves. It is nature's law.
> RICHARD: What is that to me? Did I vote it?

But this, characteristically, is a rejection of ordinary feeling. That is the interest of the failure, for it has become (though not by imitation) characteristic. A deep detachment from relationships and a rejection of ordinary communication are expressed, in a clipped brittle poise, through conventions of representation which assume their importance and reality. It is what Joyce later mocked: "writing the mystery of himsel in furniture". But it is an important and difficult phase in the evolution of naturalism: a split between an objective intention and a secretive commitment. It is there in the two meanings of "detachment", which are crucial in this period: the objective artistic discipline, which sets itself to represent the reality of others; and the imitation of this manner, to deprive others of reality in the apparent act of giving it to them— a detachment from any reality but the process of self-observation rendered as outward observation. It is a fundamentally necessary distinction, in subsequent drama, and we shall return to it. Meanwhile, since blasphemy and betrayal involve faith, Joyce's relation to the naturalist drama, and certainly to Ibsen, may be summed up in the words which pass in the first act of *Exiles:*

> RICHARD: There is a faith still stranger than the faith of the disciple in his master.
> ROBERT: And that is?
> RICHARD: The faith of a master in the disciple who will betray him.

It is a real history, this betrayal of naturalism, through and within its own forms.

4

SEAN O'CASEY

I

IRISH history had broken into revolution, a war of liberation and civil war by the time O'Casey began to write for the Abbey Theatre. His first acted play, *The Shadow of a Gunman* (1923) is at once a response to this experience of violence and, in its way, a bitter postscript to Synge's *Playboy of the Western World*. It is set in the crowded overflowing life of a Dublin tenement house which is O'Casey's major early setting. The Irish drama, in this sense, has come to town. The turbulent history through which Ireland had been living breaks into these tenements. As a direct action it is on the streets, and the people crowded in the houses react to it, in essential ways, as if it were an action beyond and outside them. This viewpoint determines most of O'Casey's early drama.

The Shadow of a Gunman is in this sense exact. It is the shadow that falls across a quite other life, but also it is the *Playboy's* action of a false hero: the frightened sentimental poet Davoren who is built up, by gossip and surmise, into a gunman's reputation:

And what danger can there be in being the shadow of a gunman?

It is the contrast between the bitter action of the history and a feckless, deceiving and self-deceiving talk that O'Casey uses as his dramatic point. Men are killed elsewhere, but within the tenement:

No wonder this unfortunate country is as it is, for you can't depend upon the word of a single individual in it.

The only victim within the play is the girl Minnie:

DAVOREN: . . . I'm sure she is a good girl, and I believe she is a brave girl.
SEUMAS: A Helen of Troy come to live in a tenement! You think a lot about her simply because she thinks a lot about you, an' she thinks a lot about you because she looks upon you as a hero—a kind o' Paris . . . she'd give the worl' and all to be gaddin' about with a gunman.

It is Minnie who is killed, after a raid on the house: found hiding arms because she believes in Davoren. The bitterness is carried right through, in that Davoren, after her death, can react only in the stereotyped "poetry" which has been his pretence and his reality:

> Ah me, alas! Pain, pain, pain ever, for ever!

With real killing in the streets, the poverty and the pretence cross to make new inadvertent victims.

This kind of irony, in O'Casey, is very difficult to follow through. The central language of *Shadow of a Gunman* is bare and taut; it is there, in reality, in the crowded life, as a tension with the endless romanticizing, boasting, sentimentality; or, again characteristically, with the simple misuse of language by the uneducated, which O'Casey always emphasizes, as here in Gallogher's letter:

> ventures to say that he thinks he has made out a Primmy Fashy case.

It is done from the inside, this tenement life, but with an eye on the audience, on external and "educated" reactions. O'Casey moves from this kind of caricature to a simpler excited naturalism—the endless overflowing talk:

> They didn't leave a thing in the kitchen that they didn't flitter about the floor . . .

It is a dramatist speaking at once from inside and outside this rush of life; in *The Shadow of a Gunman* with genuine uncertainty, and using the tension of the farcical and the terrible.

Juno and the Paycock, which followed in 1924, is in the same structure of feeling. The life is seen as farce, with death cutting across it. This can be rationalized, as in O'Casey's late description of *Shadow of a Gunman* as expressing "the bewilderment and horror at one section of the community trying to murder and kill the other". But this is never, really, what the plays show. What is there is a feckless rush, endlessly evading and posturing, while through it one or two figures—mainly women—take the eventual burden of reality. In *Juno and the Paycock* the dominant action is the talk of Boyle and Joxer: idle talk, with a continual play at importance: the false colours of poverty, which has gone beyond being faced and which is now the endless, stumbling engaging, spin of fantasy. The formal plot is rooted in this, as it might have been in Synge: the false expectation of a legacy, which will alter this world. But what comes, in the real action, is the killing from outside: first Tancred, the Republican fighter, and then Johnny, the son of the house, who betrayed him. The bereaved mothers in each case, and in the same words, call:

> Take away our hearts o' stone, an' give us hearts o' flesh! Take away this murdherin' hate, an' give us Thine own eternal love!

It is a deep, convincing, unconnected cry. It is what the mothers feel, in the terrible disturbance of the fighting. But what the play shows is not the "hearts of stone"; it is, counterpointing and over-riding these moments of intense suffering, the endless, bibulous, blathering talk.

This is, of course, an authentic structure, but it is not that which is usually presented. It is always difficult to speak from outside so intense and self-conscious a culture, but in the end we are bound to notice, as a continuing and determining fact, how little respect, except in the grand gestures, the Irish drama had for the Irish people. It was different when the people were remote and tradi-tional, as in *Riders to the Sea*. But already what comes through the surface warmth of *The Playboy of the Western World* is a deeply resigned contempt—a contempt which then allows amusement—for these deprived, fantasy-ridden talkers. Synge got near this real theme, and O'Casey is continuously dramatically aware of it. But it is a very difficult emotion to control: an uneasy separation and exile, from within the heart of the talk. And because this is so, this people's dramatist writing for what was said to be a people's theatre at the crisis of this people's history, is in a deep sense mocking it at the very moment when it moves him. The feelings of the fighters, in that real history, are not dramatically engaged at all; all we see and hear is the flag, the gesture, the rhetoric. The need and the oppression are silent, or at best oblique in some consequent action. What is active and vociferous is a confusion: the victims trapped in their tenements and abusing or flattering each other. What can be said by the mother, authentically, is

Take away this murdhering hate

—a reaction to the fact of a dead son, in whatever cause. But what is primarily and finally said is Boyle's

The whole worl's in a terrible state of chassis

—the authentic confusion translated into a refrain and a verbal error; the error and inadequacy of this people. It is strange, power-ful, cross-grained: a tension worked out, in full view, in this unusual kind of play: the facts of farce and the facts of killing.

2

The crisis of O'Casey's drama is the working-out of this compli-cated emotion. What is at issue, always, is the relation between the language of men in intense experience and the inflated, engaging language of men avoiding experience. It is a very deep disturbance, which I suppose comes out of that confused history. But what seems to me to happen, as O'Casey goes on, is the hardening of a manner-ism which overrides this crucial and difficult distinction. *Juno and the Paycock* is powerful and unforgettable because the distinction is dramatized, in the loose but authentic form which alone, within naturalism, could express it. *The Plough and the Stars* (1926) has resemblances to this, and in fact moves nearer the action that would finally have to be faced if this endless paradox—the reality of suffering and the pathetic winking confusion—was to be directly explored. But there is a change in the language, a development from the earlier plays but now exceptionally self-conscious, as if always with an eye on the audience:

> It would take something more than a thing like you to flutther a feather o' Fluther.
> Is a man fermentin' with fear to stick th' showin' off to him of a thing that looks like a shinin' shroud?

Phrases like this have been repeatedly quoted as an "Elizabethan" richness; but they are, in their origin and development, and where successful in their direct dramatic use, the consistent evidence of poverty: of a starved, showing-off imagination. I remember reacting very bitterly against them, and against the repeated tricks of colour—the naming of colours—which O'Casey carried to the point of parody. But the real point is more complex. Through all the early plays, it is the fact of evasion, and the verbal inflation that covers it, that O'Casey at once creates and criticizes: Boyle and Joxer, or again Fluther, are in the same movement engaging and despicable; talking to hold the attention from the fact that they have nothing to say. Yet then the manner spills over, into a different dramatic speech. It flares, successfully, into the shouted abuse of the overcrowded people, as here in *The Plough and the Stars*:

> BESSIE: Bessie Burgess doesn't put up to know much, never havin' a swaggerin' mind, thanks be to God, but goin' on packin' up knowledge accordin' to her conscience: precept upon precept, line upon line; here a little, an' there a little. But thanks be to Christ, she knows when she was got, where she was got, an' how she was got; while there's some she knows, decoratin' their finger with a well-polished wedding-ring, would be hard put to it if they were assed to show their weddin' lines!
> MRS. GOGAN: Y' oul' rip of a blasted liar . . .

This almost formal rhetoric, in the daily quarrels, connects with the more difficult use: the almost habitual showing-off. But it is critically different from what looks like the same manner applied to intense feeling, as in Nora in *The Plough and the Stars:*

> While your little red-lipp'd Nora can go on sittin' here, makin' a companion of th'loneliness of th' night . . .
> . . . It's hard to force away th' tears of happiness at th' end of an awful agony.

The paradoxical force of the language, endlessly presenting and self-conscious, at once to others and to the audience, drives through the play, but not as richness: as the sound, really, of a long confusion and disintegration. A characteristic and significant action is repeated: while the men are dying, in the Easter rising, the people of the tenements are looting, and lying about themselves. It is an unbearable contrast, and it is the main emotion O'Casey had to show: of nerves ragged by talking which cannot connect with the direct and terrible action. The use of random colour, of flags, of slogans, of rhetoric and comic inflation, of the sentimental song, of reminiscences of theatre (as in Nora repeating the mad Ophelia) is a rush of disintegration, of catching at temporary effects, which is quite unique: in a way, already, the separated consciousness, writing from within a life it cannot accept in its real terms yet finds endlessly engaging and preoccupying: the structure of feeling of the self-exile, still within a collective action, which can be neither avoided nor taken wholly seriously; neither indifferent nor direct.

3

Those three Abbey plays—*Shadow of a Gunman, Juno and the Paycock, The Plough and the Stars*—are a substantial but increasingly precarious achievement. The emotion is so difficult, so deeply paradoxical, that no simple development was possible. As it happened, O'Casey went away: all his remaining plays were written in exile, and there was a turning-point in his life when the Abbey Theatre, stupidly and unjustly, rejected *The Silver Tassie*. We have already seen the paradox, when the connection with Irish life and theatre was direct. That essential tension might have worked out differently, in a continuing contact. As it was, O'Casey went on elaborating his unusual forms: in a way released, in a way deprived.

The Silver Tassie (1928) is a serious experiment in a new form: an extension of naturalism to what is presented as an expressionist crisis. The first and last acts are again the crowded, overflowing talk of the Abbey plays; excited and colourful in its superficial actions—the winning of the cup, the victory dance, the songs—

but with a cold using of people, a persistent indifference to each other, that repeats, more bitterly, the paradoxical emotions of the earlier plays. The more the cry of colour and of triumph goes up, the more deprived and shut-off are the honest people. To praise the colour and excitement in abstraction is then not only critically foolish; it insults this genuine and persistent sense of loss and poverty. But the difficulty is inherent: O'Casey shows an emptiness, a terrible passivity, through the continual jerking of what presents itself as excitement. It is as if, as often in the earlier plays, he is at times himself carried away by the surface vitality; though what he always comes back to, when he shows the people, is an empty incapacity, an indifference and a cruelty.

The two middle acts of *The Silver Tassie* are a newly direct presentation—in their form critically conscious—of the determining suffering. It is the repetition, in bitter parody, of the recourse to song: the exposed soldiers finding a desperate voice, and beside them the alienated, clipped orders—the false clarity of the war. The second act is still one of the most remarkable written in English in this century, but it has the same uncertainty, the root uncertainty, of the earlier work. The critical showing, of what the war does to these men, is brilliantly achieved:

> Stumbling, swiftly cursing, plodding,
> Lumbering, loitering, stumbling, grousing,
> Through mud and rain and filth and danger
> Flesh and blood seek slow the front line.

But they are not only exposed victims. Their final chant is to the glory of the gun: they compound their suffering. And they cannot break through, at the crisis of exposure, to reason:

> But wy'r we 'ere, wy'r we 'ere,—that's wot I wants to know.
> Why 's 'e 'ere, why's 'e 'ere—that's wot 'e wants to know.
> We're here because we're here, because we're here, because we're
> here.

It is the persistent feeling: the exposed and deprived who cannot understand what is happening to them; who can talk, within limits, in their own idiom, but then fall for an alien rhetoric. It is a very deep kind of despair, and when the soldiers have become numbers, in the casualty ward, what we see again, in the reactions of others, is an indifference and cruelty. O'Casey had here his hero: the footballer who is paralysed by a wound, who watches his girl despise him and go dancing with his friend. It is the image he always returns to: of a trapped consciousness, suffering the noisy vitality of what is supposed to be a liberation. The songs point the feeling, but also, in a sense, compound it:

Let him come, let him sigh, let him go,
For he is a life on the ebb,
We a full life on the flow.

It is that ebb, that long ebb, that O'Casey writes, but through that what sounds, in inattention, like life on the flow.

4

The Silver Tassie is memorable and important. The uncertainty and the paradox find their way into parts of the form, but the general power is still there. In his later work, O'Casey experimented continually, out of touch with the theatre. What got him another kind of reputation was a play like *The Star Turns Red* (1940): a formally rhetorical communism, which overlies the difficult and incompatible social experience, the shouting frustration and loss. He dramatizes a class of attitudes, with the flags and slogans now offered in their own right. Only a careless external glance would accept them. *Red Roses for Me* (1943) is a replay of the Abbey work, with the mannerism of colour—the external colour of names and sashes—intense. But the most interesting later work is where the interest always was: in the true nature of that endless fantasy of Irish talk. There is an unusually straight dramatization of the theme—the frustration of ordinary life under the sparks of a now organized showing-off—in the post-liberation Ireland of *The Bishop's Bonfire* (1955): a directly successful play. There is also the experiment—away on his own—with an area between pantomime and folk-play, as in *Cock-a-Doodle Dandy* (1949). It is a different Irish experience that he now has in view: he has identified the enemies of the people as the Church and business and order; what crows against this is the life and play—the liberation through fancy—which he had seen, in his earlier work, shot through by the killing—at once irrepressible and their own worst enemies. It was easier, perhaps, when he could identify a cause; but it was at a distance—a felt dramatic distance—from that original confusion and intensity. It is to the Abbey plays that we still go back, but watchfully, moved and involved and yet without sentiment: seeing what happened, what so strangely happened, as the rhetoric and the reality collided, memorably, and then lurched away singing, gesturing, suffering.

PART III

Alternative Actions, Alternative Conventions

LUIGI PIRANDELLO

WHEN they advance into the theatre, these six characters in search of an author, wearing light masks which leave eyes, mouth, and nostrils free, surrounded by "a tenuous light . . . the faint breath of their fantastic reality", the central assumption of the naturalist habit in drama has at once been finally realized and finally questioned. The concept of the absolute existence of characters in a play has been set tangibly on the stage; the phrase which the characters bring with them is the echo of Ibsen's description of his aim, fifty years earlier, "the perfect illusion of reality".

Six Characters in Search of an Author is Pirandello's best-known and most challenging play. Its very title, in newspapers and similarly professional organs of outraged sanity, is a byword for the excesses of experimental art. Sanity, however, can be as elusive as any author. The whole experimental basis of Pirandello's interesting play is in fact the most universal and most orthodox prejudice of modern drama. Pirandello saw that it was a prejudice, an assumption; that was all.

> When a character is born, he acquires at once such an independence, even of his own author, that he can be imagined by everybody even in many other situations where the author never dreamed of placing him.

This speech, from the character "The Father" in Pirandello's play, is the whole basis of the experiment; but it might equally have come, not from this supposed extreme of eccentricity in drama, but from the speeches of five eminent popular writers, one after the other, at a literary luncheon.

A company of actors is rehearsing a play, an illusion of reality, in its theatre. While they are engaged in preparing certain aspects of the illusion, other aspects of it—six created characters—enter and interrupt. The resulting contrast between these various stages in the process of dramatic illusion, and the relation of the process to its context of reality, is the material of Pirandello's play.

In the course of the play's development, many of the problems peculiar to the habit of naturalism are illustrated and discussed.

There is the question of the relation of the character created by the author to its acted embodiment on the stage. When the characters have described themselves and their situation, the company begins to represent and act them:

> "THE FATHER": Yes, sir, but believe me, it has such a strange effect when . . .
> MANAGER: Strange? Why strange? Where is it strange?
> "THE FATHER": No, sir; I admire your actors—this gentleman, this lady; but they are certainly not us.

And again:

> "THE FATHER": Look here, sir, our temperaments, our souls. . . .
> MANAGER: Temperament, soul, be hanged! Do you suppose the spirit of the piece is in you? Nothing of the kind!
> "THE FATHER": What, haven't we our own temperaments, our own souls?
> MANAGER: Not at all. Your soul, or whatever you like to call it, takes shape here. The actors give body and form to it, voices and gesture. . . . The actor here acts you, and that's an end to it.
> "THE FATHER": I understand. And now I think I see why our author who conceived us as we are, all alive, didn't want to put us on the stage after all. I haven't the least desire to offend your actors. Far from it. But when I think I am to be acted by . . . I don't know whom. . . .

The issue could not have been better put, whatever conclusions Pirandello may draw from it.

Then there is the question of the degree of experience which can be communicated through drama of the type assumed. "The Stepdaughter" wants the play to concentrate on her great situation, when she is about to be taken by her stepfather:

> Ah well, then let's take off this little frock.

The Manager will not have it quite like that:

> Truth up to a certain point, but no further.

"The Stepdaughter" comments angrily:

> What you want to do is to piece together a little romantic sentimental scene out of my disgust.

But "The Father" has quite a different play in view. He wants "to get at his complicated 'cerebral drama', to have his famous remorses and torments acted".

The Manager steps in and explains:

> On the stage you can't have a character becoming too prominent and overshadowing all the others. The thing is to pack them all into a neat little framework, and then act what is actable. I am aware of the fact that everyone has his own interior

life which he wants very much to put forward. But the difficulty lies in this fact: to set out just so much as is necessary for the stage, taking the other characters into consideration, and at the same time hint at the unrevealed interior life of each. I am willing to admit, my dear young lady, that from your point of view it would be a fine idea if each character could tell the public all his troubles in a nice monologue or a regular one-hour lecture.

This is the familiar tyranny of the "neat little framework" of the orthodox theatre, with its limited versions of what is actable. It repeats points made by Strindberg and Chekhov, and develops a point central to the habit of naturalism: the "hint at the unrevealed interior life". The need for articulate, connected speech is characteristically dismissed as a "lecture". At the same time, a paradox of the whole dramatic method is realized. When "The Stepdaughter" is talking with her procurer, the actors cry:

Louder! Louder please!
Louder? Louder? What are you talking about? These aren't matters that can be shouted at the top of one's voice.

And again, when "The Father" tries to analyze his situation, the Manager protests:

I should like to know if anyone has ever heard of a character who gets right out of his part and perorates and speechifies as you do. Have you ever heard of a case? I haven't. . . . Drama is action, sir, action, and not confounded philosophy.
All right, I'll do just as much arguing and philosophizing as everybody does when he is considering his own torments.
If the drama permits.

2

Pirandello's experiments in drama were part of a general movement in the Italian theatre. Its starting-point was the revolt against romantic drama, which had been the general pattern of European dramatic reform. The romantic drama had a very firm hold in Italy, and the revolt was correspondingly extreme. Its beginning can be dated from the production of a play by Luigi Chiarelli, in 1914. The title of the play, *The Mask and the Face* (*La Maschera e il Volto*), became a slogan for the general movement which followed. Chiarelli's intention was to "expose" the romantic drama, to pull off the mask of its conventional morality, and reveal the actual form of the life which it concealed. But the mood was not that of the French realists, exposing deliberately unromantic material. The complication of the intrigue action, the nature of the dramatic situations, were largely retained. But the play was given a grotesque twist in resolution, confounding the romantic morality. For both these reasons—the retention of complicated intrigue, and the grotesque resolution—the new method came to be known as the *Teatro del Grottesco*. It went back, in the nature of its action, to the native Italian tradition of the *commedia dell' arte*; its resolution came from the deliberate experimental innovation and flouting of convention of the futurist movement in art.

Chiarelli's play is a parody, a grotesque caricature, of the romantic drama. Its characters are puppets, who are manipulated into the conventional complication, and then jerked violently into a mocking, anti-romantic resolution. This puppet nature of the characters, going back as it does to the Pulcinella and Arlocchino of the *commedia dell' arte*, is an essential element of Pirandello's dramatic method. It provides him with the means of manipulation which are essential to the realization of his fantasies. It involves, also, a dependence on certain highly skilled methods of acting, including the capacity for improvisation which was the central method of the *commedia dell' arte*. In the *commedia dell' arte* each actor was regularly assigned to a particular masked part, of which he had all the stock phrases and gestures at his command. An author then provided a framework of the plot, and the actors improvised its realization, on the basis of the stock characters whose convention they commanded. In addition to the conventional characters there were stock *lazzi*, pieces of stage business, to represent the acting of the recurrent stock situations.

Now Pirandello was very much the dramatic author, with his insistence on "the book", the text. He was, for that reason, an absolute opponent of the idea of the "producers' theatre", which was one of the characteristic ideas of the experimental theatre in Europe generally. In the play *Tonight We Improvise*, he sets a producer of this kind, Hinkfuss, in contact with the material of a drama. Hinkfuss has the characteristic attitude to his function:

> I have a greater role than the playwright, for I bring to life what is enclosed in the playwright's written work.

He tries to dictate the development of the play, to make a "production" of it, but the essence of the actual drama breaks down his schemes, and the characters end by driving him off the stage.

This is Pirandello's consistent attitude to performance. He insists on the text, and it is the author who must control its performance (cf. the Manager's treatment of the Characters in *Sei Personnagi*). As to the actors, however, they must be encouraged to improvise, in order to find the best way of expressing the written drama. When, in 1925, Pirandello founded a theatre in Rome (in the Teatro Odescalchi), his intention was to develop a technique of acting, a convention of improvisation, which would realize the tentative experience of his plays. The theatre failed financially, and the convention was never established. But Pirandello's plays remain, in an essential sense, *commedia dell' arte*. They depend absolutely, in performance, on a conventionally stylized method of acting, a subtle realization of the essential puppetry of characters and action. To see a typically straight repertory production of *Six Characters in Search of an Author* is to realize that the play can fall to pieces, in performance, because of the normal lack of achievement of any such convention. The plays are not only essentially professional; they require a professional method of a particular and specialized kind.

Pirandello's experiments were not, primarily, theatrical, although they required experimental performance of the kind I have outlined. They were always dramatic experiments aimed at the realization of a particular pattern of experience. The phrase "the mask and the face" indicates one essential element of this pattern. It can be used, of some of his plays, in the sense that it was used by Chiarelli: an exposure of the romantic drama and romantic morality. *Pensaci Giacomino* is a good example of this kind, in which the typical Pirandellian mouthpiece character, Professor Toti, expounds, against the conventions of his bourgeois neighbours, the rightness of his acceptance of his young wife's lover and the consequent *ménage à trois*. Leone Galla, in *Giuoco delle Parti*, similarly attacks the concept of honour which would send him to his death in a duel for the honour of a wife whose infidelity he is willing to accept. "You are the husband," he tells her lover; "you go and be killed."

But the concept of "the mask and the face" is not confined to this declaration of the anti-romantic. Its next development is in situations where a character agrees to play a part, for one reason or another, and then finds the mask intolerable. Baldovini, in *Il Piacere dell' Onestà*, is characteristic of this type. The situation is also the basis of the effective acting piece *Ma non è una Cosa Seria*, where the mask of a ridiculous marriage is gradually stripped into seriousness and living acceptance.

A further development is the use of the situation where a character is brought to realize that he has been playing a part, where the mask drops suddenly and he has to negotiate a revealed actuality:

> When a man lives, he lives and does not see himself. Well, put a mirror before him and make him see himself in the act of

living. Either he is astonished at his own appearance, or else he turns away his eyes so as not to see himself, or else in disgust he spits at his image, or, again, clenches his fist to break it. In a word, there arises a crisis, and that crisis is my theatre.

This is Pirandello's own definition of this particular method, which has come to be known as the *teatro dello specchio*. The play *Tutto per Bene* is an excellent example, where the mask drops, and is then consciously resumed, as the best way to go on living (cf. Synge's *The Well of the Saints*). Another example is the well-known *Henry the Fourth*.

Most of Pirandello's plays are dramatized from his own early *novelle*. This, if nothing else, would confirm that his experiments were always concerned with realizing his preoccupying experiences— the nature of reality and of illusion, the facts of man's conscious roles and disguises, the difficulty of truth in the shifting versions of any apprehension and account of what is happening. That is the experience behind the fantasy of the Six Characters:

> Your reality is a mere transitory and fleeting illusion, taking this form today and that tomorrow, according to the conditions, according to your will, your sentiments, which in turn are controlled by an intellect that shows them to you today in one manner and tomorrow . . . who knows how? Illusions of reality, represented in this fatuous comedy of life that never ends, nor ever can end.

This, then, is Pirandello's material. I have outlined the nature of his ends, and his consideration of means. It remains to offer a judgement on the degree of his success. This can be indicated by looking at *Six Characters in Search of an Author*, and at two other plays: *Henry the Fourth*; and the piece which is his most striking exposition of the problem of truth, *Così è (se vi pare)*, which is, literally, *So it is (if you think so)*, and which is usually translated as *Right you are (if you think you are)*.

3

Pirandello is a critical-naturalist writer, in the important sense which Strindberg had defined:

> I do not believe in simple characters on the stage. And the summary judgements given on men by authors: this man is stupid, that one brutal, this one jealous, this one stingy, etc., should be challenged by naturalists, who know the richness of the soul-complex and recognize that "vice" has a reverse side, very much like virtue.

Pirandello's drama is the most striking challenge that has been made to such "summary judgements". Either he turns the judgement upside down, in an explicitly anti-romantic drama comparable to Shaw's *Arms and the Man*. Or he creates situations which imply that judgement is impossible, and the attempt at judgement mere impertinence or curiosity. The first method is worth a little emphasis, because it defines one aspect of Pirandello very well. For we have not got away from summary judgements, we have not ceased to be curious or impertinent, if we merely assert a solution based upon a different morality. The morality of *Pensaci Giacomino* is as artificial as anything in the romantic drama; the dismissal of the jealous wife Beatrice in *Il Berretto a Sonagli* is either a summary joke or summarily vicious. What Strindberg had in mind, when he talked of the "richness of the soul-complex", was not simply the creation of a series of anti-romantics. He was concerned with a method of drama which would not require a type of characterization which abstracted from the complexity of experience. Pirandello's experiments, in contrast, are critical squibs against conventional morality.

The level of this kind of exploration of "life" and "truth" can be judged from the entertaining *Cosi è (si vi pare)*. Pirandello creates not so much an authentically complex situation, by which the shallowness of commonplace judgements may be revealed, as a deliberate (and brilliant) theatrical exception. The situation of Signor Ponza, Signora Frola, and the woman who may be either Ponza's first wife and Signora Frola's daughter, or Ponza's second wife and not Signora Frola's daughter, is not so much complex as confused. In order to sustain the demonstration, Pirandello has to invent the obviously theatrical device of the earthquake which has destroyed all the relevant records. One cannot help feeling, in spite of his repeated assertions to the contrary, that discovery of the records would at least have taken us *some way* nearer an understanding, except that we then realize that "understanding" is not the point; the play is a polemic against just that kind of consciousness. The woman's announcement that she is in fact both alternatives —both daughter and second wife—is a statement of what is offered as a representative alienation: she is nothing in herself; she is only the roles—even the contradictory roles—she enacts for others. And then what was formerly a critical naturalism has become a new general theory, supported by a particular theatrical method. It is, really, a mystification of a demystification, since the experience is not substantial or enacted, but depends on a theatrical special case.

Cosí è (*si vi pare*) is, in fact, simply a twist of the romantic drama. Its *raisonneur*, Luidisi, is in the authentic tradition, presiding over the usual complication of action and situation. The innovation is the negative twist, Luidisi's

> Well, and there, my friends, you have the truth. But are you satisfied? Hah hah hah hah hah hah hah!

Similarly, the conflict between "life" and "the mask" is, in Pirandello's drama, primarily theatrical illusion. In *Six Characters in Search of an Author* the contrast is not between artifice and reality, but between two levels of artifice. The characters, that is to say, cannot represent a reality against which the artificiality of the theatre may be measured; they are themselves (and Pirandello's methods insist on this) products of the theatrical method. They do not provide a convincing life-standard, but rather a different degree of abstraction:

> The Stepdaughter is dashing, almost impudent, beautiful. She wears mourning, but with great elegance.
> The Mother seems crushed and terrified as if by an intolerable weight of shame and abasement. She is dressed in modest black and wears a thick widow's veil of crepe. When she lifts this, she reveals a waxlike face.

The Characters give us an entertaining exposition of the nature of dramatic illusion, but the play remains a brilliant aside: an opportunity, and eventually an opportunism, within the general "illusion", not only of the theatre, but of any creative method. Pirandello's attempts to confound illusion and reality are carried out with great skill. His most ingenious device is in *Each in his Own Way* (*Ciascuno a suo modo*), where the inner play is a *pièce à clef*, the performance of which is commented upon by its supposed audience, which includes the supposedly real persons upon whose lives the inner play was based. The contrast of these varying aspects of characterization (they are not varying aspects of reality) is striking; but it is significant that the outcome of the action is that the play cannot go on at all.

To have contrasted reality with *delusion* (which is what he is always claiming to do) Pirandello would have needed a dramatic form through which he could have created a conviction (if not a representation) of essential reality and life-experience. But his representations of reality are nearly always of a limited, theatrical kind, so that the conflict loses its full potential power.

His most serious success is *Henry the Fourth*. There is always, in Pirandello's drama, a *potentially* tragic situation, within the circle of the comedy of illusion. But the nature of the development of the plays is such that the effect of this inner drama is usually not tragic, but simply pathetic. The laughter of Luidisi and his kind is the dominant emotional tone. *Henry the Fourth* is a play in which that element is less stressed; the external laughter is quickly and deliberately turned. A man, acting the part of Henry the Fourth in a pageant, fell from his horse; since then, for twenty years, he has continued to act the same part—for the first twelve years under a delusion, for the last eight quite consciously, because he does not see how he can take up his normal life again. The main action of the play is a declaration of his consciousness of the mask which he is wearing, and his accusation against a friend, Belcredi, who had caused the fall from the horse. There are degrees of relapse and revelation, and in the end he kills Belcredi. This is the most important point in the developed contrast between mask and face, for he has now committed an act which can only be justified within the former masquerade. It is the deepest interpenetration of actuality and delusion.

> HENRY [*who has remained on the stage, with his eyes almost starting out of his head, terrified by the life of his own masquerade which has driven him to crime*]: Ah now . . . yes now . . . inevitably [*he calls his valets around him as if to protect him*] . . . here together . . . for ever . . . for ever.

This is one of the greatest moments in Pirandello's drama: characteristically, an intensity of situation and of gesture, rather than of speech. For it is what cannot be said that compels the retreat to the mask, to the theatrical illusion. As the need for the mask becomes more urgent—not a mocking demonstration but an acted weakness—we see a structure of feeling where we had formerly seen only a theoretical polemic. It is a structure of feeling—a crisis of individualism in which the very thing that must be defended, the "personal impenetrable world", is, by the fact of its compromising existence in others, the thing that turns back and destroys oneself—which is very deeply rooted in modern experience. The stalemate of feeling and action, in which it ends, is reminiscent of Chekhov, but where that was rooted in a particular period of Russian experience, and led only to the complication of naturalism, what has happened in Pirandello is a generalization to life at any time, and a corresponding abstraction of method, to figures who exist first to demonstrate and then, as in *Henry the Fourth*, to enact a pattern. The worlds of naturalism and expressionism cross and engender what is really a new form: one which has continued to be influential. Delusion, loss of identity, the reduction of personality to a role and of society to a collective impersonation: these are the elements of a new kind of theatre: a use of the theatre to expose itself, and then in the double exposure to question any discoverable reality. What began as a twist of romantic drama became a decisive twist of a whole dramatic tradition. That, now, is Pirandello's importance.

2

FEDERICO GARCIA LORCA

LORCA was killed soon after his thirty-eighth birthday, during the early days of the Spanish civil war. He had been experimenting in drama since his earliest years: *The Butterfly's Evil Spell*; *If Five Years Pass*; *The Shoemaker's Prodigious Wife*; and *The Audience*. In 1933, he became director of the travelling theatre, La Barraca, and it was in these last years that he wrote his most connected drama: the peasant trilogy of *Blood Wedding*, *Yerma* and *The House of Bernarda Alba*. The method and design of each of the plays in this trilogy are different, and can be interestingly compared. *Blood Wedding*, of course, is the best known, but it comes to us, ordinarily, with the wrong kind of emphasis on its "Spanish" atmosphere. It is, of course, clear, everywhere in Lorca, that he drew on the life of the Spanish country people, on the national literature and on the gipsy songs and dance. It is true, also, that the traditional Spanish drama has some unique qualities, in Lope de Vega and Calderón, which mark it off from the main northern European tradition. To read the *Celestina* of Fernando de Rojas or the *Love After Death* of Calderon is certainly to recognize an important part of Lorca's ancestry. A drama of intense, complicated action, around what seem, often, the fixed points of passion, honour and blood, can be related, in that way, to *Blood Wedding*. But then the emphasis on Lorca as a Spanish dramatist goes wrong when it implies that he is so intensely national as to be incommunicable elsewhere, or that his drama relates only to an isolable Spanish temperament. On the contrary, across the distance from what he so often describes as that hot wasteland, the arid plateau, to the northern lands of Scandinavia, Lorca takes his place in a recognizable modern European tradition: working in his own language and in the imagery of his country and people, but on themes which belong to a common world. If anyone doubts this, he should go from Ibsen's *Ghosts* to *The House of Bernarda Alba*, or from Strindberg's *Lady Julie* to *Blood Wedding*. Lorca's importance is that, drawing strength from a tradition and a people, he found new dramatic forms of contemporary universal experience.

2

Blood Wedding is an action of jealousy and revenge, in which the unique notes are the creation of a dramatic poetry of intense desire and the finding of communal forms of celebration and mourning. These two kinds of dramatic poetry do not so much embody the action; they are the action. It has been argued that there was a conflict, in Lorca, between a lyric or elegiac manner and the requirements of dramatic form. It seems to me that, on the contrary, Lorca builds, with more success than any other poet in this century, from the traditional forms to an action. The variety of method in speech is notable (it makes a very sharp comparison with the "all-purpose" verse line of the later plays of Eliot). Lorca moves from realistic conversation, through speeches which outside the drama would be lyrics or elegies, to forms of song and chorus which are a collective action. Yet the variation of method is controlled, throughout, by a remarkable concentration—a bare purity of action and theme which are one. Thus the play begins with the mother talking to her only surviving son about the day's work and then about his proposal to marry. It is the formal action, beginning, but at once the knife is mentioned—

> Give me the knife.
> What for?
> To cut the grapes with.

—and as she takes the knife out she says

I don't know . . . how I let this serpent stay in the chest.

It is the need to work and to marry, and the danger in both. At the end of the play, the mother and the bride lament the death of the last son—the bridegroom—and the other man, Leonardo, with whom the bride went away. They have killed each other—

> Neighbours: with a knife,
> with a little knife,
> at a given day, between two and three o'clock,
> the two men of love killed themselves.
> With a knife,
> with a little knife
> which scarcely fits into the hand,
> but which penetrates thinly
> through the astonished flesh . . .

It is a whole movement, based on an image which is also an action. Or we can see more local examples. The second scene of the first

168

act begins with a cradle song of a horse, and this is at once followed by the next stage of the action in which Leonardo's horse has been losing its shoes, as he rides, each day, from his wife to "that waste-land" where the bride lives. In ways like this, the action is concentrated with a direct simplicity which is at once internal and narrative and yet, with a mature confidence, a dimension of reality in which the particular plot rises to the level of a general action, for which all the people have words: the song about a horse to a baby, the riding of a horse to the breaking of that family.

Or again there is the remarkable wedding scene: the song of waking the bride in which the guests join as they arrive: the traditional images of jasmine and gold, and cutting across this the bride's own uncertain, self-chosen preparations. The collective song is at once a pattern and a suppression of personal experience; it is in just this tension, between what is expected, in the traditional images and ceremony, and what the girl desires, which ends in her riding away, that the real action exists.

At the crisis of the action, when the bridegroom and his friends are searching for the bride and the man she has ridden away with, Lorca introduces a convention which is essentially a development from the dramatic imagery of the songs. It has been the whole point of his characterization that his people, moving between realistic conversation and the traditional figures of the songs, exist in a particular history which is also a conventional pattern. They are called Bridegroom, Bride, Mother, Father, Wife; only Leonardo, who breaks the conventional pattern, is given a personal name. Now, at this crisis, this element of characterization is extended to the "young woodcutter with a white face" who is the moon, and the "old woman covered by thin green cloth", who is death. It is the method of the fifth act of *Peer Gynt*, or of Strindberg's chamber plays, but in a different local tradition. What they counterpoint, essentially, are the warmth and song of the wedding; they are the cold, the night, the lonely places, the knife:

> The moon leaves a knife
> abandoned in the air . . .
> . . . I am cold. My ashes
> Of sleeping metals
> search for the crest of fire
> through the hills and the streets.
> But the snow carries me
> on her shoulders of jasper
> and the water of the ponds,
> cold and hard, drowns me.

After the killing, the old woman sees the men who had been the
dancing figures, among flowers, at the wedding:

> Crushed flowers for eyes, and their teeth
> two fistfuls of hard-frozen snow.

It is this world, a world counterpointing and related to the songs of
work, of riding, of marriage and of the cradle, which comes into
its own, is dramatically present, when an actual desire breaks the
traditional pattern and is punished, ironically, in a traditional
hunt to the death. The action is then not only played, but is given,
through the connecting imagery and conventions of character, a
whole structure of feeling. After the moon and death have appeared
in the forest, and the hunt passes, it is the woodcutters, with axes
on their shoulders, who ask:

> Leave for their love a green branch.

In the intense commitment, to love and to death, by Leonardo and
the Bride, the images return and are developed. Each says, to the
other:

> What glass splinters are stuck in my tongue.

Leonardo says:

> Nails of moonlight have fused
> my waist and your chains.

And again:

> The same tiny flame
> Will kill two wheat heads together.

This takes us back to the world of the whole action. This desire is
what the mother had praised:

> Your father, he used to take me. That's the way with men of
> good stock; good blood. Your grandfather left a son on every
> corner. That's what I like. Men, men; wheat, wheat.

The desire and the danger are in the same action; in the two senses
of blood—the passion and the killing—that make this blood wedding.

3

Blood Wedding is a remarkable example of a poetic drama in
which the imagery and the action are fused. *Yerma* is different; it is
a fusion of imagery and character. Instead of the multiple definition

of *Blood Wedding*, this is a single definition: Yerma, whose name means "barren", defines herself:

> Every woman has blood for four or five children, and when she doesn't have them it turns to poison . . . as it will in me.

The play is an unusual example of a single feeling played through again and again, in the same rhythm: the longing of a woman for a child, in a barren marriage:

> These two teeming springs I have
> of warm milk are in the closeness
> of my flesh two rhythms of a horse's gallop,
> to vibrate the branch of my anguish.
> Oh breasts blind beneath my clothes
> oh doves with neither eyes nor whiteness
> oh what pain of imprisoned blood
> is nailing wasps in my neck.
> But you must come, sweet love, my baby,
> because water gives salt, the earth fruit,
> and our wombs guard tender sons
> just as a cloud is sweet with rain.

It is her own feeling, her own nature, as the conversations with the other women make clear; but it is a feeling she writes in her land and in her life:

> A farm woman who bears no children is useless, like a handful of thorns, and even bad—even though I may be a part of this wasteland abandoned by God . . . seeing the wheat ripening, the fountains never ceasing to give water, the sheep bearing hundreds of lambs, the she-dogs; it seems that the whole country rises to show me its tender and sleeping young ones, while I feel two blows of the hammer, here, instead of the mouth of my child.

This rhythm does not change; it is irrepressible. But it goes beyond the first situation, of a woman waiting for a child of her marriage. Yerma goes on a pilgrimage to the mountains, where women pray for children, and what is enacted there is a rite of fertility, outside marriage; the Male and Female Masks, "of great beauty and with a feeling of pure earth", and at the same time the arrangement, the young unmarried men waiting in the shadows at the edge of the dance. But Yerma has waited too long:

> I'm like a dry field where a thousand pairs of oxen plough, and you offer me a little glass of well water. Mine is a sorrow already beyond the flesh.

She refuses the subterfuge, and her husband, married only to his fields, overhears her and comes to embrace her. But she is beyond reach; her response to the kiss is to kill him:

> Barren, barren, but sure. Now I really know it for sure . . .
> My body dry for ever . . . Don't come near me, because I've
> killed my son. I myself have killed my son.

It is a terrifying action, of an extending destructive barrenness. Lorca is moving here into a sense of deep contradiction between the demands of life and the rigidity of an available life. It is a hard statement, but it is not a negative endorsement of frustration; it is a terrible exposure of it; just as *Blood Wedding* is not an endorsement of the blood feud, but an exposure of the poison that runs along the veins of growth. Having come this far, he can again change his dramatic method, and present, in *The House of Bernarda Alba*, the identical rhythm, but now in a family, in a group, in a culture: "a drama about women in the villages of Spain". He underlines this emphasis: "the writer states that these Three Acts are intended as a photographic document". It is an extraordinary development, in that Lorca arrives at a naturalist form—that of the enclosed family drama—through an extension of the exploration in other forms: the acted imagery of *Blood Wedding*, the image in character of *Yerma*. It is a critical instance of a distinction we shall have to make, in the development of the drama from Ibsen; between the naturalist form and the naturalist habit. Here the structure of feeling is in the whole form: the house of Bernarda Alba: the proud barren house, occupied only by women: the five daughters, from twenty to thirty-nine, all unmarried, and the mother, class-ridden and hating, who prevents their weddings. The father has just died, and money has come, in the largest portion, to the eldest girl, who can now be courted by the man we do not see, the shadow in the courtyard. He follows the formalities, at the open window, but he goes in to the youngest daughter, Adela. The bitter jealousy of the daughters, embroidering for their hope-chests under the barren discipline of their mother, breaks the whole situation open. The mother shoots at the shadow in the yard, and Adela takes her own life, thinking her lover killed. The family reassembles, under the mother's direction, in a barren confirmation:

> Cut her down. My daughter died a virgin. Take her to another
> room and dress her as though she were a virgin. No one will
> say anything about this. She died a virgin.

The daughter, Martirio, who called her mother because Adela had found love, says only:

A thousand times happy, she who had him.

But the rule is reimposed:

> We'll drown ourselves in a sea of silence. She, the youngest daughter of Bernarda Alba, died a virgin. Did you hear me? Silence, silence, I said. Silence!

4

In this trilogy of Lorca, we have an extraordinary range of dramatic experiment and achievement. In his discovery of forms, he is strikingly original, and yet he seems to range, with creative confidence, over the many possibilities of the modern dramatic tradition. It is an intensely personal and identifiably national achievement, yet it makes us look again, with new eyes, at the forms now available to us. What Lorca has most to show us is the flexibility of form when it is determined, precisely, by a structure of feeling. There is no compromise, at any point, with external form, and then what Lorca creates, out of acted imagery, out of the character as image, out of the family as image, has a defining purity that is an unusual kind of permanence. In the intense power of his creative effort, against the negatives of the wasteland, he extended dramatic possibility, beyond the conventional frontiers.

3

T. S. ELIOT

MOST of T. S. Eliot's mature work was in drama: in the plays from *Murder in the Cathedral* (1935) to *The Elder Statesman* (1958). These had been preceded by the experiments of *Sweeney Agonistes* (1926-7) and *The Rock* (1934), but, just as clearly, by his early poems and by his critical essays on the drama. One of the central preoccupations of the early poems was the discovery of an idiom of the speaking voice:

> Shall I say, I have gone at dusk through narrow streets
> And watched the smoke that rises from the pipes
> Of lonely men in shirtsleeves, leaning out of windows? . . .
> I should have been a pair of ragged claws
> Scuttling across the floors of silent seas.

This is already, in one sense, a dramatic idiom: a questioning, ironic rendering of conversation and commonplace observation, and, as it were darting under it, the unspoken voice of private thought. Several of the most successful early poems are dramatic monologues, records of conversation, overheard self-questioning. Their structure, from *Prufrock* and *Portrait of a Lady* to *The Waste Land*, is of a dramatised consciousness: juxtaposed scenes, overheard voices, remembered words and gestures: fragments of a play rehearsed and re-enacted in the mind. The surrogate characters, from Prufrock to Gerontion, are ways of distancing, often grotesquely, an intense private feeling; or a scene is played, as with three voices—

> Would it have been worth while,
> To have bitten off the matter with a smile,
> To have squeezed the universe into a ball
> To roll it toward some overwhelming question,
> To say: "I am Lazarus, come from the dead,
> Come back to tell you all, I shall tell you all"—
> If one, settling a pillow by her head,
>   Should say: "That is not what I meant at all.
>   That is not it, at all".

Here an intensely private, even an isolate, feeling—as if a voice from the dead—is communicated by distancing it, in an ironic

174

commentary, and by juxtaposing it with a bored, indifferent consciousness. Or again:

> And so the conversation slips
> Among velleities and carefully caught regrets
> Through attenuated tones of violins
> Mingled with remote cornets
> And begins.
> "You do not know how much they mean to me, my friends,
> And how, how rare and strange it is, to find
> In a life composed so much, so much of odds and ends,
> (For indeed I do not love it . . . you knew? You are not blind!
> How keen you are!)
> To find a friend who has these qualities,
> Who has, and gives
> Those qualities upon which friendship lives . . ."

This is not only the imitation of a particular speaking voice. In the whole poem the carefully mocked self-pity of the lady is a device for inspecting—at once distancing and examining—the protagonist's guilt and nostalgia. What Eliot then found was not only an idiom—"how people of the present day would speak, if they spoke verse"—but also a preliminary method of dramatising a conflict, in contrasting rhythms and states of mind. Meanwhile, in his dramatic criticism, he was trying to extend this, into the possibility of a whole form; trying to imagine a drama in which, essentially, states of consciousness would be an action. Though in his critical work he looked back to Shakespeare and the Jacobean dramatists, and in his contemporary observation looked at such forms as classical ballet and the mass, his interest can be seen as belonging, essentially, to the dramatic experiments which had begun in late Ibsen and in Strindberg. He was, that is to say, looking beyond the naturalist theatre for a new kind of dramatic form: a "form to arrest, so to speak, the flow of spirit at any particular point before it expands and ends its course in the desert of exact likeness to the reality which is perceived by the most commonplace mind".

These, then, are the bearings, for any critical inquiry into Eliot's work in the drama: the experiment in an idiom, of speech in verse; the experiment in form, to dramatise consciousness rather than behaviour. These are the reasons for his choice of a verse drama:

> The tendency of prose drama is to emphasise the ephemeral and superficial; if we want to get at the permanent and universal we tend to express ourselves in verse.

Moreover, underlying all the experiments, there is the fundamental distinction between what he saw as authentic experience and a familiar, commonplace reality.

2

Eliot's first specific experiment in drama, *Sweeney Agonistes*, exists only in fragments. The *Fragment of a Prologue* and *Fragment of an Agon* were designed, he tells us, as part of an "Aristophanic melodrama". Here, as in *Portrait of a Lady* or *The Waste Land*, the idiom was to be contemporary, but the structure one of contrasted states of consciousness (indicated, Eliot hoped, by the reference to a traditional action and suffering; it is just the memory and the contrast between Samson and Sweeney that are intended to make the dramatic point). The immediate contrast was to be achieved by a method which Eliot was to retain in several of his later plays: a device of levels of consciousness as between characters, within the action. He proposed

> one character whose sensibility and intelligence should be on the plane of the most sensitive and intelligent members of the audience; his speeches should be addressed to them as much as to the other personages in the play—or rather, should be addressed to the latter, who were to be material, literal-minded, and vision-less, with the consciousness of being overheard by the former.

Sweeney himself answers to this description; he is shown as preoccupied by the problem of communication:

> I gotta use words when I talk to you.

He is, moreover, the essential pattern of the action, himself the "meaning" of the play. But in the fragments as we have them, this form is largely inferential; it would have very little clarity if it were not pointed by elements outside the play, the keys of the epigraphs. Orestes' phrase from the *Choephoroi*—

> You don't see them, you don't—but *I* see them

—is a statement of the experience which separates Sweeney and gives him the formal status described above. The sentence from St. John of the Cross—*Hence the soul cannot be possessed of the divine union, until it has divested itself of the love of created beings*—embodies a judgement of the whole action and of Sweeney himself. The fragments are incomplete, not only in themselves, but in their considerable dependence upon these external written aids. Sweeney is a fragment of the Orestes experience, and *Sweeney*

Agonistes is a brilliant dramatic aside on the contemporary context of such experience. But it is probable that the fragments will be remembered as important, not for this creation, but for the experiments in language. A form is discovered, not so much in characters and action, and not in any conclusive way in a pattern of experience, but rather in an inclusive ordering of speech. It is in the success of rhythms like these that *Sweeney Agonistes* marks a notable advance:

DORIS: There's a lot in the way you pick them up.
DUSTY: There's an awful lot in the way you feel . . .
DORIS: You've got to know what you want to ask them.
DUSTY: You've got to know what you want to know.

SWEENEY: I tell you again it don't apply.
  Death or life or life or death,
  Death is life and life is death.
  I gotta use words when I talk to you,
  But if you understand or if you don't,
  That's nothing to me and nothing to you.
  We all gotta do what we gotta do.

SWEENEY: That's what life is. Just is
DORIS: What is?
  What's that life is?
SWEENEY: Life is death.

Eliot is breaking very sharply from the tradition of English poetic drama, trying to find a contemporary idiom. He is rejecting the Shakespearean blank-verse line which had been the main English medium for dramatic poetry: not because he did not greatly admire it, but because its dominant memory pulled writers back to the experiences and rhythms of the past. His own idiom, in this early experiment, is contemporary American: perhaps the last time he used overtly American forms. The real basis for the rhythms of *Sweeney Agonistes* is jazz:

SWEENEY: Birth, and copulation and death.
  That's all, that's all, that's all, that's all,
  Birth, and copulation, and death.
DORIS: I'd be bored.
SWEENEY: You'd be bored.
  Birth, and copulation, and death.
DORIS: I'd be bored.
SWEENEY: You'd be bored.
  Birth, and copulation, and death.
  That's all the facts when you come to brass tacks:
  Birth, and copulation, and death.

In the same way, the real basis for the characters of these fragments is the comic strip (by which Eliot had always been fascinated): the jerky, angular outline figures, going through a stylised routine of ordinary life.

Eliot's next experiment was disappointing. *The Rock*, which is described as a pageant play, was written for a charity performance, and Eliot received much collaboration. One would like to think that his prefatory disclaimer of full responsibility is substantial rather than merely polite; there is indeed a fleeting tone of irony in the courtesy. But one's surprise is not that he retains only a joint responsibility, but that he retains any. The worst thing in the "book of words" is the prose dialogue of the modern workmen. In speeches like—

> . . . people is still born very much the same. There's some new notion about time, what says that the past—what's be'ind you— is what's going to happen in the future, bein' as the future 'as already 'appened. I 'aven't 'ad time to get the 'ang of it yet; but when I read about all those old blokes they seems much like us. . . .

—the hand is the hand of Eliot, but the voice is the voice of Sir Arthur Pinero and of the Robertson of *Caste*. The tradition is not the vitality of the popular music-hall which Eliot had acknowledged, but rather the debility (a patronizing humanitarian "charity") of *Punch*.

The verse choruses are more important. The writing of the final Chorus on a base of the *Gloria* of the Mass is a significant presage of the success of *Murder in the Cathedral*. There is a brilliant dramatic movement in some of this verse:

The soul of Man must quicken to creation.
Out of the formless stone, when the artist united himself with
    stone,
Spring always new forms of life, from the soul of man that is
    joined to the soul of stone;

and:

In our rhythm of earthly life we tire of light. We are glad when
    the day ends, when the play ends; and ecstasy is too much
    pain.
We are children quickly tired: children who are up in the night
    and fall asleep as the rocket is fired; and the day is long for
    work or play.
We tire of distraction or concentration, we sleep and are glad to
    sleep,
Controlled by the rhythm of blood and the day and the night and
    the seasons.

And we must extinguish the candle, put out the light and relight
it;
Forever must quench, forever relight the flame.

But these are isolable passages of intensity, drawing attention to
themselves rather than to any total form in the work as a whole.
In deference to the received temporal sequence of the pageant play,
there is no integral creation of form. The incompleteness permits
an enormous variation of level, and the corruption of "the past—
what's be'ind you" comes to dominate. *The Rock*, indeed, is a case
of "versifying the drama", for local effect; Eliot's substantial work
was to move in a quite different direction, towards the discovery of
a dramatic method which would have the status of poetry.

3

Murder in the Cathedral is Eliot's most assured dramatic success.
It has a completeness which springs from the perfect matching of
material and form; and a certainty of communication which depends
on the use of a living convention of action and speech. A play
written for performance in a cathedral, which explicitly invites
the collaboration of its audience in the celebration of the martyrdom of an archbishop, assumes the inheritance of Christian ritual
so easily that we are likely to overlook the actual process of the
convention. A continuity of traditional form was available to the
poet because of the subject of the play, and Eliot exploits this
continuity to great effect. It is not simply that the story of the
martyrdom of Becket was already almost universally known,
although this strengthened the invitation to participation. The use
of traditional form is most important as an assured convention for
both speech and action.

The best dramatic conventions are usually those which the
audience do not recognize as conventions; which we accept and
assume so completely that our participation is immediate. The
chorus, for example, is one of the most difficult conventions to
establish in modern drama. Where it is based simply on a lost
tradition it has to fight against its own unfamiliarity. Eliot uses
the chorus in *Murder in the Cathedral* in part according to Greek
practice, as an expository device:

> Seven years and the summer is over
> Seven years since the Archbishop left us,
> He who was always kind to his people.

If he had had to depend on this function, it is doubtful whether
he could have established any substantial degree of communication.
But the function is merged in a larger method in which a tradition
is still available. The chorus becomes a link between ritual and
believers; chorus is choir, the articulate voice of the body of
worshippers:

> Forgive us, O Lord, we acknowledge ourselves as type of the
>   common man,
> Of the men and women who shut the door and sit by the fire; . . .
> We acknowledge our trespass, our weakness, our fault; we
>   acknowledge . . .

The dramatic possibilities of this function of the chorus may have
been suggested to Eliot by the Greek drama, but the dramatic
realization is in terms of the Christian ritual: the accepted, familiar
relationships of priests, choir, and congregation. Thus a convention
of choral speech, which is of great dramatic value, so far from being
an unfamiliar barrier is the actual convention of participation.
The convention is more; it is the actual form of the play. It embodies
one of the principal dramatic movements, from the early—

> For us, the poor, there is no action,
> But only to wait and to witness—

through the intermediate

> In our veins our bowels our skulls as well—

to the final—

> . . . the blood of the martyrs and the agony of the saints
> Is upon our heads

—a movement from passivity to involvement to participation.
This is one element of the ritual tradition, and it is powerfully
reinforced by the use of verse rhythms based on Christian hymns,
as here on the *Dies Irae*:

> The agents of hell disappear, the human, they shrink and dissolve
> Into dust on the wind, forgotten, unmemorable; only is here
> The white flat face of death, God's silent servant.

The formal language is acceptable because of its context and
its familiar rhythms, and this acceptance extends itself to the degree
of formalization in the language of the play as a whole. There are
other structural elements which permit dramatic experiment while
appearing familiar to the audience. Here, for example, is an
exchange of dialogue based on the responses:

SECOND PRIEST: Your Lordship will find your rooms in order as
you left them.

THOMAS: And will try to leave them in order as I find them.

The sermon, a familiar and natural form of direct address, gives
the dramatist a convention for soliloquy which, in any other terms,
might have been impossible.

The action of the play has great formal beauty of design, but it
is not a design that has to be imposed on the audience; it is a formal
movement, a succession of balances, which springs naturally from
the fundamental relationships within the ritual. It is indeed "a
form to arrest the flow of spirit" and to communicate it; but its
design does not seem contrived, because the audience is from the
beginning within the formulation. Its correspondences are as clear
as those of a morality play, and similarly acceptable; for both depend
upon the same originating form within the church.

The verse of the choruses is an obvious success. Its movement is
an exciting realization of a kind of dramatic experience which the
ordinary theatre had lost:

Here is no continuing city, here is no abiding stay.
Ill the wind, ill the time, uncertain the profit, certain the danger.
O late late late, late is the time, late too late, and rotten the year;
Evil the wind and bitter the sea and grey the sky, grey, grey, grey.
O Thomas return, Archbishop; return, return to France.
Return. Quickly. Quietly. Leave us to perish in quiet.
You come with applause, you come with rejoicing, but you come
   bringing death into Canterbury:
A doom on the house, a doom on yourself, a doom on the world.

            We do not wish anything to happen,
            Seven years we have lived quietly,
            Succeeded in avoiding notice,
            Living and partly living.

The most important dramatic advance of verse of this kind is
that language reasserts control in performance. The problem of
performance is the application of these rhythms, within which all
the visual elements of performance are contained and prescribed.
This is perhaps Eliot's most important general achievement. There
is the same control over character. The persons are individualized
so far as is necessary, but they are contained by the total pattern.
The device of character permits a full communication of consciousness, because speech is not limited to representation, but is made
fully articulate within the dramatic form:

They speak better than they know, and beyond your understanding.

They know, and do not know, what it is to act or suffer.
They know, and do not know, that action is suffering
And suffering is action. Neither does the agent suffer
Nor the patient act. Bot both are fixed
In an eternal action, an eternal patience
To which all must consent that it may be willed
And which all must suffer that they may will it,
That the pattern may subsist, for the pattern is the action
And the suffering, that the wheel may turn and still
Be forever still.

The achievement of *Murder in the Cathedral* is dramatic pattern,
a pattern which "is the action". Only at times is this completeness
threatened, perhaps most notably in the Sermon and in the speeches
of the Knights. In the Sermon, when one comes to phrases like
these—

A martyrdom is always the design of God, for His love of men,
to warn them and to lead them, to bring them back to His ways.
It is never the design of man . . .

—one feels that the "meaning" which they bear is a crude addition
to the fully dramatic communication which is the total action. It is
natural self-explanation by Becket, and natural exposition; but it
lacks the intensity of the play as a whole. Similarly, the speeches of
the Knights to the audience can be theoretically justified, as a
dramatic device to indicate the speciousness of their reasoning; and
the tone is an interesting variation in the movement of the play.
But there is a distinctly Shavian element of "knowing comedy"
which seems to me essentially sentimental.

When we look at the whole action of *Murder in the Cathedral*, we
find that Eliot, though using the familiarity of the Canterbury
theme, is not writing the history of Becket, but is dramatizing a
contemporary consciousness of separation and martyrdom; Becket
is in that sense a Sweeney. The Tempters, matching the Knights,
who come to dissuade Becket, offer not only the usual rewards of
material power, but also the false glory—the intellectual pride—
of wanting to be a martyr. It is this that is finally rejected, in what
is described as a total submission to the will of God. This is the
action, in formal terms, but in its substance *Murder in the Cathedral*
is based on yet another rhythm: not so much of martyrdom as of
sacrifice. The dominant imagery is of the land and the seasons:
of the relation between the lives of men and the lives of beasts;
of what can be seen as redemption but also as increased fertility
through the spilling of blood. Redemption is an awareness that the

natural and human order, without this kind of sacrifice, is merely bestial. It is the act of blood, and the receiving of blood, which creates consciousness and separates man from the beasts. The whole drive of the play is to gain acceptance, through the chorus, of this feeling. We have already seen the movement from

> no action
> But only to wait and to witness

to

> the blood of the martyrs and the agony of the saints
> Is upon our heads.

The participation is formally in a Christian recognition, through the acceptable and familiar phrases of orthodoxy. But the substantial design is the need for sacrificial blood, for the renewal of common life. This need is not discovered within a common experience, but is brought to the people by an exceptionally conscious man: Becket. This is, in another form, the variation of levels of consciousness we have seen described in *Sweeney Agonistes*: it is the structure of feeling on which all Eliot's work is based—the many unconscious, the few conscious. The act of martyrdom, but more crucially the act of drama, as Eliot conceives it, links the two groups, in an achieved common action.

The power of *Murder in the Cathedral* is that it succeeds in communicating a personal structure of feeling as if it were traditional and even conventional. The strangeness of Eliot's vision—the rejection of ordinary life, the insistence on separation and sacrifice— is made to seem familiar and acceptable:

> We thank Thee for Thy mercies of blood, for Thy redemption by blood.
> For the blood of Thy martyrs and saints
> Shall enrich the earth, shall create the holy places.

When Eliot moved on to his explicitly contemporary plays, the problem was not only one of dramatic convention, without the basis of the liturgy. It was also of conveying a strange consciousness— here masked by orthodoxy—in its own surprising and even shocking terms.

4

The Family Reunion, if not a wholly new start, is a different kind of success. In theme it is related to *Murder in the Cathedral* and, very closely, to *Sweeney Agonistes*. Its difference is indicated in one sense by the label which it has acquired: "a drama of contemporary people speaking contemporary language". The persons of the play, with the important exception of the Eumenides, are certainly contemporary; they are, moreover, characters of the contemporary drama and theatre. The phrase "contemporary language" is similarly true, but it must not be taken as an antithesis to Eliot's earlier work. Once again, the phrase is best understood in relation to the contemporary drama and theatre; in the lower reaches of *The Family Reunion* the small talk (and this is the innovation) is our own.

The scene of *The Family Reunion* is the family drawing-room of naturalism. The persons of the play include several "everyday, insignificant characters", such as Ibsen had introduced. These elements are framework rather than structure, however. The play draws a measure of initial acceptance from the familiarity of its surface; from its resemblance, indeed, to the conventional country-house detective play. But there is a further relation to naturalist method, and particularly to Ibsen. The close-knit family drama; the *incidental* revelations of certain aspects of character; the development through retrospect so that the present is continually deepened to include the past: these are manners inherited, directly or indirectly, from Ibsen; and perhaps also from the novel. The drama has moved out of the church, and the former continuity and contact is not available. New links have to be forged.

The critical issue is raised sharply by these now notorious lines:

What's the use of asking for an evening paper?
You know as well as I do, at this distance from London,
Nobody's likely to have this evening's paper.

On their own, certainly, these lines are flat. It is easy to object that for so commonplace a remark, verse is not necessary, or is even ridiculous. And it would be possible to make an anthology of passages from the play, of similar apparent vapidity. No proper critical conclusion could be drawn from them, however, for it is the total verse-form that is important.

Consider an example from the first scene:

                      I.: The younger generation
Are undoubtedly decadent
                      C.: The younger generation
Are not what we were. Haven't the stamina. . . .

This minutely stylized deadness is very characteristic of Eliot's earlier work, and indeed of *Sweeney Agonistes* itself. The imitation and repetition of commonplace speech, and then its contrast with intensity, is one of Eliot's permanent methods. The organization of different kinds of statement can be seen very well in an exchange of this kind:

GERALD: That reminds me, Amy,
　　When are the boys all due to arrive?
AMY: I do not want the clock to stop in the dark.
　　If you want to know why I never leave Wishwood
　　That is the reason. I keep Wishwood alive
　　To keep the family alive, to keep them together.
　　To keep me alive, and I live to keep them.
　　You none of you understand how old you are
　　And death will come to you as a mild surprise
　　A momentary shudder in a vacant room.
　　Only Agatha seems to discover some meaning in death
　　Which I cannot find.
　　—I am only certain of Arthur and John,
　　Arthur in London, John in Leicestershire:
　　They should both be here in good time for dinner.

The sudden deepening of level with the first line of Amy's speech is the test of Eliot's essential organization. The verse-form of the whole play must be such that it can, when necessary, be intensified into the statement of a complex experience, while retaining its affinity with the verse of ordinary conversation through which the audience is led into the play. It is a form designed to express the interpenetration of different levels of reality; not merely as a dramatic device, but because this interpenetration is the condition of experience of the play as a whole. The passage I have quoted seems to me successful in its aim, and it succeeds very largely because the transition of level is not consciously pointed by the author. When attention is drawn to the transition, there is dislocation, because the uncertainty of the convention is revealed. Here, for example:

AGATHA: When the loop in time comes—and it does not come
　　for everybody—
　　The hidden is revealed, and the spectres show themselves.
GERALD: I don't in the least know what you're talking about.
　　You seem to be wanting to give us all the hump.

This play for laughter as a smooth transition, back to "normality" from too great an intensity, is of the same order as a significant passage in a play of Granville-Barker's: *Waste:*

T: I'm offering you the foundation of a New Order of men and

women who'll serve God by teaching His children. Now shall
we finish the conversation in prose?

c: What is the prose for God?

or the end of a speech in Denis Johnston's *Moon in the Yellow River:*

. . . I suppose the Devil can do nothing for us unless God gives
him a chance. Or maybe it's because they're both the same
person. Those glittering sorrows, eh? Asleep? Well, here endeth
the first lesson.

The level of experience, and so the character of the language, has
gone beyond the tone of established probability. But then instead
of contrast—the dramatic contrast of kinds of experience—the
mixing of levels is accepted as uneasy, and is manipulated, negotiated, by a self-conscious—a falsely self-conscious—uneasiness.
There are several such manipulations of tone in *The Family Reunion*,
typified perhaps in Aunt Violet's conscious play with the audience:

I do not understand
A single thing that's happened.

The failure is in fact a dramatic timidity, an uncertainty of the
audience's acceptance of the convention, so that a need is felt to
offer reassuring explanations in naturalist terms. It is a serious
corruption of a possible form. When Harry and Agatha, after
virtual soliloquies, ask:

What have I been saying?

the effect is perhaps right; but the interpenetration of levels is most
successful when Eliot is confident of his convention, and offers no
explanation. When a writer is launched into a form of this kind, the
middle of the play is no place to express technical hesitations.

This kind of failure is what might be expected of Eliot's attempt
to come to terms with the methods of the naturalist theatre. Within
the total form which he has attempted, the attraction of certain of
the superficial elements seems to have been too great. The policeman, for example, is a weary caprice, hoping that the audience will
be reassured by having the familiar figure around. Similarly, the
chauffeur's exposition of the death of Harry's wife involves an over-
familiar piece of business:

But you know, it is just my opinion, sir,
That his lordship is rather psychic, as they say.

It is the familiar comic exercise, the *Punch* tradition; a character
in the shadow of Mr. Forster's Leonard Bast and Mrs. Woolf's

sudden insensitive charwomen. The fault is partly social, a real corruption of the common language. More immediately, it is part of the general anxious reassurance of the audience; and the question is not whether the audience is in fact reassured, but whether such reassurance helps the communication of the play. Comic episodes may serve communication, by setting the central experience in relief (it is in this sense that the serious use of comic relief is best understood); they may also, like Mr. Eliot's policeman, simply distract. The experience of *The Family Reunion* is revelation, but the coincidence of the word does not demand that this should involve character-revelation of the familiar naturalist kind. The "inside stories" of the newspapers are revelations, and for spiritual auto-biography of the special interview variety one does not need the talent of an Eliot.

> I shall have to stay till after the funeral.
> Will my ticket to London still be valid?

This is one of Eliot's theatrical aunts; and while it is an amusing appeasement of certain appetites of the contemporary theatre, it is the kind of thing which blurs the significant communication of the play.

The problem which faces the critic is of deciding whether these things are mere blemishes, a minor residue of confusion as to means; or whether they are local indications of some more fundamental disharmony in the play. Harry's experience is the search for redemption, which cannot come while he flies from the pursuing Eumenides, but only when he recognizes them and their significance. This he is able to do, with Agatha's help, in a moment of illumination when his own and his family past becomes realized in the present. In this revelation his guilt is transformed; the Furies will not continue to pursue him, but he, instead, will "follow the bright angels". The series of events which Eliot has created to embody this experience is in a way adequate; but there is also a sense of the form being fitted, as a secondary process, to an already considered experience. This is why we ask how Harry's wife really died: not because guilt requires some overt crime, but because we get the impression of a sustained bluff, and even a certain arrogance: what has happened is too difficult for *us* to understand: "I gotta use words when I talk to you." Some part of this difficulty is inherent in the nature of the experience, but it is too persistent to be dismissed with a gesture towards the "incommunicable". For we have, as it happens, an immediate basis for comparison, in the *Four Quartets*. The central experience of the poems is similarly "incommunicable", but in fact, in each of the poems, and particularly in *The Dry Salvages*, there is a convincing achievement of resolved experience beside which *The Family Reunion* pales.

The play is, nevertheless, very interesting, technically. Its greatest positive achievement is in certain scenes, of which the middle scene of Part Two is perhaps the best example. If we take a great scene from some prose play—say that between Ella and Gunhild in Ibsen's *John Gabriel Borkman* (a play which has certain affinities with *The Family Reunion*)—we find, when we compare the two, that it is not only Eliot's language which is finer, but that in Eliot the emotions of the drama itself are more intense and more precise. It is in such local achievements that the potential importance of the dramatic method is most clearly seen, and in the richness and flexibility of such dramatic speech as this:

Not yet! I will ring for you. It is still quite light.
I have nothing to do but watch the days draw out,
Now that I sit in the house from October to June,
And the swallow comes too soon and the spring will be over,
And the cuckoo will be gone before I am out again.
O Sun, that was once so warm, O Light that was taken for
    granted
When I was young and strong, and sun and light unsought for
And the night unfeared, and the day expected
And the clocks could be trusted, tomorrow assured
And time would not stop in the dark!
Put on the lights. But leave the curtains undrawn.
Make up the fire. Will the spring never come? I am cold.

5

Ten years separated *The Family Reunion* and *The Cocktail Party*, and the new play was awaited with more than ordinary interest. Eliot's influence at this time was considerable, and his choice of method was certain to have important effects. He might have returned to the deliberately formal pattern of *Murder in the Cathedral*, which had been his most complete success; or he might continue with the experiment of using current theatrical forms and trying to raise them to the status of poetic drama by the use of a flexible overall verse convention, as he had done in *The Family Reunion*. His choice, as we now know, was the latter. *The Cocktail Party* almost entirely abandoned even those elements of ritual which had been retained in *The Family Reunion*: the use of an occasional chorus, of interspersed lyrics, and of "runic" recital. The chorus of

The Family Reunion had not been very satisfactory: the verse was adequate, but the formal convention depended upon a sudden change of function by the aunts and uncles, who had been set in a deliberate comic characterization and were required suddenly to become agents of a formal commentary; this was not easy to accept. The lyrics had been used to express certain of the moments of illumination; a good example is given to Mary, beginning:

> I believe the moment of birth
> Is when we have knowledge of death.

The "runes" had been used as a formal ending to each part, spoken by Agatha:

> Round and round the circle
> Completing the charm
> So the knot be unknotted
> The crossed be uncrossed
> The crooked be made straight
> And the curse be ended.

Unlike the lyrics, the placing of these passages had made transition into conversational speech unnecessary, and for this reason they were more successful. This is the only formal device of the kind retained in *The Cocktail Party;* it is used in the libation near the end of Act Two:

> ALEX: The words for those who go upon a journey.
> REILLY: Protector of travellers
>   Bless the road.
> ALEX: Watch over her in the desert
>   Watch over her in the mountain
>   Watch over her in the labyrinth
>   Watch over her in the quicksand.
> JULIA: Protect her from the Voices
>   Protect her from the Visions
>   Protect her in the tumult
>   Protect her in the silence.

With this exception, *The Cocktail Party* uses no formal devices which are not already familiar from the average prose play. Its main formal device is the overall verse convention.

The verse of *The Cocktail Party* is similar in function to that of *The Family Reunion*, with its capacity for sudden change of level from light conversation to conscious statement:

> EDWARD: Celia? Going to California?
> LAVINIA: Yes, with Peter.

Really, Edward, if you were human
You would burst out laughing. But you won't.
EDWARD: O God, O God, if I could return to yesterday
Before I thought that I had made a decision.
What devil left the door on the latch
For these doubts to enter? And then you came back, you
The angel of destruction—just as I felt sure.
In a moment, at your touch, there is nothing but ruin.

The function is similar to that in *The Family Reunion*, but the quality of the verse is very different. In the first place, the verse of conversation, particularly at the beginning of the play when the measure needs to be established, is very closely stylized, in the manner of *Sweeney Agonistes:*

PETER: I like that story.
CELIA: I love that story.
ALEX: *I'm* never tired of hearing that story.
JULIA: Well, you all seem to know it.
CELIA: Do we all know it?

or, again:

JULIA: The only man I ever met who could hear the cry of bats.
PETER: Hear the cry of bats?
JULIA: He could hear the cry of bats.
CELIA: But how do you know he could hear the cry of bats?
JULIA: Because he said so. And I believed him.

The device is obvious in print, but in speech it is virtually an unconscious form, since the repetitions on which the rhythm depends are normal elements of conversation.

The second and more important difference in the verse of *The Cocktail Party* is that it is always, at every level, *statement*, of a deliberate lucidity, and with the minimum of imagery and evocation. In *The Family Reunion* the speech of Harry and Agatha is full of the characteristic imagery of Eliot's general poetry: the corridor, the footfall, the door opening into the garden. The words

have often a network of tentacular roots, reaching down to the deepest terrors and desires.

In *The Cocktail Party* the language is never, or hardly ever, of that kind. It is verse of the surface, although not superficial. It is conscious, lucid statement, with a generality which is quite unlike the normal verse of *The Family Reunion*. Here, for example, is a speech which will illustrate the change:

EDWARD: No—not happy; or, if there is any happiness,
  Only the happiness of knowing
  That misery does not feed on the ruin of loveliness,
  That the tedium is not the residue of ecstasy.
  I see that my life was determined long ago
  And that the struggle to escape from it
  Is only a make-believe, a pretence
  That what is, is not, or could be changed.
  The self that can say "I want this—or want that"
  —The self that wills—he is a feeble creature.
  He has to come to terms in the end
  With the obstinate, the tougher self; who does not speak
  Who never talks, who cannot argue;
  And who in some men may be the *guardian*—
  But in men like me, the dull, the implacable,
  The indomitable spirit of mediocrity.
  The willing self can contrive the disaster
  Of this unwilling partnership, but can only flourish
  In submission to the rule of the stronger partner.

The third and fourth lines of this speech are in the recognizable manner of *The Family Reunion* and of much of Eliot's poetry, but the dominant tone in the passage is something quite different; it is deliberate, contained statement. It is a remarkable achievement, for it is both eminently speakable and also the instrument of complete precision in the expression of feeling. This distinct manner is the main strength of the play; it can be very widely exemplified from the best scenes, those between Edward and Reilly; Edward and Celia; Edward, Lavinia and Reilly; Reilly and Celia. However the play as a whole may be judged, this development of a flexible, lucid verse manner, based very closely on speech and yet capable of great precision, is an important achievement.

The speech of Edward which I have quoted provides one key to the theme of the play: the concept of the *guardian*. The play is concerned with the salvation, not of an individual, but of a group, and the elements of this salvation are the guardians Reilly, Alex, and Julia. The word is certainly *salvation*, although for a considerable part of the play one could substitute *cure*. This double sense is an important element of the play, and it is this above all which has caused difficulty. The double sense is most clearly expressed in the character of Reilly, who is at once psychiatrist and confessor. Reilly's treatment of Edward and Lavinia is in the familiar psychiatric tone, even if it is never quite orthodox:

  I learn a good deal by merely observing you,

And letting you talk as long as you please,
And taking note of what you do not say.

The cure of the delusions and dishonesties of Edward and Lavinia
is a cure *within* society:

> . . . my patients
> Are only pieces of a total situation
> Which I have to explore. The single patient
> Who is ill by himself, is rather the exception.

What Reilly does is to bring Edward and Lavinia to knowledge
of themselves and their situation, and to forward the process of
reconciliation:

> The best of a bad job is all any of us can make of it.

This is Eliot's familiar description of the unreality of commonplace experience, and the limited possibilities of any growth in its
terms. These are the "unconscious majority", brought to local
recognition. And beyond them, as before, is the "conscious minority":
the exceptional person:

> The best of a bad job is all any of us can make of it,
> Except of course the saints.

Delusion, irreconcilability, have been seen with the others as part
of the habitual mask; health lies in acceptance of the reality. But
delusion must be carefully defined: Reilly says to Celia:

> A delusion is something we must return from.
> There are other states of mind, which we take to be delusion
> But which we have to accept and go on from.

This is Celia's case:

> CELIA: It's not the feeling of anything I've ever *done*
> Which I might get away from, or of anything in me
> I could get rid of—but of emptiness, of failure
> Towards someone, or something, out of myself;
> And I feel I must . . . *atone*—is that the word?

This is not delusion, but

> a sense of sin.

It is, as Reilly comments, "most unusual".
    Celia chooses, not the first way of "cure", of reconciliation; but
the second way, of atonement:

REILLY: The first I could describe in familiar terms
Because you have seen it, as we all have seen it
Illustrated, more or less, in lives of those about us.
The second is unknown, and so requires faith—
The kind of faith that issues from despair.
The destination cannot be described
You will know very little until you get there;
You will journey blind. But the way leads towards possession
Of what you have sought for in the wrong place.
CELIA: . . . Which way is better?
REILLY: Neither way is better.
Both ways are necessary. It is also necessary
To make a choice between them.
CELIA: Then I choose the second.

The way of atonement need not necessarily lead outside society.
Some who have chosen it—

                        . . . lead very active lives
Very often, in the world.

But Celia's way leads to isolation and to a terrible death.

Here the shock that had been masked in *Murder in the Cathedral*—
the intense insistence on separation and sacrifice—is made open and
explicit. The details of the death were softened, after the first
production, but there is still a direct preoccupation with an exposed
physical suffering, and this is ratified:

                        she paid the highest price
In suffering. That is part of the design.

What Eliot does, in *The Cocktail Party*, is to bring to the level of
recognizable action the structure of feeling by which he had always
been determined, but which had been mainly expressed, elsewhere,
as a rhythm or as an image. This is the real irony of his acceptance
of the methods of the naturalist theatre. The comic-strip figure of
Sweeney could be made to say

                I knew a man once did a girl in
                Any man has to, needs to, wants to
                Once in a lifetime, do a girl in

without involving, with any closeness, a human death. In *The
Cocktail Party*, in what is offered as a probable life, the pattern is
the same, but the effect is different. And yet it is not the death that
is most shocking; it is the consequent version of life. The play shows,
convincingly, an empty round: the superficial society of the title.
It is a world of temporary relationships, transience and bright

emptiness: the "unconscious majority", for all their sophistication. But then there is a further irony. For this kind of life, which is Eliot's image of a common condition, is particularized in a place and among people who belong, essentially, to the theatrical mode which he has chosen as his dramatic means. Anxiously reassuring his audience about the surface of his play—here the bright talk of a London flat; there the known habits of an English country house—he involves himself in a profound deception: what he is offering as a surface becomes the substance, and the intended counter-statement, of the separation and sacrifice of Celia, has, in its turn, to be negotiated in just such a world. "The soul cannot be possessed of the divine union, until it has divested itself of the love of created beings": this is still the pattern, but the substance of the play is in fact an attachment, to a chosen social mode. Whatever the ultimate action means, the visible action accepts the world from which Celia is separated. The scene in which her death is reported, as the guests reassemble and go on with the cocktail party, is no longer, dramatically, the interpenetration of states of consciousness; it is the absorption, the negotiation, of that savage death, and the reduction of its meaning to a story at a cocktail party. In moving so far into the conventional theatre, giving its modes and tones an effective priority, Eliot succeeded in displacing the lonely intense experience, which had always been his essential concern, to a reported event: a story to point at. It is not only the guests, coming together and going on with the familiar round, but also the dramatist, who is making the best of a bad job. The play could have followed "the bright angels", pursued the "agony in the desert"; but it chooses not to; it delights too much in its chosen particulars, its reassuring social tone. What was once a dramatic tension has become a theatrical compromise.

6

The Confidential Clerk appeared in 1953. It represented a decadence in manner which was, in its way, startling. "If one wanted to say something serious nowadays it was easier to say it in comedy", Eliot remarked on its production. But though the form of this remark is an arguable critical truth, its content is a surrender to a particular social mode: that West End sense of humour which is supposed to be a saving grace. Since grace had meant something, in Eliot, this parody of a play was especially shocking. In any other circumstances, its slightness would leave it unnoticed.

For the theme is again that of John of the Cross: "the soul cannot be possessed of the divine union until it has divested itself of the love of created beings". There are again the two worlds, of illusion and reality: the unconscious majority and the conscious minority:

> I dare say truly religious people—
> I've never known any—can find some unity.
> Then there are also the men of genius.
> There are others, it seems to me, who have at best to live
> In two worlds—each a kind of make-believe.
> That's you and me.

The action is a breakthrough to identity, by at least one person, after the discovery of false identities:

> Of course, there's something in us,
> In all of us, which isn't just heredity,
> But something unique. Something we have been
> From eternity. Something . . . straight from God.
> That means that we are nearer to God than to anyone.

But the detail of the action is a farcical complication of lost and wrongly identified children, as in the old intrigue drama (it is to the nineteenth century, as also in the archaic title of "confidential clerk", rather than to classical or Renaissance precedents, that reference must really be made). And then the point is not so much the improbability of the revelations and coincidences, by the standards of normal life, as the *dramatic* improbability. We are asked to accept as a dramatization of the relative unreality of temporal relationships a world in which in any case no substantial relationship exists. Just as, in *The Cocktail Party*, the emptiness of a particular group is made to stand for, is falsely asserted as, the emptiness of all available ordinary living, so here the unreality of human relationships is asserted, not, where the dramatist would be called to real effort, in a substantial life, but in a group to whom relationships of any kind obviously do not matter, and in a convention of farce in which assumed relationships are by definition mere counters of the plot. It is not the surface tricks, but this deeper deception, which must be emphasized.

The tone of the play corresponds to this complicity. It is a repertory of West End gestures:

> E: And you're thinking no doubt that Lady Elizabeth
>   Would be put in mind of the child *she* lost.
> C: In a very different way, yes. You might say *mislaid* . . .

The emphasis is a cue to an old, false gesture; as again, here, in a falsely tentative, sentimental "deepening":

L: But you've something else, that I haven't got:
Something of which the music is a . . . symbol.

The damned dots are for the lurch of breath and the meaning look: a dramatist in full retreat before a false style of acting. Eliot, in every important detail, is now within this sensibility, which at the level of theme he still abstractly rejects.

And when she's abroad
She is apt to buy a house. And then goes away
And forgets all about it. That can be complicated . . .

I didn't want to belong there. I refused to believe
That my father could have been an ordinary earl!

He was run over. By a rhinoceros
In Tanganyika.

This is not, as similar lines had once been, a stylized deadness; it is an acceptance, for its own sake, of a theatrically familiar style. The scattiness and yet the "something about her" are matinee exercises: that old way of building a false presence, in a character, by the hyperbolic chatter of others:

It's no use telling anybody about you:
Nobody'd ever believe in your existence
Until they met you.

This is spoken, characteristically, in the presence of two other people, but, more crucially, in the presence of hundreds of others: an audience accustomed, in just this way, to being suggested into significance.

All this was described, at the time, as Eliot learning the "wisdom of the theatre". What he had actually learned was the inertia of a convention he had begun by attacking. His decisive innovation had been the remaking of a fully expressive dramatic speech; but this was a writer's reform, and the problem of performance had still to be solved. The speech was dramatic verse, in a contemporary rhythm and idiom, but it is clear that this can only be performed as written if the dramatic movement has been conceived in the same dimension. Such movement, however, depends on conventions of action which are wholly different from the imitation of behaviour, and from the styles of gesture and pose which belong to another kind of theatrical speech. Eliot had developed a verse-line which was intended to allow variations of emphasis, from the relaxed to the intense, according to the progress of the real action.

But it was the intensity, increasingly, that could not be performed, and its elements were then steadily cut out: first the chorus and other formal devices; then the extended dramatic imagery; finally the central rhythm and precision. There are moments of emphasis— of an isolated thematic seriousness—in *The Confidential Clerk*; but they are little more than pauses in the swirl of another rhythm, that of theatrical mannerism. When the more deliberate verse had to be played, one noticed that the actors sat down; indeed they had, in some way, to stay still, for there was no movement, no dramatic action, to which these saving clauses could correspond. When such an episode was over, they got up again and went on with the conventional business of a theatrical drawing-room, and of course this is what had been written for them: not only in the action, but now finally in the verse, which had been adapted to that kind of mannered slackness. At the end of *The Confidential Clerk* there is an important question, to which there is no spoken answer, but the stage directions indicate a nod. It was from just that world, of wished significance, that the articulacy and intensity of verse drama had been intended to deliver the theatre. In that sense, the confidential nod marked not only the end of a play but the end of a period.

7

The Elder Statesman, in 1958, was a dramatic epilogue. It brings together the two themes of the epigraphs to *Sweeney Agonistes*: the relation between human and divine love; and the consciousness of the Furies. The first of these themes is beyond Eliot's power, though for different reasons from the failures in *The Cocktail Party* and *The Confidential Clerk*. The love of Monica and Charles is defined, it is true, by them being Monica Claverton-Ferry and Charles Hemington; a dry, tight-lipped idiom, in a world of social formali- ties, which makes the talk of love like the faint rattle of spoons; dry sticks, saying the words to each other, as the old man dies in the garden. But the consciousness of guilt, in the elder statesman himself, waiting for death, brings a return of some of the earlier power. The Furies, it is true, are theatrically negotiated; the endless trouble of having them materialize in the window recess, in *The Family Reunion*, has been avoided by making them Federico Gomez and Mrs. Carghill: a cross between the grotesques of the early poems and familiar theatrical types. It is not in that action that any significance is achieved, but in what has been forced back— after all the years of dramatic experiment, after the still conscien- tious construction of a theatrical framework—to monologue:

> But waiting, simply waiting
> With no desire to act, yet a loathing of inaction.
> A fear of the vacuum, and no desire to fill it.

As nearly forty years before, in *Gerontion*:

> Here I am, an old man in a dry month,
> Being read to by a boy, waiting for rain.

When this feeling is touched, Eliot's recognizable verse returns:

> Say rather, the exequies
> Of the failed successes, the successful failures,
> Who occupy positions that other men covet.

> What is this self inside us, this silent observer,
> Severe and speechless critic, who can terrorise us
> And urge us on to futile activity,
> And in the end, judge us still more severely
> For the errors into which his own reproaches drove us?

The ostensible action, which provokes and resolves this emotion, never begins to be convincing. It is a given emotion, to which the memories and the hauntings of Gomez and Mrs. Carghill are no more than a rough correlative sketch. Its issue again is private:

> They are merely ghosts:
> Spectres from my past. They've always been with me
> Though it was not till lately that I found the living persons
> Whose ghosts tormented me, to be only human beings,
> Malicious, petty, and I see myself emerging
> From my spectral existence into something like reality.

It is Eliot's familiar conclusion: the release, through consciousness, from an unreal ordinary life, "only human beings"; the acceptance, in death, of another reality. It can be spoken with a shadow of his old conviction, but it can not be enacted; Claverton must die, off stage, under the beech-tree, in a traditional literary reminiscence; while on the stage the spectres of a dying theatre go through the motions of being human. And what we then see is a tragedy of another kind, in which this powerful voice—intense, articulate, memorable—finds and then loses, in experiment and accommodation, a new and serious dramatic form.

4

POETS AND PLAYS, 1935-55

(a) Auden and Isherwood

THE three plays written in collaboration by W. H. Auden and
Christopher Isherwood—*The Dog Beneath the Skin, The Ascent of F6*
and *On the Frontier*—are now obviously related to a particular,
unmistakable period: the 1930s in England. But the plays have a
more than temporary importance, and can be usefully looked at as
experiments in a kind of verse drama, based mainly on expressionism, which is quite different from the line that was to be followed
by Eliot.

Before the collaboration with Isherwood, Auden had written
two dramatic pieces: *Paid on Both Sides* and *The Dance of Death*.
Certain features of the later plays are prominent in these. In *Paid
on Both Sides*, which the author calls a charade, there is a mixture of
popular songs, slapstick, and serious intentions. The piece is in
many ways obscure, and some of this obscurity seems wilful. Yet
much of it is accomplished and original, and its dramatic possibilities are obvious. The achievement of *The Dance of Death* is
tenuous. In performance it was exciting to English audiences in its
use of various expressionist techniques which are always well
suited to satire; and it had much topical interest. But also it was the
first production of the Group Theatre, which was later to produce all
the joint plays. The first of these was *The Dog Beneath the Skin*,
which appeared in 1935.

What is most interesting in the three main plays is the use of
existing conventions of popular entertainment. *The Dog Beneath the
Skin* opens in the manner of a musical comedy, and this atmosphere,
sustained by the frequent songs and choruses, persists. Here, in the
first scene, is the musical-comedy technique operating as exposition:

IRIS: And here am I, Miss Iris Crewe,
    I live in Pressan Ambo too,
    The prize at village dances.
    From Honeypot Hall, the haunt of doves,
    In my blue Daimler and white gloves
    I come to take your glances.
CHORUS: With nose and ear and mouth and hair
    With fur and hat and things like that
    She takes our loving glances.

The tradition, of course, is that of burlesque (with a certain residual reference to the self-introduction of the characters in morality plays). But the question one comes to ask of it is to what degree the formula is used or simply exploited. For in the end, if you set out to burlesque a musical burlesque you find that you have written a musical burlesque.

There are other intentions. In the Chorus which precedes the first scene, we find a characteristic pattern. There is the satiric statement:

> Tourists to whom the Tudor cafés
> Offer Bovril and buns upon Breton ware
> With leather work as a sideline: Filling stations
> Supplying petrol from rustic pumps;

and the affirmative counter-statement:

> Man is changed by his living; but not fast enough.
> His concern today is for that which yesterday did not occur.
> In the hour of the Blue Bird and the Bristol Bomber, his
>   thoughts are appropriate to the years of the Penny Farthing:
> He tosses at night who at noon-day found no truth.

This kind of verse, particularly as it appears in affirmation, is thin. The seriousness has an inescapably casual air, or is as if thrown at one:

> The sky is darkening like a stain,
> Something is going to fall like rain,
> And it won't be flowers.

There remains another element of this play, which is, indeed, formally the central element:

> For walk he must the empty
> Selfish journey
> Between the needless risk
> And the endless safety.

The thematic intention of *The Dog Beneath the Skin* is, clearly, the Quest. A young man is elected and sent out in search of the missing baronet who would normally be head of the village:

> Would he were here! We badly need him.

One of the rewards for success is marriage with the baronet's sister. Formally, this is close to the Fairy-Story Quest, which Mr. Auden himself has since described:

The rescue of the magical object, the marriage with the princess . . . are of benefit, not only to the hero himself, but to society as a whole; as long as the magical object is in the wrong hands the crops will not grow, the people are unhappy and their future is dark, for there is no heir to the throne.

So the search for Sir Francis Crewe is easily identified with the search for a better society: even when Francis has been found, the Quest continues, led by him:

GENERAL [*shouting after them*]: You're traitors to Pressan!
FRANCIS [*shouts back*]: Traitors to *your* Pressan, General, not to ours!

The actual quest is, of course, generalized; it operates, not towards "the centre of dreams", but towards a political commentary. If one seeks its real dramatic antecedent, one arrives at the fourth act of *Peer Gynt*. It is not only that the mad scene in the English play is strongly reminiscent of the similar scene in the Norwegian, but that, in this part of *Peer Gynt*, and in *The Dog Beneath the Skin*, we find the same method and intention. The method is that of identifiable caricature; the intention topical satire. It seems impossible that the authors did not have Ibsen in mind, especially when the end of the play—the transformation of the respectable villagers into animal faces—provides a further important reminiscence (of *When We Dead Awaken*—"Just the dear old farmyard, Maia").

Since Ibsen, of course, many new technical devices had been discovered—particularly by Strindberg and the German expressionists—and some of these are effectively used (in, for instance, the animal transformation just referred to). And further, the authors' talent for comic verse makes the play much more lively than, in abstract, it sounds. Such scenes as those in the Nineveh Hotel (Act III, Scene 2), and especially the figure of Destructive Desmond, retain their brilliance. But everywhere, one feels, it is no more than a local success which is being registered. The play becomes a revue, and the choruses which are clearly intended to stabilize the action take on increasingly the character of a hectoring compère:

But already like an air-bubble under a microscopic slide, the film of poverty is expanding
And soon it will reach your treasure and your gentlemanly behaviour.
Observe, therefore, and be more prepared than our hero.

Then the edges between scenes and choruses become ragged, and there are critical problems of tone. Consider:

[i] Men are falling through the air in flames and choking slowly in the dark recesses of the sea to assuage our pride. Our pride!

[ii] Sons, see your aged father who has taught you to reverence truth and purity; see him caught as the house collapses, his skull smashed like an egg before your eyes by a falling beam.

[iii] O lion, O sun, encompass me with power,
Feed lion, shine sun, for in your glory I flower,
Create the huge and gorgeous summer in an hour.

[iv] Where time flows on as chalk stream clear
And lovers by themselves forgiven
The whole dream genuine, the charm mature
Walk in the great and general light
In their delight a part of heaven
Its furniture and choir.
—To each his need: from each his power.

[v] Our sails are set. O launch upon love's ocean,
Fear has no means there of locomotion
And death cannot exhaust us with his endless devotion.

[vi] "There you see! I knew it! You don't like me. None of them like me. Wherever I go I see it.

[vii] I was fascinated and horrified by you all. I thought such obscene, cruel, hypocritical, mean, vulgar creatures had never existed before in the history of the planet.

It is difficult to estimate, from the tone of these passages, their respective intentions. About the first, a reservation has been made for the rhetoric, but the context clearly indicates that the intention is positive. Yet in what sense is it distinguished from the next extract, which is from the hysterical speech of the leader of Westland to the madmen? Similarly, the third and fifth extracts are spoken by the tailor's dummy in the seduction scene at the Nineveh Hotel; but the fourth, which lies between them without any clear disparity, is from the concluding chorus of the play and contains, presumably, the most positive note of all. The sixth extract is from the self-pitying sentimentality of the financier; but the seventh, which is irresistibly reminiscent of it, comes from the final, and positive, speech of Francis. Whether its tone is also the basis of this whole kind of satire is a question worth asking; we have seen many similar examples, in what was called the "revival" of satire, from Osborne's *The World of Paul Slickey* to the weekend television shows.

The Ascent of F6, which appeared in 1936, is more substantial than the two other joint plays, and is probably the authors' most considerable achievement. Thematically, it has many links with *The Dog Beneath the Skin*. The central figure, the climber Ransom, is clearly involved, when he attempts the peak F6, in a kind of

quest. And like the search for Francis, the ascent of F6 has consciously general implications. Ransom is able to say near the end:

F6 has shown me what I am,

and the general emphasis is on this kind of discovery, on self-
knowledge. Yet the ascent, beside having immediate political
point, is also a search for the salvation of society. Ransom's final
settlement with his mother and brother on the last slopes represents
a highly individual experience; but at the same time the brother is
the Dragon and Ransom the liberator.

Let the eye of the traveller consider this country and weep.

It is to end the despair of society that the liberator has come.
The reward for slaying the dragon is conventional:

The princess' cheek burns red for your love.

But Ransom's reward is also salvation, achieved through discovery of his mother, who is the demon-figure at the peak. The
discovery is death and solitude.

Parts of the achieved work are valuable. Yet its limitation is
certain, in its kind of gesture towards universality, where significance
is sought by the direct imposition of comment rather than by
growth from within the dramatic body. And this tendency in the
structure finds confirmation in the substance, where the process of
experience is more often the exhibition of the label than any actual
realization.

Thus the ascent of the mountain is a convincing representation of
Ransom's personal quest, and the mother-figure at the peak
corresponds. But between the ascent and the summit lies the twin
brother, and here the key changes, and he is the Dragon, with
appropriate fairy-tale attachments. But he is more, he is imperialism;
and F6 is political power. And in the political exploitation of the
ascent—its transformation to a commercially heroic event—appears
the theme of the scapegoat: the hero who vanquishes both despair
and the varieties of desperation which are suburbanism (enter the
clerk).

We are, of course, asked to believe that these are not different
themes and different levels, but have an essential unity. The authors
work with cross-reference to confirm this; but in the end it is perhaps
only clever juggling. The tone of the work as a whole is uncertain,
even at times defensive. It is like watching, in the same movement,
a Dance of the Seven Veils and simple commercial strip-tease.

The popular parts of the play are clearly the comic verses,

which are still interesting, although inferior to the comic invention of *The Dog Beneath the Skin*. The successful parts are a few isolated scenes: the early soliloquy of Ransom; the death of Gunn; the meeting of Ransom and the Abbot. It is perhaps significant that two of these are in prose.

Ransom's soliloquy, on the summit of Pillar Rock, is the first scene, and sets the substance of the tragedy:

> "Deny not, to this brief vigil of your senses that remains, experience of the unpeopled world behind the Sun". . . . One can picture Ulysses' audience . . .; glad they must have been to believe it, during the long uneventful voyage westward: yes, even up to the very end, when the last deceptions were choked from each in turn by the strangling Atlantic.

This is the context of the quest, and the prophecy of its end, as again:

> Friends whom the world honours shall lament their eternal losses in the profoundest of crevasses, while he on the green mountains converses gently with his unapproachable love.

But the apparent search for Virtue and Knowledge can be represented as a search for power. In Ransom, this leads to a reversal of roles between himself and his political brother, so that in their final exchanges on the mountain each speaks the words the other had spoken at the beginning. Similarly, the mother had sought by withholding love to give Ransom the "power to stand alone". She won, but must ask herself—

> Was the victory real?

In the chess-game on the mountain, the Liberation provokes the same question:

> Was the victory real?

In the trial, Ransom and his mother seem identified, and are accused of spiritual pride and found guilty. With the verdict comes release.

> At last his journey ended
> Forgiven and befriended
> See him to his salvation come.

The various identifications only convince in their own right on one or two occasions: the rest get merely abstract support. There is also a disturbing knowingness, briefly represented in such games as the "psychrometer" which the climbers consult, and the mountain flowers with names like Frustrax Abominum. This is all very much on the level of:

> The croquet matches in summer, the handshake, the cough, the kiss,
> There is always a wicked secret, a private reason for this.

These general weaknesses are repeated in much of the verse. The suburban couple chant:

> Moments of happiness do not come often,
> Opportunity's easy to miss.
> O, let us seize them, of all their joy squeeze them,
> For Monday returns when none may kiss;

and the passage slips by, within the customary defensive irony, without much question. More seriously, at a climax of the play, there is this kind of bathos:

> Do you think that it was easy
> To shut you out? I who yearned to make
> My heart the cosiest nook in all the world
> And warm you there for ever, so to leave you
> Stark to the indifferent blizzard and the lightning?

Once again, the edges between distinct elements in the play become blurred; and just as fairy-tales and political satire are mixed with a private theme, so are contrasting levels of poetry. It is not that the play is a welding of these diverse elements, but that they seem to run together, each affecting the other, because of some fundamental uncertainty of control. So that in the serious statement of the mother, on the substance of which the play pivots, such a phrase as "my heart the cosiest nook in all the world", which would slip naturally into one of the comic lyrics or the satiric diversions, intrudes and destroys. It is a local indication of the more general failure.

Individual salvation, at the end of the quest, was at least conceivable to Auden and Isherwood; and according to the rules of their attitude this would imply social salvation also. What, in detail, this might be was less certain. Perhaps the choice was made when the first version of *On the Frontier*, which ended in a revolution and the seizure of power by the people, was redrafted into the inconclusiveness of a protracted civil war, and the lament:

> Will people never stop killing each other?
> There is no place in the world
> For those who love.

On the Frontier, as a play, is simpler. It is made up of political satire and a minor descant on Love, and is the dullest work which the collaboration produced. The substance is war and high politics: it can be interestingly compared to C. K. Munro's *The Rumour*. There are two or three lively episodes, but the general interest seems to have gone, and we approach the flatness of the living newspaper.

The phrase "living newspaper" leads us back to the important critical problem. The contribution which Auden and Isherwood made was definite. They set a lively action against the simple character-revelation with which the ordinary playwrights were concerned, and against the constricting influence of naturalist stage practice. But what they offered in its place, when the dust of the high spirits had cleared, was subject to limitations which, though different from those of orthodox naturalism, were equally fatal. Through conventions which corresponded to the techniques of commercial popular culture—the radio announcer, the loud-speaker, the pair of commentators, the headline, the slogan, the dance-tune—certain points about society could be forcibly made. In *The Ascent of F6* the dramatic issue was joined, and the possibility of handling more connected experience in a fully dramatic way was apparent in one or two scenes. But the local interest appears to have been stronger. It is in the achievement of any adequate dramatic *integrity* that Auden and Isherwood failed. Whether or not this integrity would have been achieved, in the maturing of their collaboration, we cannot now say. When its immediate context disappeared, and the political climate changed, the experiment ended, and the quest went elsewhere.

(b) Christopher Fry

In the late nineteen-forties and early nineteen-fifties, verse drama was represented in the English theatre not so much by T. S. Eliot as by Christopher Fry. His comedies were an intense theatrical fashion, which, in the way of fashion, were then suddenly dropped. An achievement which had been greatly exaggerated was then simply pushed aside, but it retains some relevance, as an example of one way in which the idea of a poetic drama was understood.

In his plays for the West End theatre, Fry added a variation of style to a kind of drama which was already popular. This was the comedy of manners in its weakened modern sense, in the descent from Wilde and Shaw. Instead of a critical comedy, with a public tone based on the edges of contemporary values, the form had become one of incidental wit, of fashionable conversation, and, typically, of costume (as in the constant revivals of Wilde). Fry took this form, and added the play of verse to it. He wrote a comedy of local incident and attitude and of a self-dedicated verbal humour —pun, epigram, burlesque. Meanwhile the action and characters were familiar. Thomas Mendip, in *The Lady's not for Burning*, was a direct descendant of the protagonist of *The Devil's Disciple*, and Jennet Jourdemayne, in the same play, has more than a casual relation to Saint Joan. The Chaplain is a typical minor character out of Chekhov; Bates, in *Venus Observed*—

> There are faces
> As can be mauled about wiv, and there are faces
> As can't be mauled about wiv. Mine can't
> Be mauled about wiv.

—is in the tradition of the comic uneducated of Shaw and Gilbert and popular twentieth-century prose comedy. The Duke, also in *Venus Observed*, is primarily the "mature" figure of the dramatic world of Shaw. As for Wilde, such phrases as these—

> RICHARD: All I can claim as my flesh and blood
> Is what I stand up in. I wasn't born,
> I was come-across.

and

> THOMAS: Your innocence is on at such a rakish angle
> It gives you quite an air of iniquity.

—leave us in very little doubt of this part of Fry's ancestry. It is true that from such plays as *The Lady's not for Burning* and *Venus Observed* it is possible to construct a kind of theme:

> Over all the world
> Men move unhoming, and eternally
> Concerned: a swarm of bees who have lost their queen.

> . . . this great orphanage
> Where no one knows his origin and no one
> Comes to claim him.

> . . . the question is a man's
> Estrangement in a world
> Where everything else conforms.

> And of course you're right.
> I have to see you home, though neither of us
> Knows where on earth it is.

These are persistent moods, but the plays do not, in their substance, either concentrate on or embody them. The sense of loss
of origin is genuine, but as an element of the drama it is offered
diffidently, almost casually. There is a certain concern with death,
but it is an essentially genteel eschatology. The dramatist is as if
surprised by the nature of existence, but he keeps his surprises well
under control, and permits himself only a few unexceptionable
doubts. The apprehensions fall

> as airily as lime flowers, intermittently,
> Uninterrupting, scarcely troubling
> The mild and fragile progress of the sense.

What then needs emphasis is that the verse is not, in the general
meaning of poetic drama, dramatic at all. I do not mean that it is
a different kind of dramatic verse, inadmissible because of its lack
of reference to some orthodox canon. I mean that the drama is not
in the verse as verse; its root is in moods and phrases, which the
verse bears but does not embody. In discussions of the quality of
the language, it was usually phrases which were cited:

The lanterns, Rosabel. They'll be very pale
Compared with the foment of wild flamboyant rose
We have in the sky tonight.

Horses . . . the caves of their nostrils blowing
Bright clouds of breath.

. . . I, as unlaborious
As a laburnum tree, hang in caresses of gold.

. . . the river
Where the water gives those girlish giggles around
The ford.

Our English sun, convalescing after passing
Through the valley of the shadow of the moon.

I, the little heretic as he thinks,
The all unhallows Eve to his poor Adam.

Such white doves were paddling in the sunshine
And the trees were as bright as a shower of broken glass.

. . . I've an April blindness.
You're hidden in a cloud of crimson catherine-wheels.

What was said at the time, by most reviewers, was to the general
effect that "Mr. Fry . . . can let down his bucket into a sea of
dazzling, verbal invention where he wishes, and bring it up brim-
ming". But the colour and richness were fairly obviously *external*,
and the exuberance not so much intensification as a defect of precise

imagination. The *cloud of crimson catherine-wheels*, the doves *paddling in the sunshine*, the *girlish giggles* of the water, the *caves . . . blowing* bright clouds, the *foment of wild flamboyant rose*: these are a straining after effect which is seen as straining precisely because no real structure of imagination is achieved in the writing as a whole. They have the air of contrivance because they add so little but a vague diffusion of fancy. The *caresses of gold* and the *shower of broken glass* are commonplace romantic incidentals; the *valley of the shadow of the moon* is a reminiscence of profundity which the image as a whole not only does not sustain, but to which it has no reference. *All unhallows Eve* is a different kind of phrase, in a manner in which Fry was more often successful than the manner of romantic fancy. It is not very successful here, but it is seen pleasantly enough in:

> The Society for the Desecration
> Of Ancient and Modern Monumental Errors

in

> An occasional signpost of extreme prejudice
> Marked "No Thoroughfare"

and in Jennet Jourdemayne's mathematical biography of her father. The reference here is not to romantic poetry, but to Auden and—

> Give us our trespassers as trespassers will be prosecuted for us

—to Joyce. This kind of interest is seen again in the playing with unfamiliar terms—

> God give me a few
> Lithontriptical words

—which is very apt when the meaning can be taken. The scatter of verbal jokes was responsible for much of the incidental success of the plays, but there was a persistence about it which became tedious.

To see the final effect more clearly, we need some examples of extended speech:

> There it is,
> The interminable tumbling of the great grey
> Main of moonlight, washing over
> The little oyster-shell of this month of April:
> Among the raven-quills of the shadows
> And on the white pillows of men asleep:
> The night's a pale pastureland of peace,
> And something condones the world, incorrigibly,
> But what, in fact, *is* this vaporous charm?

The movement of this passage, if studied closely, is based on what we can call a refusal of the noun. At every point, adjectives, or adjectival phrases, are used to usher in the objects; and their cumulative effect is a relaxed, almost careless rhythm, moving always on the outside of statement. Whether the adjectives are "striking" or not, the effect of this dulling rhythm is an unmistakable vagueness. Its main variant is the persistent

> Anyone would think I had made some extraordinary
> Suggestion.

or again,

> Which were excellent and bright and much to be
> Remembered.

But the general measure is a loose sliding away from speech; a monotone of seeming; with slow, wide meanders into adjective and adjectival phrase. There is hardly any variety in the movement of the plays, so that even the felicities come to be blurred. It has been said that *The Lady's not for Burning* is an April mood, and *Venus Observed* the mood of November, but both moods *sound* very much the same:

> I can see
> The sky's pale belly glowing and growing big,
> Soon to deliver the moon. And I can see
> A glittering smear, the snail-trail of the sun
> Where it crawled with its golden shell into the hills.

> Branches and boughs,
> Brown hills, the valley faint with brume,
> A burnish on the lake; mile by mile
> It's all a unison of ageing,
> The landscape's all in tune, in a falling cadence,
> All decaying.

No matter that in any theatre the valley would be faint with another kind of brume; the falling cadence exerts its own characteristic effect.

The movements of fashion, in the commercial theatre, are not in themselves important. But they can succeed in confusing, often for several years, more important dramatic developments. It was from the experience of these plays, and of their temporary mannerism, that the idea of an English verse drama was rejected. The complex problems of action and dramatic design, which it had initially raised, were then brushed aside, only to reappear, after a brief interval, in new forms. This development will be traced, but it is still worth saying, about Fry's work, that he was the victim of fashion, as well as its beneficiary. His *Sleep of Prisoners*, written for performance in a church, was an interesting experiment in a dramatic tradition very different from that of the fashionable comedies. It is a series of interlocking dreams, by four prisoners of war, in which each enacts for the others, through successive Old Testament stories, a response to violence. It is a more serious design than anything else Fry has written, and it is rooted in an authentic crisis of feeling:

> swaying and troubled figures.
> The flames are men: all human. There's no fire!
> Breath and blood chokes and burns us. This
> Surely is unquenchable. It can only transform.

The weakness, again, is a mannerism: a scatter of superficial verbal jokes and correspondences. But the play has dramatic movement, and genuine experiment, in ways that the comedies had not. An alternative design and a conscious feeling are trying to come through, past the screen of defensive and nervous mannerism. It is worth comparing, in this respect, with a successful later play: John Arden's *Serjeant Musgrave's Dance*. It was there, at the time, that the line of growth really lay, and it is worth remembering that it was mainly fashion—the confident superficial orthodoxy of the commercial theatre—that overrode it.

(c) Dylan Thomas's Play for Voices

Experiment passed, in this period, into broadcasting: significantly, not only because it was an alternative cultural base, but because one central problem of poetic drama, as it had been developed in England—the problem of acted and visible performance of new conventions of speech—could be sidestepped. For an action created solely by voices, radio, as a medium, cancelled several intractable problems of acting and action. The point was made at the time by Louis MacNeice:

> The all-important difference between visual and non-visual drama, while discouraging some, may encourage others towards radio, for here and here alone can one listen to calculated speech divorced from all visual supports or interferences—even from a printed page.

In practice, most radio drama supplied a range of supporting representational sounds, of an evocative atmospheric kind, which were the exact equivalent of visual props. Problems of dramatic movement were avoided, but the use of the voice, to suggest an essentially familiar action, remained the ordinary use of the naturalist theatre. Louis MacNeice's own plays were the most sustained experiment in the medium; *The Dark Tower* and others can be usefully read as a continuation of the experiments of Auden and Isherwood. But the most interesting single work, that came out of the radio experiment, is Dylan Thomas's *Under Milk Wood*. And it is then interesting that it was first actually performed in a theatre, and, after a radio production, was successfully transferred to the stage and to television.

Under Milk Wood, in approximately its published form, was first played in New York only a few weeks before Dylan Thomas died there. His work on it, during the last months of his life, was work against time and breakdown, yet in essence we can regard it as complete. The marks of the history of the play are, nevertheless, quite evident, and in particular the many revisions which the plan of the play underwent remain as separable layers, if not in the total effect of the work, at least in its formal construction. The play grew from a broadcast talk, *Quite Early One Morning*, which described the dreams and waking of a small Welsh seaside town. Daniel Jones, in his preface to *Under Milk Wood*, describes the stage through which this developed towards the work as we now have it. There was the insertion, and subsequent abandonment, of a plot in which the town was to be declared an insane area, and the blind Captain Cat, at a trial of sanity, was to call the inhabitants in their own defence. The defence was to be abandoned, finally, after the prosecution's description of a sane town, the inhabitants of Llaregyb at once petitioning to be cordoned off from such sanity. Thomas worked on this scheme, under the title *The Town was Mad*, but later changed the action back to a simple time-sequence description of Llaregyb itself. This was published, as far as it had been written— up to the delivery of letters by the postman Willy Nilly—as *Llaregyb, a Piece for Radio Perhaps*, in 1952. Then this was again revised, the title changed to *Under Milk Wood*, and performed, again incomplete, in May, 1953. John Malcolm Brinnin has described the last-minute writing and revision for this performance, which was part of Thomas's American reading tour. By the following October, having left aside certain things he had planned to include, Thomas had finished the play as we now have it.

This confused history seems not to have affected the spirit of *Under Milk Wood*, though the loss of *The Town was Mad* is a thing to regret. It is in construction that the different intentions are evident, and in particular in the multiplication of narrators. The original narrator, the blind Captain Cat, was an obvious device for radio. Then, in the scheme of *The Town was Mad*, Captain Cat became a central character, so that eventually another narrator was necessary.

With his public readings in mind, and following also the habits of this kind of radio play, Thomas moved steadily back towards emphasis on the narrative voice. In the final version there are two narrators, First Voice and Second Voice, and there is also narration by Captain Cat and the Voice of a Guidebook. Formally, this is confusing, though part of the difficulty lies in the whole concept of a play for voices.

The idea of the play for voices, primarily developed in terms of sound broadcasting, is one of many attempts to make a new convention which is not limited to a single dimension of reality. It is a very difficult undertaking, and it is not surprising that the device of narration should have gained such a crucial importance. In terms of recent stage drama, narrative can be called undramatic, but on a longer view it can be seen that in some of the most satisfactory dramatic forms ever achieved—in Athenian tragic drama in particular—narrative has had an important place. The rehabilitation of narrative, in broadcast drama, was a sound instinct, and *Under Milk Wood*, in spite of the crudity of its narrative structure, is the most successful example we have of its dramatic usefulness.

There is another reason for the emphasis on narrative. The craft of dialogue, in modern drama, has been ordinarily so much practised in terms of naturalism, that to a poet, or a writer with similar intentions, it has come to seem the hardest and most baffling part of drama: not only because it is in any case difficult, but because to lapse into the dialogue of a single dimension is so easy and so frustrating. Narrative, in comparison, is free, and in a way is turned to in relief. There is a similar turning, wherever possible, to such devices as chorus and song, because these again follow relatively directly from kinds of writing practised elsewhere. In the case of *Under Milk Wood*, the narrative structure must be seen, finally, as in part a successful convention for a particular kind of play, in part a residue of weakness following from both general and personal inexperience in this kind of dramatic attempt.

I have distinguished three elements—three kinds of writing—in *Under Milk Wood*: narrative, dialogue, song. The narrative of the first and second voices is relatively unsuccessful—perhaps, indeed, because it was too well-known, too easy a manner. This sinuous, decorated, atmospheric writing had become commonplace in broadcast drama, and I think it is ordinarily unsatisfactory, and particularly so in Dylan Thomas, where it opens the gate to certain observable weaknesses of his poetry. Near the beginning, for instance, we find

the hunched, courters'-and-rabbits' wood limping invisible down

to the sloeblack, slow, black, crowblack, fishingboat-bobbing
sea.

The "sloeblack, slow, black, crowblack" device seems a nervous
habit rather than actual description; a facile assonance rather than
a true dramatic rhythm. This can be seen more clearly by contrast
with a piece of successful narration, where Thomas is involved
with action and character rather than with suggestion of an
atmosphere:

> The Reverend Eli Jenkins, in Bethesda House, gropes out of bed
> into his preacher's black, combs back his bard's white hair,
> forgets to wash, pads barefoot downstairs, opens the front door,
> stands in the doorway and, looking out at the day and up at the
> eternal hill, and hearing the sea break and the gab of birds,
> remembers his own verses . . .

The suggestiveness of the former piece is strictly casual, a simply
verbal device, whereas in the latter piece the rhythms point and
make the action, and the verbal order plays its part in character.
"His bard's white hair" is not merely decorative, like "sloe-black";
it contains both relevant meanings, the man's appearance and the
sense, in the word order, of the bard's part he is acting. The rhythmic
stop and surprise, so casually placed, of "forgets to wash", is again
serving the whole situation being presented. It is the difference
between dramatic writing and unattached tremolo.

There is some significance in this distinction, when extended to
Thomas's work as a whole. *Under Milk Wood* is important because
it seems to break a personal deadlock, a long imprisonment in a
particular kind of practised effect, in much the same way that Yeats's
plays mark the development from the imprisoning "wan, pale,
languishing" world of his early poetry to the fine hardness and
clarity of his later work. It is a movement out of a self-regarding
personal rhythm into a more varied world. Whenever Thomas
touches the action of his town and its people, there is a sudden
sharpening and deepening, very different in effect from the posing
rhythms of the anxious, word-locked, suggestive observer. The
actual voices are very different from the atmospheric voices of the
narrators:

> 1W.: And look at Ocky Milkman's wife that nobody's ever seen
> 2W.: he keeps her in the cupboard with the empties
> 3W.: and think of Dai Bread with two wives
> 2W.: one for the daytime one for the night.
> 3W.: Men are brutes on the quiet.

It is ordinarily this one sharp comic lilt, but it is markedly better than

> the lust and lilt and lather and emerald breeze and crackle of the bird-praise and body of Spring.

The imprisoning rhythm is broken whenever the drama is actual, and it is interesting to notice that it is also broken for the songs, which are not set romantic pieces, but ballads in the mood of the successful dialogue:

> In Pembroke City when I was young
> I lived by the Castle Keep
> Sixpence a week was my wages
> For working for the chimbley sweep.

It is in the achievement of other rhythms, other voices—in part traditional, in part those of his actual community—that Dylan Thomas found the beginnings of a dramatic action.

Yet the main source of *Under Milk Wood* is literary; is indeed a passage from a novel. I refer to the "play for voices" in the Circe episode (Part Two, section twelve) of Joyce's *Ulysses*. The parallels are remarkable, and some of them should be cited. I will put what in *Ulysses* is printed as stage-direction (though of course it is not this) into the narrative-voice form which Thomas adopted:

N: Ellen Bloom, in pantomime dame's stringed mobcap, crinoline and bustle, widow Twankey's blouse with muttonleg sleeves buttoned behind, grey mittens and cameo brooch, her hair plaited in a crispine net, appears over the staircase banisters, a slanted candlestick in her hand and cries out in shrill alarm.

EB: O blessed Redeemer, what have they done to him! My smelling salts!

N: She hauls up a reef of skirt and ransacks the pouch of her striped blay petticoat. A phial, an Agnus Dei, a shrivelled potato and a celluloid doll fall out.

EB: Sacred Heart of Mary, where were you at all, at all?

N: Bloom, mumbling, his eyes downcast, begins to bestow his parcels in his filled pockets but desists, muttering. A voice, sharply

V: Poldy!

B: Who?

N: He ducks and wards off a blow clumsily.

B: At your service.

N: He looks up. Beside her mirage of datepalms a handsome woman in Turkish costume stands before him . . .

If we compare this with the ordinary method of *Under Milk Wood*, the technical continuity is obvious:

> *N:* Mr. Pugh reads, as he forks the shroud meat in, from *Lives of the Great Poisoners*. He has bound a plain brown-paper cover round the book. Slyly, between slow mouthfuls, he sidespies up at Mrs. Pugh, poisons her with his eye, then goes on reading. He underlines certain passages and smiles in secret.
>
> *Mrs. P:* Persons with manners do not read at table.
>
> *N:* says Mrs. Pugh. She swallows a digestive tablet as big as a horse-pill, washing it down with clouded peasoup water.
>
> *Mrs. P:* Some persons were brought up in pigsties.
>
> *P:* Pigs don't read at table, dear.
>
> *N:* Bitterly she flicks dust from the broken cruet. It settles on the pie in a thin gnat-rain.

The continuity, moreover, is in more than technique. Compare:

> Mr. Pugh minces among bad vats and jeroboams, tiptoes through spinneys of murdering herbs, agony dancing in his crucibles, and mixes especially for Mrs Pugh a venomous porridge unknown to toxicologists that will scald and viper through her until her ears fall off like figs (THOMAS).

> I shall have you slaughtered and skewered in my stables and enjoy a slice of you with crisp crackling from the baking tin basted and baked like sucking pig with rice and lemon or currant sauce. It will hurt you. (JOYCE)

> Soon it will be time to get up.
> Tell me your tasks in order.
> I must put my pyjamas in the drawer marked pyjamas.
> I must take my cold bath which is good for me. (THOMAS)

> You will make the beds, get my tub ready, empty the pisspots in the different rooms. You'll be taught the error of your ways. (JOYCE)

There is an evident similarity between *Under Milk Wood* and *Ulysses* (each covering the life of an ordinary day), not only in kinds of imagination, but also in certain marked rhythms. I do not make the comparison to show Thomas unoriginal, though that he learned from Joyce is obvious. The interest is rather in the kinds of speech both are able to develop, as alternatives to one-dimensional "public" conversation. Thomas is writing for speaking, rather than writing speech (conversation) in the ordinary sense. The ordinary poetic alternative to conversation has been rhetoric, but this is by no means the only variant. There is the chorus of cries:

Try your luck on spinning Jenny! Ten to one bar one!
Sell the monkey, boys! Sell the monkey! I'll give ten to one! Ten
to one bar one! (JOYCE)

How's it above? Is there rum and laverbread? Bosoms and
robins? Concertinas? Ebenezer's bell? Fighting and onions?
(THOMAS)

Or the simple, hard chanting:

> I gave it to Molly
> Because she was jolly
> The leg of the duck
> The leg of the duck. (JOYCE)

> Boys boys boys
> Kiss Gwennie where she says
> Or give her a penny.
> Go on Gwennie. (THOMAS)

By weaving a pattern of voices, rather than an ordinary conversational sequence, the reach of the drama is significantly enlarged.
It can include not only things said, but things left unsaid, the
interpenetration of things seen and imagined, the images of memory
and dream, the sharp rhythmic contrasts of this voice and that, this
tone and that, this convention and others. When we first read
Ulysses, it seems that we are reading actual conversation, hearing
our own full voices, spoken and unspoken, for the first time. The
ordinary dialogue of a naturalist play seems, by comparison,
artificial and theatrical. *Under Milk Wood* is much slighter than
Ulysses, but there is the same achievement of a living convention:
the voices, in their strange patterns, are among the most real we
have heard. This success raises interesting possibilities for the drama
as a whole, when we remember that, in England, the ordinary
modern alternative to naturalism has been, not a pattern of voices,
but the single general-purpose poetic rhythm of Eliot or Fry. It is
significant that the varied pattern of voices has been achieved only
in the context of an abandonment of ordinary naturalistic action.

It remains true, in the drama and the theatre, that we do not
know what we can do until we have tried; our ordinary conceptions
of what is theatrically possible, what is properly dramatic, remain
timid and custom-bound, and constant experiment is essential.
Under Milk Wood justifies itself, if only as this. Yet in substance, also,
it is not inconsiderable. It is true that it is very much a boy's-eye
view, like most of Thomas's writing of this kind. Yet there is a
warmth of acceptance in the experience, a willing return to the
absorbed absolutes of boyhood, which deserve recognition in a

period soured by a continual, prematurely-aged rejection. It is not a mature work, but the retained extravagance of an adolescent's imaginings, a confused rehearsal of experiences, the acceptance and elaboration of shaping fantasies.

Is it an expressionist play, dramatizing a mind, or a poetic documentary, dramatizing a way of life? In form, of course, it is the latter, but through the medley of voices, through the diverse experiences, a single voice and a recognizable experience emerge. The play can be seen in three parts:

(a) *Night and Dreams:* "you can hear their dreams"; pp. 1-22
(b) *Waking and Morning:* "rising and raising . . . the shops squeak open"; pp. 22-61
(c) *Afternoon, Dusk and Night:* "the sunny slow lolling afternoon . . . down in the dusking town . . . dusk is drowning for ever. It is all at once night now"; pp. 61-86.

The distribution of interest is characteristic. The strong feelings are of dream, hiding, the effort of waking to the pretences of the day. Single feeling, in these modes, flows through the many voices. Near the beginning and near the end are the drowning memories of the blind Captain Cat—the private poetry; and again, by contrast, the morning and evening verses of Eli Jenkins—the public poetry of woken self-conscious sentiment. The neighbours' chorus (pp. 9-13) clacks through the day with its hard, waking judgements. The three fullest portraits—of Mog Edwards and his Myfanwy, of Mrs. Ogmore-Pritchard and her dead husbands, of Pugh obsequiously hiding his hatreds—have a clear family likeness: the rejection of love, in whatever terms—money, house-pride, cold self-sufficiency. These are the hated, woken world, set in relief by the exceptions—the loving, fighting Cherry Owens; the dreamers of love—Lily, Gossamer, Bessie, Waldo and Sinbad; Dai Bread and his two wives; Polly Garter. The town is mad because the exceptions are so many, but only because we hear their dreams. Briefly, at the climax of the day, another world breaks through, and "the morning is all singing"—the three songs, two by the children, one by Polly Garter, between morning and night.

It is not a formal structure, but the shape of the experience is clear. The little town is observed, but in a curve of feeling familiar from Thomas's poems: a short curve from darkness to darkness, with the songs and dreams of the day cut through by the hard, mask-ridden uproariously laughed-at world. This, in the end, is the experience, in a single voice, and the chosen technique, which we have discussed formally, must now be seen as necessary to the experience. The language of dream, of song, of unexpressed feeling is the primary experience, and counterpointed with it is the public language of chorus and rhetoric. The people, in the end, hardly talk *to* each other; each is locked in a world of dream or a convention of public behaviour. The play for voices has many uses, but for experience of this kind it is the most evident form. Its limitations, in turn, follow the character of the experience: the impossibility of significant relationship is directly related to the miscellany of self-enclosed voices, parodied and enacted in a single internal voice; and the impossibility of action—of struggle and change in the world—is at once taken for granted and ratified. Only the voice and its variations are left, to the despairing poet.

5

PLAYS AND MYTHS

MYTH has meant many things, from "plot" and "tale" to "fable". In modern usage, its meaning has specialized in this last direction: it is "a false version of reality" but also "a representation of a different kind of reality". In this latter use, it is an available term for several kinds of drama, but it is again commonly specialized to the stories of earlier periods of civilization: particularly Greek and Hebrew; and to the former especially, since these are already embodied in major drama. It is difficult to distinguish this specialized use from certain kinds of historical play, in which a known or traditional action is used to express, in a particular and distanced dramatic form, a structure of feeling that has been cut free from contemporary detail yet is still expressing contemporary experience. There are many examples of this use, from Ibsen and Strindberg to Camus and Brecht. But where "myth" as a word is in question, the simplest reference is to that continuity and reworking of the dramatic tradition which has led to many plays in which the stories of Greek drama are used again, as a form of contemporary expression. It is worth considering some examples of this, because it is subject, in practice, to important variations of method and purpose, which myth, as a word, too often overrides.

We have first to notice certain qualifying facts. The Greek myths have been used not only for drama but for psychological theory: Oedipus, since Freud, has been not only the strange original story but also the contemporary psycho-analytic interpretation. "Myth", Jung argued, "is an involuntary statement of an unconscious process"; but that, presumably, is the myth itself. It is not always clear whether a reference to Electra is to the person of that story or to the pattern implied in "the Electra-complex"; the apparent reference to the myth may be the didactic reference to the interpretation. Further, it is clear, in the Greek plays themselves, that what we now call "the myth" is subject to real variation. The most evident example is, precisely, Electra, for if we compare the *Oresteia* of Aeschylus, the *Electra* of Sophocles and the *Electra* of Euripides, we find radical differences: not only of detail but of experience. In the *Oresteia* the emphasis is on the pollution of the house by the murder of Agamemnon; Electra greets Orestes not only as the cleanser but the unifier—the son who carries, through the bitter difficulties of the action, the loving kinship relations of a disrupted household. The insoluble difficulty is the need to cleanse and re-establish the house by its own norms, and the relation of the inevitable matricide to these norms and to other conceptions of justice. In Sophocles, the emphasis is much more on the personal feelings of Electra and Orestes; the motive of Clytemnestra's murder of Agamemnon is in the same way personalized—it is not only a chain of events in the history of a house, but a compounded husband-murder and adultery; the reaction is then of a son and daughter, as well as of an avenging and cleansing generation. In Euripides, the emphasis has again shifted: Electra is married to a farmer, and the vengeance and murder come as if from a different dimension, a tragedy necessarily but with a degree of bitterness and malignity breaking into an apparently settled life. In each of these cases (a much fuller account would be necessary to show the full extent of the variation) it is not just detail that is altered; it is the dramatic meaning of the experience. It is then not possible to abstract a single "orthodox" meaning of "the myth".

When we look, then, at contemporary examples of plays based on these "myths", we shall, when we find variations, not be measuring them against an orthodoxy, though the taking of a relatively familiar story legitimately draws attention to the particular emphasis that is given. There is often a critical difficulty, in that we have to attend to the emphasis, but cannot criticize it through the myth; each play's action stands in its own right. But then, at the same time, the action has to justify itself in its own right. Where it fails to do so, no defence is available by pointing to "the myth": that is a stratagem of the same order as writing a play wholly about con-temporary experience and then, as an addition, calling its persons Prometheus or Jason, or, by a device of title or external allusion, hinting that the action is that of the Last Supper or the Road to Emmaus. The real difficulty, in many cases, is a critical determina-tion of just these points. Strindberg's *Road to Damascus* is an internal reference, pointing to the essential action; Graham Greene's *The Third Man* is an external reference, hinting at an action which is not really present. The problem is structurally similar to the analysis of the seagull, the wild duck, the white horses, in Chekhov and Ibsen; indeed the use of myth, in some cases, is precisely of that kind. There is then a very fine line, as with "symbol" and "atmosphere", between the use of myth and its exploitation.

We can turn now to look at four examples: three based on the story of Electra and Orestes—O'Neill's *Mourning Becomes Electra*, the *Electre* of Giraudoux, and Sartre's *The Flies*; and an important, rather different experiment—Anouilh's *Antigone*.

(a)

O'Neill said that he was trying

to get modern psychological approximation of the Greek sense of fate into such a play, which an intelligent audience of today, possessed of no beliefs in gods or supernatural retribution, could accept and be moved by.

The description is revealing. It confirms, what the play indeed makes clear, the derivation of the formal action, which is quite evidently from Freud rather than Aeschylus. Vinny, the "Electra-figure", is jealous of her mother because she also is in love with Adam Brant. The relationship of Orin and Christine is that of Freud's "Oedipus". There is no valid reason against these dramatic patterns, but it remains to ask what the "Greek" reference is then being used for. There are several local indications that it is essentially an external gesture: the "Mannon face, which resembles a life-like mask rather than living flesh" is a gesture to the masked actor; the "Greek" façade on the New England house is a gesture to an architectural style; the chorus of townspeople is a formal reminiscence. But none of these would be more than incidental if the main pattern did not confirm what they are doing. For we are given, in the real action, an inherently self-destructive family, in the particular circumstances of New England puritanism and the effects of the civil war. What is given by the "Greek" reference is the imposed universal pattern. It is called fate: a direction of attention to forces outside these characters. But, most characteristically, there is an identification between "fate"—the external universal design—and "the unconscious"—an internal universal pattern.

The conventional association between the names of the myth and a Freudian theory of motive is then used, rhetorically, to unite these conceptions. The questions which the action raises, moving inwards, are not resolved by but referred to this external association. The real drive of the play is behind this façade. The structure of feeling that is actually operative is of a different kind again: not so much that the relationships are destructive as that they are illusory:

MANNON: Me as your husband being killed, that seemed queer and wrong—like something dying that had never lived.

What comes through, as the decisive feeling, is the damage people do to each other because they can never really know or understand each other: a rather different version of "the unconscious", though one which has become conventional. It is a structure of feeling on which much modern drama rests, but it is the weakness of *Mourning Becomes Electra* that it not only rationalizes the feeling, by the external references, but that it is deeply confused, in its own essential feeling, by these very gestures, pointing in several directions at once. The "myth", that is to say, confuses rather than clarifies, though it then, in a familiar way, recommends the confusion. We can see the point most clearly when we compare the directly dramatized structure of feeling in *Long Day's Journey into Night*. In *Mourning Becomes Electra* the last line gives the real clue, to this kind of use of myth:

It takes the Mannons to punish themselves for being born.

For the decisive reference here is of course not to Agamemnon, but to this particular destructive family and, in a gesture through the name, to Man.

(b)

In Alfieri's and in Voltaire's dramas of *Orestes*, the complication is one of action. Retaining the reported death of Orestes, in the Greek versions, which Sophocles had used to provoke the passionate recognition of Electra, they developed the action towards stratagem, uncertainty, intrigue: the hazards of action. It is like the pre-Shakespearean Hamlet story, in which the madness is a device to get near to Claudius, rather than the condition of division and uncertainty which defines what action at all is possible. In Alfieri and Voltaire, the action turns by external accident: Orestes is seized, at what seems the last moment, and then liberated by a revolt of the people of Argos; he goes on to kill Aegisthus and, inadvertently, his mother.

O'Neill, as we have seen, had changed the inwardness of the action: the motive of fate is not in history but in complicated family relationships overlying an essential human isolation. In the *Electre* of Giraudoux, the complication is again, at first sight, one of motive. Only Electra believes that Aegisthus and Clytemnestra are lovers: Argos is peaceful, self-deceiving, asleep. Orestes returns, to his place and his power, but it is Electra who calls him to life as the avenger. For she is, as she puts it, the widow of her father; she loves everything which comes from Agamemnon, but her relation to Clytemnestra is no more than equivocal: a complicity which binds a mother and daughter in indifference and hatred. What is then revealed is a web of relationships, uncertain and ambiguous, which becomes dangerous only because Electra transforms it, driven by "a hatred which is not mine". There is a baffling element, in Giraudoux' whole treatment, which rests on this point. The action takes place, as it were, in two dimensions, under the cover of the myth. It is an action of complicated human frustrations, jealousies and desires, yet as such incompletely established: the daughter's hatred of the mother for not loving (as much as for killing) her father; the daughter's suspicion of her mother's relationship with the new king; the focus of attraction and antagonism between a daughter and the suspected lover of her mother. Yet the persons do not come through to make these relationships substantial; and this is not because Giraudoux has failed to develop them, but because he is interested, ultimately, in something else. He complicates the myth, by altering the relationships, but it is in just the level of uncertainty at which it then materializes that his real dramatic question is posed. Against the royal family he poses a bourgeois family, in which the same infidelities occur and through which, ironically, the infidelity of Clytemnestra is revealed. But the bourgeois settlement is one of composition, and the royal ideal, as expressed by Aegisthus, is ultimately of the same kind: a secure and a settled city. It is this that Electra challenges, as the bearer of the myth.

> You who pretend to know me: you think me one of those to whom you can say "Lie and permit lying, and you will have a prosperous country. If you hide crimes, your country will be victorious". What is this poor country that you are sliding between us and the truth?

It is a country, evidently, of a common condition. It is only pushed to tragedy, in spite of its crimes and lies, by Electra's demand for full consciousness. And this is, again, the contrast between the royal and the bourgeois family:

> With kings you can achieve experiences which are never achieved with ordinary people: pure hatred, pure anger. Always purity. That's what it is, tragedy, with its incest and murders of parents ..

PLAYS AND MYTHS

The myth, that is to say, permits a dramatic action which expresses the pure result of what is otherwise impure; but at the same time this is turned, in a persistent irony, to a contrast of the relative possibilities of life, in the contrasted conditions. Ordinary life is seen as a kind of sleep, but a sleep in which men put on

the armour of happiness: satisfaction, indifference, generosity, appetite. But a spot of sun reconciles them with all the spots of blood. A bird's song with all the lies.

It is an awakening, a morning, that Electra forces, so that when, in the end, Clytemnestra and Aegisthus are killed, and the city is sacked and burning, it can be described as the dawn. This is what happens when men declare themselves, when they "make a sign to the gods", when they take responsibility. Electra can say, over the death and ruin:

I have justice, I have everything.

Giraudoux' use of the myth, then, is at once a clarification and an irony. The formal action of the play is a forcing of consciousness, of a destructive truth, through the sleepy compromises of ordinary life. But the substantial action is a continual reflection of this process, as it were in infinite mirrors: a multiplicity and suggestion of motive; an irony and an unconnected lyricism. The Furies are girls who get bigger as the action develops: playful, even arch; but it is only they who can speak the direct words of the action, taking the roles of the principals; the leading actors themselves are caught in their two dimensions, of their uncertain relationships and their ominous names. Where, in many cases, myth is used to simplify, to a universal pattern, Giraudoux uses it to complicate an existing complication, in the uncertain traverse between experience and metaphysics, an ordinary day and the permanent abstractions. The mood of the play is then very strange: opportunist, for effects which are almost immediately rejected; reflective, but carried along by an action mainly seen as external: the myth not as exposition but as introspection, on a common experience which at the same time it makes uncommon. The structure of feeling, finally, is a central indecision, and the taking of positions, attitudes, towards a series of possibilities which are only ever partly realized: an incomplete and uncertain action, which succeeds in dramatizing an incompleteness and uncertainty.

(c)

The contrast with Sartre's *The Flies* is then very marked. Sartre returns the myth to the central fact of Aeschylus: the pollution of the city. He then describes this pollution differently: an unhealthy fear of the dead; a collective refusal to accept responsibility for the crimes of the past. His Jupiter wants this, as he explains to Aegisthus:

> We are among kings, and I will speak frankly. . . . I like crimes that pay . . . For one dead man, twenty thousand others plunged into penitence . . .

It is the "sad secret of gods and kings": that men are free, but by oppressions and demonstrations like this can be prevented from knowing it. Orestes returns, but as the liberator, not the avenger. Electra is prepared to be talked out of her revenge, but Orestes is determined to regain his country by killing Aegisthus and Clytemnestra and taking full responsibility for everything he is doing. He confronts Zeus, who shows him the power of the created universe. Orestes replies:

> You are the king of gods, king of stones and stars, king of the waves of the sea. But you are not the king of men . . . You made me, but you made me free . . . I am my freedom . . . Outside nature, against nature, without excuse, with no remedy but in myself . . . The people of Argos are my people. I must open their eyes.

Ironically, then, in fulfilling the abstract destiny of the myth, he is refusing the orthodox destiny: that men will suffer and be guilty because they refuse to take their freedom. When he kills, he takes on himself all the crime and guilt of the city. The swarm of flies—the Furies—attach themselves to him, and he leads them away, like rats, leaving the city cleansed.

The power of Sartre's play is its clarity of attitude. It is of course significant that the structure of feeling from which the argument is mounted lends itself to just the theatrical gesture which is the play's climax. It is not the revolt of the citizens, as in Alfieri or Voltaire, which liberates the city. Their freedom is brought to them, by the desperate outsider, who in acting for himself is acting for them. Thus the grandiose terms of the myth, and in particular the name of Orestes, permit a reasoned rhetoric which in more direct terms might be vulnerable. Sartre's Orestes can do what Ibsen's Brand cannot do; and the alteration of possibility is in terms of the fable. The single desperate act, which will liberate a whole people, is converted from fantasy to a persuasive theatrical action. The reality of a crime is qualified by its status in the myth as justified and liberating. Thus, by what is in effect a brilliant opportunism, a contemporary feeling is released without substantial consequence, because the myth reserves the action to a reasoned rehearsal of things already done and distanced; only the argument alters, the action can be assumed.

(d)

It is in just this seizing of the theatrical possibilities of myth that we can see the importance of a very different experiment: Anouilh's *Antigone*. This is played in "a neutral setting", which indicates the purpose of the use of the myth. Its most striking achievement is its easy adoption of conventions which allow a critical distancing—a taking of roles—and yet also, through this, an essential contemporary action. The play begins with all the characters on the stage, in an informal group. Prologue detaches himself from the group, and steps forward:

> There! These characters are going to act out for you the story of Antigone.

It is as easy and confident as that, and yet immediately the whole necessary convention for the dramatic method of the play is established. Immediately, Prologue is able to accomplish all the necessary exposition of characters and situation. He points out the various characters of the group:

> Antigone: she is that thin little one sitting down there, saying nothing. She is looking straight in front of her. She is thinking. She is thinking she is soon going to be Antigone . . . Nothing can be done about it. She is called Antigone, and she is going to have to play her role to the finish . . . And, since the curtain has risen, she feels that she is distancing herself, at a speed that makes her dizzy, from her sister Ismene, who's chatting and laughing with a young man; from all of us, who are very calm, watching her: we who don't have to die tonight.

The convention, both of commentary on the various characters in turn, and of establishment of the play and the characters as action and parts which only begin "now that the curtain has risen", is very impressive. By the end of Prologue's speech, the audience has been firmly introduced to the conventional nature of the play, and also to each of the characters:

> That powerful man, with white hair, thinking, close to his attendant, is Creon . . .
> That pale boy, down there at the bottom, dreaming, leaning against the wall, on his own: that's the Messenger. He doesn't want to talk or mix with the others. He already knows.

—and to the situation:

> And now that you know them all, they can act out their history

for you. It begins at the moment when the two sons of Oedipus—Eteocles and Polyneices—who should have reigned over Thebes in alternate years, each taking his turn, have fought and killed each other under the walls of the city.

Prologue steps back out of sight, the characters leave the stage, the lighting changes, and the persons of the play begin to enter, each in his turn in the course of the action. It is very simple, and completely convincing. It gains an immediate dramatic concentration, and the conditions of intensity; it also provides the major resource which the naturalist drama has lacked, that of commentary. Prologue has begun this; it will be continued by Chorus, who enters at several points in the action to continue the form. Not the least of the achievements of this method is that it restores to the dramatist major control of the form of his play.

The main events of the play are foretold by the device of commentary. This is a deliberate choice with reference to the play's nature:

> Tragedy is clean, calm, flawless. It has nothing to do with melodrama—with traitors, villains, persecuted innocence, avengers, sudden revelations, gleams of hope: making death horrible, like an accident. They might have saved themselves, the hero might have arrived in time with the police. But in tragedy you can be calm. There is a fellow-feeling among the characters, and they are all innocent. It isn't that one kills and one gets killed. It's a matter of casting: of the part you're playing.

The explicit rejection of an intrigue action, subject to arbitrary causes, only echoes the rejections, sixty years earlier, of Ibsen and Strindberg and Hauptmann. But now the rejection had found an alternative form: that is Anouilh's innovation in the prose drama, as it had been Eliot's innovation in *Murder in the Cathedral*.

The drama is played without intervals, and the central scene is the confrontation of Creon and Antigone, when Antigone has persisted in her attempts to bury her brother and has accordingly forfeited her life to the law. The scene is an intense realization of the experience of choice:

ANTIGONE: I have not said "yes". What do you expect them to matter to me: your politics, your necessity, your meagre histories? I can still say "no" to everything I don't like, and I am the only judge. You, with your crown, your guards, your whole show, you can only kill me, because you have said "yes".

As in *Murder in the Cathedral*, the form of the play is not a matter of abstract technical choice, but, in its certainty of what is to come, a finely operative context for the particular experience of choice which the action embodies. The intensity of the form is the intensity of Antigone:

> We are the people who push questions right through.

The inevitability is the inevitability of Creon's conception of order. It does not matter to him which of the bodies lies rotting and which is buried in state; one must rot, so that the citizens may smell the end of revolt. This must be done, for order; the attempt to "manage people". And Antigone must act as she does, for herself:

> CREON: Not for others, not for your brother? For who then?
> ANTIGONE: For nobody. For myself.

Thus the design of the characters and of the action is integral with the design of the play. Chorus enters at the end, reminding the audience of the "calm" which has been recommended as the mood of watching:

> There! Without Antigone, it is true, they would all have been calm. But now, it's finished. And they are calm, all the same. All those who had to die are dead. Those who believed one thing, and those who believed the opposite—even those who believed nothing and found themselves taken by this history without understanding it. All dead alike: stiff, useless, rotting. And those who still live are beginning quietly to forget them, and to get their names mixed up. It's finished.

What the myth then serves, through its distancing, its inevitability, is a contemporary feeling: simpler than that of Giraudoux, less positive than that of Sartre: the inevitable struggle of those "who say yes" and those "who say no" to an order and system of life; the catching up of others in a struggle they don't understand; the indifference, the ironic calm, of those who are outside the struggle, watching it like a play. It is made a play—a taking of roles—because it is not a play and yet is turned into a play, by the mood of detachment. The actors are dead and yet are only acting their parts: the myth is the irony of necessity but also the more immediate irony of the abstract, name-given action. It is not a contemporary action swollen to myth, but a way of defining contemporary action, and a range of attitudes to it, through a precise dramatic form. It is, that is to say, just because it is theatre that it is at once possible and intolerable.

PART IV

Social and Political Drama

I

GEORG BÜCHNER: A RETROSPECT

GEORG Büchner's plays, *Danton's Death* and *Woyzeck*, seem clearly now to belong to the modern dramatic movement. The fact that they precede it, by half a century, is in part explained by their history. Büchner died in 1837, at the age of twenty-three. *Danton's Death* had been published, in an altered form, in his lifetime. *Woyzeck* was not published until 1879, and even then in an uncertain text. The plays were first performed, in Germany, in 1902 and 1913. Thus the work of a late Romantic dramatist, of great originality, became fully known only in a period in which the new forms of naturalism and expressionism were already active. His work was recognized, rightly, as connecting with these movements, and a power which had lain dormant became a known achievement and an active influence. Whenever this happens (as in English poetry, with Gerard Manley Hopkins) there are difficult critical problems. There is an obvious tendency to abstract the innovating genius altogether from its period, though in the case of both Hopkins and Büchner this is in the end misleading. What has primarily to be done, in any event, is to look at the plays in their own terms, before their place in any tradition can be decided.

Danton's Death and *Woyzeck* are very different from each other, though certain thematic connections are obvious. *Woyzeck* is very difficult to judge, because its arrangement is uncertain, and the modern edited versions differ in important respects. Though very powerful, it is then in an essential way fragmentary; indeed there seem to me to be signs in it of two or three related but different conceptions, which exist at different levels of realization. Interpretation can compound them, but the more relevant exercise is their distinction, since this shows us much more clearly the major experimental quality in Büchner's art. At a simple level, it is in effect a ballad-play, in which Woyzeck is the poor soldier, exploited and cheated, who kills his wife when she is unfaithful to him. The scenes of the dance, the killing at the pond, the wading into the pond to get rid of the knife (in the common version, the wading until he drowns) are in that mode of romantic drama which derives, not from the sophisticated romances, but from the folk-tale. It is simple, effective and limited, because it draws on the resources of common intense experience, in which the individual is not even representative; he is so integrated with ordinary humanity, and with its normal crises, that neither representation (an individual standing for others) nor individuality (in its modern sense, a man distinct from others) arises. This is clearly an important part of Büchner's inheritance, some of it directly through folk-song; but though in a technical sense experimental it is not innovating: the crisis of popular literature was not the transposition of folk-literature, that experience of a stable world in which certain traditional crises occur (husband, wife, lover); but was the redefinition of common experience in a changing, socially and philosophically conscious world. The nostalgia for ballad-experience is a nostalgia for pre-revolutionary society; it is understandable and powerful, and some kinds of literature can be made from it. But the point about Büchner is that though he received this tradition, and drew strength from it, he lived also, consciously, in a revolutionary period, philosophically and socially.

The ballad-play is there, as a late action. But the defining scenes of *Woyzeck* are in a different mode. The fact of exploitation is made actual, in a major originality. In the presence of the captain and the doctor, Woyzeck is the man being used like a trained animal: "yes, sir, Captain"; "yes, sir, Doctor": the Captain's body-servant and the Doctor's experimental creature. Woyzeck is presented in a rigidity of response against the fluent dominance of his trainers and exploiters; but he is given also—the convention gives him—an ironic radical consciousness:

> Our kind is miserable only once: in this world and the next. I think if we ever got to Heaven we'd have to help with the thunder.
>
> Us common people, we haven't got virtue. But if I could be a gentleman, and if I could have a hat and a watch and a cane, and if I could talk refined, I'd want to be virtuous, all right.

Woyzeck is not, that is to say, singly defined: he is the rigid servant, and the ironic critic. And this is not a question of complexity of character; it is a process of variation of dramatic viewpoint (what Brecht, whom these scenes indicate, called a century later "complex seeing"). The point can be reinforced by a characteristic scene, which, like the social naming of Captain and Doctor, anticipates clearly an expressionist mode. The captain and doctor are projected in a self-defining, self-exposing mode, and this is extended to the scene at the fair in which the charlatan presents a trained monkey:

> You see before you here a creature as God created it. But it is nothing this way. Absolutely nothing. Now look at what art

can do. It walks upright, wears coat and trousers, even carries a sabre. This monkey here is a regular soldier. So what if he isn't much different!

As Woyzeck the trained soldier, is shown watching this presentation of the trained animal, there is a characteristic shift of dramatic viewpoint and method: the isolation and conscious inspection of a distortion which repeats, in an acted image, a distortion already directly presented. In scenes like this, Büchner is pioneering an objective-critical mode which is a deeply innovating dramatic response to a changed position in popular experience. It is what he had expressed in simple argument in his revolutionary pamphlet *The Hessian Courier*.

These two modes—of the folk-tale and of conscious and self-conscious criticism—are interwoven with a third: the confused relation between Nature and man's nature—the animal and the social being. This association of themes is a particular structure of feeling, which is as much historical as it is personal: the three themes commonly occur, in very complex relations, in romantic literature (they are all present, for example, in Wordsworth). At the same time, Büchner's intensity is so great that each element, as it is expressed, rises to a temporary dominance. It is interesting that he does not express the complicated relations to nature in the consciously recovered simplicity of the ballad. Where Woyzeck speaks traditionally in his folk-role, and with a clear bitter irony in his critical role, he speaks, in this natural relation, in a desperate inarticulate imagery:

Like when the sun stops at noon, and it's like the world was going up in fire? That's when I hear a terrible voice saying things to me.

Did you ever see the shapes the toadstools make when they grow up out of the earth? If only somebody could read what they say.

A fire's sailing around the sky and a noise coming down like trumpets.

And he passes through this imagery—of an unrealizable relation to natural forces—into a self-questioning, a general questioning, which is the philosophical revolt:

What is Man? Bones. Dust, sand, dung. What is Nature? Dust, sand, dung. But poor stupid Man, stupid Man. We must be friends. If only you had no courage, there would be no science. Only Nature: no amputation, no articulation. What is this? Woyzeck's arm, flesh, bones, veins. What is this? Dung. Why is it rooted in dung? Must I cut off my arm? No, Man is selfish, he beats, shoots, stabs his own kind.

And he arrives through this at an alienation and a despair:

> Every man's a chasm. It makes you dizzy when you look down in.
>
> Look, a beautiful, hard, grey sky. You'd almost like to pound a nail in up there and hang yourself on it.

He becomes, in this despair, what the Captain had taunted him with being:

> Running through the world like an open razor, you're liable to cut someone.

What Büchner is then doing, in *Woyzeck*, is reaching out, through an intense association of themes and images, to the dramatization of a complicated process which he seeks to embody in this single figure: materializing him first this way, then that. The fertility of the play, in later minds, is not only the persistence of this intense inquiry; it is also, in the main tradition, a separation of elements that were there historically united, so that each of the themes can be taken up and taken further. Woyzeck is a "raid on the inarticulate" in the full sense: that what is created and connected out of intense feeling is only later available for deliberate explanation. Dramatically, the excitement of *Woyzeck* is its reaching in so many directions at once; not the grasp of a single vision, from which new total conventions could be built; but the tumbling experimental touching of one intense vision after another, and the achievement of conventions which for a scene, for a group of scenes, express and control this, and then this. When the play is used, by later writers and critics, any one of these achievements can be isolated and abstracted; indeed this is commonly so, in the process of tradition, and especially, as here, when it leaps a historical gap.

Woyzeck reaches farther than *Danton's Death*, but is for just this reason essentially fragmentary where *Danton's Death* is essentially complete. It is true that the form has been difficult to describe, but this is because it relates to a structure of feeling which has an exceptional historical precision. Woyzeck, though he reaches an objective-critical consciousness, has reached also (the dramatic stages are indistinguishable) an existential despair. When he takes the knife, it is not, as it ought to have been, in the new consciousness, to the Captain, or perhaps to himself, but, in the folk consciousness, to another victim, to his wife. Danton, by the fact of history rather than the folk-tale, has taken the knife to the exploiters; it is on the consequences of this, at once historical and existential, that Büchner's imagination is concentrated. He takes what is at first the open chronicle form, the narrative juxtaposition of scenes, of

Shakespearean history: the Shakespearean reminiscences, in the crowd-scenes and in the introspection, are obvious. But what he defines through this is original: a unique though now recognizable kind of post-revolutionary experience: at once the acceptance of historical forces, and a personal alienation from them. Both factors must be stressed. In modern Marxist criticism, Danton is seen as being called to account for his turning-away from the revolution. In modern bourgeois criticism, Danton is seen as discovering a permanent human isolation, against the noisy rhetoric of change. Each interpretation is reductive, and quite evidently wrong: the Marxist because what arraigns Danton is in explicit detail corrupt and corrupting; the bourgeois because the isolation is in the same explicit detail depraved and depraving. The action of the play is in fact the connection between these processes: a relation, and a tension, between the revolution and its consequences. What is taken, characteristically, is not a history in the chronicle sense, but a history in the critical sense: a revelation of a movement at its crisis.

It is a counterpoint, of a terrible kind. Danton says, rightly:

> Everything we build today is of human flesh.

And this is also what Saint-Just says:

> Every link in the chain of this argument translated into reality has cost human lives.

It is the moment at which this is clear, after the revolutionary break-through, that Büchner chooses:

> For how much longer must the footprints of Liberty be graves?

If it were not a necessary revolution, this would not be a necessary question. It is what happens inside the revolutionary consciousness, not at an indifferent or conservative distance, that then counts in the play. Arguing for the continuation of the terror, Saint-Just says:

> Is it so astounding then that the great flood of the revolution tosses up its dead at every bend and turn?

Danton, facing execution, is thinking in the same terms:

> What does it matter? The flood of the Revolution can toss up our bodies where it likes, but they'll still be able to pick up our fossilized bones and smash in the heads of kings with them.

On that general movement, the action agrees, but within it, necessarily, there is another movement: what Danton summarizes, in a defining phrase:

Liberty and whores are the most cosmopolitan things under the sun.

In the breakdown of normal relationships, in the direct disruption of change, ideas and people are in fact disintegrated. Danton can contrast his life among the whores with Robespierre's deformed puritanism; but then both are destructive: the people still cry in the streets that their daughters are being turned into whores by the supposed leaders of the revolution; they cry also for bread, and are given another head in a basket. At the level of formal distortion, the rhetoric of liberty becomes more abstract, more hating, more irrelevant. Meanwhile, in the personal distortion, Danton reaches a stage of exhaustion, of a collapse of the centre of his being, which prevents him from acting in time to save his own life, and which makes every voice and action absurd: "enough to make you burst out laughing in the street". He is executed, after a valid denunciation of his executioners in the name of the revolution, which is also a denunciation of his own inaction—an effort made too late. Lucille's defiant cry at the end—"Long live the King"—is a reaction, strictly, to which the terror has brought her and others. It follows, in its absurdity, from a genuine recognition:

Everything has the right to live . . . The stream of life would stop if even a drop were spilt.

But the terrible realization is that it does not stop: that life goes on, through the screams of the dying, against the screams of the outraged. It is the image of man which Lucille has seen earlier, looking up at Camille in the high barred window in the prison wall:

with that long stone coat and the iron mask on your face.

It is this, in the process of revolution, which defines the need for revolution; but flesh and blood can bear only so much: in a real confusion, in the actual rush of history, they are all masked. Büchner's method is directly related to this extraordinary expression of a paradoxical stasis and loss of self in the very rush and noise of historical change. Danton's prolonged self-inquiry is absurdist and nihilist; it is also an insight, into a real condition. The scenes in the street and in the political meetings are confused, rhetorical, destructive; they are also an historical change. In this remarkable counterpoint of two modes of experience, two kinds of feeling and language, Büchner finds a form which exactly expresses and clarifies a structure: a deep internal tension, at once personal and historical, which is not resolved, but dramatized. *Woyzeck* was best understood in a desperate period of collapse and stagnation: a loss of personal identity in an arbitrary time. *Danton's Death* is being best understood in a different period: after another revolution and another terror. But then it is worth emphasizing, finally, that Büchner's genius was rooted in his own time. It was because he responded so intensely, there, that the structure of feeling became dramatic fact. What he discovered, remarkably, in dramatic method, comes through now not as a single form, but as a range of possibilities. As he is learned from, in different ways, it is also worth emphasizing that he is not only an influence; he is a dramatist standing in his own terms and in his own time.

GERHART HAUPTMANN: "THE WEAVERS"

THE writer of *Michael Kramer*, of *The Beaver Coat* and *Drayman Henschel*, of *Ulysses' Bow* and *The Sunken Bell* and *Iphigenia in Delphi*, cannot be set down as a representative of a single dramatic style. Hauptmann's work is as various as that of Strindberg, and, although deficient in power in such a comparison, is of undoubted force. I wish to treat him here, however, solely as the author of *The Weavers*. In this play Hauptmann made a significant innovation in naturalist drama, which is still of commanding importance. He looked back to Büchner, and evidently learned from him, but still what he created was new in kind.

The naturalism of *The Weavers* is not new in theory. By 1892, when the play was written, the idea of the absolutely realistic treatment of a particular segment of life was a commonplace among dramatists and critics. The work of Ibsen and Strindberg and Dumas *fils*, to mention only the most influential names, had, in its different ways, brought to maturity the naturalist drama of the family, of personal relationships. *The Weavers* was different; not only (following Zola and the novelists) did it go outside the bourgeois world in which the earlier naturalist dramatists had commonly moved; it went also outside the limited group of persons, or the family, and attempted to deal with a community. Further, it was not merely a community, in the older sense, with which Hauptmann was concerned, but a *class*. There had been earlier attempts at the dramatic treatment of working people, but none with this particular emphasis, and none of comparable power.

The action of *The Weavers* is the gathering and final eruption of a revolt among the pauperized fustian weavers of the Eulengebirge, in the 1840s. It is action, rather than plot; and this is the first of Hauptmann's major innovations. *The Weavers* is the first important example in naturalist drama of a method of realistic treatment which is fully emancipated from the ideas of plot of the older romantic drama. Strindberg's domestic plays, it is true, had abandoned plot as Ibsen had learned to understand it; but the abandonment went along with an intensification of experience and characters which was already an essential rejection of naturalism in its popular sense. Hauptmann maintains the traditional realism, but *The Weavers* is almost bare of plot and situation, in the normal definition. The one possible exception is the accidental killing of Old Hilse, which ends the play; this is very like the ironic coincidence of the intrigue drama. In general, however, *The Weavers* is a deliberate chronicle, without surprise, without uncertainty, without complication, except in so far as these are generated by the collective action of the weavers. The diverse and complex interaction of individuals, on which the romantic plot rested, is set aside here for the determinism of the operation of a class. The first act shows the weavers bringing their work for sale, and sets them in contact with their employer, his manager, the cashier, and a regular apprentice. The second act draws the circle tighter, concentrating on a pauper weaver's home. The third act moves out again, into the wider community at the inn, bringing the weavers into contact with a commercial traveller, a joiner-employer, the inn-keeper, the policeman, a smith, and a ragman. The fourth act begins from the other side, in the home of the employer, where the parson is a guest, and where a superintendent of police is called to deal with the rioting weavers; it ends with the weavers taking possession of the house. The fifth act moves the revolt to another village, and its action is set in the house of another weaver, as the rebel weavers approach to continue their destruction of the employers' houses and the factories, led by the returned soldier; it ends with the weavers fighting the soldiers who have been sent to put the revolt down. Through the whole play, within this chronicle framework, the mainspring of the action is not a matter of individuals, but of the revolt of the body of weavers, springing from their poverty.

This is an authentic dramatic theme, and Hauptmann's treatment of it, with its concentration on a general movement, is a convincing artistic decision. If one compares *The Weavers* with an almost exactly contemporary "social" play, *Widowers' Houses*, Hauptmann's method is seen to have a clear advantage over that of Shaw; *The Weavers* does not need a Lickcheese. The moving power is the event, the action, the class articulate in revolt; where this is so, situation, plot, "spokesman" characters are forms which cannot express the new theme. *The Weavers*, in this respect, is the perfect expression of its substance, and it is a very considerable achievement.

It is obviously difficult, within dramatic forms as we know them, to articulate an entire class upon the stage. This was what Hauptmann was trying to do, and it is here that we must make distinctions of success. There are two methods used in the play: first, the isolation of a smaller, representative group, the isolation of persons;

this may be seen in the Baumert family, in Becker, in the Hilse family. And second there is a method that one can perhaps best define as choral, which is the method of the first act. The first method is in the main tradition of naturalism; it is successful because the characters are not required to be anything but weavers, preoccupied with a crushing poverty and with the defences against it. It is a method, however, which challenges comparison with the novel. Hauptmann works with the characteristic fictional aids of description of scene and person, and with the commentary description of speech. The acts are convincing and powerful, but we are always aware in them of the essential limitation of the method; not only by comparison with the fuller substance of the novel, in dealing with the flow of a common reality; but also in the dependence of the dramatic effect upon visual elements which the play itself cannot finally control. In this sense, the method of the first act is most dramatic. The coming of a number of weavers to sell their webs; the creation on the stage of this group—"the weavers", the interaction of the group *as a whole*, through the successive bargainings, with the employer and his creatures; the speech which is less the speech of individual workers than a pattern of speech of the whole group; in these and similar ways Hauptmann creates in this act a sense of class—the substance of his play—with complete dramatic effect. It is a deliberate impersonal convention for the expression of an essentially impersonal force.

These two methods—the realistic presentation of the lives of workers and workers' families, and the impersonal expression of a class—have both been used in subsequent drama; the former, of course, very much more widely. They are, in fact, both present in a single later play: Sean O'Casey's *The Silver Tassie*. The first method is the most familiar, and if we judge, as I think we must, that it has produced little significant work, it is because most writers who have essayed it have lacked one or both of the two essential elements of Hauptmann's success. They have lacked his conception of action, and have blurred their effects with devices of plot of the older, romantic kind (and hardly anything could be less suitable to such a theme). They have usually lacked also Hauptmann's sureness of language. The success of attempts in the impersonal convention has also been limited by this same failure of dramatic speech.

Hauptmann's language is authentically realistic, and only rarely forced. He is not striving for *effect*, of the usual kind, but is recording. It is often believed that recording speech is the simplest of writing tasks; but it demands, in fact, an unusual kind of integrity.

I do not say that it is the highest integrity; the greatest dramatic speech is something essentially different from the process of recording. But it requires, nevertheless, an impersonality and a control, which are rare enough. It is a quality, unfortunately, that one cannot represent adequately by quotation; it is a matter of general key and tone. But it is worth emphasizing that it is through his control of recorded speech, and the significantly detailed use of dialect (see *Before Dawn* and *The Beaver Coat*) that Hauptmann is able to realize his deliberate chronicle form. It is not that he does not occasionally use speeches and songs—the traditional devices of intensification—but in *The Weavers* these are set so firmly in the continuity of recorded speech that they are themselves transformed. The revolutionary song is a proper intensification corresponding to the rising spirit of the weavers; it is not a sentimental accompaniment. The speeches at the inn have a clear difference in kind from Dr. Stockmann's speech at the audience, in the public meeting in *An Enemy of the People*.

The Weavers, then, is a successful example of a type of drama, in which, if one judged from theory alone, there should be scores of similar successes. It is a successful realistic play because its realism operates at every level of creation—action, persons, and speech, instead of being reserved merely for the convenient elements. If for nothing else (and there the judgement is more complicated) Hauptmann will be remembered in modern European drama for this rare and particular achievement.

3

BERNARD SHAW

I

THE Thing, which was foretold in the Metabiological Pentateuch, almost Happened. In 1950, Bernard Shaw, the younger contemporary of Ibsen, the contemporary of Strindberg and Chekhov, the elder contemporary of Synge and Pirandello, was still alive: outliving his epoch but also continuing to appear to embody it: a political dramatist, a socialist writer, though in European terms that now seems absurd. In real terms, the plays run from the 1890s to the 1920s, but Shaw was so able and persistent an advocate (including, of course, a steady advocacy of himself) that it was not easy to find bearings: Shaw, self-evidently, was a Modern: indeed "modern", as a description, stuck quite generally, and has continued to stick, in that self-conscious and very local transition from a Victorian to a post-1918 world.

Shaw's work in the drama began with his lively theatre reviews, and with his programmatic book, *The Quintessence of Ibsenism*, which was published in 1891. The book has to do with Ibsen only in the sense that it seriously misrepresents him; but it was one of the forces which produced in England what was known at the time as the "new drama"—a movement which was identified with J. T. Grein's Independent Theatre. At this point Shaw's position was intelligent. He was, of course, preoccupied by the censorship (a preoccupation which his personal encounters with it fully explain) and placed it as the main contributory factor in the decline of English drama. Since the suppression of Fielding's dramatic ambitions, he argued, and the driving of serious authors to the uncensored form of the novel, "the English novel has been one of the glories of literature, whilst the English drama has been its disgrace".

Shaw's analysis of the decline was not even a half-truth; but on the related question of interaction of the drama and the theatre he was right. Of the Independent Theatre he wrote:

> Every attempt to extend the repertory proved that it is the drama which makes the theatre, and not the theatre the drama. Not that this needed fresh proof, since the whole difficulty had

arisen through the drama of the day being written for the theatres instead of from its own inner necessity. Still, a thing that nobody believes cannot be proved too often.

So he proposed to re-establish the drama as a literary form, and his arguments in favour of publishing plays are powerful so far as they go. But in fact it was at this point that he surrendered to the illusions and prejudices of the theatre he was attacking.

> The fact that a skilfully written play is infinitely more adaptable to all sorts of acting than available acting is to all sorts of plays (the actual conditions thus exactly reversing the desirable ones) finally drives the author to the conclusion that his own view of his work can only be conveyed by himself. And since he could not act the play singlehanded even if he were a trained actor, he must fall back on his powers of literary expression as other poets and fictionists do.

Shaw's intuition of the acting situation, which offered either a realism which was open to the changing personalities and "interpretations" of successive actors, or on the other hand a simple theatrical virtuosity which was virtually independent of the play —the tradition of the actor-managers and actor-producers—was acute. But he seemed unable to conceive that things could be otherwise. He continued:

> So far this has hardly been seriously attempted by dramatists. Of Shakespeare's plays we have not even complete prompt copies, the folio gives us hardly anything but the bare lines. . . . If we had . . . the character sketches, however brief, by which he tried to convey to the actor the sort of person he meant him to incarnate, what a light they would shed, not only on the play, but on the history of the Sixteenth Century. . . . For want of this elaboration . . . Shakespeare, unsurpassed as poet, storyteller, character draughtsman, humorist and rhetorician, has left us no intellectually coherent drama, and could not afford to pursue a genuinely scientific method in his studies of character and society.

What (leaving aside the characteristic assumption of the "genuinely scientific method") Shaw is complaining about, is that Shakespeare did not write nineteenth-century novels. He cannot see that the "bare lines", as he calls them, constitute a work of literature that is sufficient in its own right. Shakespeare's views about his plays would, of course, be illuminating. But the plays do not suffer because Shakespeare was not his own Bradley or Verity. What Shaw calls "literary treatment" is the method of fiction rather than of drama. And he is completely characteristic in this of the views of his allies and opponents alike: for what no one seemed able to believe was that drama is capable of being a self-sufficient literary form.

> Anyone [he asserts] reading the mere dialogue of an Elizabethan play understands all but half a dozen unimportant lines of it without difficulty—

this is a proposition which it would be interesting to test—

> whilst many modern plays, highly successful on the stage, are not merely unreadable but positively unintelligible without the stage business. Recitation on a platform with the spectators seated round the reciter in the Elizabethan fashion would reduce them to absurdity.

About many modern plays he is right; but he is so much at one with the dramatists he has criticized that the only suggestion for improvement he can make is that "intellectual meaning and circumstantial conditions must be supplied by the author so that actors can understand".

In practice this means reforming the drama by making it something else. The "mere dialogue" will stay as it is, but because it is inadequate, the dramatist will turn his text into a pseudo-novel by supplying descriptions of scenery and characters, and prefaces on the subject of the drama as a whole, within which the "lines" will be interspersed. The issue, of course, is neither novel nor play, but a thing inferior to both.

In *The Quintessence of Ibsenism* Shaw misrepresented Ibsen's work as avowedly didactic. For the same reason he admired Brieux, whom he did not misrepresent. He quickly proclaimed his own similar intention:

> I must however warn my readers that my attacks are directed against themselves, not against my stage figures.

And, having rejected clandestine adultery as a subject, he

> tried slum-landlordism, doctrinaire free-love (pseudo-Ibsenism), prostitution, militarism, marriage, history, current politics, natural Christianity, national and individual character, paradoxes of conventional society, husband-hunting, questions of conscience, professional delusions and impostures, all worked into a series of comedies of manners in the classic fashion.

From this alone, the character of Shaw's work ought to be clear. It is the injection of seriousness in the drama, and seriousness means "a genuinely scientific method": "we wanted as the basis of our plays . . . a really scientific natural history". Shaw is able to tell us, by naming a problem, what each of his plays is about; and the phrase is always an adequate explanation. This is his affinity with Eugène Brieux, whose stage-manager (in *Les Avariés*) is instructed to appear and say to the audience:

> Ladies and gentlemen . . . the object of this play is a study of the disease of syphilis in its bearing on marriage.

One need not go outside the modern period to define this kind of abstraction; Ibsen had made the point, if Shaw had been prepared to listen:

> Everything which I have written as a poet has had its origin in a frame of mind and situation in life. I never wrote because I had, as they say, "found a good subject".

What Shaw was concerned to do, when he had "found a good subject", must be determined by a closer look at certain of his plays.

2

Widowers' Houses ("slum-landlordism") need not detain us; it is not Shaw at his best. It is a crude intrigue melodrama, mechanically contrived to allow Lickcheese, the rent-collector, to be explicitly rhetorical about slums, and to involve everyone on the stage in a condonation of criminality. It is very thin stuff. *The Philanderer* ("doctrinaire free-love") is more interesting, not indeed as a play, but as an element in Shaw: because whenever Shaw had to deal with personal emotion, as in this play he chose to do, certain radical weaknesses appeared. It is important to remember that when he wrote this play, he was already mature in years.

Conventional stage romance is rejected.

CRAVEN: What the dickens did he mean by all that about passing his life amid—what was it—"scenes of suffering nobly endured and sacrifice willingly rendered by womanly women and manly men"—and a lot more of the same sort? I suppose he's something in a hospital.

CHARTERIS: Hospital! Nonsense! He's a dramatic critic.

Well and good; but what are we offered instead?

JULIA [*vehemently and movingly, for she is now sincere*]: No. You made me pay dearly for every moment of happiness. You revenged yourself on me for the humiliation of being the slave of your passion for me. I was never sure of you for a moment. I trembled whenever a letter came from you, lest it should contain some stab for me. I dreaded your visits almost as much as I longed for them. I was your plaything not your companion. [*She rises, exclaiming*] Oh there was such suffering in my happiness that I hardly knew joy from pain. [*She sinks on the piano stool, and adds, as she buries her face in her hands and turns away from him*] Better for me if I had never met you.

The ideology may have shifted, but is the emotional quality of this speech (in all its stated sincerity) distinguishable at any point from the familiar rant of romantic melodrama? "Pay dearly; revenge; slave of your passion; trembled; stab; dread; your plaything not your companion; hardly knew joy from pain"; the phrases form the conventional declamatory pattern, leading up to the great theatrical moment with its familiar rhythm: the heroine turns away: "Better for me . . ." etc.

Shaw was conscious of the mechanism of such moments, as indicated here:

JULIA [*with theatrical pathos*]: You are right there. I am indeed alone in the world.

But what is the difference between that and this?

JULIA [*with deep poignant conviction*]: He cares for only one person in the world and that is himself. There is not in his whole nature one unselfish spot. He would not spend one hour of his real life with [*a sob chokes her: she rises passionately crying*] You are all alike, every one of you. Even my father only makes a pet of me.

One begins to see the point of the stage directions, of the "literary treatment": they indicate whether what is being said is burlesque or high passion. Without them, we would be hard put to know.

JULIA [*exhausted, allowing herself to take his hand*]: You are right. I am a worthless woman.
CHARTERIS [*triumphant and gaily remonstrating*]: Oh why?
JULIA: Because I am not brave enough to kill you.
GRACE [*taking her in her arms as she sinks, almost fainting away from him*]: Oh no, never make a hero of a philanderer.
[CHARTERIS, *amused and untouched, shakes his head laughingly. The rest look at Julia with concern, and even a little awe, feeling for the first time the presence of a keen sorrow.*]

That is the end of *The Philanderer*. We have been told with great care exactly how to feel and respond. Melodrama has been laughed out of court, and then brought in again by the front door, with drums playing, to be acclaimed as the all-new goddess of genuine feeling. The quality of Mr. Shaw's rejection of the current theatre, and his motives, certainly need to be questioned.

Arms and the Man is a sentimental burlesque, and much of it is very funny. It is negative, like most burlesque, and Shaw owes its success to a wise policy of rejecting romance by statement rather than by example. It is not a policy to which he was to adhere. Because:

> When a comedy is performed, it is nothing to me that the spectators laugh: any fool can make an audience laugh. I want to see how many of them, laughing or grave, are in the melting mood.

In such an interest, it would seem, he wrote *Candida*. This play is generally taken as the major work of his early years; and many of his critics have called it "a little masterpiece". In his Preface to the *Plays Pleasant* Shaw rejects certain of his earlier work (or rather comes as near rejection as his personality would allow):

> Certainly it is easy to dramatize the prosaic conflict of Christian socialism with vulgar unsocialism.

And he instances *Widowers' Houses*. But

> to distil the quintessential drama from pre-Raphaelitism, mediaeval or modern, it must be shown in conflict with the first broken, nervous, stumbling attempts to formulate its own revolt against itself as it develops into something higher. . . . The eyes of men begin to turn to a new age. Discernible at first only by the eyes of the man of genius, it must be focussed by him on the speculum of a work of art, and flashed back from that into the eyes of the common man. Nay, the artist himself has no other way of making himself conscious of the ray; it is by a blind instinct that he keeps on building up his masterpieces until their pinnacles catch the glint of the unrisen sun. . . . He cannot explain it; he can only show it to you as a vision in the magic glass of his artwork. . . . And this is the function that raises dramatic art above imposture and pleasure hunting, and enables the dramatist to be something more than a skilled liar and pander.

Of this vision, he tells us, he availed himself in *Candida*. The conflict is between Christian socialism and the magic vision: personalized in the conflict of Morell and Marchbanks for the love of Candida. What, then, are these pinnacles, on which we may concentrate to the exclusion of the Cockney speculator and Prossy the typist and Lexy the curate? (It is one of Shaw's recurrent techniques to shorten the names of his characters: either his grand personages, like B.B. in *The Doctor's Dilemma*, for an obvious deflationary effect; or his young women, like Savvy in *Back to Methuselah*, for an effect which is perhaps not so obvious.)

Here is one important moment:

CANDIDA: Are you ill, Eugene?

MARCHBANKS: No, not ill. Only horror! horror! horror!

BURGESS [*shocked*]: What! Got the 'orrors, Mr. Marchbanks! Oh that's bad at your age. You must leave it off grajally.

CANDIDA [*reassured*]: Nonsense, papa! It's only poetic horror, isn't it, Eugene? [*Petting him.*]

BURGESS [*abashed*]: Oh, poetic 'orror, is it? I beg your pardon, I'm shore. . . .

CANDIDA: What is it, Eugene?—the scrubbing brush? . . .

MARCHBANKS [*softly and musically, but sadly and longingly*]: No, not a scrubbing brush, but a boat—a tiny shallop to sail away in, far from the world, where the marble floors are washed by the rain and dried by the sun; where the south wind dusts the beautiful green and purple carpets. Or a chariot! to carry us up into the sky, where the lamps are stars, and don't need to be filled with paraffin oil every day.

MORELL [*harshly*]: And where there is nothing to do but to be idle, selfish, and useless.

CANDIDA [*jarred*]: Oh, James! How could you spoil it all?

MARCHBANKS [*firing up*]: Yes, to be idle, selfish, and useless: that is, to be beautiful and free and happy: hasn't every man desired that with all his soul for the woman he loves? That's my ideal: what's yours? . . .

CANDIDA [*quaintly*]: He cleans the boots, Eugene. . . .

MARCHBANKS: Oh, don't talk about boots! Your feet should be beautiful on the mountains.

CANDIDA: My feet would not be beautiful on the Hackney Road without boots.

BURGESS [*scandalized*]: Come, Candy: don't be vulgar. Mr. Marchbanks ain't accustomed to it. You're givin' him the 'orrors again. I mean the poetic ones.

The kind explanation of all this would be that it is burlesque again; but that it is not, that it is meant to be accepted seriously— as the "magic vision" or as the words of what William Archer called "a real poet on the stage"—is clear from the comment/ stage-direction which immediately follows:

[MORELL *is silent. Apparently he is busy with his letters: really he is puzzling with misgivings over his new and alarming experience that the surer he is of his moral thrusts, the more swiftly and effectively Eugene parries them. To find himself beginning to fear a man whom he does not respect afflicts him bitterly.*]

This, then, is the conflict. I do not know how it is possible to assume that it is a real conflict: an experience, that is to say, which survives serious attention. Both attitudes are abstract; and one, at least, is hollow: a modish adolescent romanticism. Conflict of an unresolved kind, however, is certainly there; although it is not the formal conflict. The question is whether the romantic reformism of Morell is anything more than a different aspect of the naïve idealism of Marchbanks: whether the deflation of abstract conventions is not rooted in the same complex as the afflatus of conventional sentiment. One cannot understand, to put it another way, why Marchbanks and Morell should quarrel: they have so much in common, and share at least one fundamental characteristic: emotional credulity. Whether, further, they share this with their creator is a matter for investigation.

The famous scene of Candida's choice is not reassuring: the emotional discrimination is again mechanical:

CANDIDA: And you, Eugene? What do you offer?
MARCHBANKS: My weakness! My desolation! My heart's need!
    [. . . MORELL, *whose lofty confidence has changed into heartbreaking dread of Eugene's bid, loses all power of concealing his anxiety.* EUGENE, *strung to the highest tension, does not move a muscle.*]
MORELL [*in a suffocated voice—the appeal bursting from the depths of his anguish*]: Candida!
MARCHBANKS [*aside, in a flash of contempt*]: Coward!
CANDIDA [*significantly*]: I give myself to the weaker of the two.
    [EUGENE *divines her meaning at once: his face whitens like steel in a furnace.*]

And:

CANDIDA: One last word. How old are you, Eugene?
MARCHBANKS: As old as the world now. This morning I was eighteen. . . . In a hundred years we shall be the same age. But I have a better secret than that. Let me go now. The night outside grows impatient.
    [. . . *He flies out into the night. She turns to Morell, holding out her arms to him.*]
CANDIDA: Ah, James!
    [*They embrace. But they do not know the secret in the poet's heart.*]

Flying out into the night, with a secret in the poet's heart, is often likely to produce, as its literary complement, a certain flippancy. From this play onwards, the alternating pattern of Shaw's dramatic career was set.

3

Like Shakespeare. . . . I was a born dramatist. . . . Like Shakespeare, I had to write potboilers until I was rich enough to satisfy my evolutionary appetite . . . by writing what came to me without the least regard to the possibility of lucrative publication or performance. . . . In writing *Back to Methuselah* I threw over all economic considerations. . . .

Of Shaw's later work, *Back to Methuselah* and *Saint Joan* are the landmarks. *Back to Methuselah* was chosen by Shaw himself as his masterpiece: and *Saint Joan*—which, more than any other play, is the basis of his wide popularity—has been called "the one modern tragedy".

The link with *Candida* in *Back to Methuselah* is clear:

THE SHE-ANCIENT: Yes, child: art is the magic mirror you make to reflect your invisible dreams in visible pictures. You use a glass mirror to see your face: you use works of art to see your soul. But we who are older use neither glass mirrors nor works of art. We have a direct sense of life.

This discovery—this direct sense of life—was perhaps the secret in the poet's heart for which the night grew impatient. But is it discovery, or is it rejection?

THE HE-ANCIENT: Look at us. Look at me. This is my body, my blood, my brain; but it is not me. I am the eternal life, the perpetual resurrection. . . .
THE SHE-ANCIENT: It is this stuff [*indicating her body*] this flesh and blood and bone and all the rest of it, that is intolerable. . . .
LILITH: They have accepted the burden of eternal life . . . after passing a million goals they press on to the goal of redemption from the flesh, to the vortex freed from matter, to the whirlpool in pure intelligence that, when the world began, was a whirlpool in pure force.

Now Shaw's play, although it goes back to Eden and forward "as far as thought can reach", must not be exempted from its inevitable conditions on those grounds. It must not, that is to say, in spite of its Preface, be accepted as scientific history or prophecy. It is, inevitably, a criticism of life as we know it: but the biology does not matter, the emotional pattern does. The He- and She-Ancients (it is not only the prefixes that remind us of goats) are simply conventions of a dramatic judgement of life as Shaw had experienced it. In the play, creative evolution is merely a device: "I exploit the eternal interest of the philosopher's stone which enables men to live for ever". When this is realized, the nature of Shaw's discovery is clearer; and it does not seem unreasonable to describe it as rejection. For the experiences which Shaw explored

BERNARD SHAW

in his earlier work raised problems of adjustment which, although the night was impatient, he could not make. And now, as far as his thought could reach, all he could offer was an obliteration of the actual human situation in terms of a fantasy of "pure intelligence". The best comment is that of W. J. Turner:

> Was it an insufficiency of vital energy which led to this conservation, this shrinkage into two planes—an instinctive process of self-preservation and of self-development founded upon ambitious vanity—vanity being the isotope of passion? This may explain the peculiar forms of exhibitionism Mr. Shaw has always displayed. Passion needs an object exterior to itself by which the self is enriched. Vanity extends itself objectless in space, and *Back to Methuselah* is such an extension on a tremendous scale. As Lilith says of the Ancients (*alias* Mr. Shaw):
> "They press on to the goal of redemption from the flesh, to the vortex freed from matter, to the whirlpool in pure intelligence."
> In other words, to vanity—pure, unadulterated vanity! . . . Why does Mr. Shaw hate all "matter"—nature, the human body, works of art, all *objects*? Because matter fills space and gets in the way of the unlimited extension of Mr Shaw's thought. Mr. Shaw would fill the whole of space. Such is his vanity.

It only remains to add that this desire to be freed from the body, from this "degrading physical stuff"—is a typical fantasy. And the persistent desire to substitute some abstract ideal for the tangible facts of human living is a typical process of romanticism. The iconoclast of Romance ends, not merely as its ikon, but as its slave.

But he took a last romantic heroine—Jeanne d'Arc—and in a Preface attacked the romancers who had misrepresented her. Yet

> this, I think, is all that we can now pretend to say about the prose of Joan's career. The romance of her rise, the tragedy of her execution, and the comedy of the attempts of posterity to make amends for that execution, belong to my play and not to my preface, which must be confined to a sober essay on the facts.

"The romance of her rise"; "the tragedy of her execution"; "the comedy of making amends": these stages are a useful framework for an examination of this baffling play. Of the six scenes, the first five are devoted to Joan's rise and military career; the sixth to her trial and execution, and the epilogue to the amends. The successful part of the play is Shaw's characteristic comedy: the deflation of great names—

> Polly!! You impudent baggage, do you dare call Squire Bertrand de Poulengey Polly to my face?;

explicit satire by statement—

> We were not fairly beaten, my lord. No Englishman is ever fairly beaten;

the unromantic prince—

> If you are going to say "Son of St Louis: gird on the sword of your ancestors, and lead us to victory", you may spare your breath to cool your porridge; for I cannot do it.

All this is as good as anything he had done in his funniest plays, like *The Devil's Disciple* and *John Bull's Other Island*. The historicism (as in the discussion between Warwick and Cauchon) is more successful than anywhere else in his work; and the excellent forensic of the trial scene is mature when placed against its forerunners: Lickcheese, Caesar, the brothers Barnabas. But it is clear that Shaw has made all those qualities dependent on the success of his central figure: Joan. Unless she is positively realized, even the successful elements fall in the general disintegration.

Now the ancestry of Joan, in terms of Shaw's work, may be traced to such different figures as Marchbanks and Bluntschli; or may be represented as the projection of the Superman in human terms. We are not limited, in this genealogy, by differences of sex; with Shaw, these do not greatly matter. Joan, at one level, is energetic and free from romantic conventions. She shows up the French Court as Bluntschli showed up the Balkan army. And while the play is moving on this general plane, it is successful. Bluntschli, it will be remembered, was left largely negative: what positives he had were those of a successful businessman, to which Shaw, for ideological reasons, would not render any stressed assent. The Ancients are more complex, representing the shift from burlesque to drama. Their positive qualities, as Shaw sees them, are not only political common sense and freedom from conventional illusions (which Bluntschli shares with the early Joan); but also a rational rejection of physical complexities (a willed "redemption from the flesh") and a yearning towards the ideal of "pure force". Now these latter qualities are also the achieved positives of Marchbanks— the "secret in the poet's heart". They are also—it is by now surely obvious—the positive elements of the creation of Joan.

Joan is Shaw's conception of a Saint (the conventional name for a Superman). With her common sense about politics and fighting she is merely a sensible country girl, uncorrupted by the romantic Court. But the positive qualities of her inspiration, as Shaw sees them, are her singleness of purpose and her sexlessness. It is this latter fact which is given to account for her control over the army:

> There hasn't been a word that has anything to do with her being a woman.

For Shaw, Joan is a saint because she has subordinated the facts of her person in order to become an uncomplicated instrument of the Life Force, of "Creative Evolution". She represents the ideal of the rejection of those tiresome facts of human behaviour which complicate the conception of Progress. She represents, that is to say, a fantasy.

But the fantasy is heavily disguised, and Shaw uses all his dramatic skill to prevent it being recognized as such. He gives Joan an earthy "country accent" (Mummerset):

> Coom, Bluebeard! Thou canst not fool me. Where be Dauphin?

He gives her a solid peasant background, and an implication of normality. The result is that even those to whom the Ancients are unacceptable find Joan captivating. Yet the disguise is superficial. One remembers Marchbanks:

> This morning I was eighteen. [I am] as old as the world now.

He, too, is an Ancient. The genealogy of the Ancients, the composite Ancient of Days, is Marchbanks, the He and She, Saint Joan.

The central fact of Joan, that is to say, is no more positive than that of Marchbanks, and *Saint Joan* as a whole is very far from being the major play for which it has been taken. Her voices are acceptable: they are recognized human experience. But the full creation of Joan has no direct relation to experience: she is an uncomplicated romantic heroine, a figment.

It remains probable that the attraction of Shaw's play has only indirectly to do with the fantasy of Joan—the knight in shining armour—and most to do with the simple romance of the burning. For she passes to the simple romantic heroine in her relapse, with a very typical speech:

> I could let the banners and the trumpets and the knights and soldiers pass me and leave me behind as they leave the other women, if only I could still hear the wind in the trees, the larks in the sunshine, the young lambs crying through the healthy frost, and the blessed blessed church bells that send my angel voices floating to me on the wind. But without these things I cannot live. . . .

These familiar phrases are simply conventional romantic pathos: the mechanical evocations of nature place Shaw firmly in his period—the nature-poetics of the late Victorians and Georgians. It is the pathos which moves on precisely to the "glow and flicker of the fire . . . reddening the May daylight", and to the "heartrending sobs" of the Chaplain who has watched her execution. With the fantasies of "pure force" superseded, and faced by the human fact of death, Shaw collapses into melodrama. And when, in the Epilogue, he has made the point about the mechanics of her canonization, he pushes home his advantage with the characteristic appeal to the sentiment of the audience—the structure of the *play*'s emotion set aside:

> O God that madest this beautiful earth, when will it be ready to receive Thy Saints? How long, O Lord, how long?

The rhetoric finds its mark at the pit of the stomach, hammering the audience into consciousness of an experience. For Joan's self-pity involves the accepting audience; she has behaved as we would like to behave (but do not) and the pity of the world's rejection of her is the pity of the world's rejection of that imagined element in us. Shaw has redeemed and embellished our fantasies, and we are properly grateful. But for how long, how long?

4

Shaw's dynamic as a dramatist has now largely weakened, and it is difficult to believe that it ought, as a major force, to survive the period of which he was a victim. Respect for his ability to laugh at a great deal of persistent nonsense will certainly endure; and respect for his great wit and for his skill in forensic and burlesque which made the willingness literary fact. But the emotional inadequacy of his plays is increasingly obvious, as the Edwardian screen falls. He withered the tangible life of experience in the pursuit of a fantasy of pure intelligence and pure force, and even these, as we look back at them, seem no more than conventional gestures. In this sense, a comment of his own in another context is apt:

> One hardly knows which is the more appalling: the abjectness of the credulity or the flippancy of the scepticism.

As one always expected, Shaw himself has the last word.

4

D. H. LAWRENCE:
"THE WIDOWING OF MRS. HOLROYD"

BETWEEN 1909 and 1914, when he was writing his first novels
and stories, D. H. Lawrence wrote several plays: *A Collier's Friday
Night* (1909); *The Daughter-in-Law* and *The Widowing of Mrs.
Holroyd* (1911); *The Married Man, The Merry-go-Round* and *The
Fight for Barbara* (1912-13). He said in a letter in 1913:

> I believe that, just as an audience was found in Russia for
> Tchekhov, so an audience might be found in England for some
> of my stuff, if there were a man to whip 'em in. It's the producer
> that is lacking, not the audience. I am sure we are sick of the
> rather bony, bloodless drama we get nowadays—it is time for a
> reaction against Shaw and Galsworthy and Barker and Irishy
> (except Synge) people—the rule and measure mathematical
> folk.

In effect the audience was not found, and Lawrence left the plays.
He wanted to revise *The Widowing of Mrs. Holroyd* when it was
eventually produced in the twenties, on the strength of his reputation
as a novelist, and he revised *The Married Man* in 1926. He went back
to drama only in 1920 with *Touch and Go*, and a scriptural play,
David, in 1926.

Lawrence identified the problem correctly. He was writing plays
of working class life, outside the modes of the contemporary theatre.
It was natural for him to think of Chekhov as a predecessor, and he
admired Synge, who had found a theatre:

> Tchekhov is a new thing in drama.
> *Riders to the Sea* is about the genuinest bit of dramatic tragedy,
> English, since Shakespeare, I should say.

He was interested in a kind of play which, without theatrical
devices, embodied a rhythm of ordinary life.

> I don't want to write like Galsworthy nor Ibsen, nor Strindberg,
> nor any of them, not even if I could. We have to hate our im-
> mediate predecessors, to get free from their authority.

But in fact he had found his relevant predecessors, and given their relations with a theatre could have extended not only his own plays, but the possibilities of English drama at that time.

As it is, the plays overlap with the novels and stories. *A Collier's Friday Night* is very close to *Sons and Lovers*; *Touch and Go* is an extension of the Gerald of *Women in Love* into a miners' strike; *The Daughter-in-Law* belongs with the early mining stories. In this last play, particularly, all Lawrence's gifts for a precise form of speech— the rhythms of a dialect which is not just a variant of printed English but the shape and sound of a particular way of living—are as evident as anywhere in the stories, and he is able to isolate the open tensions and subtle shifts of relationship in a dramatic rhythm which belongs with the speech. He was driven back from the attempt, by a cultural barrier; in this as elsewhere he had to endure the reaction represented by Katharine Mansfield's reaction to *Touch and Go* as "*black* with miners". And it is then not easy to separate this kind of cultural difficulty—the lack of a people's theatre; the prejudice against working life in its own terms—from the other kind of difficulty which would in any case have been there: the adequacy of this particular naturalist form to his whole range of experience. By the time of *Touch and Go* it is the later, separated Lawrence: attitudes *to* mining life, general social argument, speechmaking explicit and implicit, in the shape of the dialogue. *A Married Man*, *The Merry-go-Round* and *The Fight for Barbara*, though relatively early, are the other available tone: a jollying, slangy talk, around the relationships. The real test comes when he is writing from the direct rhythms of the experience, as in *The Daughter-in-Law* and *The Widowing of Mrs. Holroyd*. And for the particular point that has been raised—the relation between what could be done in fiction and in this kind of dramatic naturalism— *The Widowing of Mrs. Holroyd* is the play to consider, because it is another version of the experience in the fine early story *Odour of Chrysanthemums*.

Lawrence defined the experience differently, in the play and the story. In the story he begins from the mining country, and the train moving through it. This is not simply landscape: it is a definition of the relations between men and things in this place—

> The trucks thumped heavily past, one by one, with slow inevitable movement, as she stood insignificantly trapped between the jolting black waggons and the hedge.

In the play, in what is in effect a trapped interior, this cannot be shown, though in a way the crisis depends on it. And yet it is not that it is undramatic; it is simply that there is an absence, in this stage-as-room, of the necessary dramatic scene: the pressing visual and auditory rhythm. Lawrence describes the interior with his usual care (he is even more specific in *A Collier's Friday Night*), but this, though it can be built, is a static environment, whereas in the story he can move, for emphasis, from point to point within it: again a dramatically feasible method, but not in this mode.

In the play Lawrence extends and complicates the action. Mrs. Holroyd, in the play, has the young electrician, Blackmore, as the responsive man who shows her the inertness that her marriage has become. In the story this is assumed, in description: "her mouth was closed with disillusionment". Again, in the play, her husband brings home two women he has met in the pub; the relationship is acted right through, to the point where the husband comes home drunk and is settled for sleep in the living-room: the action which prefigures the climax when he is brought home dead from the pit accident, and is laid out and washed in the same room. It is a fuller action, and prepares more deeply for the crisis.

But then it is just in this crisis that Lawrence is able to write in the story what he could not write in this kind of play. As the dead man is brought home, the play is stronger: the miners' world enters, fully and substantially; achieved in speech where the story, as shown earlier, worked by movement and description. But the crisis is when she is left alone with the naked body: the flow of pity and shame over the dead relationship that is now, momentarily, in the flesh, alive again. Lawrence is held back, here, in the play. The woman speaks, alone, but briefly, in a limited convention:

> . . . Did it hurt you?—oh, my dear, it hurt you—oh, I can't bear it. No, things aren't fair—we went wrong, my dear. I never loved you enough—I never did . . .

In the story, at the same point:

> her mind, cold and detached, said clearly: "Who am I? What have I been doing? I have been fighting a husband who did not exist. *He* existed all the time. What wrong have I done? What was that I have been living with? There lies the reality, this man."

But this detached voice is not the only one, for the story can use several voices, to show both the confusion and the intensity of the response, and to move between the woman as defined by her immediate circumstances and the woman in the deeper rhythms of her life and a common life:

> The eyes, half shut, did not show glazed in the obscurity. Life with its smoky burning gone from him, had left him apart and

utterly alien to her. . . . In her womb was ice of fear, because of this separate stranger with whom she had been living as one flesh.

It is an experience the play can represent only obliquely: by the silent product of the action. The story is so much stronger, in this last crisis, that there is hardly a comparison; it moves into a different world. We can see, clearly enough, the limitations of the form Lawrence chose for the play, at just this point of intensity and extension. Yet it is more than a negative point. Lawrence, more than any other English novelist, brought the speaking voice and every-day language into his narrative, descriptive, analytic prose. It is only just a step—but a step the narrowness of dramatic habit prevents him from taking—to this control by the voice through the whole dramatic rhythm, reaching out, at crisis, to the woman speaking to the body and to herself in a number of voices. It is not, that is to say, some intrinsic superiority of "impersonal" prose; it is just the failure of a speech convention, in the limited form he was trying to adapt to, and from which he got all the available strengths. He did not choose a more common solution: the projection into atmosphere; the overt theatrical shaping. As he said later:

> To me, even Synge, whom I admire very much indeed, is a bit too rounded off and, as it were, put on the shelf to be looked at. I can't bear art that you can walk round and admire.

It was a refusal of what had seemed a solution, but it is not, neces-sarily, a refusal of drama. He stays close to the internal rhythms, as carried by voices; unemphatic, ungestured, ending very quietly: a dramatic connection, if the full rhythm of voices, and especially a corresponding rhythm of the life which is there all around them, in the mining country, counterpointing the voices, could have been carried right through. It was not carried through, for the different reasons we have noted; but the relevant conclusion is not that Lawrence was "always really a novelist; the novelist got the upper hand in his plays". It is that the dramatic climate, in audiences and expectations, in habits and external conventions, prevented him, clearly, from carrying through a very serious intention: to the disadvantage of English drama as much as to his own disadvantage. What he did, as many others have done, was to settle for that form —the novel—in which he could make his own rules, on his own, without negotiation: a liberation, since the novels are very important; but also a separation, a loss, since those voices, directly, had mattered so much, and needed, dramatically, to be heard.

5

ERNST TOLLER:
"HOPPLA! SUCH IS LIFE!"

WHAT we now understand by expressionism is a complicated movement, and we shall have to distinguish its different and even contradictory phases. The essential creative turn, towards a method that can be called expressionist, had been made in the later work of Strindberg. But the consciousness of a movement belonged to Germany, from the years immediately before 1914. As one looks from, say, Wedekind to Kaiser, a common element is quite clear, but there are also marked differences, beyond the personal variations. It is indeed necessary to distinguish what can be called an individual expressionism, in which the modes of polarization, typification and distortion are related to the exploration of subjective and even isolate experience. This, after all, is where Strindberg had begun, in *The Road to Damascus*, and its emphasis continued, in what were called both "expressionist" and "symbolist" plays. Yet the same modes were widely used for a different exploration: the characterization, often critical and even revolutionary, of a social system. Certainly the landmarks of the expressionist theatre are primarily social plays: Kaiser's *From Morn till Midnight*, Capek's *R.U.R.*, Rice's *The Adding Machine*. In England O'Casey built expressionism into a realistic play, in *The Silver Tassie*. Auden and Isherwood united the personal and social modes of analysis in plays like *The Ascent of F6*, which show, among other influences, the very direct influence of Toller.

Masses and Man is perhaps the most striking theme in Toller's drama, but its dramatic method is relatively narrow. The character of Gene in *Hinkemann* is a very powerful creation, and the interpenetration of pity and laughter has considerable effect. *The Machine Wreckers*, a play about the Luddites, is not very successful; among other things, it challenges too close a comparison with Hauptmann's *The Weavers*, and its inferiority in the comparison is clear. *Draw the Fires* is similarly based on a realistic set of events, but modified by expressionist presentation. The best example, however, is none of these, but *Hoppla!* which appeared in 1927.

The action of the play passes in Germany in 1927, with a prologue set in 1919. The prologue shows a group of condemned revolutionaries, waiting for execution. At the last moment, the death-sentence is commuted to imprisonment, for all the condemned except one, Wilhelm Kilman, who is secretly released. In the play, Karl Thomas, one of the condemned, is just released from his detention. Kilman, meanwhile, has become Prime Minister, and an enemy of the revolution. The action consists of the exploration and rediscovery of society by Karl Thomas, and ends with his imprisonment on a false charge and with his suicide.

The function of the play, clearly, is the analysis of society, with Karl Thomas as its agent. It is this analysis that the various expressionist devices serve. The first and most surprising device is the use of film, projected on to a screen on the stage. This is designed to show the larger outline of social events, within which the particular events of the stage action are to be understood. Thus:

On the screen

SCENES FROM THE YEARS 1919-27

Among them Karl Thomas, walking backward and forward in a madhouse cell, wearing the uniform of the institution.

1919: Treaty of Versailles.
1920: Stock Exchange uneasiness in New York—People go mad.
1921: Fascism in Italy.
1922: Hunger in Vienna—people go mad.
1923: German Inflation—people go mad.
1924: Death of Lenin in Russia. Placard. Death of Luise Thomas.
1925: Gandhi in India.
1926: Fighting in China. Conference of European leaders in Europe.
1927: Face of clock. The hands move, first slowly, then more and more quickly. Noises. Clocks.

This is the use as historical outline. Elsewhere, film is used, first to show the present social condition of women, as a prelude to the reintroduction of Eva Berg, one of the revolutionaries; and second, to show the conditions of the workers, as a prelude to an election.

Similar to the use of film is the use of wireless. There are loud-speaker reports of contemporary world events:

Unrest in India. . . . Unrest in China. . . . Unrest in Africa. . . . Paris. Paris. Houbigant the fashionable perfume. . . . Bucharest. Bucharest. Famine in Romania. . . . Berlin. Berlin. Elegant ladies delight in green wigs.

At times these wireless reports are reinforced by films of the events which they describe. The wireless is also used in the election, to announce the results of the voting. In other plays, such as *Hinkemann*, Toller uses newspaper headlines as a similar background.

Late-night final. Sensational news. New night club opened. Stomach dances. Jazz. Champagne. American bar. Late-night final. Latest sensation. Jews massacred in Galicia. Synagogue burnt down. A thousand burnt to death.

Within an outline described in this way, Toller sets his specific scenes. In *Hoppla!* these range from bedroom to police court, but the principal are a lunatic asylum and a Grand Hotel. These are staged in a general structure of a scaffolding divided into several floors. The hotel, for example, has the wireless station at the top of the scaffolding, three lines of rooms below, which are illuminated in turn as the scenes turn to the various characters occupying them, and at the base the staff room and the vestibule. The same structure is used for the prison in which the play ends, with particular cells illuminated in turn. To observe Toller's method in specific scenes, we can look at part of the second scene of Act Three, which is set in the hotel. The first episode is in a private room, where Kilman, the former revolutionary, is being entertained by a financier:

KILMAN: The Service wears me out. People think it means sitting in armchairs and smoking fat cigars. Forgive me for being late. I had to receive the Mexican Minister.
FINANCIER: Let's make a start.
[*They all sit at table. Waiter brings food.*]

The second episode is in the wireless station. Karl Thomas, who is a waiter at the hotel, listens with the operator to the world reports that have been quoted. The third episode is in a Clubroom, a meeting of the Union of Brainworkers:

PHILOSOPHER X: Listen, Comrade Waiter, young proletarian, would you be willing to consummate the sexual act with the first attractive young woman you met, or would you first consult your instincts on the subject?
[KARL THOMAS *laughs aloud.*]
CHAIRMAN: This isn't a laughing matter. The question is serious. Moreover, we are customers of your employer and you are the waiter.
KARL THOMAS: Oho, first "Comrade Waiter" and now "Keep your place". You wish to redeem the proletariat? Here, in the Grand Hotel, eh? What would happen to you if it were redeemed? Where would *you* be? Back in the Grand Hotel? Eunuchs!

VOICES: Scandalous. Scandalous.
   [KARL THOMAS *goes.*]
PHILOSOPHER X: Lower-middle-class idea merchant!
CHAIRMAN: We come now to the second item of the agenda.
   Proletarian communal love, and the problem of the intelli-
   gentsia . . .

The fourth episode returns to the financier's entertainment of
Kilman; he is advising the Prime Minister to play the stock market.
A political innocent from the provinces, Pickel, enters to seek
advice, and is sent away. The fifth episode shows a briefing of
journalists for a propaganda campaign; the sixth a nationalist
Count in bed with the daughter of the Prime Minister—the girl is
also a Lesbian. The seventh episode is in the staff-room: the hotel-
porter has had his life's savings reduced to the price of a box of
matches by inflation—he has turned to gambling.

Karl Thomas is called with drinks to the Count's room, and then
takes a revolver to answer a call to the room in which the Prime
Minister is being entertained. An intermediate episode shows the
Count preparing a student to assassinate the Prime Minister for the
nationalist cause. The final episode shows Thomas confronting
Kilman:

> THOMAS: . . . When we waited together in a common grave
> we didn't stand on ceremony. . . .
> KILMAN [*to Financier*]: Owing to some romantic episode in his
> youth he went off the rails.

The Student, disguised as a waiter, enters the room quietly,
switches off the light, and shoots Kilman over Thomas's shoulder.

A play like *Hoppla!* requires considerable discrimination in
judgement. A common reaction is to call Toller's political views
extremist, and so dismiss the play. But this is evasion: "extremist"
and "moderate" are simply names for different sides. In any
complicated society, in which major social forces are bound to
appear as in many respects impersonal, the schematic, typifying
method of expressionism may in fact reveal more than immediate,
"unexaggerated" description or reproduction. It is not at that
general level that the difficulty comes. It is a question, really, of
consistency between this particular convention and the underlying
reading of social experience. In *Hoppla!* the panorama unrolls, but
increasingly one has the impression that it *shows* nothing. For there
is at the root of Toller's art a profound doubt:

> In my political capacity, I proceed upon the assumption that
> units, groups, representatives of social forces, various economic

functions have a real existence; that certain relations between human beings are objective realities. As an artist, I recognize that the validity of these "facts" is highly questionable.

And again:

The plays collected in this volume are social dramas and tragedies. They bear witness to human suffering, and to fine yet vain struggles to vanquish this suffering. For only unnecessary suffering can be vanquished, the suffering which arises out of the unreason of humanity, out of an inadequate social system. There must always remain a residue of suffering, the lonely suffering imposed upon mankind by life and death. And only this residue is necessary and inevitable, is the tragic element of life and of life's symbolizer, art.

It is a known and persistent uncertainty, but it is difficult to feel that Toller ever resolved the tension which the recognition implies, or expressed its irresolution, in his art. The intelligent doubt, the personal reservation, remains in the social plays, not as an element of communication, but as an almost sardonic disintegrator. The frantic typification seems at times, in *Hoppla!*, in *Hinkemann*, in *Transfiguration*, a deliberate, virtually hysterical attempt to repress an alternative consciousness. This very real hysterical element in Toller does not reside in the violence and clarity of his political views, but rather in the attempt to repress a part of the pattern of his experience, which has too much vitality to be simply and easily neglected.

The power of *Hoppla!* and of the other plays is primarily a spectacular power. The language is as deliberately general and unspecific as the visual panorama. Its method is essentially that of the slogan; it very rarely has any power to surprise or, in its own right, to convey emotion. It is a slogan summary of experience, and too many of the slogans are too familiar even to interest. This is especially so in his deliberately expressionist episodes, such as those in the hotel; it is true also of his longer single scenes, where he writes in an explicit kind of naturalism. Hinkemann's whole experience is summed up in his saying:

The world has lost its soul and I have lost my sex

—the slogan again.

It is very common, in England, to be patronizing about the expressionist experiment, and to remind readers that it was mainly *German* expressionism, which presumably settles its inferiority. It depends where you criticize from. When expressionist drama is set against the classics of naturalism, it seems angular and one-dimensional: a lively but temporary art. Yet, in certain of its methods, it surpassed naturalism in its capacity for consciousness, and it is this that indicates its lasting importance: a possibility—of course at some cost—of penetrating customary relationships and a known world. Out of what seemed a breakdown—a lively break-down—a new dramatic world was in fact to come.

6

ARTHUR MILLER

IN the vigour of American life and speech, many elements of European drama found new variants and successes. Eugene O'Neill was directly inspired by Strindberg, but in *Anna Christie* and *Desire under the Elms* the significant element is the liveliness of the vernacular: a discovery of the resources of popular speech comparable in strength and intention to that of the Irish dramatists. O'Neill, in fact, had other and complicating dramatic purposes: the paradox of his work is his success in the vernacular and his increasing attachment to what is essentially isolated experience—a discovery or imposition of internally determined and abstract patterns (the success and failure of these modes is indicated in the analyses of *Mourning Becomes Electra* and *Long Day's Journey into Night*). In the 1920s, there was a vigorous American expressionist theatre, moving from O'Neill's *Emperor Jones* and *The Hairy Ape* to Elmer Rice's *The Adding Machine*, and in the 1930s there was a further lively experiment in radical dramatic forms, as in Odets' *Waiting for Lefty*.

This important and native experimental tradition is not easy to bring into focus with the contemporary European tradition in which many of the innovating forms had been discovered. It was perhaps only after 1945, and then from the cinema even more than the theatre, that the current of serious influence began to flow the other way. The major American dramatist remains Eugene O'Neill, but it was in Arthur Miller, in those post-war years, that the American tradition seemed most lively and fertile. While lacking O'Neill's range, he was also easier to understand. The strange and restless genius of O'Neill was perhaps only clearly understood in the posthumous plays of the middle-late 1950s.

Meanwhile the work of Tennessee Williams was intensely influential in the theatre: following Strindberg and early O'Neill it remains a classic instance of the dramatization of intensely private and destructive passion; it is, in a literal sense, drama on a hot tin roof: the direct communication, to the nerves of an audience, of raw and essentially inarticulate experience: with the strengths of popular music and of an intensely personal kind of acting or acting-

267

out; but with the dramatic design, often locally effective, revealing itself essentially as a highly professional theatrical contrivance. The line from *Lady Julie* to *Cat on a Hot Tin Roof* is obvious enough, in its strengths; but it represents also a domestication of that strangeness, a professional appropriation and exploitation of the methods of dramatic disturbance. It has of course in this respect been very widely imitated. There is now an effective sub-culture of just this kind of direct exposure of harsh and disintegrated feeling. In its strengths and weaknesses it seems to relate directly to an assenting structure of feeling in its audiences, and it is understandable that in this sense it has broken out of drama and the theatre and is finding, as it must find, less conventional and less independent forms: the completion of its own internal logic, which requires an assenting participation in a temporary accentuation and release of disturbance.

Arthur Miller, by comparison, is a traditional figure, but his works have an independence of occasion which contrasts very markedly with this alternative American tradition. His first two published plays—he had written seven or eight others before getting the recognition of production—were *All My Sons* (1947) and *Death of a Salesman* (1949). These show very well some of the problems of the post-war dramatist, in relating method to experience. For their themes, obviously, are very deeply linked, but their methods show a very marked contrast. *All My Sons* has been described as an Ibsenite play, and certainly, if we restrict Ibsen to the kind of play he wrote between *The League of Youth* (1869) and *Rosmersholm* (1886), it is a relevant description. The similarities are indeed so striking that we could call *All My Sons* pastiche if the force of its conception were not so evident. It is perhaps that much rarer case, of a writer who temporarily discovers in an existing form an exact way of realizing his own experience. At the centre of the play is the kind of situation which was Ibsen's development of the device of the "fatal secret". Joe Keller, a small manufacturer, has (in a similar way to Consul Bernick in *Pillars of Society*) committed a social crime for which he has escaped responsibility. He acquiesced in the sending of defective parts to the American Air Force in wartime, and yet allowed another man to take the consequences and imprisonment. The action begins after the war, and is basically on the lines of what has been called Ibsen's retrospective method (it was always much more than a device of exposition; it is a thematic forcing of past into present). The Ibsen method of showing first an ordinary domestic scene, into which, by gradual infiltration, the crime and the guilt enter and build up to the critical eruption, is exactly followed. The process of this destructive infiltration is carefully worked out in terms of the needs of the other characters—Keller's wife and surviving son, the girl the son is to marry, the neighbours, the son of the convict—so that the demonstration of social consequence, and therefore of Keller's guilt, is not of any abstract principle, but of personal needs and relationships, which compose a reality that directly enforces the truth. If Keller's son had not wanted to marry the convicted man's daughter (and they had been childhood friends; it was that neighbourhood which Keller's act disrupted); if his wife, partly in reaction to her knowledge of his guilt, had not maintained the superstition that their son killed in the war was still alive; if the action had been between strangers or business acquaintances, rather than between neighbours and neighbouring families, the truth would never have come out. Thus we see a true social reality, which includes both social relationships and absolute personal needs, enforcing a social fact—that of responsibility and consequence. This is still the method of Ibsen in the period named, and the device of climax—a concealed letter from Keller's dead son, who had known of his father's guilt—is again directly in Ibsen's terms.

The elements of theatrical contrivance in Ibsen's plays of this kind, and in *All My Sons*, are now sufficiently clear. Yet the total effect of such a play is undoubtedly powerful if its experience truly corresponds to its conventions. In historical terms, this is a bourgeois form, with that curious combination of a demonstrated public morality and an intervening fate, evident in the early eighteenth-century domestic drama, and reaching its maturity in Ibsen. To a considerable extent, *All My Sons* is a successful late example of this form, but a point is reached, in Miller's handling of the experience, where its limits are touched. For, as he rightly sees it, the social reality is more than a mechanism of honesty and right dealing, more than Ibsen's definition—

The spirits of Truth and Freedom, these are the pillars of society.

Miller reaches out to a deeper conception of relationships, which he emphasizes in his title. This is something more than honesty and uprightness; it is the quite different social conception of human brotherhood—

I think to him they were all my sons. And I guess they were, I guess they were.

Moreover, Miller sees this in a social context, as he explains in the Introduction to his *Collected Plays:*

> Joe Keller's trouble . . . is not that he cannot tell right from wrong
> but that his cast of mind cannot admit that he, personally, has
> any viable connection with his world, his universe, or his society.
> He is not a partner in society, but an incorporated member, so to
> speak, and you cannot sue personally the officers of a corporation.
> I hasten to make clear that I am not merely speaking of a literal
> corporation but the concept of a man's becoming a function of
> production or distribution to the point where his personality
> becomes divorced from the actions it propels.

This concept, though Miller does not use the term, is the classical
Marxist concept of alienation, and it is with alienation both in a
social action and in a personality that Miller is ultimately concerned.
The true social reality—the needs and destinies of other persons—
is meant to break down this alienated consciousness, and restore
the fact of consequence, of significant and continuing relationships,
in this man and in his society. But then it is at this point that the
limits of the form are damaging. The words I have quoted, expressing Keller's realization of a different kind of consciousness, have to
stand on their own, because unlike the demonstration of ordinary
social responsibility they have no action to support them, and
moreover as words they are limited to the conversational resources
so adequate elsewhere in the play, but wholly inadequate here to
express so deep and substantial a personal discovery (and if it is
not this it is little more than a maxim, a "sentiment"). It is at this
point that we see the naturalist form—even a principled naturalism,
as in Ibsen and Miller and so rarely in others; even this substantially
and powerfully done—breaking down as it has so often broken down,
because the consciousness which the form was designed to express
is in any serious terms obsolete, and was already, by Miller himself,
being reached beyond.

There is an interesting account, in Miller's Introduction, of the
genesis of *All My Sons*, relating it to a previous play and the discovery
that

> two of the characters, who had been friends in the previous drafts,
> were logically brothers and had the same father. . . . The overt
> story was only tangential to the secret drama which its author
> was quite unconsciously trying to write. . . . In writing of the
> father-son relationship and of the son's search for his relatedness
> there was a fullness of feeling I had never known before. The
> crux of *All My Sons* was formed; and the roots of *Death of a
> Salesman* were sprouted.

This is extremely important, not only as a clue to the plays named,
but as indicating the way in which Miller, personally, came to the

experience expressible as that of human brotherhood. In any sense that matters, this concept is always personally known and lived; as a slogan it is nothing. And the complicated experience of inheritance from a father is perhaps one of the permanent approaches to this transforming consciousness. There is the creative complexity of the fact that a son, in many senses, replaces his father. There is dependence and the growth to independence, and both are necessary, in a high and moving tension. In both father and son there are the roots of guilt, and yet ultimately they stand together as men—the father both a model and a rejected ideal; the son both an idea and a relative failure. But the model, the rejection, the idea and the failure are all terms of growth, and the balance that can be struck is a very deep understanding of relatedness and brotherhood. One way of looking at *All My Sons* is in these universal terms: the father, in effect, destroys one of his sons, and that son, in his turn, gives sentence of death on him, while at the same time, to the other son, the father offers a future, and the son, in rejecting it, destroys his father, in pain and love. Similarly, in *Death of a Salesman*, Willy Loman, like Joe Keller, has lived for his sons, will die for the son who was to extend his life, yet the sons, in their different ways, reject him, in one case for good reasons, and in effect destroy him. Yet the failure on both sides is rooted in love and dependence; the death and the love are deeply related aspects of the same relationship. This complex, undoubtedly, is the "secret drama" of which Miller writes, and if it is never wholly expressed it is clearly the real source of the extraordinary dramatic energy.

Death of a Salesman takes the moment of crisis in which Joe Keller could only feebly express himself, and makes of it the action of the whole play. Miller's first image was of

> an enormous face . . . which would appear and then open up, we would see the inside of a man's head. In fact, *The Inside of His Head* was the first title.

This, in dramatic terms, is expressionism, and correspondingly the guilt of Willy Loman is not in the same world as that of Joe Keller: it is not a single act, subject to public process, needing complicated grouping and plotting to make it emerge; it is, rather, the consciousness of a whole life. Thus the expressionist method, in the final form of the play, is not a casual experiment, but rooted in the experience. It is the drama of a single mind, and moreover,

> it would be false to a more integrated—or less disintegrating—personality.

271

It is historically true that expressionism is attuned to the experience of disintegration. In general dramatic history, as in Miller's own development, it arises at that point where the limits of naturalism are touched and a hitherto stable form begins to break. Yet *Death of a Salesman* is actually a development of expressionism, of an interesting kind. As Miller puts it:

> I had always been attracted and repelled by the brilliance of German expressionism after World War I, and one aim in *Salesman* was to employ its quite marvellous shorthand for humane "felt" characterisations rather than for purposes of demonstration for which the Germans had used it.

This is a fair comment on one aspect of, say, Toller, and the split of expressionism into "personal" and "social" kinds is related to an important general dissociation of contemporary experience. *Death of a Salesman* is an expressionist reconstruction of naturalist substance, and the result is not hybrid but a powerful patricular form. The continuity from social expressionism remains clear, however, for I think in the end it is not Willy Loman as a man, but the image of the Salesman, that predominates. The social figure sums up the theme of alienation, for this is a man who from selling things has passed to selling himself, and has become, in effect, a commodity which like other commodities will at a certain point be economically discarded. The persuasive atmosphere of the play (which the slang embodies so perfectly, for it is a social result of this way of living) is one of false consciousness—the conditioned attitudes in which Loman trains his sons—being broken into by real consciousness, in actual life and relationships. The expressionist method embodies this false consciousness much more powerfully than naturalism could do. In *All My Sons* it had to rest on a particular crime, which could then be seen as in a limiting way personal—Keller the black sheep in a white flock—although the fundamental criticism was of a common way of living and thinking. The "marvellous shorthand" is perfectly adapted to exposing this kind of illusion and failure. At the same time the structure of personal relationships, within this method, must be seen as in a sense arbitrary; it has nothing of the rooted detail which the naturalism of *All My Sons* in this respect achieved. The golden football hero, the giggling woman in the hotel, the rich brother and similar figures seem to me to be clichés from the thinner world of a work like *Babbitt*, which at times the play uncomfortably resembles. The final figure of a man killing himself for the insurance money caps the whole process of the life that has been demonstrated, but "demonstrated", in spite of

Miller's comment on the Germans, is the word that occurs to one to describe it. The emotional power of the demonstration is considerable, and is markedly increased by the brilliant expressionist staging. Yet, by the high standards which Miller insists on, and in terms of the essential realism to which he seems to be reaching, the contrast of success and failure within both *All My Sons* and *Death of a Salesman* points finally to the radical and still unsolved difficulties of form.

The Crucible (1952) is a powerful and successful dramatization of the notorious witch-trials of Salem, but it is technically less interesting than its predecessors just because it is based on a historical event which at the level of action and principled statement is explicit enough to solve, or not to raise, the difficult dramatic problems which Miller had previously set himself. The importance of the witch-trials is that in them, in a clear and exciting way, the moral crisis of a society is explicit, is directly enacted and stated, in such a way that the quality of the whole way of life is organically present and evident in the qualities of persons. Through this action Miller brilliantly expresses a particular crisis—the modern witch-hunt—in his own society, but it is not often, in our own world, that the issues and statements so clearly emerge in a naturally dramatic form. The methods explored in the earlier plays are not necessary here, but the problems they offered to solve return immediately, outside the context of this particular historical event. *The Crucible* is a fine play, but it is also a quite special case.

In *A Memory of Two Mondays* (1955), Miller returns to the direct dramatization of modern living, and as if to underline the point made about *The Crucible* (of which, as the Introduction shows, he was completely aware) seeks to make a new form out of the very facts of inconsequence, discontinuity and the deep frustrations of inarticulacy, which is at once a failure of speech and the wider inability of men to express themselves in certain kinds of work and working relationship. Instead of concentrating these themes in a particular history, pointed by plot or single crisis, he deploys them in the scattered form of a series of impressions, with the dramatic centre in memory rather than in action or crisis. The work atmosphere is in some ways significantly caught, and there is always the mark of Miller's insight into the importance and passion of what many others dismiss as "ordinary" lives. There is an occasional flare of dramatic feeling, as in the last speech of Gus, but in general the tension is much lower than in the earlier plays, and the dramatic methods seem often mere devices. The Irish singer and reciter; the insets of flat sub-Auden verse; the lighting and scenic devices

of the passing of time: these, at this tension, seem mechanical. And
a central image of the play—when the workers clean the windows
to let in a sight of sun and trees, and let in actually a view of a
cat-house (brothel)—seems contrived. Miller's fertility of experiment
is important, but experiment, as here, involves failure.

A View from the Bridge (1955; revised 1957) brings back the
intensity. The capacity to touch and stir deep human feeling was
marked in the earlier plays, but Miller has said, interestingly, (it is
his essential difference from Tennessee Williams, with whom he is
often linked):

> The end of drama is the creation of a higher consciousness and
> not merely a subjective attack upon the audience's nerves and
> feelings.

The material of *A View from the Bridge* is to most people deeply
disturbing, and Miller's first impulse was to keep it abstract and
distant, to hold back

> the empathic flood which a realistic portrayal of the same tale and
> characters might unloose.

But, in his own view, he went too far in this direction, and subsequently revised the play towards a more intense realism. The
distancing element remains, however, in the use of a commentator,
or *raisonneur*, and, though there are false notes in the writing of
this part, it is an important reason for the play's success.

A View from the Bridge follows from the earlier works in that it
shows a man being broken and destroyed by guilt. Its emphasis is
personal, though the crisis is related to the intense primary relationships of an insecure and partly illegal group—a Brooklyn waterfront
slum, with ties back to Italy, receiving unauthorized immigrants and
hiding them within its own fierce loyalties. Eddie Carbone's breakdown is sexual, and the guilt, as earlier, is deeply related to love.
And the personal breakdown leads to a sin against this community,
when in the terror of his complicated jealousies Eddie betrays
immigrants of his wife's kin to the external law.

At the centre of the drama again is the form of a relationship
between parent and child, but here essentially displaced so that the
vital relationship is between a man and the niece to whom he has
been as a father. The girl's coming to adolescence provokes a
crisis which is no more soluble than if they had really been father
and child, yet to a degree perhaps is more admissible into consciousness. Eddie is shown being destroyed by forces which he cannot
control, and the complex of love and guilt has the effect of literal

disintegration, in that the known sexual rhythms break down into their perverse variations: the rejection of his wife, as his vital energy transfers to the girl, and then the shattering crisis in which within the same rush of feeling he moves into the demonstration of both incestuous and homosexual desires. The crisis burns out his directions and meanings, and he provokes his death shouting "I want my name". This establishment of significance, after breakdown, through death, was the pattern of Joe Keller and Willy Loman; of John Proctor, in heroic stance, in *The Crucible*; of Gus, in a minor key, in *A Memory of Two Mondays*. We are at the heart, here, of Miller's dramatic pattern, and his work, in this precise sense, is tragedy—the loss of meaning in life turns to the struggle for meaning by death. The loss of meaning is always a personal history, though in Willy Loman it comes near to being generalized. Equally, it is always set in the context of a loss of social meaning, a loss of meaning in relationships. The point is made, and is ratifying, in the commentary in *A View from the Bridge*:

> Now we are quite civilized, quite American. Now we settle for half . . .

and again, at the end:

> . . . Something perversely pure calls to me from his memory—not purely good, but himself purely, for he allowed himself to be wholly known and for that I think I will love him more than all my sensible clients. And yet, it is better to settle for half, it must be! And so I mourn him—I admit it—with a certain alarm.

Tempted always to settle for half—for the loss of meaning and the loss of consequence endemic in the whole complex of personal and social relationships, the American way of living as Miller sees it—the heroes of these plays, because, however perversely, they are still attached to life, still moved by irresistible desires for a name, a significance, a vital meaning, break out and destroy themselves, leaving their own comment on the half-life they have experienced. It is a powerful and connecting action.

Yet its dramatic problems remained considerable, and were illustrated, retrospectively, by Miller's most confused play, *After the Fall*, which appeared in 1964. This was said to be intensely autobiographical, but the more important point is that, under the tension reached in *A View from the Bridge*—between a virtually uncontrollable guilt and confusion, and a way of seeing just these experiences in a communicable pattern of relationships—Miller moved, in effect, to the alternative tradition: the direct exposure of inarticulate private feeling, and beyond this the essentially abstract imposition of a pattern of universal guilt. This pattern is strictly suggestive: an incoherent phrasing and gesturing of a metaphysical meaning—the separateness of every human being, the inevitability of betrayal, the reduction of social guilt to a common but incommunicable private neurosis. What had been dramatically present in the earlier plays—an undogmatic, substantial point of view towards the action, which sustained a consciousness other than the take-it-or-leave-it confession of disturbance—is now absent; what replaces it is a confusion between the main actor and the narration, which is then itself at the level of the disturbed and suggestive confession. It is very significant, historically, that Miller should have moved to this alternative method, which has the weight and disturbance of a culture behind it:

QUENTIN: Murder?
> (*His mother stumbles into darkness, her hands in prayer, whispering "I will die, I will die". He turns to Maggie who is now getting to her hands and knees, gasping. He rushes to help her, terrified by his realization, but she flails out at him, and on one elbow looks up at him in a caricature of laughter, her eyes victorious and wild with fear.*)
MAGGIE: Now we both know. You tried to kill me, mister. I been killed by a lot of people, some couldn't hardly spell, but it's the same, mister. You're on the end of a long, long line . . .

It is hardly any longer dramatic writing. It is the notation of a different convention: the alternative tradition of semi-articulate exposure. It cannot be taken as an epilogue to Miller, and it does not cancel his earlier work, but it shows both the difficulties of development of the form he had chosen and the intense disintegrating pressures of a powerful contemporary structure of feeling.

7

BERTOLT BRECHT

BRECHT'S work is the most important and original in European drama since Ibsen and Strindberg, but it is in many ways difficult both to understand in itself and to relate to a tradition which it at once develops and criticizes. The major plays—*Mother Courage, The Good Woman of Sezuan, The Life of Galileo* and *The Caucasian Chalk Circle* belong to a remarkable period between 1937 and 1945, but Brecht had been writing almost continuously since 1918, had produced his important theory of an "epic form of the theatre" in 1931, and, after the major writing period, influenced theatrical production, very widely, through the Berliner Ensemble founded in 1949. In this long and complicated development there are many obscurities and contradictions, and there are very marked variations in dramatic success. I propose here to consider the two major and related contributions—the idea of "epic form" and the plays of 1937-45—in a primarily analytic rather than historical aspect; and then briefly to relate them to Brecht's own development and the general situation in drama and theatre.

2

When a writer tries to set down the general principles of his work, he is often tempted to define it negatively: by rejecting his predecessors and often collecting them, arbitrarily, into a "tradition". Brecht certainly did this: not only because it is an obvious form for an artistic manifesto; but also because the whole cast of his mind was critical—many of his plays, though not indeed the most important, are in effect critical replayings of the work of others. We need to remember this at the very beginning, when Brecht distinguishes his "epic" form from a "dramatic" or "Aristotelian" form. It would in fact be possible to take Brecht's list of distinguishing characteristics, of the two kinds, and find more of the "epic" characteristics corresponding to Aristotle and the methods of Greek drama than to the work of any other critic or period. But this is not the main point (although when the terms are transferred beyond Brecht that kind of correction has to be firmly made). What matters, in the manifesto, is the positive content. For the rest, there is really no doubt, to any historian of the drama, that what is being attacked as "Aristotelian" or "dramatic" is the dominant naturalism of the European drama after Ibsen. Brecht lists many points, but four can be taken as decisive. The drama he opposes involves the spectator in a stage-action and consumes his capacity to act; the drama he recommends makes the spectator an observer but awakens his capacity to act. Again, the drama he opposes presents experience, drawing the spectator inside this until he is experiencing the action with the characters; the drama he recommends presents a view of the world, in which the spectator confronts something and is made to study what he sees. Further, the drama he opposes makes one scene exist for the sake of another, in what is seen, under the spell of the action, as an evolutionary inevitability; the drama he recommends makes each scene exist for itself, as a thing to be looked at, and develops by sudden leaps. Finally, the drama he opposes takes man, in the run of its action, as known, given, inevitable; the drama he recommends shows man producing himself in the course of the action, and therefore subject to criticism and to change.

What is being basically attacked here is the central naturalist thesis of the "illusion of reality", in which an action is created that is so like life that the verisimilitude absorbs the whole attention of both dramatist and audience. It is not true to say, of course, that this is necessarily uncritical: the observed reality can shock, by its concentrated power, and has again and again done so, in the naturalist theatre. What Brecht seized on was the exclusion, by particular conventions of verisimilitude, of all direct commentary, alternative consciousness, alternative points of view. At the simplest level, he is calling for their restoration: historically, these had been the conventions of chorus, narrator, soliloquy; or, in more compli-cated movements, the achievement of a dramatic design which was more than the design of the action. Brecht sometimes confused the issue by concentrating on the spectator's reactions: actually, in a tradition derived from neo-classical dramatic criticism, which is probably where he picked up the "Aristotelian" tag. In fact the issue is not in the spectator but in the play: whether in its dramatic design it is an essentially single, presented or suggested, experience; or an essentially complex, multi-dimensional, presented and internally valued action. The spectator (as Brecht learned, bitterly, when his *Threepenny Opera* succeeded for what to him were the wrong reasons) is the one element the dramatist cannot control, in any form. It is in the action, the dramatic design, that the choices Brecht insists on must be made.

The alternative term, "open" theatre, is in some ways preferable to "epic". Essentially, what Brecht created, after long experiment, was a dramatic form in which men were shown in the process of producing themselves and their situations. This is, at root, a dialectical form, drawing directly on a marxist theory of history in which, within given limits, man makes himself. Correspondingly, the pure naturalist form (which in many actual naturalist plays is diluted or qualified) depends on a simpler materialist view, in which man discovers the truth about himself by discovering his real environment: the literal presentation of this environment is then a means to human truth.

To show men in the process of producing themselves and their situations, as opposed to discovering themselves in a given situation, Brecht developed methods of writing, producing and acting which embodied a critical detachment: hopefully, as we have seen, in the spectator, but more radically in the immediate nature of the play. The production and acting methods have been widely discussed, around his concept of "verfremdung"—"making strange". On the stage, the emphasis on an "open" presentation gives the right stress. Brecht's methods varied, widely, but were consistent in their intention to show the action in the process of being made: that is to say, to confront an audience with a performance, a deliberate action in a theatre, often with the machinery of effects visible and with the passing of time and place conventionally indicated rather than assumed and recreated: a continual and explicit contrast with all those means to a suspension of disbelief before an illusion of reality. What happens on the stage is not so much lived as shown, and both the consciousness of an audience, and the distance between that audience and the deliberately played action, are made central to the style. In acting, Brecht emphasized the same elements of distance and demonstration. Stanislavsky, developing a style for Chekhov's work (to which it was not, as it happened, particularly appropriate; Chekhov, though very different from Brecht, often wrote in terms of this same self-consciousness and distance) had encouraged the actor to "live the part", to "become the character", not only on the stage but off it, while the production was being prepared: asking himself what the character might have done or said in situations other than those in the play, until, in effect, he was so wholly inside the character that everything he did showed this completely assumed personality. Brecht encouraged the same kind of thinking about the character, but for an objective rather than a subjective understanding:

> He has merely to show the character; or, better, not merely to experience it; but this does not mean that when he has to act passionate people he must himself remain cold. It is only that his feelings should not be fundamentally the same as those of his character, so that the feelings of his audience do not become fundamentally those of his character.

He encouraged this objective relation, in rehearsal, by getting actors to precede their words with "he said", or to translate them into the third person and the past tense, or to exchange parts. Then instead of subjective involvement there would be objective, critical presentation.

These emphases are important, and as theatre techniques have been widely influential (though it is more, there, than the simple influence of Brecht; it is part of the general influence of the producer's rather than the actor-manager's theatre). But what has then to be said is that to be more than techniques, to be dramatic conventions, they have to be applied to plays which are written in the same terms. It is possible, that is to say (and had indeed happened widely, before Brecht's influence was felt) to apply a critical-objective treatment to any play, by letting the techniques of production take priority. It is what Brecht himself said, in another connection:

> Today we see the theatre being given absolute priority over the actual plays. The theatre apparatus's priority is a priority of means of production. This apparatus resists all conversion to other purposes, by taking any play it encounters and immediately changing it so that it no longer represents a foreign body within the apparatus. The theatre can stage anything; it theatres it all down.

This has been, in practice, quite as true of the "open", objective-critical, presented theatre, as of older theatres in which the play was reduced to a vehicle for a star actor or to an occasion for the designers of scenery and costumes, or to a "script" for a company's orchestration. At the level of theatrical style only, Brecht's emphases are possibilities among others: a contribution to an eclectic repertory. They become more than that only when they are related to plays designed to use the methods as conventions, so that the production, the acting and the writing depend, necessarily, on a particular structure of feeling.

3

The key to Brecht's real originality is a phrase he used looking back on the production of *The Threepenny Opera*:

> Complex seeing must be practised . . . Thinking *above* the flow of the play is more important than thinking from *within* the flow of the play.

In this latter sentence, he is still prescribing an attitude for the spectator: characteristically, after a failure of just that kind, in which the "cheerful amorality"—"eats first, morals after"—of the post-Gay whores and highwaymen had been accepted and enjoyed rather than looked at and criticized. "Complex seeing", in fact, had to be more than enjoined on a spectator; it had to be realized in a play.

We can mark the passage from a theatrical technique to a dramatic convention by taking some examples. In *The Threepenny Opera* we can see a technique becoming a local convention, in Peachum's commentary on pity:

> (*A large board is let down from the flies and on it is written:* "*It is more blessed to give than to receive*")
> PEACHUM: What's the use of the finest and most stirring sayings painted on the most enticing boards if they get used up so quickly? There are four or five sayings in the Bible that really touch the heart. But when they're used up, one's daily bread's just gone.

This direct, self-revealing address to the audience, on pity as a calculating trade, is an open irony which sets a tone for the action. It provides a certain local consciousness, but it is objective-critical only if it can be prevented from becoming an "engagingly cheerful dishonesty, frankly confessed". In the play as a whole, this was not prevented; indeed a cynical amorality could not only expose exploitation but appear to ratify it.

The case of the chorus in *The Measures Taken*, when Brecht had turned to an explicit morality, is different. It is used as a commentary on a persistent Brechtian theme: the choice between sympathy, accepting a local reality, and revolt, contradicting both the local reality and immediate human need and convenience. Each of four professional revolutionaries acts out, in turn, a decision to turn aside from revolutionary work to immediate charitable aid. Because this threatens the mission, it is decided to execute the generous one: to isolate that feeling and destroy it. This is "complex seeing" of a kind, in its dramatization of a common impulse rather than the particularity of one character, but the chorus, instead of allowing the action to be seen in its many aspects, in the end merely ratifies the decision to execute: the critical-objective element is then counter-seeing rather than complex seeing: a limited anti-romantic action rather than a new whole form.

The emphasis on acting out a role, to see what it is like and how others respond, is an important means to Brecht's aim of showing men producing themselves and their situations. But here again, there is an important difference between what is really a device of exposition or of local revelation of character, and the method as a structure of feeling. In one of the early scenes of *Fear and Misery in the Third Reich*, a stormtrooper encourages a worker to act out a grumbler in a food-queue, to show how the stormtroopers deal with malcontents. It is locally brilliant, but it is a device of exposition because after the acting-out the characters resume their original roles and relationships—a kind of wary banter. In other words, they have been acting, in an enclosed experience, rather than producing a new situation. A related comment can be made on a later scene in the same play, where a Jewish wife decides to leave Germany, to avoid harming the career of her non-Jewish husband. This interesting scene is played, first, by the wife on her own, imagining a conversation with her husband, and then, on her husband's return, in an actual conversation. This in part dramatizes a whole situation, critically seen: the representative acquiescence by the husband in the norms, though not the practices, of the persecution. But it is mainly, as presented, character-revelation: an insight into a relationship, with objective implications rather than actualities. A comparable method in the same play is more success-ful, where a husband and wife, suspecting their son has gone out to inform on them, produce the mutual suspicion and abandon-ment of primary relationships which allows the regime to control them. The irony, when the son returns from an ordinary errand, with no thought of informing, is characteristic, but again in part cancels, as action, the full realization of consequence.

It was in the major plays, from 1937 to 1945, that Brecht broke through to a complex seeing which was the dramatic action itself. One of the simplest and most brilliant examples is *The Good Woman of Sezuan*, where the idea of acting out alternative roles is developed into an action. The story, in a simple sense, is about the problems of a good woman in a bad society: personal generosity can be so easily exploited, leaving the romantic figure of the isolated heroine destroyed by the greed of others. Brecht could easily have substituted for this (as in so many of his earlier plays, from *Baal* onwards) the anti-romantic version, in which the woman, realizing that her society was like this, adopted a cheerful, tough amoralism—"eats first, morals after"—and kept alive. Each of these versions is simple seeing, from alternative points of view. But what Brecht now does is in effect to embody both versions: Shen Te, the good woman, invents her tough cousin, Shui Ta—first as an alternative, relieving role, but then, in effect, as an independent person who coexists with her. It is not fixed goodness against fixed badness—a cops-and-robbers morality—but goodness and badness in the act of being produced in the turns of an action, as coexistent possibilities. This is genuinely complex seeing, and it is deeply integrated with the dramatic form. No resolution is imposed; the tension persists, as it must, and the play ends with a formal invitation to consider it. The evasive responses, covering or weakening the tension, are expressed by other characters, so that we can see their inadequacy while the fact of Shen Te and Shui Ta is still evident. The methods of expressionist drama, which had normally been used to show an intolerable tension within a single consciousness, are extended to show the tension of a common experience: a method of critical examination rather than sensational exposure. The play does not show the world through the actions and tensions of a single mind, but through an objective action in which Shen Te and Shui Ta are at once created characters and yet, by this fact of creation, reveal the processes by which they have produced themselves. It is the alternative responses, but then also the hard independence of consequence, which are simultaneously dramatized.

It is important that Brecht, who was so deeply concerned with a contemporary political world, turned so often to fable and to history, to achieve complex seeing. In his major plays, he is able to isolate, especially from history, a particular form of crisis in which men produce themselves and their situations in a rather special way. For although he was ostensibly concerned with the whole range of historical development, and practically concerned with most of the forms of contemporary social crisis, his main creative energy went into the realization of a particular crisis, which has his own unique stamp. The use of fable and of history is connected with this, as well as being a device of distancing, of making strange, comparable to the more evident distancing conventions and techniques. But it is then necessary to distinguish between the use of fable and of history. In the fable plays—in *The Good Woman of Sezuan* or *The Caucasian Chalk Circle*—the issues are characteristically simpler. The survival qualities of goodness and evil; the definition of justice by the needs of life: these have a centrality in Brecht, but are presented in the fable-plays as cases for debate: the simplest, most discursive version of complex seeing. Issues are looked at in new ways, by the turns of the action and by a consciously available argument. In the history plays—in *Mother Courage* and *The Life of Galileo*—similar issues can be abstracted, but the mode of their dramatization is different. And then what needs to be stressed, critically, is that while the most evident examples of the open, critical-objective drama are the fable plays, they represent only a minor, readily recognizable and imitable, originality. They belong, at this level, with the important theatrical innovations: a lively achievement and tendency, but not in themselves a full dramatic discovery. The major originality is in the history plays, for a precise reason in the central structure of feeling.

It is impossible to understand Brecht as an artist (though he can be understood as a pamphleteer) if the claims of immediate satisfaction—of an immediately available vitality—are abstracted and counterposed to the claims of history. He knew the arguments on this, sometimes only too well: that immediate satisfaction can come through as personal selfishness, indifference to the political struggle and to history. In the fable plays he could dramatize these arguments, in a many-sided way. In *The Caucasian Chalk Circle* he could even override the argument, by making the judge in the case of disputed maternity, Azdak, an unpredictable and amoral vitality. The formal conclusion, that the child should go to whoever is best for her (as in the political analogy—"the valley to the waterers, that it shall bear fruit"), is complex seeing of an abstract kind: we see the legal claims, and the human claims, and the latter, in a familiar dialectic, are shown as stronger. But the main dramatic conclusion, through the figure of Azdak, is arrived at almost by impulse: an essentially unpredictable vitality, concerned, really, with neither formal law nor human morality, gives the child to the woman who loves her, in "a brief Golden Age that was almost just". That is indeed how it could happen, in the fable plays: life would find the right way, as in all fable conventions. The intellectual backing, that life finds the right way through the struggles of history, can be produced on demand, but, in creative terms, is only marginally present. Thus, though formally the seeing is complex, the chosen action is a simplification.

We cannot say, with any certainty, why Brecht did not embody his major dramatic conflicts in a contemporary action. His distancing, there, produces effective scenes, but not a whole action, and the technique of distancing may itself be connected with this. It seems

to me at least possible that the full dramatic action was too painful
to see in contemporary terms: not that he drew back from dramatizing brutality and betrayal—those painful scenes were, paradoxically, the easiest to realize; but that the claims of immediate
satisfaction, not as argument but as experience, were at once
undeniable and insupportable, in the realities of contemporary
struggle. What could be seen as the claims of immediate life, in
historical situations, translated too quickly, in a structured contemporary world, into evasion. Brecht could, in this view, only
release his full dramatic action, giving all its impulses a full creative
weight, by this particular kind of distancing: an action away from
immediate issues and names.

The point is very complicated, for this kind of historical distancing is so normal in dramatic art, is indeed so much more common
than the realization of contemporary action, that in any case but
that of Brecht no particular notice would need to be taken. It is
just the paradox of a contemporary urgency and a profound distancing that irresistibly holds the attention. And it must be made clear,
also, that Brecht does not, by his historical distancing, express
what can be called a "creative truth" as opposed to what is often
called his "doctrinaire truth". On the contrary, the actions of
Mother Courage and of *Galileo* are at the heart of Brecht: not only
integrating the creative impulse and the political beliefs, but also,
by this fact, enabling a major dramatic achievement, the triumphs
of his particular form.

Complex seeing, in *Mother Courage* and *Galileo*, is not an attitude
to the action, or a battery of separable techniques and effects; it
is the action, in a profound way. We obscure this when, for example,
in a convenient brevity, we shorten the title of *Mother Courage and
her Children* to *Mother Courage*, the separable figure. But then it is
just in the fact that she can be separated, that in one (and her own)
way of seeing the action she can be isolated, and is isolated, as a
heroically persistent figure, that the complexity of the action reveals
itself. She has to persist, and she has to be isolated, so that the full
action can be shown. What has to be created, as communicable
experience and not merely as an argument, is just her hard lively
opportunism (it is the recognizable voice of Peachum or Azdak),
until it engages; until it not only seems but is a way to live. And
then the depth of the drama is not what is said about this, by some
device of exposition or commentary; it is in the rest of the action,
in what *other things* happen. The point is then not (as in so much
discussion of the play) whether Mother Courage, as a person, is
meant to be admired as heroically persistent, or despised as wickedly

opportunist. That separable moral judgement is precisely what the play confounds. For not an attitude but an experience drives through the action: what else can be done, here, in this war across Europe? The formal submission to an uncontrollable power; the preservation of life by going on with the system, dragging the cart after the armies: these not only seem but are inevitable; they have to convince, as experience, before the full dramatic shock can come: that life isn't preserved; that a family, before our eyes, is destroyed; that the cart is dragged on, but the dead are multiplying. It is not the abstract question, "are they good people?", or "what should they have done?". It is, inescapably, at once "what are they doing?" and "what is this doing to them?". It is in this way that a complex seeing is integrated in the action itself:

CHAPLAIN: Mother Courage. I see how you got your name.
MOTHER COURAGE: The poor need courage. They're lost, that's why. That they even get up in the morning is something, in *their* plight. Or that they plough a field, in wartime. Even their bringing children into the world shows they have courage, for they have no prospects. They have to hang each other one by one and slaughter each other in the lump, so if they want to look each other in the face once in a while, well, it takes courage.

It certainly takes courage: not the isolable moral quality, but this character, this action. Past the justifications, the excuses, the "bad luck", the inevitabilities, it takes this action—of a mother destroying her family with the aim of preserving life—to see what is happening; to be able to bear to see it. If she were not so strong and persistent, there would be no life at all; and at the same time, because she is strong and persistent, in a destructive society, she destroys the life that she has herself created. This deep and complex image, in a character and in an action, is Brecht's central structure of feeling, directly dramatized. It is by looking this action, this character, in the face, that we see what we are doing: the essential contradiction; the destructive acquiescence in the name of life; the persistent vitality in a continuing destruction. The desperate urgency, of the real preservation of life, is articulated only in the drumming of the dumb girl, to waken and save the city: a defiance that gets her killed, but that is as inevitable as her mother going on with the cart. It is to that experience, of a crushed revolt, as well as to the other experience, of a desperate acquiescence, that the soldiers sing, in the same essential action:

And though you may not long survive
Get out of bed and look alive.

The vitality and the danger are inseparable; the reality and the pretence, until the action is played through, are indistinguishable. The conflict is pushed through, seen from every side, until it connects with our own conflict.

The dramatic action of *Mother Courage and Her Children* is Brecht's major achievement. The achievement of *The Life of Galileo* is different: a dramatic consciousness. Thematically, the connection is clear: Galileo, under pressure, renounces what he knows to be the truth; gains two things—the physical continuity and satisfaction he must have, and also the time to write the "Discorsi"; and loses the connection of his truth, his science, with the needs—the physical continuities and satisfactions—of the majority of men. In saving his life he has destroyed a connected life: in saving his science he has altered it. The dramatic method is not historical reconstruction: Galileo, and the action surrounding him, are specifically created so that we can see, in a proper complexity, the complexity of the real choices. Galileo stripped to the waist, explaining the rotation of the earth with an apple, is the claim of immediate life, in the most direct way: physical satisfaction and understanding. It is there, undeniable, except that a corrupt system denies it. Once again, as in *Mother Courage and Her Children*, we are then "torn in two": except that this is only ever a metaphor—the tearing happens, between the body and the mind, the satisfaction and the truth, but both are still in one person, one need, one consciousness. What is then especially brilliant is that the intolerable tension is overcome, as it must be in life, by a specific distortion: a partial validity extended until it is a false but effective consciousness. Galileo had asked:

Could we deny ourselves to the crowd and still remain scientists?

The answer, of course, is yes: but scientists of a different kind. In the beginning there was a connection between the truth about the solar system and the truth about the social system: a falsehood in one had been used to maintain an oppression in the other; Galileo, in challenging one, is challenging both:

The most solemn truths are being tapped on the shoulder; what was never doubted is now in doubt. And because of that a great wind has arisen, lifting even the gold-embroidered coat-tails of princes and prelates, so that the fat legs and thin legs underneath are seen; legs like our legs.

It is this connection that Galileo betrays, taking science out of the street and into the service either of a court or of a private study.

The images of this resolution are powerfully created, in their own terms: Galileo the survivor, going on with his work in his exiled intelligence; the manuscript of the "Discorsi" crossing the border to freedom. But they are not simple images; they are seen, in the action, in complex ways. The vitality of the earth and the apple, in the first scene, are the smearing fat of the goose in the fourteenth. In the last scene, when the manuscript crosses the border, it is hidden in a coach, and the boys playing at the frontier—the boys who would have been Galileo's audience—are talking of devils and witches. Both things happen: a way of continuing science, and a way of detaching it from ordinary life. And the solution is in the service of Galileo's ordinary life: the goose and the opportunity to work, both of which he had every right to. A complex consciousness, in which not only this but also that must be said, is then brilliantly created.

4

Brecht's important dramatic conventions can be briefly summarized. He is able to use with a new freedom, at many points in his work, conventions of exposition and commentary which belong to a contemporary consciousness, rather than to an imitation of older forms. Again, with a new freedom, he is able to range, in language, from a vigorous naturalism, through the formalities of argument, to the intensity of song. In learning to present characters, rather than assuming and developing their existence, he found ways of combining an intense physical presence, backed up with all the vigour of an intensely physical imagery, with the possibility of detachment, of suspension, allowing the presence to be examined and looked at, yet without abstraction. And what, in his major work, holds these conventions together, is a form so simple, at first sight, that we can easily overlook its originality. To see the open action of *Mother Courage* or *Galileo*—the sequence of scenes which are "for themselves", sharp and isolated, yet connect in a pattern that defines the action—is to see what can appear an unstudied form: a mere series: a setting-down of scenes. But what has gone, from the ordinary shape of most modern plays, is more noticeable, as we look closer. What has gone is a form that encloses the characters, in fixed places and at fixed times. The shape of separable, enclosed acts, with fixed beginnings and climaxes, has been replaced by this open sequence of scenes, which is not only technically flexible and mobile, undominated by fixed scene and persistent situations, but is basically a movement corresponding to a flow of action—a process rather than a product. The form is not, of course, an innovation by Brecht; it derives, essentially, from the Elizabethan drama and especially from Shakespeare; through Büchner and others. But it is a form which corresponds exactly to the realization of process—an isolation, a contrast but then a connection of scenes—which is the determining dramatic experience. Put one way, Brecht's drama is that of isolated and separated individuals, and of their connections, in that capacity, with a total historical process. He is hardly interested at all in intermediate relationships, in that whole complex of experience, at once personal and social, between the poles of the separated individual and the totally realized society. His dramatic form, isolating and dialectic, serves this structure of feeling exactly; it is his precise development of an expressionist mode, and the dimension of social realism is absent in his work, both in substance and in any continuing contemporary experience, because the structure is of that kind. Put another way, Brecht's expressionism is unusually open, is a development of possibilities and even at times a transformation of effective conventions, because he took up the position of explaining rather than exposing: an overall critical-objective position, rather than the intensity of special pleading on behalf of an isolated figure. Retaining the characteristic poles of expressionism—the isolated suffering individual and the totality of the world in which he suffers—he reversed the normal positive and negative references. The previously over-whelming positive reference—the isolated individual—becomes negative: is seen not subjectively, as in conventional expressionism, but objectively, as a characteristic even symptomatic figure. The positive reference, the source of values and explanation, is at the other pole: the totality, the historical process. The strength of his form is that it permits this kind of clarification: at once clipped, bitter, distant, and yet, in its assumption of a common complicity, a common weakness, connecting and humane in very general ways: a human need and satisfaction ironically known and recalled. Because the polar relationship is still there and decisive, the drama is retrospective, in a deep sense: the intolerable isolation is a fact, and when we see men producing themselves and their situations it is this, essentially, that they produce; that is seen as inevitable and yet is rejected. The dramatic form is not oriented to growth: the experiences of transforming relationship and of social change are not included, and the tone and the conventions follow from this: men are shown why they are isolated, why they defeat themselves, why they smell of defeat and its few isolated, complicit virtues. It is a major originality, not because it enters a new world, but because it values an old world differently: the world created directly, in drama, by Ibsen and Strindberg and Chekhov—a world of defeat, frustration, isolation; a world rationalized by Pirandello and the absurdists to a total condition, an inherent insignificance and loss of values; a world purged now, by Brecht, of pity and acceptance—held at arm's length, criticized, explained. On to an alienated world, that had been dramatized mainly from the inside, Brecht turned àn alienated consciousness: meeting a negative with a negative; intransigent, detached, open. It is this connection between a structure of feeling and conventions that we must end by emphasizing: the Brechtian mode, in any serious sense, belongs to that consciousness; its particular methods, without the consciousness, are merely fashionable techniques. What comes through, as always, when the consciousness and the conventions are deeply connected, is the power of a major writer: a way of seeing that permanently alters dramatic possibilities. Looking back from Brecht, we see the drama of the last hundred years differently: see its consciousness and its methods from the outside, in a fully critical light. We do not, because of that, at all lessen our respect: the power of the masters is what it was. But the power of this different master is conclusive. With this last shift, a particular dramatic world—that of the individual against society—is now wholly seen. Without the substance created by others, Brecht's critical epilogue—his dramatic negative—could not have been written. But now that it has been written, in two or three great plays and in a wider achievement of a powerful and unforgettable dramatic consciousness, we have to struggle to enter, as Brecht himself insisted, a new kind of world.

PART V

Recent Drama

I

SIX PLAYS

1. *Long Day's Journey into Night* : Eugene O'Neill

WHEN Eugene O'Neill died in 1953, he left three plays in manu-script, and among them *Long Day's Journey into Night*, dated 1940 on the manuscript but first produced in Stockholm in 1956. The play has a haunting effect: the re-establishment, as a living voice, of a dramatist whose main work had belonged to the 1920s and early 1930s; but also, in its power, the adding of a dimension, a necessary dimension, to all that earlier work. What came back into the theatre, in this posthumous play, was not only the voice of O'Neill, now especially intense and convincing. It was also the voice of that fully serious naturalism of the first epoch of modern drama: of Ibsen and of early Strindberg. It might have seemed like a ghost walking, but in all essential respects this was a powerful contemporary voice.

The sense of return, of the *revenant*, is of course overpowering, but as a direct dramatic experience. O'Neill spoke, in a note to his wife on the manuscript, of "the faith in love that enabled me to face my dead at last". It is the voice of late Ibsen, though not in imitation. The paradox of O'Neill's work, always, had been the strength of his realism, in a vernacular which created the modern American theatre, and his devices of distance, artifice, theatre in quite another sense. There is of course still power in *The Hairy Ape* and *Anna Christie*, in *Desire under the Elms*, *The Great God Brown*, *Strange Interlude* and *Emperor Jones*; but what I think is clear in O'Neill throughout, until these last plays, is a crisis of form which makes him a significant figure. As in *Mourning Becomes Electra*, there is a sense of an intense experience just behind the play, just beyond what seemed the daring formal or theatrical experiment. Cast into what seemed, at the time, the new exploratory forms, the intensity in fact stiffened, became awkward: not gauche, which is on every count the wrong thing to say, but often falsely self-conscious, carrying out a literary act, surprising a theatre. There were many dramatists who used these new forms in a direct relation to a structure of feeling which supported them. The paradox of O'Neill was a sense of projection when all the substantial feeling was direct; of formalism, when all the driving emotion was in a different, more immediate voice. My own sense, when I came to *Long Day's Journey into Night*, was of release and discovery: that hidden drama, of the earlier work, was at last directly written, and the power flowed, now at last in its authentic channels.

Many voices are heard in this play which was new in the mid-1950s: the Ibsen reckoning, the calling-to-account of a family; the Strindberg intensity, as direct confrontation breaks through the prepared defences; and also, unexpectedly, the experience of that Irish drama, now set in another country, where the persistent tension is between an intense reality and a way of talking, of talking well, to avoid it. It is an autobiographical play: that is one way of describing it. O'Neill faces his dead—the Tyrone family, the O'Neills. But though the correspondences are obvious, it is not the autobiography that makes the play important it is that what is commonly faced in displaced forms is now faced directly, not as a documentary record but as an imaginative summoning. What comes out elsewhere as a conclusion—the sense of deadlock, of isolation, of insubstantial and destructive relationships—comes out here as a process: not those static forms dramatized, as a single act, but their complex formation pressed deeply into a consciousness which is the controlling convention. Much of the drama of the last forty years has been the last act, the last scene, of an earlier phase, presented, with increasing sophistication, as a whole history. Men are lost, frustrated, isolated, in a world of illusion and self-deception, a world they have distorted and is now only distorted: that condition, which is always a consequence, has become an assumption, is where the new conventions start. O'Neill, who had made this assumption as powerfully and as conventionally as anyone else, now goes back behind it, and shows the experience as active. The action takes place in one day—the day's experience of the title. But the convention is not of a static situation, or of the last stage of deadlock. It is a calling to account, a facing of facts, inside this family; but not to prove anything, by some retrospective formula. It is a searching of the past, to define the present, but because all the family are speaking, it is not one selected past, but a range of past experiences now relived and altering the present: not memory but recreation, with the possibilities as well as the failures acted out.

This essential and liberating strength can be seen most clearly in the writing of the mother: now drugging herself with morphine against the pain of present and past. The pain and the drugging are directly powerful, but they release—as in different ways in the others—at once the intense confession, the necessary involvement with the pain of what the family has become, and the detachment from it: the ability to find both the truth and the fantasy of the past. Under the drug she is "detached", but it is a detachment in active presence, and this is the necessary dramatic means: that she can be the girl before her marriage but also, from her pain now as a wife and mother, the false idea of that girl—an involuntary, painful self-deception which has fed into the long destruction. Her husband, similarly, exists in his several possibilities and self-accounts: coming in poverty from Ireland and still buying land—irrelevant land—against the fear of dying in the poorhouse, in what is at once a substantial experience and a practised excuse; or as the actor, the man who can play a role—at once his gift, from which they live, and his power to deceive himself and others, in a continual shifting uncertainty. Each mode of the parents appears, disappears, comes back to be seen differently: this is the real haunting, the live haunting, of the many possibilities out of which a life is made and through which it can be seen: not separate possibilities, but interacting within each person, and, crucially, between them, where the weaknesses interlock. The two sons, Jamie and Edmund, can be taken as contrasting characters, and indeed have this immediate substance; but they are also two living possibilities, of response, shaping and self-shaping to that parental relationship and, just as much, those shifting parental identities. There is the hard cynicism, or the lonely walking in the fog: neither able to realize a self: not mature, or not born, in this unfinished, unresolved parenthood.

In a later dramatic form, the roles would be separated, would be separately played, as conditions. What is replayed here, in the rush of the present, is the range of modes, in a still active process. It is defined in different ways: through the idea of the theatre, which has made and destroyed this family—so that when Mary comes in, drugged and in pain, in the last scene at midnight, both playing and being the hunted, remembering, day-dreaming girl, Jamie can say "the Mad Scene. Enter Ophelia!", and it is both true and false, about the scene and about her. Again, an element of Tyrone's deception is not only his acting manner—which he briskly resumes after the intervals of pain—but his willed Irish charm, a false consciousness, which can yet be contrasted with the rejection of Ireland, the rejection of the father, in Jamie—

TYRONE: Keep your dirty tongue off Ireland. You're a fine one to sneer with the map of it on your face.

JAMIE: Not after I wash my face. (*Then before his father can react to this insult to the Old Sod . . .*)

—and with the false consciousness of the cynicism of the new country, as in Edmund's parody:

They never come back! Everything is in the bag! It's all a frame-up. We're all fall guys and suckers and we can't beat the game!

Each way of speaking is at once the truth of their experience and a way of avoiding the truth, in the conventional patter of one or other dialect.

What is said under drink or drug, or in anger and then in apology, or then soberly and honestly, is made part of the range: the interaction, of all the ways of speaking, is the dramatic truth. The true poetry and the false poetry, the feeling, the pretended feeling, the lie and the white lie, the substance and the performance: this, essentially, is the medium. It is bound to be uneven, but in scenes like that between Tyrone and Edmund at the beginning of the fourth act, which yet does not stand out but is an intensification of the continuing action, it has a power which reminds us what serious naturalism—the passion for truth, the relentless directness—was and is, as a dramatic movement. What the play relives, in its substance, is not only the history of a family, but of a literature. It is the long crisis of relationships, in a family and in a society, now again enacted directly, in and through a disintegration, while at the edges of this consciousness the forms of a late phase, of the consciousness of midnight after the long day's journey and pain, stand burning and ready:

as if I had drowned long ago.

2. *The Lesson* : Eugene Ionesco

The Lesson (1951) is described by Ionesco as a "tragic farce", and in this respect is not new. The spectacle of a kind of brutality which has become absurd, or of a violent obsession which has become a domestic routine, had been realized in drama, as a direct form, in the chamber-plays of Strindberg. What is really new in Ionesco is the reworking of this form by a particular use of language. The dramatic form he creates is perhaps most successful in *The Rhinoceros* (1960), and the use of language is at its clearest, its most isolated, in *The Bald Prima Donna* (1950). *The Lesson* is interesting because it shows, in a simple form, the development of a particular use of language into a dramatic convention.

The "plot" of *The Lesson* is at once simple and unreal: in dramatic terms, not by some external probability. It can be summarized as the visit of a student, a young girl, to a professor: a first visit;

they go through questions and answers, the professor gives an explanation of the relation between language and objects, produces a knife to illustrate it, and kills her; the maid, who has been expecting and fearing this, helps him to carry the body away; notes that this is the fortieth victim that day; and answers the door to admit the next student. But to describe this as an action is already to misrepresent it, to alter its dramatic dimension. The knife the professor produces is imaginary, like the imaginary blackboard on which he has been teaching her arithmetic. That he kills with it is then the whole point: it is the mimed truth, not the represented truth, on which the play insists. What he actually kills with is words, and the whole action has that particular and limited verbal status.

But what is transparent, as a method, in *The Bald Prima Donna*, is relatively opaque, as a convention, in *The Lesson*. In the earlier play, the "action" is built directly from commonplaces, of a recognizable social kind, which in repetition and multiplication create an effective vacuum, in which anything can appear to happen and yet is overridden by the sheer imposition of false descriptions. Ionesco has described this directly:

> the secret of "talking and saying nothing" . . . because there is nothing personal to say, the absence of any inner life, the mechanical soullessness of daily routine. . . . The Smiths and the Martins have forgotten how to talk because they have forgotten how to think; and they have forgotten how to think because they have forgotten the meaning of emotion, because they are devoid of passions; they have forgotten how to be, and therefore they can "become" anyone, anything, for, since they are not in themselves, they are nothing but other people, they belong to an impersonal world, they are interchangeable,

What the method then embodies is a manifestation, a critical manifestation, of a condition which can be pointed to outside the play: a condition of conformism, and of mechanical conversation, which the play counts on us recognizing.

The Lesson is different, because the critical method has become in itself a convention. There can be no reference, within the world it creates, to any other conceivable condition. A structure of feeling is put directly on to the stage. It is what Ionesco described, in another comment:

> As plots are never interesting, it is my dream to rediscover the rhythms of drama in their purest state.

He was thinking, there, of a drama of "pure scenic movement", but the emphasis on rhythm, and the opposition to plot, are wholly relevant to *The Lesson*. The play is carefully written to emphasize a very simple rhythm: what is described, in the initial directions to the actors, as the establishment of confidence and uncertainty, in a manner of speaking, in the student and the professor, and the slow development of these manners until they are transposed, and the professor becomes dominant and the student inert. It is that rhythm which is the action: not the "plot" of the visit and the killing; or at least, that is what Ionesco intends.

What the rhythm "means", that is to say, is another question. It is obviously a form of many relationships: the shifting relationships of dominator and dominated: a professor and a student, as Ionesco directly reminds us; or a much wider world, as we are again reminded, when the maid offers the professor a political armband, after the killing, as a way of not being frightened of what he has done. But the point is not to treat the relationships directly, nor at all "symbolically". It is to isolate the rhythm, the forms of words, through which relationships between people become displaced, in what is also an unconnected relationship with objects.

> *The Professor goes quickly to the drawer and finds a big imaginary knife; he takes hold of it and brandishes it exultantly.*
> PROFESSOR: Here's one, Mademoiselle, here's a knife! It's a pity this is the only one; but we'll try to make it serve for all the languages. All you need to do is to pronounce the word Knife in each language, while you stare closely at the object and imagine it belongs to the language you're using.
> STUDENT: I've got the toothache.
> PROFESSOR: (*almost chanting*): Come along then: Say Kni, like Kni, Fff, like Fff . . . and watch it carefully, don't take your eyes off it . . .
> STUDENT: What is it, this one? French, Italian or Spanish?
> PROFESSOR: It doesn't matter . . . It doesn't matter to you. Say Kni.
> STUDENT: Kni.
> PROFESSOR: Fff . . . Watch it.
> *He moves the knife in the student's face.*

What is being imposed, here, is an alienation of thing from idea, of thing from word, of person from person, until in their alienated forms the disconnected words, things and ideas can kill; the life of persons is overridden by them.

It is a difficult convention to transpose to the stage. Ionesco's verbal rhythms are subtle and brilliant, creating their own kind of hypnotic attention. But what is then interesting is that precisely through these rhythms an action of a particular kind emerges, and it is not only the professor who brandishes the knife. The deep and determining structure of feeling is what Ionesco described in his memory of a puppet-theatre:

> The spectacle of the *guignol* held me there, stupefied by the sight of these puppets who spoke, who moved, who bludgeoned each other. It was the spectacle of life itself which, strange, improbable, but truer than truth itself, was being presented to me in an infinitely simplified and caricatured form, as though to underline the grotesque and brutal truth.

Ionesco's rhythms are not verbal games, to be enjoyed for their own sake as in *The Bald Prima Donna* and in several English imitations. They are dramatic rhythms with this specific meaning: "the grotesque and brutal truth". The alienation is so deep that it is continually pushed away into the categorizing complacency of "the absurd", or the equally abstract complacency of "pure non-representational theatre". What is being said and done here is the action of a single mind: not the expressionist distortion—the static fury—of the Strindberg chamber-play; not the demonstration of illusion of Pirandello; though in elements and tradition it is related to both. The "illusion of reality", under severe tension, has become now wholly internal; is in the dramatic language, in new ways; making the play into an object, an alienated object, which in the hypnotic rhythms can be moved in the audience's face. Whatever is said, this is what is done: the "grotesque and brutal truth" is directly communicated, by consuming the very action, the words, the stage-objects in the act of demonstrating them; turning the power of the theatre against itself, so that what is done is displaced and yet, as was always the intention, is still done; a world seen and shared while we are looking at the impossibility of seeing and sharing; a lesson which after all its content and consequences people go on turning up to be taught:

> I'll go and tell him you've arrived. He'll be down in a minute. Come in, won't you, Mademoiselle?

3. *Waiting for Godot* : Samuel Beckett

Samuel Beckett's *Waiting for Godot*, which appeared in 1952, is a unique development of a traditional form. Any adequate critical description must begin from its unusual combination of speech and design. Consider this early sequence:

VLADIMIR: What are you doing?

ESTRAGON: Taking off my boot. Did that never happen to you?

VLADIMIR: Boots must be taken off every day, I'm tired telling you that. Why don't you listen to me?

ESTRAGON: (*feebly*) Help me!

VLADIMIR: It hurts?

ESTRAGON: Hurts? He wants to know if it hurts!

VLADIMIR: (*angrily*) No one ever suffers but you. I don't count. I'd like to hear what you'd say if you had what I have.

ESTRAGON: It hurts?

VLADIMIR: Hurts! He wants to know if it hurts! (*Stooping*) Never neglect the little things of life.

ESTRAGON: What do you expect, you always wait till the last moment.

VLADIMIR: (*musingly*) The last moment . . . (*he meditates*). Hope deferred maketh the something sick, who said that?

There are three immediate points. First, the simplicity of the every-day speech, in a real way about the "little things of life". Second, as if edging this simplicity but also defining it, patterns of repetition and recurrence, an emphasis of key phrases which go beyond what is otherwise the simple exchange of conversation between the two tramps: a technique very clear here because the particular repetition —"It hurts?". "Hurts! He wants to know if it hurts!"—transposed between the characters, is also another kind of address: an appeal as if to someone or something beyond them, which is also, in immediate convention, the technique of the stage figure, traditionally the comedian, appealing to and involving a theatrical audience. Third, moving in the same direction, the half-reminiscence of "hope deferred": the reference to a system of traditional words and meanings which ultimately define the action but which define it precisely because they are at once present and absent: remembered but only half remembered.

It is the fusion of these methods in what communicates as a single form that makes description difficult. For example, the play cannot be wholly understood unless the possibility of completing that remembered phrase is actual.

Hope deferred maketh the heart sick, but when the desire cometh, it is a tree of life.

(PROVERBS, XIII, 12)

The feeling and the imagery are indeed the action of the play. It is the hope deferred, that Godot will come, that keeps the tramps where they are: recurrently waiting and being disappointed. They are waiting under a bare tree, which in the second act has some four or five leaves. Yet it is not only the relevance of this traditional design and image that must be noticed; it is also its incompleteness, which is a crucial part of its meaning.

The difficulty, not so much in the play but in any critical account, is then the function of this underlying design and imagery which, in exposition, can become more complete than they are in the action. If, for example, someone argues that much of the play is haphazard and incomprehensible, it is necessary to show how each element has this kind of reference, yet in giving the precise reference an essential part of the structure of feeling—that the design is blurred and in effect lost—can be missed altogether, by a false clarity. This problem is acute when the convention changes, as it does in the middle of each act with the arrival of Pozzo and Lucky. The tramps alone might be seen in a very simple way: I have read a programme note which indicated that the play's subject was an unusual and interesting kind of French vagrant. The bizarre figures of Pozzo and Lucky put paid to that; but there is of course nothing wilful or haphazard about them, and the change of convention, to the overtly exaggerated character, is very closely related to the experience which their coming represents. The reference is again offered, in their whole appearance:

> For they bind heavy burdens and grievous to be borne, and lay them on men's shoulders; but they themselves will not move them with one of their fingers.
> Ye fools and blind! for whether is greater, the gift or the altar that sanctifieth the gift.
> (MATTHEW, XXIII; verses 4 and 19)

The burden on Lucky, and Pozzo's total ease, in the first act; the alteration of condition, in which the fool leads the blind, in the second act: these are real correspondences. But they materialize at the level of direct dramatic presentation; it is not the commentary (on the scribes and pharisees) but the immediate action that is decisive.

What then needs emphasis is the dramatic rather than the referential form. It is not that the relation to Christian tradition is unimportant, but that this misleads us when we go on to describe *Waiting for Godot*, in traditional terms, as a morality play. It has some methods in common: the concentration of general qualities and modes of being and behaviour into personal images, set in an acted design. But the structure of feeling on which the morality form is based acts from a common centre outwards; it is a demonstration of a faith. The structure of feeling of *Waiting for Godot* is the loss of this faith, and an essentially uncertain waiting; it is not, from a centre, a demonstration; but is peripheral, fragmentary, blurred. The real dramatic relation is not to the morality but expressionism. The play is an unusually clear example of that expressionist method in which an essentially private feeling—incommunicable in direct terms because of its very isolation—is dramatized by its projection into contrasting characters which are also contrasting modes of action. It is in fact a double pattern of this kind: the opposition of two contrasting pairs of characters, with a further contrast and opposition within each pair. The nature of the action depends on this set of contrasts.

There is first the basic contrast between the tramps and the travellers. Pozzo and Lucky are conscious of time and subject to change, while Vladimir and Estragon are not:

VLADIMIR: How they've changed! Those two.
ESTRAGON: Very likely. They all change. Only we can't.

This comes out most clearly in the contrast between the two acts. For the tramps, in each act, there is only another day of waiting: "for night to fall or for Godot to come". For the travellers there is radical, seemingly arbitrary change: from master and slave to the blind led by the dumb. "Do I look like a man to suffer?", Pozzo had asked in the first act; "Pity . . . Pity . . . Help", he cries in the second. These are contrasting worlds: of waiting beyond time, and of change in time.

The contrasting worlds define the contrasting kinds of relationship, within each pair. Pozzo and Lucky are in a formal world and in an orthodox social relationship: dominating and being dominated. They are tied to each other, both ways, not by their natures but by their external conditions. The slave is led but (as Hegel had argued, in another remembered image) the master is also tied, because he must hold the rope. In the second act this is the rope leading the blind. Vladimir and Estragon have a different essential relationship: informal and outside society (this is the real vagrancy); at once loving, doubtful and resentful, wanting to break away yet still anxiously returning to each other; a voluntary relationship, but with binding natural ties. There is a major contrast, in tone, between the cold formality of what the travellers can say, in either condition, and the warm only seemingly haphazard conversation of the tramps. Each pair is on the road, but the cries of Pozzo and Lucky, in either condition, are "On, on", while Vladimir and Estragon conclude each act with a return on themselves, to a fixed but indefinite point:

ESTRAGON: Well, shall we go?
VLADIMIR: Yes, let's go.
(*They do not move*)

VLADIMIR: Well? Shall we go?
ESTRAGON: Yes, let's go.
(*They do not move*)

At the same time, within this basic contrast of worlds, relationships and possibilities, there is the further contrast, within each pair. Between Pozzo and Lucky the contrast is characteristically overt and absolute. It was Lucky who gave Pozzo a higher consciousness:

> But for him all my thoughts, all my feelings, would have been of common things . . . He used to be . . . my good angel . . . and now . . . he's killing me.

But the enslaved and exploited mind has broken down into delirium and then dumbness, though it can still terrify the apparently satisfied and consuming body, and in the end drags it down into its own collapse. This actual relationship (in traditional terms between soul and body) is echoed, in a less formal, less exposed way, in the different world of the tramps. It is Vladimir, primarily, who is waiting for Godot. Estragon, primarily, is waiting for death. Since in fact they are tied, though less formally than Pozzo and Lucky, each is waiting for both, but the emphasis is different. It is Estragon who proposes suicide, and Vladimir who replies "Not worth a curse" (the orthodox damnation). At the end, in hope deferred, Vladimir provisionally consents:

> VLADIMIR: We'll hang ourselves tomorrow. Unless Godot comes.
> ESTRAGON: And if he comes?
> VLADIMIR: We'll be saved.

It is keeping body and soul together, in an uneasy relationship, waiting for what are defined as alternative ends but are the same end: not moving, coming back to each other.

This formal design is the basic structure of the play, but its realization depends, as we have already seen, on an immediately involving speech and imagery, which follows the movement of uncertainty, revelation, uncertainty again. Beckett's power in this play is the finding of an action and an imagery which are virtually universal: not by a scheme of reference, and not even (though that is his own control) by a formal design; but by directly communicated experience. The central experience of waiting, of hope deferred, of "he won't come this evening but surely tomorrow" is so authentically general that both its conscious and unconscious power are considerable. The experience could not be shared, in the same way, if this were really a morality: if the thing awaited, rather than the actual experience of waiting, were definite. "Godot", that is to say, is not to be translated or even interpreted; it is an indefiniteness that defines what the real experience is: not the coming but the waiting. This general quality is again evident in the figure of master and slave, which cuts deep into all our experience: the Pozzo of the first act, the complacent sentimental consumer, is deeply recognizable. In his fixed relation, he has also the whip and the rope. The terror of breakdown—the blind stumbling Pozzo, or the gabbling Lucky—is again general.

But while drawing on this wide area of quite general experience, Beckett controls, with extraordinary skill, his particular action. The famous speech of Lucky is a good example. It is a mind in breakdown, haunted by the scraps of traditional learning—

> man in Possy . . . man in Essy . . .
> . . . Acacacacademy of Anthropopopometry . . .

but though cut across by compulsion and fatigue as well as by the whirling phrases from the schoolmen and scientific scholarship, its preoccupation is still evident and is the groundline of the play. This can be set out, for convenience of reference:

> Given the existence of a personal God who loves us dearly, with some exceptions for reasons unknown but time will tell;
> And suffers with those who are plunged in torment;
> And considering that it is established beyond all doubt that man in spite of the progress wastes and pines;
> And considering what is much more grave, the great cold, the great dark, the air and the earth, abode of stones, in the great world;
> Alas alas, on, on;
> To shrink, pine, waste;
> Alas alas, on, on;
> The skull, the skull, the skull.

"Given" and "considering": these are the bearings of a traditional explanation, cut across and confused by the present; and that they can not be got clear—either the existence of God or the historical scheme of decline (like the sun of the Macon country, the paradise, "when the world was young", which Vladimir remembers but Estragon has forgotten)—is the whole experience; there is only the terror, the lonely but common terror, of darkness and death. At every point in the play, this essential movement, which is also a deadlock, asserts itself. The design itself, though the dramatist's control, is a form and a blurring of form, over "all the dead voices":

Like wings. Like sand. Like feathers. Like ashes.
Like leaves.

Or again:

> Astride of a grave and a difficult birth. Down in the hole, lingeringly, the grave-digger puts on the forceps. We have time to grow old. The air is full of our cries. (*He listens*) But habit is a great deadener.

It is in this recurrent paradox—for of course as Vladimir listens he hears nothing, in a condition he knows to be general—that the terror and the habit are fused. This fusion, dramatically, is a particular tone. For the pattern is desperate and yet the movement, paradoxically, hopeful; the feeling is bitter and dark, yet the speech lively, irrepressible; in an essential way comic and accepting. It is then not that the pattern cancels the movement, or the tone the feeling; it is just their tension that is the real action, the real language of the play.

Beckett's work as an innovator is well-known and remarkable. It belongs, in many ways, to an earlier period: dramatically, to the world of late Strindberg; culturally, to the exile of Synge and then Joyce (compare the image of the grave with Synge's *Deirdre* and the speech of Lucky with Joyce, but compare also the experience of a lost country and a lapsed but still determining faith). It is in these ways a last voice from an old time, and the innovation, which is real, is itself a paradox: the discovery of a tone which depends on that world but is then closely contemporary; an expressionist form in a naturalist theatrical language; an unrepeatable but also unique and very powerful achievement.

4. *The Balcony* : Jean Genet

Jean Genet's *The Balcony* (1956) is a triumph in a form which, to judge by discussion, would be widely and powerfully represented, but which in fact now exists only in isolated examples. It is a taking of the possibilities of theatrical presentation, in direct relation to the idea of role-playing, and making from this not an entertainment, not a diversion, but a point of entry into an explosive consciousness.

The "Balcony" of the title is a brothel; it is also a theatre and a form of public action and representation:

> The Grand Balcony has a world-wide reputation. It's the most artful yet the most decent house of illusions.

Its rooms are studios in which, with costumes, properties and with the whores as actresses, clients can enact, for a private need, a public fantasy:

> They all want everything to be as real as possible . . . Minus something indefinable, so that it won't be real . . . I'm only the manager. Each individual, when he rings the bell and enters, brings his own scenario, perfectly thought out. My job is merely to rent the hall and furnish the props, actors and actresses.

The theatrical possibilities of this bizarre house are brilliantly taken: the rooms swing through sacristy, lawcourt, battlefield and slum; the clients are dressed and undressed in magnifying, enhancing theatrical costumes, as bishop, judge, general, beggar, But then the image swings both ways: outwards, into the world, where the real public roles are no more than these functions and images; inwards, into the theatre, in the continual repetition of mirrors, where the unmade bed which has its crucial role in the fantasy is, by reflection, in the front rows of the audience, and where the spectacle of roles—images of life—is presented for these other clients. It is not, as it has been described, any kind of analogy; it is too dramatic for that. The act of theatre, over the whole range, is made at once actual and critical.

The concept of role-playing, and of its difficult relations to reality, has been central in a modern mode of consciousness, for at least three generations. What Genet brings to it is not only unusual insight and flair, but a hardness that breaks its complacent orthodox version: that if all is role, then there is no reality. What is pressed, continually, is the distinction made by the acted Bishop:

> A function is a function. It's not a mode of being.

But the functions that are rehearsed, in the vain and humiliating urgency of private desire, are in fact the functions of power. It is the Establishment figures, of bishop, judge and general, who are identified with, and who release this form of living energy:

> My big, long, sterile girls . . . Their seed never ripens in you, and yet—if you weren't there?

Against that establishment, that power, there is a revolution, driving through the city: the people "on the brink of ecstasy". The life released there is different, or seems different:

> Those gentlemen—and this seems a new phenomenon—aren't playing, or rather, don't realise what they're playing. They calculate. Their faces are pale and sad, their gestures sharp and precise, their speech always exact. They don't cheer. They have tremendous power over the people.

And yet the real power, the power which has not yet found its function in fantasy, is not the traditional figures, but the chief of police. The figures of authority are puppets, images, manœuvred by the police and the officials: the reality of projection:

> Not even for myself, but for my image, and my image for its image, and so on.

When the "real" Queen, Bishop and Judge are lost, in the fighting, their places can be taken from the brothel: the manageress and the two clients accustomed to those roles. Given the robes and signs, they are accepted by the crowd, even when their former identity is directly known. The real question is not what happens to them, but to power—to the Chief of Police. As the court official explains, on behalf of the traditional rulers:

> Our resources are inexhaustible . . . we need only choose from the storehouse of mummery. But we must act fast.

In the crisis of power, what is always possible seems to happen. As one of the revolutionary leaders puts it:

> If we behave like those on the other side, then we *are* the other side. Instead of changing the world, all we'll achieve is a reflection of the one we want to destroy.

After the production of the "Queen", the "Bishop" and the "Judge" has gained time, it is this revolutionary leader, dressed as the Chief of Police but with appropriately magnified theatrical uniform, who comes to play "the Hero" and to enact in another studio of the brothel the triumph of history over the slave:

> My history was lived so that a glorious page might be written and then read. It's reading that counts.

Or to put it another way:

> Everything always takes place in the presence of a woman. It's in order for a woman's face to be a witness that, usually . . .

His exhibition of himself, in this new role, has that kind of desire. But as he speaks a cock crows, and he asks:

> Is life so near?

Or as the slave puts it, enacting his humility:

> We try hard just to stand and rot. And, believe me, it's not always easy. Life tries to prevail.

Everyone is looking in on this crisis: voyeurs and audience; actors and agents. At the crisis of his act, the revolutionary shouts:

Outside, in what you call life, everything has crashed. No truth was possible.

It is in this disillusion that he plays his role as chief of police, and his own role, to the end; he makes the gesture of castrating himself; the connection is finally broken. And yet when this has happened, and when the chief of police has achieved his apotheosis—to be impersonated in a brothel—there is blood on the carpet, and the fighting starts up again, as if at a signal. Life tries to prevail. But of course against odds, for the whole apparatus of illusion is in effect intact, though the sound of the machine-guns shows it is still being challenged. The manageress of the Balcony turns to the audience, as she puts out the lights at the end of the play:

> In a little while, I'll have to start all over again, put all the lights on again, dress up (*A cock crows*) Dress up—ah, the disguises! Distribute roles again, assume my own. Prepare yours: judges, generals, bishops, chamberlains, rebels who allow the revolt to congeal. I'm going to prepare my costumes and studios for to-morrow. You must now go home, where everything—you can be quite sure—will be even falser than here.

And she gives the same directions—"by the right, through the alley"—to the audience leaving the theatre as to the clients leaving the Balcony.

The central action of the play—an action of power and its images, of potency and its fantasies—is of course disturbing: the audience is involved in it, and then exposed to it, with a kind of savagery: the relentless, wholly uncompromising vision of the outsider who is also a rebel. Compared with this force, most versions of this theme are literally tame: an insight into roles has been made revolutionary where it is commonly the last sophisticated rationalization of orthodoxy. The theatrical methods, the dramatic means, then become authentic conventions, in this urgent structure of feeling; it is finally not the force but the control of the play that is impressive; the parts are distributed and enacted, but then their world is exploded, into a critical consciousness, a direct challenge: to go out and look at the real world. In *The Balcony* at least, Genet is not acting a role for others; he is creating a dramatic action.

5. *The Fire Raisers* : Max Frisch

Max Frisch's *The Fire Raisers*, which was first produced in 1958, is an ingenious ironic fable: what he himself describes as a "morality without a moral". The phrase is the key to an analysis, for this is a deliberately representative action, intended to connect with a generation of political violence in Europe, and yet what is represented, both in the action and in the dramatized attitudes to it, is an ironic detachment from reality: a kind of negative universality.

The theatrical idea is very powerful. In front of the chorus of firemen—the watchers and guardians who should protect the city, but who mainly, in an ironic development of the manner of the Greek chorus, observe and react—

> Questioning merely, polite
> Even when danger dismays us,
> Warning merely, restrained
> In spite of our anguish,
> Helpless though watchful, the Chorus
> Offers its help till the fire
> Is beyond all hope of extinction

—a free citizen admits into his house first one and then a second obvious fire-raiser, who in effect identify themselves with the exact forms of burning that have been spreading through the city. The dramatic point is the certainty of what is happening, and the citizen's stubborn and complacent detachment from the truth. This familiar idea is raised to a persistent intensity by the very openness of the danger; it is not obliquely, or in hints, implications and guesses that the danger is conveyed, but in the most gross direct forms. This has the effect of shifting attention from the fire-raising itself—that open action—to what is offered as a representative response to it: a refusal to believe that "it can happen here"; jokes and bribes covering the growing apprehension; in the end complicity—even handing over the matches—with those who are destroying him. The only reasons are a fear of giving offence, of acting on suspicion, and a kind of vague goodwill. As the action develops, the contrast between the fire-raising and the response to it becomes, and is meant to become, preposterous: Biedermann's self-deception is a common absurdity, a savagely open farce:

BIEDERMANN: What's in these drums?
EISENRING: Petrol.
BIEDERMANN: Stop joking! I'm asking you for the last time, what's in these drums? You know as well as I do that an attic isn't the place for petrol—
(*He runs his finger over the drum*)
There—just smell for yourselves!
(*He holds his finger under their noses*)
Is that petrol or isn't it?

(*They sniff and look at each other*)
Answer!
EISENRING: It is.
SCHMITZ: It is.
BOTH: No doubt about it.

The tone, here, is decisive. It is the laconic, self-evident, resigned
tone, of a generation which has seen the fire-raisers, not in the
theatre but in history. As such it connects, to contemporary
audiences: a history into a fable; a fable into a tone.

What has then, I think, to be observed is some complacency in
the form. Just because the tone establishes itself so brilliantly, we
can at first overlook the assumptions which are being made, in
effect conventionally, between action and audience. At a simple
level, *The Fire Raisers* is a morality *with* a moral. The chorus says in
the prologue:

> Bestow not the name of Fate
> Upon man's mistakes.

Biedermann is not just Everyman, though the play, at one point,
makes that association by name. He is not only a citizen but a
bourgeois citizen: a comfortable employer, who admits the fire-
raisers but refuses to admit an employee whose patent he has in
effect stolen. He is afraid to call the police, one of the fire-raisers
argues, because

> he has committed an offence himself . . . Strictly speaking, every
> citizen above a certain level of income is guilty of some offence.

When the chorus insist on the danger of fire, he replies:

> What happens under my roof is my business; I mean to say, I
> am the house-owner!

And the chorus reply:

> Sacred to us what is sacred,
> Property,
> Even if out of it springs
> A fire that we cannot extinguish
> That reduces us all to a cinder,
> Sacred to us what is sacred.

They go on to argue:

> He who fears change
> More than disaster
> What can he do to forestall
> The threatening disaster?

It is a dimension of social reference, beyond the generality of the fable, but it is not clear that it is more than a gesture. The fire-raisers evidently recall the Nazis, but they could equally be communists: the Doctor of Philosophy, who accompanies them but later formally dissociates himself, is described by the chorus as

> Resolved to perform any action
> Convinced as he is that the end
> Justifies fully the means . . .
> Cleaning his glasses to lengthen his view
> He sees in the drums full of fuel
> Not fuel—
> He sees the idea!
> Till it's all blazing.

No precise identification can be made, within the terms of the fable, and it could be argued that none is needed. But we are bound to notice that the play operates both in its own terms, as a fable, and by this kind of external reference, pointing in several directions, in what is really theatrical opportunism. The fire-raisers, as a result, are strangely "given": they come with their drums and fuses, and are let in; what looks like history, and is accorded historical allusions, is then emptied of history, and the fire-raisers are, as it were, agents of fate. The ambiguity is there in the epilogue, as the fires spread through the city:

> What all have foreseen
> From the outset
> And yet in the end it takes place,
> Is idiocy,
> The fire it's too late to extinguish
> Called Fate.

This is underlined in an afterpiece, in hell, in which the fire-raisers are traditional devils, who have to go up to earth because traditional sins have been compounded, in the modern world. At the same time, the historical allusion is again made, in the rebuilt city

> Gleaming with glass and with chrome
> But at heart just the same as before.

The laconic tone is that of a world which has "seen it all", but explains only by multiplying allusions and analogies, from the metaphysical to the political, at once conscious and half-made. Not only the fire, but the reasons for it, have been seen and heard before: the tone rests on an exhaustion beyond both; an exhaustion which as in so much post-war European drama is expressed as irony.

In this essential structure of feeling, *The Fire Raisers* is then at once representative and opportunist, and its essential conventions correspond to this: an engaging surface realism in an absurd action; a critical chorus, and internal self-consciousness, which rests not on critical explanation but on making every possible point and letting them all interact. It is the dramatic method of Brecht adapted to a quite different consciousness, which is in the end not critical but paradoxically reassuring: that characteristic contemporary distancing which says in the end "stupid man". At the same time, because this is a real structure of feeling, and not just an idiosyncrasy, the play has an energy, a theatrical brilliance, which makes it a major example of this dramatic kind. Saying "shut the door, we have seen it before", it replays history as farce, to let us see it again, "experimentally", in a safe theatre.

6. *The Physicists* : Friedrich Dürrenmatt

Dürrenmatt's *The Physicists*, which first appeared in 1962, is a further and again brilliant example of a kind of post-war drama which assumes a post-war historical consciousness and at the same time expresses it as a compounded unreality. Where from *The Fire Raisers* we could look back to Brecht, through an important altera- tion of consciousness and tone, from *The Physicists* we can look back to Pirandello, with a continuity of emphasis on "the playing of roles" —the relations between fantasy and reality—yet with an altered edge of conscious and perhaps critical social reference.

The scene is a private sanatorium for mental illness, and is given that sense of a microcosm of the European condition which has spread, in so many forms, from Thomas Mann's *The Magic Mountain*. But this is not a place of philosophical confrontation; it is the characteristic post-war dramatic scene in which absurdity and violence co-exist: an uncertainty, of everything except the killing. Each of the three physicists who are patients kills his nurse; but who they are, and what are their motives, is not only uncertain, in detail; it is uncertain, as a condition. The third physicist and murderer, Mobius, persists in a single role, but is like Pirandello's Henry the Fourth, who is at once mad and conscious of his madness, and who in the end is trapped, after the killing, to go on with the simplest version of his role. What is revealed to him, in visions, by King Solomon, is at once a mad universal theory and a scientific discovery. The discoverer is at once paranoiac and protecting a too dangerous knowledge from a careless and brutal world. Neither role is "real", as against the other; each is potentially real and a potent fantasy; what finally determines him is not a decision, but the trap of a situation. The other two physicists have three roles each: as the patient Beutler, the spy Kilton, and the fantasy-character Sir Isaac Newton; and as the patient Ernesti, the spy Eisler, and the fantasy-character Einstein. Here, again, no single role is more real than the others: the fantasy-characters are transparent, but in the trap of the action are finally assumed; the patients are spies and the spies are patients—in each case, in the action, with supporting corroborative detail (the real sanatorium, the real wireless transmitters). The police inspector, who calls after the murders, is a neutral representative from "outside", whose own role is reversed, however, as the Superintendent, Fraulein Doktor Mathilde von Zahnd reverses hers: what had been seen by one as murder and the other as accident is seen, in the final instance, by one as accident and the other as murder. The Doctor herself alters her role and the very scene of the action: she is at once the medical superintendent and the head of an industrial trust, using the discoveries of the physicists; the sanatorium is also the headquarters of an insane destructive international enterprise. Here, again, though the beginning of the play has established the reality of the sanatorium, this is not more real, in the action, than the destructive enterprise: what is imagined in this world, even in madness, is done.

The conscious edge of the play, through the idea of the physicists, is nuclear weapons: a vast and conscious destructive potential which is also a major intellectual achievement. The same consciousness was at the edge of Brecht's *Galileo*, and was related to it by an argument, on the social connections of science. Here the universal violence is replayed, with a kind of foreseen, mechanically repetitive absurdity, in the killing of the nurses. This is now a familiar type of image (it has affinities with Frisch's fire-raising). It is not the enacted connection, between the historical consciousness and the particular action; it is a "given" connection, in which the historical consciousness is used, but at the level of reference and analogy, while the particular action takes its private and arbitrary course. What is unusual and impressive in *The Physicists* is the continually involving substitution of roles, until it is not this single image, but a whole internal complex of images, that determines the action. Given the inherent theatrical trick, as in Pirandello, that we are who we say we are, that we can so represent ourselves to others as to alter both their and our condition, the ordinary turns of the action, however surprising, follow an internal logic. The formal mode of *The Physicists* is one of presentation, but the substantial mode is a continual disturbance, connecting with false identities, the terror of multiple deception, and the pervading terror of violence. It is a world in which all are using and used: in that literal sense a mad world, of a persistently internal kind. This is connected, formally, with the title-theme:

> "NEWTON": All I do is to elaborate a theory . . . on the basis of natural observation. I write down this theory in the mathematical idiom and obtain several formulae. Then the engineers come along. They don't care about anything except the formulae. They treat electricity as a pimp treats a whore. They simply exploit it. They build machines—and a machine can only be used when it becomes independent of the knowledge that led to its invention. So any fool nowadays can switch on a light or touch off the atomic bomb.

This mechanical "independence", from natural observation, is in a real sense the mental condition of the characters, who are also exploiting, as in the deaths of the nurses, "as a pimp treats a whore". The means of release into fantasy are again related:

> MOBIUS: New and inconceivable forces would be unleashed, making possible a technical advance that would transcend the wildest flights of fancy if my findings were to fall into the hands of mankind.

Or again:

> MOBIUS: For us physicists there is nothing left but to surrender to reality. It has not kept up with us. It disintegrates on touching us.

Consequently:

> MOBIUS: Either we stay in this madhouse or the world becomes one.

There is indeed, through the lines of this "argument" a simple way of seeing the play: as a warning about nuclear physics; an argumentative warning, with supporting murders. But the play is more complex and more disturbed than that. Below all the assigned roles is another consciousness, which can be reached by saying that one does not, at any time, believe these men to be physicists, of a mad, spying, historical or any other kind. The physics is really an "independent" machine; "independent of the knowledge that led to its (dramatic) invention". It is a thing to talk about, to switch on, while a different underlying drama takes its course: that drama which culminates, at the level of a tag, in:

"EINSTEIN": The world has fallen into the hands of an insane
  female psychiatrist.

What is directly communicated, from behind the screen of talk,
is a caged world, in which any role is assumed, under temporary
pressure, and all that is deeply known is an alienation in which
hands are laid on others only to kill. The condition is rationalized,
by each of the characters, and some of their rationalizations are
exposed, or at least contradict each other. But the "physics",
finally, is the play's rationalization: a way of connecting, in a
dramatic image, a formal public violence and an inarticulate
private violence, and of communicating the latter in the guise of,
and with a reference to, the former. It is not quite what Dürrenmatt
said about art and power: "two mirrors which reflect one another
remain empty". It is, rather, his belief that art, now, can reach
"only the victims", not the agents. It is "in this extreme form of
human existence, this last, most miserable form, that the audience
is to see the human being also, indeed itself". He was not there
writing about *The Physicists*, but this is still the essential form of the
play. These imprisoned madmen, and their mad superintendent,
are not agents but victims. Agency, in any dramatic sense, has
gone elsewhere, and is beyond reach. What we see is a state of
mind in which agency and connection have collapsed, and in
which reality and identity are indifferent. This would have been
presented, in early expressionist drama, through a single dominating
consciousness. Now it is presented as it were objectively, and through
what can pass for a public metaphor. The traditional recognition
scenes, in their intrigue form, are replayed, bewilderingly, but there
is nothing and nobody to recognize; the last identity is merely the
most convenient, in a common trap. History, and personal names,
are confidence tricks; the more explicit the attachment, the more
deluded it finally is. The physicists, Dürrenmatt is finally saying—
in a last repetition of that dramatic form in which men explain
themselves to an audience—are not who they say they are; they
are our unrecognizable selves.

2

FOUR PLAYS

1. *Marching Song* : John Whiting

JOHN Whiting's *Marching Song* (1954) is an interesting development of a familiar theatrical form: the house-party of representative
characters, in which a phase of society and a crisis of conscience
can be enacted. It is what Shaw made of Chekhov in *Heartbreak
House*, and there are innumerable minor examples. Fry's *The Dark
is Light Enough*, which appeared in the same year, is a related
example. What is unusual, about Whiting's play, is the tone: an
understatement, in the direct terms of naturalist theatre and acting,
in a form which is normally, by its whole stance, rhetorical.

The scene is a room above a European capital city: "a web of
glass and steel". The house belongs to a rich woman, Catherine de
Troyes, who is waiting for the return from prison of a disgraced
soldier—a war criminal who is her former lover—Rupert Forster.
The country is now ruled by an old, manipulative leader, Cadmus—

> The way to prevent revolt is to stop men living in the present
> time. Given a sad song they drift off with their wives and sweet-
> hearts and resolve their misery in quite the oldest way.

To prevent a public trial of Forster, which would disturb stability
by its inquiry into the past, he has released him and now invites him
to commit suicide. Everything turns on this decision, and the play
is essentially the experience of this kind of decision, between
available ways of living and dying, under a variable but persistent
and overwhelming political pressure. It is then a late version of an
early naturalist structure of feeling: men and women trapped in a
room which is the stage, their fate determined by an unseen but
reported action from elsewhere. In the simplest version of this
form, the audience is similarly trapped, in the room which is the
theatre, looking at the action from only one point of view. The
variant, in this "representative" group, is the flow of the argument:
different possible responses, within the overall constraint, are
embodied in the representative characters: here a priest, a doctor,
a young officer, a sentimental film director, a young girl. In the

end, in this argument, Forster kills himself, in a kind of negative lesson:

> I faced the same problems over the same ground as that man (*the wearer of the helmet*) and young Hurst will face them in the future. They are unchanging but the time and place of decision is personal.

He has killed children who got in the way of a tank attack; the murder, and the failure of the attack, are both held against him. What comes out of the representative action is then a complex of violence, success, humanity, guilt, which is seen as permanent and subject to individual decision. It is a late re-enactment of an essentially liberal question. The representative form and the generalized theme are matched.

Characteristically, the representative form is given overtones of permanence:

> If you listen very hard both of you, you'll hear the sounds of war. Coriolan—Coriolan. You'll hear the soft stumbling tread of returning men. Men out of order and out of heart. There's no trumpet call left will call them to attention. There's no drum can fit the broken rhythm of their march. But they are come back—they have come home.

This, now, is the marching song: uneven and demoralized. It is given the contemporary shapes of a tank attack, government by loudspeaker, the glass and steel room; but it is given historical overtones by the ancient bronze helmet and by the names—Cadmus, Troyes, Dido. It is the representative gesture to contemporary Europe and the allusive gesture to a permanent condition: the creative strategy of Eliot brought into more manageable focus on a naturalist theatrical form. The claim of life is the girl—the representative girl—of this repeated action. It is also the memory of a goat song, heard by Forster in prison: which kept him alive because it was a human voice, but which as an actual song was obscene. These are the representative images of a version of civilization: the goat-song, the Greek names, the bronze helmet, Coriolan; the massacre of the children, the free girl, the rich house in which nobody now can live fully. Through these images, the liberal theme moves: formally, the decision of an individual conscience; substantially, the intolerable choice between human "freedom" and human "entanglement": the trap of human arms and the necessary warmth of relationship—as in Forster's decision when the child climbed on to his tank, or in the contrary decision, of Dido and Catherine, to seek some warmth against the invading cold.

Marching Song is unusual in a special sense: in its concentration, into a single and restrained form and tone, of the representative themes and gestures of a late liberalism, a settled naturalism. It is not penetrating: not the savagely exposing, disturbed and distorted action of the post-liberal collapse. It is a late compression, internally honest and serious and restrained, of an achieved structure of feeling and its essential conventions. The tension, that is to say, has all gone inwards: into a stasis of mood and image; an un-rhetorical heartbreak house, at the very end of a period. It is less showy, less crude, than the forms which succeeded it; its professional compression has that assurance that is possible in a stalemate of feeling and action, within which the words and movements and references are known. At the same time its anxious restraint shows clearly, if negatively, what would happen, to this complex, if the controls were relaxed: a rush of feeling, and a loss of form.

2. *Look Back in Anger* : John Osborne

"To put ourselves and our situations on the stage": this ambition of naturalism, in its ordinary forms, is recurrent. The locally convincing speech and atmosphere, of one generation, becomes first dated, then theatrical; a new local style is then launched against it. This is the central importance of John Osborne's *Look Back in Anger*, which when it was produced in 1956 had the appearance of a breakthrough, but which was essentially a delayed recognition of an already altered style: a recognizable environment, and a recognizable idiom, that had not broken through to the stage though outside the theatre it was already known. It is always, in one sense, a remarkable play that achieves this public alteration of style; only a genuine power can effectively dramatize the necessary sense of release. At the same time, any particular play which achieves this gets a historical weight, a representative importance, which is often more than in itself it can bear.

A general definition of *Look Back in Anger* is not difficult; it has indeed been widely made. Its details of talk and atmosphere, and through these its expression of an intense feeling—a frustrated anger, a prolonged waiting, which must be broken, at any cost, by a demonstration, a shout—have an authentic power. It is that traditional room of the naturalist theatre: the room as trap, with the sounds and messages of a determining and frustrating world

coming in from outside; the people staring from a window, looking
on and raging at their world. But what comes is not the wistfully
confident—

the spirits of truth and freedom, these are the pillars of society

—nor the sad refrain—

To Moscow, Moscow . . . If only we knew, if only we knew

—nor the resigned

The whole worl's in a terrible state of chassis.

It is the trapped angry slang of people shut up too long, in just this
condition, and of one man raging, in a way on behalf of them all
but in default of a visible general condition at each and all of them
as victims, reflections, symptoms: a necessary but intolerable
audience. Jimmy Porter is raging at himself, through the raging at
others and at an intolerable general condition. The sickness of a
society is re-enacted in this particular enclosed form, as the sickness
of available relationships and of this sick man at their centre.

This emphasis on the form is necessary if we are to define *Look
Back in Anger*, and the dramatic movement which followed from it,
in relation to the general tradition. It has been called the emergence
of working-class drama, at a particular stage of cultural and social
change in Britain. But it is not that. The life that comes through is
of people disorganized and drifting; youth and poverty are factors
in this, but the general state of feeling matters more, in these plays,
than any precise social setting. The true social experience is of a
general restlessness, disorganization and frustration, which had
elements in common with the utterly different dramatic style which
it replaced. In Eliot and Fry, also, the dominating themes had
been restlessness and loss of direction, but in the late plays of Eliot,
and in the decorated sentences of Fry, this condition had been
displaced and indulged, in a distant and theatrical mannerism.
What came through in *Look Back in Anger* was a new voice and a
different edge: not the sweet hopelessness, and the measured
despair, but the directly disordered talking and crying—the social
criticism, the cruelty, the sentimentality—of a trapped, identifiable
group. The plays are then not (as they have been sometimes
described) experiments in social realism. A locally convincing
detail and atmosphere are used, but, as always in the mainstream
of naturalism, to be the immediate circumstance for something
very different from description or report. The plays are not docu-
mentaries of youth and poverty, but are intensely personal cries in

the dark: a sentimental drama turned bitter and almost hopeless: a set of blues rhythms rather than a set of social problem plays.

There are then obvious critical difficulties, after the first recognition of an authentically contemporary rhythm and idiom. In any generation (and this was especially marked in the new English writers of the mid-1950s) the first signs are in rhythm and idiom, which appear to give a community to work that later separates into many tendencies. Moreover, recognition of a contemporary style—a crucial act of the theatre—can override the form of a particular play, and be confused with it. This confusion can even occur internally, within the work itself; the matter is never so simple as in Strindberg's analogy of the wine and the bottles.

What is central and memorable in *Look Back in Anger* is the sound of a voice:

> I suppose people of our generation aren't able to die for good causes any longer. We had all that done for us, in the thirties and the forties, when we were still kids. (*In his familiar, semi-serious mood*). There aren't any good, brave causes left. If the big bang does come, and we all get killed off, it won't be in aid of the old-fashioned, grand design. It'll just be for the Brave New-nothing-very-much-thank-you. About as pointless and inglorious as stepping in front of a bus. No, there's nothing left for it, me boy, but to let yourself be butchered by the women.

In this now famous speech, it is interesting that what is communicated, in a way from behind the effective idiom, is an unusual complex, in fact evident throughout the play, of a kind of social despair and a fear and hatred of women. The sharp edge of this voice, at every point, draws on these apparently separable emotions which are felt as one emotion. It is at this point that we encounter the limitation of the description of the play as a blues rhythm; for of course the play is not only a voice; it is an action around this voice. And what is then interesting is that this complex of emotion, which the play as a whole is designed to express, comes to be seen, in continuing work, not as an idiosyncrasy but as the structure of feeling of a group. It is now almost a convention, in Britain: the play of overt social criticism in which the only enemy in sight, though always against a background of generalized social experience, is a wife or girl-friend. What was present as an intense disturbance in Strindberg, and again often in Lawrence, has hardened to something that is almost taken for granted, and that commonly resists explanation. It has been described, in orthodox terms, as a "fusion of the class-war and the sex-war", but the abstractions are

absurd: in this particular complex, there is certainly no class-war
—it is too trapped and passive for that—and what is characteristic
about the abuse of the women is that it is in pseudo-social terms;
not a fusion but a displacement. It may well be that the complex is
too close for analysis, but it is now of major symptomatic importance, and this play is its most important contemporary example.
What seems crucial is that the woman is made the bearer of society,
in a literal way:

> She just devours me whole every time, as if I were some over-
> large rabbit. That's me. That bulge around her navel—if you're
> wondering what it is—it's me. Me, buried alive down there, and
> going mad, smothered in that peaceful looking coil.

To an ordinary kind of sexual disturbance, something is added:
the disturbance as metaphor. The fear of adult relationships, the
willing relapse—as at the end of the play—into a child's game, the
incoherent shifting from one girl to another—from Alison to Helena
and back to Alison—are made, by the idiom, into a criticism of the
world: of a stupid establishment, of a lack of causes, of a general
emotional incapacity. In a sense, always, women are the bearers of
society; of its continuing life, of its settlements, of its practical
inheritance. A rage against a frustrating society, which is in fact
never fought but is shouted at from a distance, might then express
itself through this particular available symbol: the woman is seen
as the society which traps and swallows a particular self, and is
only acceptable (like Alison, when she has lost her baby) when she
renounces that social role and will play in a hiding, frightened
isolation. If he can destroy that continuity, that physical fact of
men born into relationships, the isolated man can find a possible
if childish role. Any other available identity is not only rejected; it
is made, by an idiom, into a common rejection, enlisting the support
of others. What can be said, in apparently direct ways, about a
middle-class establishment, about reactionary ideas, about the loss
of effective causes and feelings, is then swept, by the rhythm, into
an identity with this lonely fear.

It is then important to remember that this structure of feeling is
neither recommended nor valued; the whole form of the play allows
it to be taken as a case, without necessary endorsement. It is very
similar, in this respect, to those first-person novels which at once
communicate an emotion, a way of responding to the world, and
yet, by their form, can detach themselves from its understanding.
This particular relationship between a voice and an action is then
the necessary critical point: the action serves only to release the

voice, but at the same time the voice can hide itself behind an apparent action. A world has been reduced to these symptomatic relationships, and the shouting inside them—even the direct indifference and cruelty—is heard as a shouting past them, a shouting from that trap of a room at an unseen, representative world. Indeed the idiom itself—a continual free association of ideas, a rough overriding of precision, an engaging, disturbed rage and parody ("his familiar semi-serious mood")—is an exact expression of a carefully prepared dramatic situation: the rough shouting at cruelty and indifference through cruelty and indifference; the loss of feeling in an acting-out of feeling; the humiliation of self and others as a response to a humiliating, intolerable society.

"To put ourselves and our situations on the stage": the orthodox claim comes back like an echo. "The joy of life in its tense and cruel struggles": the emphasis persists, from that early to this late naturalism. The voices and the atmosphere of each period of breakthrough become period voices and a period atmosphere, in direct relation to the original shock and excitement of recognition. And then what stands out is a situation, inseparable from the idiom but defining itself in much wider terms: a late stage of that crisis of isolation and terror, in which the victims turn on each other and on the weakest, and their cries for freedom are the painful, ugly, hysterically powerful cries from the trap.

3. *The Birthday Party* : Harold Pinter

There is a point in the development of many dramatic forms when the original strangeness can be mastered, the difficult convention learned as a method, and the unusual structure of feeling assumed. The form is then available, in quite new ways, for use in the theatre.

This seems to me the essential history of Harold Pinter's plays. They are strange only in the absence of a tradition in European literature, of the last fifty years. What they represent is the domestication, in an English theatrical idiom, of what had been a strange form. *The Birthday Party*, written in 1957, is an example of just this skilful adaptation. It is what had been the strange world of Kafka, now in an English seaside boarding house. The characteristic pair of attendants, the strange agents or messengers, come to break and carry away a young man. The menace of what they are doing is tangible but unexplained; it is the irruption of a bizarre and arbitrary violence into an ordinary life. The structure of feeling is familiar: the precarious hold on reality, the failures of communication, the inevitability of violence and exploitation. In drama, this world had already been realized: most evidently in Ionesco, but also in Eliot's *Sweeney Agonistes* and in Beckett. It is always in a sense recalcitrant, this world of the absurd, in which it is in the gaps between what can be said that the arbitrary action, the overwhelming preoccupation, pushes through, and in which language, across the gaps, takes the form of a comic nightmare. What Pinter is able to do is to assume this structure, and to find a way of communicating it in terms of the English theatre. At the beginning of *The Birthday Party*, the philosophical absurd is already an old friend: the deck-chair attendant and his landlady wife:

> Petey?
> What?
> Is that you?
> Yes, it's me.
> What? Are you back?
> Yes.
> I've got your cornflakes ready. Here's your cornflakes.
> Are they nice?
> Very nice.
> I thought they'd be nice.

This is the theatrical idiom of socially inarticulate people, as conventionally presented, for a kind of comedy, on the English middle-class stage. It is through this lead, in what is already a known game, that the gap is opened, and when the strange agents arrive they are also, in the first instance, familiar theatrical characters: a stage Irishman and a stage Jew. The ordinary counters, of a conventional English naturalist comedy of the lower classes and of foreigners, are used to initiate an action which in its direct terms would lack these essential connections: a known absurd calls to an unknown, and the necessary trick is turned.

What then happens, in *The Birthday Party*, is that the idiom of naturalist comedy—the deck-chair attendant, the landlady, the lodger, the tart, the Irishman, the Jew—is developed to the point where the irruption of another consciousness—a malignant universal bullying—is not, and has no need to be, an irruption into an everyday world; that acceptance has already been gained, by the conversion of ordinary life into this kind of theatre. The opportunity to show menace—an inarticulate menace—is then fully taken. The birthday party, with its drum, its switching-off of lights, its game of blind-man's buff, releases the violence, in a further stroke of theatre. The shock of bringing together these two idioms—virtually of

farce and of melodrama—is controlled by their separate, prepared familiarity. With the conventions loosened, by the theatrically
acceptable evasion of probability, the central scenes of interroga-
tion, the human breaking and bewilderment, can occur in their
own terms. Names are confused, identities shuffled; miscellaneous
charges, at once grave and ridiculous, are hurled in a rapid stage
patter:

> Why did you change your name?
> I forgot the other one.
> What's your name now?
> Joe Soap.
> You stink of sin.
> I can smell it.
> Do you recognize an external force?
> That's the question!
> Do you recognize an external force, responsible for you, suffering
>   for you?
> It's late.
> Late! Late enough! When did you last pray?
> He's sweating!
> When did you last pray?
> He's sweating!
> Is the number 846 possible or necessary?
> Neither.
> Wrong. Is the number 846 possible or necessary?
> Both.
> Wrong! It's necessary but not possible.
> Both.
> Wrong! . . .

It is the edge of metaphysical menace of Beckett, crossed with the
terrifying platitudes of Ionesco. But the point is always the theatrical
effect. The menace is of the agents of an unnamed organization,
and the fact that it is unnamed allows every effect at once: criminal,
political, religious, metaphysical. Behind the effects is an effective
conviction, now in its turn a cliché, but there to be drawn on as an
active unlocated experience: that "they" will get you—drag you
back to a wife, a shop, striped trousers and black jacket, duty,
respectability, death. It is Mr. Polly raised to a pseudo-metaphysical
status; a social experience abstracted to an idiom of isolation and
the breakdown of language. He is secretive and dangerous anyway;
furtive as all men are furtive; the dragging to grace or to death,
or simply back to striped trousers, is in a final sense indifferent.

Pinter's theatrical projection of the difficult conventions of the
absurd is consistently successful, in these essentially minor ways.

But his most substantial achievement is something quite different, below the conventional levels of the absurd. There was a point, in the evolution of naturalist dialogue, when the repetitions, the questionings, the dead phrases, the gaps of an accepted inarticulacy could be worked on, reduced and stylized, to a conventional idiom. Eliot worked on it, in his early comic-strip characters, and it is still there, as a style, in the first scene of *The Cocktail Party*. Pinter took this further, in the different context of ordinary English speech: a fragmentary rhythm, in a particular interest: the deluded and dangerous comedy of ordinariness; the dead strangeness and menace of a drifting, routine-haunted, available common life. It has been widely imitated, in many different forms:

Had they heard about us, Petey?
They must have done.
Yes, they must have done. They must have heard this was a very good boarding house. It is. This house is on the list.
It is.
I know it is.

What this offers is at once the attachment to ordinary life—the conviction of normality, of the everyday—and a covert valuation, beyond the anxious imitation—of a loss of significance, a loss of reality: a naturalism at once confirmed and emptied of content, given a different content: the hollow men not masked and chanting, but in ordinary clothes, speaking ordinary words; a loss of spiritual connection now at last domesticated; the strange idiom of the absurd become a theatrical method.

4. *Serjeant Musgrave's Dance* : John Arden

Any break from naturalism is a break from the room: from that representative room, above a capital city; from that trap of a room, in which the victims torment each other; from that everyday room, in which the menacing agents arrive unexplained. It is not, of course, mainly a question of staging; it is a question of consciousness. What is enacted in the room is a state of mind in which things happen to people from a determining world beyond them. Those external forces can be a loudspeaker government, or the sound of church bells, or mysterious emissaries: what is crucial, always, is the passive consciousness, accepting certain limits, devising trapped styles. It is so powerful and ordinary an experience that it still determines our majority drama, at the point where action—a willed action—is felt to be impossible. What is essentially dramatized in *Serjeant Musgrave's Dance*, and what gives it its distinction, in the English drama of its generation, is the attempt at willed action, against the sources of the determining world. This is so in plot, in the simple sense: the sergeant who leads his deserters to bring the truth and the crime of a colonial war to an ordinary town. It is so, also, in feeling: not the look from the window, at where violence and exploitation are happening, but the attempted enactment—the re-enactment—in a suddenly open theatre. What is then interesting is that Arden, following Brecht, uses the form of a fable: what he calls, in his sub-title, "an un-historical parable". He removes the action from any precise location or period, to avoid, paradoxically, the distance, the cut-offness, of history; yet to avoid, also, the arguable contemporary detail. He then uses, frankly, the costumes of rank, the badges of occupation, the identifying marks of a known social world: simplified, isolated; an identifying and challenging action.

What is thus brought into the play, as an explicit dramatic idiom, is a popular history, which by its deliberately theatrical form is made visible and even transparent. The subsidiary characters are sketches of attitudes, in a few brief strokes: mayor, parson, constable—the phrases and gestures of "order"; "a slow collier", "a pugnacious collier", "an earnest collier"—the range of simple attitudes among the working men; three soldiers contrasted in mood—Sparky, Hurst, Attercliffe. It is not so much a representative as a mimed world, drawing in a simple way on popular song, popular stories, popular attitudes. What drives through this, as in *Woyzeck*, is a disturbed consciousness: a bizarre, critical, willed action: Serjeant Musgrave's dance.

A parable, then, in a way based on pantomime: on a deliberate, explicit staging, to isolate an action which in being willed is already theatrical: an extravagant gesture against a conventional world. What the form allows, and what the action shows, is a complex seeing, not of the world that is acted against, but of the character of the action.

Musgrave's plan is to bring home death, literally, to the social order which sanctions it. But this is already understood, by his companions, in different ways: as the shock of the bones of a soldier from this town; as the affront of this hung skeleton; as the case for continuing the killing, in the mad logic of progression—five citizens had been killed, in that other town, in revenge for the death of this soldier; let there now be five times five, in this same ordinary town. The demonstration, that is to say, can be differently seen; the dance of death, as a willed action, is always subject to this hazard. Thus a critical consciousness—of the nature of the action—is there, from the beginning, past the mystery, the strange brooding presence, of Musgrave himself. It is not a question, in this form, of the rightness or wrongness of the action: of rightness and wrongness as given. As it is worked through, the play gives its impulses, and then gives its effects. Its climax is when the skeleton hangs in its soldier's tunic, and Musgrave dances under it, "waving his rifle, his face contorted with demoniac fury". This is the man who had seemed to be God, the avenging angel, the bringer of a terrible saving truth:

> Dead man's feet
> Over the street
> Riding the roofs
> And crying down your chimneys . . .
> . . . Up he goes and no one knows
> How to bring him downwards.

At the point of the revelation, and because of the kind of revelation it is, everything is still uncertain, and anything can still happen: all that is there and certain is the fact of the dead soldier:

> *and* it'll go on, there or elsewhere, and it can't be stopped neither, except there's someone finds out Logic and brings the wheel round.

Musgrave's logic—the apparently simple impulse of extending the truth of death—is in practice insane; the demand for order, that he has learned from the rigid training for killing, can be called a demand for justice but is simply a continuation of the hated order by other means. What is against it is the persistent thought of a human alternative:

> it *wouldn't* be anarchy, you know; he can't be right there! All it would be is: *you* live and *I* live—we don't need his duty, we don't need his Word—a dead man's a dead man! We could call it *all* paid for! Your life and my life—make our *own* road, we don't follow nobody.

But this is said by Sparky just before he is killed, not in the execution of Musgrave's design but in an accident in a jealous and irritable fight. The impulse for order, the perception of real anarchy, goes and comes back; is seen both ways round. This is the method throughout: its most evident immediate example is the Bargee's parody of Musgrave's discipline and of Musgrave's prayer—to see both, simultaneously, is to be critically conscious of both actions. Or again,

Mrs. Hitchcock and Annie, who speak throughout for "life or love",
bring it in the end to the dead and condemned:

> ANNIE: His blood's on my tongue, so hear what it says. A
> bayonet is a raven's beak. This tunic's a collier's jacket. That
> scarecrow's a birdcage. What more do you want!

—a truth not unlike Musgrave's; or again:

> MRS. HITCHCOCK: Look at it this road: here we are, and we'd
> got life and love. Then *you* came in . . . *you* brought in a
> different war . . . Those men are hungry, so they've got no
> time for you. One day they'll be full, though, and the Dragoons'll
> be gone, and then they'll remember.
>
> MUSGRAVE: No.

It is a continuing uncertainty, letting each action, each feeling,
go its whole run. Musgrave's last dance will be when he is hung for
robbery and desertion:

> Crooked Joe Bludgeon having his dance out in the middle of
> fifty dragoons.

But, as against that, Attercliffe can ask, in the last words of the
play:

> They're going to hang us up a length higher nor most apple-
> trees grow, Serjeant. D'you reckon we can start an orchard?

The seed of the death may be a tree of fruit, for the action remains
open.

It has been clear for some years that John Arden is the most
genuinely innovating of the generation of young English dramatists
of the fifties. The intense consciousness and the theatrical invention
are unusually integrated, but in a situation in which this kind of
integrity is tentative and precarious: a situation, in English drama
and theatre, in which, like the serjeant's dance, the meaning is one
thing and its success another: an open and doubtful action, which
can go either way.

Conclusion

CONCLUSION

I

WE can now look again at the real relations, in modern drama, between structures of feeling and conventions. These relations imply, analytically, questions of consciousness and audience: of dramatic form and the theatre.

To define the history in this way is a critical choice. We cannot usefully apply, to any modern art, the critical terms and procedures which were discovered for the understanding of earlier work. A theory of kinds, which still haunts dramatic criticism, is now obviously null. Its inherent notions—of hierarchy, separation, fixed rules for each kind—belong to a social and philosophical order built on exactly those principles. The order and the theory have fallen together. The terms that succeeded, in art as in society, were of movements: self-originating movements, which defined their own characteristics. From the manifesto of Strindberg to the manifesto of Brecht; from Ibsen's critical description of his decision to write the "language of real life" to Eliot's critical arguments for dramatic verse; from the self-criticism of theatre in Büchner and Chekhov to a later self-criticism in Pirandello and Anouilh: these bearings indicate our initial survey. It is part of a deep inner history, in repeated struggles, that this century of new drama is directly and indirectly self-conscious: critically aware of its own problems and forms. Very few modern dramatists, whose work has survived their immediate place and time, have failed to write critically about dramatic form and the theatre. Yet no real history can be written from the critical pronouncements alone: there is too much evident tension between the critical positions and the varying creative practices. The substance is always in many hundreds of plays, or, to put it another way (which is already a beginning of history) in the life's work of many scores of dramatists. But then these are interpreted, not only externally but also internally, not in kinds but in movements. It is where a critical survey begins.

It will take us some way, but no longer far enough. It is not only that as the names of movements get known—naturalism, expressionism, epic theatre, the absurd—they harden, inevitably. They acquire external associations; become a shorthand of classification;

tend to blur and confuse essentially different practices, and certain
necessary connections. About the past, always, they have a look
of calm certainty; but in any active present they can decline to
meaningless repetition, or become rigid, desperate: a barrier where
work is now done. It is also that each of the movements is, intrinsi-
cally, a recommendation: an offered completion of the creative
effort; a way of forming and training an audience. In the competition of offers there is already confusion: where the kinds stare
inertly, from another history, the movements penetrate, organize;
find workers, supporters, hangers-on. To accept the terms of those
offers is to make any critical history impossible. It is receiving a
tradition as opposed to living it. Any real tradition is a selection,
a revaluation, a critique of the orthodox survey. Now, when we
have looked at the plays, we can go back behind the names, and
make our own history, in our own terms.

2

It is commonly said that we have got beyond naturalism. Yet the
argument, here, has scarcely even begun. For it is clear, in practice,
that naturalism means several different things. In its widest sense,
it is an absorbed interest in the contemporary everyday world, and a
corresponding rejection or exclusion of any supposed external
design or system of values. It is then an absorbed recreation of the
ways in which people, within human limits, actually speak, feel,
think, behave, act. By these criteria, many of the supposed rejections
of naturalism are in fact variations on it. Conventions are changed,
not because some other view of the world, or some other creative
purpose, is now proposed, but because existing conventions are
no longer *true enough*, by essentially similar criteria. It must be
obvious that what is meant by the "rejection of naturalism" is
ordinarily a rejection of its earliest particular conventions. The most
evident emphasis, of those early conventions, was the dramatic
representation, the theatrical reproduction, of "lifelike", "probable"
speech, behaviour and environment. It can then seem a rejection
of naturalism to use conventions of speech, action and scene which
are not, in immediate terms, probable, or superficially lifelike. But
these new conventions, normally, have the same central purpose:
a true representation of life. Strindberg, proposing his experimental
conventions, made the distinction in that way:

false naturalism, which believes that art consists simply of
sketching a piece of nature in a natural manner; . . . true

naturalism, which seeks out those points in life where the great conflicts occur, which rejoices in seeing what cannot be seen every day.

These intense isolated moments, and the conventions needed to give them dramatic expression, are then not evidence of an alternative structure of feeling, but of the development of the heart of the original naturalist claim. Strindberg's definition, clearly, could be applied as it stands to Ibsen's major naturalist plays.

Or take Yeats, again recommending quite new conventions:

There, where no studied lighting, no stage-picture made an artificial world, he was able to recede from us into some more powerful life. Because that separation was achieved by human means alone, he receded, but to inhabit as it were the deeps of the mind . . . Our unimaginative arts are content to set a piece of the world as we know it in a place by itself, to put their photographs, as it were, in a plush or plain frame, but the arts which interest me, while seeming to separate from the world and us a group of figures, images, symbols, enable us to pass for a few moments into a deep of the mind that had hitherto been too subtle for our habitation.

This "deep of the mind", again, is not evidence of an alternative structure of feeling; it is a human discovery, "by human means alone". We can compare it with Ibsen saying:

My play is no tragedy in the ancient acceptation. My desire was to depict human beings and therefore I would not make them speak the language of the gods.

It is not the creative purpose, but the creative means, that are at issue. We can compare, in this precise respect, Eliot arguing against the kind of speech that Ibsen had chosen, and for a return to dramatic verse:

The *human* soul, in intense emotion, strives to express itself in verse. It is not for me, but for the neurologists, to discover why this is so, and why and how feeling and rhythm are related. The tendency, at any rate, of prose drama is to emphasise the ephemeral and superficial; if we want to get at the permanent and universal we tend to express ourselves in verse.

The offered contrast is sharp, but the "permanent and universal" is not a world outside man; it is "the *human* soul, in intense emotion", and subject—in a characteristically naturalist reference—to the understanding of the neurologist.

We can evidently, then, avoid some confusion if we make certain initial distinctions about naturalism. Nobody who knows the major naturalist plays can believe, seriously, that their impulse is technical: that their particular conventions for putting human beings and their environment on the stage were a choice of style, subject to rejection by choice of a different style. It is this, above all, that we now underestimate: under the influence, of course, of important arguments for different conventions. The driving force of the great naturalist drama was not the reproduction of rooms or dress or conversation on the stage. It was a passion for truth, in strictly human and contemporary terms. Whatever the later argument, about particular conventions, it was the decisive moment, in all modern drama. A long prepared redefinition, of the sources of human understanding and of the objects of human concern, found at last, in this form, its decisive realization. It is one of the great revolutions, in human consciousness: to confront the human drama in its immediate setting, without reference to "outside" forces and powers. It is so difficult a revolution that it is still, in some ways, incomplete. Dramatic methods and theatrical practices, drawn from an earlier consciousness, persist, as we have seen, in the greatest dramatists: in Ibsen more clearly than anywhere. But, in spite of these difficulties, it is a successful revolution, and it is from its central purposes that nearly all serious modern drama derives. There are important secondary arguments, on the dramatic means of this confrontation, even on the particular sources of this decisive human truth. But it is deeply significant that the creative purpose is now so widely accepted that it is hardly even noticed; indeed that it is often taken for granted.

It can never be taken for granted, as we can show, at once, by considering another meaning of naturalism. There is always a precise internal relation between a structure of feeling and its effective conventions: in the great naturalist drama, between the strictly human definition of truth and the direct representation of human actuality. To achieve this, as we saw in Ibsen, certain external conventions, mechanically persisting from an earlier major consciousness, had to be rejected and altered: conventions deriving ultimately from a design, a fate, outside man, intervening beyond his terms. These were dismissed as "theatrical": an opposition to truth. But the new naturalist conventions had to be established in the theatre; learned as practices. What then happened, in turn, was the establishment of new external conventions: methods and practices without precise relation to the consciousness they had been designed to express. Representation, verisimilitude, probability became, in these terms, self-sufficient. A dramatic setting must be "right"—the sort of room people like this would live in. An actor's movements must give the effect of "the expected"—what that person, in that situation, would probably do. Dramatic speech must be "like conversation"—what those people, in that situation, would say, and no more. These conventions and practices, which in effect still govern our majority drama, can be seen as external because they are self-defining dogmas. We are in fact as likely to see them employed without consideration of the structure of feeling from which they derive, as to see them *necessarily* following from the consciousness of the play. Thus what are authentic conventions, in major naturalist drama, become inauthentic, by simple habit; as can be seen in performances of what are essentially intrigue plays, melodramas, fantasies; in the development of Eliot, where the consciousness and the conventions come to open contradiction; in the ordinary season of Shakespeare. There are then comic paradoxes. A naturalist scene is abandoned but naturalist speech is retained; or naturalist speech abandoned, but naturalist scene and movement retained: yet all, in the jargon, going "beyond naturalism". It is then important to distinguish naturalist drama from what we can call the naturalist habit. It is not in the separated conventions that naturalism defines itself; it is in the structure of feeling to which, as serious conventions, they relate.

3

What is the naturalist structure of feeling? We have described the revolution in which the whole consciousness and concern of modern drama were altered. It was called the naturalist revolution, and the term is still accurate. But a particular distinction, of its earliest phase, needs to be clearly made. In any precise analysis of the structure and its conventions, a particular relation between men and their environment is evidently assumed. If we see, in its detail, the environment men have created, we shall learn the truth about them. That is one way of putting it, and it is deeply relevant to Ibsen and Chekhov, where the dramatic tension, again and again, is between what men feel themselves capable of becoming, and a thwarting, directly present environment. It is even possible to feel that Ibsen had to make rooms on the stage in order to show men trapped in them. For he certainly did not make them in a kind of competition with furnishers. It is perhaps a particular stage of bourgeois society, in which the decisive action is elsewhere, and what is lived out, in these traps of rooms, are the human consequences: in particular, the consequences of a relatively leisured society. To stare from a window at where one's life is being decided:

that consciousness is specific, in this great early phase. The rooms are not there to define the people, but to define what they seem to be, what they cannot accept they are. This is of course radically different from the reproduction of a room to try to persuade us (it is usually hard going) that if the room is right the people are real; if the phrasing is right, something is being said; if the gesture is right, it means something.

But then the authentic naturalism, of this early phase, reached a necessary limit. It is what we saw in the discussion of Lawrence's plays, or in the problem of Synge's *Riders to the Sea*. When the action is really elsewhere, and begins to engage the exploring consciousness of a writer, the trap of the room is a real trap; the interior life—not only the domestic interior but the corresponding consciousness, reflecting, reacting—is no longer an adequate truth. There must be a break to action: to a made and making rather than merely received environment; and then the early conventions, within a room and among people waiting and watching, are dangerously in the way. Many of the simple limitations, of this early naturalist form, can be overcome, at once, in a different convention of performance: with the cleared stage, allowing a different range of actions; or with the film or television cameras, offering a new range and mobility. At the same time, the will to move in this way, for dramatic rather than for spectacular reasons, is quite another matter. We have gone on being trapped, by that same early consciousness, in the more crowded and moving streets.

We can perhaps best see that room—the room in which one watches at a window, to which people call saying what is happening in the world, in which one's fate is decided—as intermediate, between two possible dramas. It was a real situation, a real conscious-ness. It was also an attempt to bridge two radically different worlds, which, for historical reasons, were now difficult to integrate: a world of action, in which an environment is made; and a world of consciousness, in which a consequence is realized. Dramatists have struggled, throughout, to bring these worlds together; but no real integration is within a gift. If the separation were not real, the conventions would not have needed to be changed.

What was at stake, in that early phase, was a more difficult claim: to be representative; to create a unique history which was a general truth. The claim has persisted, yet it belongs, deeply, to a particular history, a particular consciousness. The major and irreversible change, between renaissance and modern drama, is an alteration in the terms of that "typicality" on which all drama depends. The former typicality was "universal" in character:

depending at once on a social and metaphysical order, it took the prince (the hero) as in this sense representative of human destiny. The liberal revolution against the social and metaphysical order overthrew any such definition. The insistence on the drama of ordinary life, on the dramatic importance of people without formal rank, altered action and character in a single movement. The change from the "universal" to the "representative" is one way of describ-ing this; each mode has deep ties to other characteristic institutions and forms of thought in its kind of society. Yet each mode, in real situations, is a mystification, or, if we prefer it, an ideal. It would be possible in some simple communities to create a unique history which was also a general truth; but all drama has been made in already complicated societies: it is a willed form, not a self-evident or traditional fact. In the period of early naturalism, the complica-tion was exceptional. It was a class society, in which the "middle" class was dominant. While the drama could remain, by isolation, within a single class, it could offer to be representative, in simple ways; it could assume an effective common understanding of a human situation and human claims. Some isolated popular drama (early Synge and early Lawrence, or Büchner and Hauptmann, are relevant) could make a similar, though always temporary, assumption. The inner history of naturalism is really this: that it developed *as a style*—a characteristic way of handling the world—in bourgeois society, but that it developed *as a form*, capable of major dramatic importance, in a period in which bourgeois society was being fundamentally criticized and rejected, mainly by people who nevertheless belonged in its world. There is then a contradic-tion in naturalism, but also a tension out of which the great drama of Ibsen directly came. The style assumed an understandable, recognizable, manageable everyday world; the form, while linked to this, discovered a humanity which this same world was frustrating or destroying. It is easy to see, by contrast, how little tension there is in the simple majority drama of what we have called the naturalist habit. Take that explosive discovery away, and the people are indeed as they seem, and everything necessary can be said or, even more crucially, done. There have been hardly any difficulties with naturalism in the majority middle-class theatre and its deriva-tives; it is a self-evident, though to others mainly boring, tradition. But important naturalist drama developed, historically, in just that period of liberal revolt against orthodox liberalism, of individual revolt against an orthodox "individualist" society, of bourgeois revolt against the forms of bourgeois life. Its means were the "free theatres" which sprang up across Europe (often interwoven with nationalism, but still connecting with each other) between 1860 and 1900. What was becoming available as a style was used to push an action beyond the ordinary terms of the beliefs on which it depended. The self-evident reproductive element in naturalism was joined by the alternative emphasis of direct exposure. The passion for evident truth burst beyond the forms of self-evident truth. We have seen, in detail, what then happened: in Ibsen and in Chekhov; a repeated search for some means of defining the humanity that cannot be lived, in these well-ordered rooms—the forces outside, the white horses or the seagull, the tower or the cherry orchard, which have meaning because there are forces inside these people in these rooms, which can not be realized in any available life. This is the paradox of the unique history which is also a general truth, in early naturalism: that it is of an individual who is breaking away from what is offered as general truth: a uniquely representative figure (representative of "humanity", of "Man") who is in revolt against the representative environment other men have made. The world of action, characteristically, is then the action of others; the world of consciousness is one's own. Out of this separation, and out of its terrible tensions, these men trapped in their rooms make their only possible, their exceptionally powerful, drama.

4

This real contradiction, between style and form, could not last for ever, in serious drama. Ibsen, towards the end, is already breaking, externally, what he had broken internally by sheer tension and force. Strindberg, in a younger generation, soon abandoned the given environment, and made a dramatic form out of the internal struggles. The subsidiary characters—the characters as environment—are excluded, and then, in a new major innovation, a dramatic form is made wholly from the already isolated consciousness: what we call, in defining that kind of early expressionism, the drama of a "single mind". Instead of an understandable, recognizable, manageable everyday world, there is the creation, from separation, of a world which is still everyday—which is still offered for recognition—but which is now unmanageable, strange, hostile. The suppressed tension, of those many trapped rooms, now breaks to a redefinition of what any environment is. A dramatic world is made (and we are still mainly in this phase) in which it is human isolation that has become representative: another unique history, offered, even more paradoxically, as a general truth. What was still, in the patient reproduction of naturalism, a self-evidently man-made world, is now a phantasmagoria, a hostile projection, a parody of order. Out of this structure of feeling—in historical terms, out of the failure of bourgeois revolt against bourgeois society—comes a new confidence: a confidence of despair. The techniques were available, from traditional romantic literature, from the fragments of a supernatural order: visions, transformations, superhuman powers, a malignant nature. But the techniques became conventions by a major creative reworking. It was not now in an order beyond man that these manifestations occurred; it was inside him, deep inside him, in dreams and in visions, in his own irreducible and most personal and significant life. What in orthodox fantasy or romance (of which, in the commercial theatre, there are still many examples) were still theatrical tricks, a kind of conscious play in the relaxation from reality, became now a reality of its own: the direct projection, into a dramatic action, of man's inner history. It is the abandonment of naturalism, in one ordinary sense. Yet the new conventions establish themselves because what is shown is integrated by an inner personality, an inner vision. They are more than techniques because they have this organizing principle: not a way of looking at reality, a way among other ways, but reality itself: what life is like when the external pretences are dropped. We can all see the difference, in dramatic method, between say *Ghosts* and *The Road to Damascus;* but we must also now see the connection. It is in the same passion for a strictly human truth that each play is conceived, but the suspicion of Mrs. Alving—"I sometimes think that we are all ghosts"—has been put directly on the stage, in quite different conventions but in what is really only a development of the structure of feeling. This early expressionism, and the whole powerful drama of "internal vision, external distortion" which has followed from it, is the action that succeeds to, rather than contradicts, the great tensions of the major naturalist play. The person looking from the window of that trapped room is still there; but the room around him has gone, the other people in his direct dimension have gone, and what he sees from the window, now through his own eyes, is not the orthodox world but his own necessary version of it: a look from the window that is now, in essence, the dramatic form.

5

It is not then really surprising that two apparently different forms—serious naturalism and psychological expressionism—should have come to coexist in the same drama: often, indeed, in the same theatres, the same companies, the same actors, the same writers. The conventions are different, as well as the local techniques, but they relate, essentially, to historically connected structures of feeling. Thus we can turn from what Strindberg was doing, in his late plays, to Stanislavsky's version of the naturalism he developed from and applied to Chekhov:

> This imaginative truth was formerly achieved by us mostly externally; it was the truth of objects, furniture, costumes, stage property, lighting and sound effects, the outward image of the actor and his external physical life.

That is indeed the convention which Joyce mocked in his "writing the mystery of himsel in furniture". Stanislavsky moved on to direct human means, in acting, to express what he called an "inner realism" (though in fact he never abandoned the "truth of objects", any more than most modern theatre). Expressionism, on the contrary, moved on to transform, in a surprising way, the "truth of objects", using the stage physically to realize "inner" images. This is basically the completion of the movement we have already discussed: in which there was first a tension, then a separation, between the decisive consciousness and the available world. What was dramatized, in major naturalism, was a tension which still drew much of its force from the physical existence of an unacceptable world, and from the presence in it of others, in the same dimension, with whom the attempt at a common understanding, a common recognition, must continue to be made. (This form, of course, has continued, down to the drama of our own day; it is the naturalist form—as in Pinter—of what is called the drama of "non-communication"). What was dramatized in expressionism was a related tension which remade the world and its persons in its own terms: not for liberation from it—it was still consciousness and not action—but to show what it really was, what it felt like; to expose it.

There are, of course, two clear meanings of exposure, and throughout this history they have both been important. We have already seen how major naturalism was an inherently critical form; it showed the world as unacceptable by showing directly what it was like, and then how impossible it was when people really tried to live in it. Major expressionism was also inherently critical; it said not only "this is what my world is like" but, in a persistent anguish, "because it is like this it is intolerable to me". This is true in naturalism from Ibsen to O'Neill, and in expressionism from Strindberg to Beckett. Yet, in all these cases, though the critique is evident, it is also implicit. It is in tensions within the form that the critique is expressed. What we have now to look at is a succeeding phase, still deeply connected, in which dramatists attempted to make the critique explicit, by a new variation of form, requiring new conventions.

Once again, techniques and methods were in fact available, from earlier drama: chorus, narrator, commentator, raisonneur. Any of these, of course, might be used simply as techniques: available variations of style, as still in many examples. But in some major experiments these methods became true conventions; were related, organically, to an altered structure of feeling. Yet what could this be? The internal critique, like the internal tensions, seems to have depended, historically, on the situation we have described: a "rejection" of bourgeois society which was also, factually, a resigned or angry acceptance of it as inevitable. The dramatists could have done nothing else, from real experience, and yet the nature of the "solution" is one of the reasons for the development of more frankly separated and isolated forms: to speak the whole truth at last, in one's own terms and no others. By definition, of course, there could not be an internal critique, of one's own vision, in the same way: what is present in Ibsen, as a continually implied point of view, is present in late Strindberg or Beckett as an impotent anguish.

What had to be done, to get truly outside? This is the later history, of social expressionism, and of the experiments of Brecht. The isolated consciousness, seeing the world in its own way, had to try to become, to identify itself with, an objectively critical or revolutionary consciousness. This is a phase of profound importance, but it has been more often imitated than achieved. We have seen in Toller, or in Auden and Isherwood, how the conventions can fail, can decline to techniques, if there is any real doubt about the truth of that objective viewpoint; or if it is only negatively identified with a still subjective and anguished consciousness. There have been two main solutions: in summary, those of Pirandello and Brecht. The objective viewpoint, in Pirandello, as in later writers like Ionesco, is a total criticism of the possibility of a knowable world: this is the centre of what is now called "absurdism", though many essentially different things have been confused with it. Not this society but any society; not this relationship but any relationship; not these words but any words: all these thwart men, inevitably; and that "universal" condition is then critically seen. In Pirandello the critique is formal: against the attempts at reality which prove to be illusions. In Ionesco, the critique is a self-sufficient form: a world openly mocked in a set of cliches and self-deceptions which are the only available words and actions.

The objective viewpoint in Brecht, on the other hand, is revolutionary and historical: the thwarting and destruction are shown, but are then explained, critically: a point of view is established, by what are now not techniques but conventions, and this viewpoint controls the dramatization. We can then see the development—in the rush of work of course very complicated—from naturalism to critical naturalism; from personal expressionism to social expressionism; from an "absurd" private drama to an "absurd" social drama; from the subjective-critical to the objective-critical. It is a development that is still very far from complete, for what has persisted throughout, in a majority of cases, is the original difficulty: of the real experience: of a man trapped in bourgeois society and unable to escape from it; of the conviction, after so long a persistence, that this is not a social but a "universal" condition; of the precarious and often ambiguous character of actual change and revolution.

There have been, of course, certain clear periods of development. There is a clear difference, in action and tone, between the generously angry, the bitterly humane naturalism of the liberal period, at the end and at the turn of the century, and the kinds of despair, contempt and rejection which have multiplied since the first war. There has been a steady development of theories but also processes of illusion and alienation, to the point where they have become an orthodoxy. The preoccupation with violence and degradation has not always been either critical or humane; in a good deal of minority work—now sedulously imitated in commercial entertainment—it is often brutally exposed and even rationalized: a pseudo-tough modernity which is the mark of a broken spirit—a broken general spirit. As it has penetrated the crisis, in new dramatic forms, modern drama has also found ways of playing with it: reducing it back to a trick of theatre. The possibility of a controlling illuminating form, so often glimpsed and in some important cases realized, has been repeatedly contradicted by a kind of sensational displacement. This real history is still a history of crisis.

But then it is also an indication of the character of the crisis that its forms and problems so often recur: that European drama, since 1945, is so close to the world of Strindberg, some fifty years earlier; that, in particular situations, the break to naturalism—the passion for truth, in a real situation, against an artificial theatre—can be still authentically made, as in some of the new English drama of the fifties and sixties; that the trap of a room, of a street, from which a man looks at a world that at once determines and is beyond him, should go on being experienced, in comparable dramatic actions; that certain illusions hold, and can be replayed but newly experienced. Within and across the lines of development, there are these continuities, recurrences, new breaks to an already realized position. It is this double character of the history that defines the nature of the movements: there is a historical succession of naturalism, private expressionism, social expressionism, the theatre of illusion and of the absurd; but there is also a continual coexistence, in authentic work, of each one of these tendencies, in the struggle for a common form.

6

It is then necessary to emphasize the difficult relation between what are not only historical but socially alternative structures of feeling, and the consequently complex relations between conventions, theatrical methods and audiences. My essential argument is on the relation between a structure of feeling and a convention: the first critical task is always that necessary analysis. This brings to our attention, as the first kind of fact, problems of form and method which reveal themselves, ultimately, as problems of content and viewpoint. To clarify these relations is a main critical purpose, for it is then possible to see the choice between structures of feeling, and the consequent choice of conventions, as a substantial and still active history and experience, rather than a random variation of viewpoints and styles.

This is especially important, and especially difficult, in the history of the theatre. For there is a continual attempt to abstract a general "dramatic" method, a "true theatrical use", and this is frequently supported by the prestige of a successful theatre in a particular time and place. It is in fact abundantly clear, from modern drama alone (and of course from the whole wider history of drama and performance) that there is no such special orthodoxy: virtually anything can be done, virtually any method become a convention, in the pressure of actual experience. What is continually but variously defended as the special art of the theatre is always the local material-ization of particular conventions, and the history of modern drama is, to a large extent, the repeated breaking and altering of those conventions, to allow a different form to come through. Of course, when this has been done, the theatre itself is usually the first to identify with it; to dismiss, with a fine confidence, old "theatrical" methods, and to reannounce the "true" possibilities of theatre. In practice, of course, the new orthodoxy is simply repeating the posi-tion of the old orthodoxy, in relation to newly discovered dramatic forms.

The forms and conventions we have seen in such variety, in so many plays, can not, then, be reduced to varying theatrical styles. Each form and convention has to solve the problem of performance;

there is no dramatic solution until that has been done. But the method of performance is not a style applied to the play; it is, in its central importance, the necessary realization of the play's essential form. We cannot then reduce naturalism or expressionism to methods of production: to the look of the stage; to particular kinds of scenery or design; to particular ways of speaking and moving. Given that abstracted autonomy, the methods lack a dimension, and to speak of "going beyond naturalism", or "dropping all that expressionism", will often be a merely external change —a temporary fashion in the theatre—which while giving opportunities to particular kinds of drama will merely frustrate or break the back of other important kinds. What happened to Eliot's drama is a major example of this, but it is only one among many.

This false autonomy of theatrical method is in itself a symptom of the general situation that has been described. It is the absence of a reasonably common form, in modern drama as a whole, that has led both to waves of fashionable emphasis or eclecticism, and to the supposed autonomy of an internally determined production. The repeated tension between dramatists and theatres, which has been so marked in this century, is an aspect of the problems of dramatic form itself. This is especially clear in those movements of literary reform which, concentrating on the problems of dramatic speech, have neglected the central problems of dramatic action. To change a speech convention, but no other convention, is to disintegrate a form which already has its theatrical methods, and so to leave a gap which "production" is forced to fill. The problem, throughout, has been the writing of a whole form, and in the absence of any reasonably common conventions (which are of course not received, but have to be made) this raises severe problems: at root creative, but involving also the method of notation. As we pass from Ibsen's detailed stage directions to Strindberg's writing of a flow of images we see a major example of just this problem. What in orthodox naturalism is stage direction is in later forms either a creation of mood for the reader (and for that crucial reader, the producer) or an attempt to realize an action for which no theatrical notation (as opposed to a dramatic notation) was, as yet, available. Brecht's success is directly related to his willingness to make the notation in practice with a company, and this is obviously admirable. But there are real social reasons why this direct relation is often unavailable, or breaks down: not least the characteristic discontinuity of experimental theatres, and the social failure to support the institutions from which new work can come. We can look back, in this century, at enough successes, where a dramatist worked with a theatre, to see how important this opportunity can be. But we have also to look back at repeated failures and false connections, which have radically affected dramatic development.

The question of convention is, in practice, often, just this question of a relation between form and performance, which the dramatist, where possible collaboratively, has to learn to solve. But to put the matter in this way is to realize also that it is a question of audiences; it is there, in the theatre as a social institution, that conventions are really made. It is then necessary to argue for properly based and continuing dramatic companies, with the necessary time and autonomy, which are now being attempted, in many different ways, in many countries.

But it is also necessary to realize that drama is no longer coexistent with theatre, in the narrow sense. We have been used to their equation, for some centuries, but for half a century now, and with increasing effect, other means and places of performance have been discovered. The largest audience for drama, in our own world, is in the cinema and on television, and in many countries these are explicitly popular forms where the theatre is self-consciously, even willingly, a minority form. It is then very important that many of the developments we have observed, in dramatic forms and conventions, have been, in a deep way, towards these new media. For one particular kind of drama, that of early naturalism, the framed-stage theatre was exactly suited: the group trapped in a room—that substantial experience—could be immediately staged; and the audience, essentially, was in the same position. Of course, as the stage was cleared of its furniture, the frame taken down, the audience encouraged to react and participate rather than sitting trapped, many new conventions were possible. Expressionism, in particular, was well served in this kind of theatre, often with the addition of devices of film projection and broadcasting, allowing new relations between speech and action, or action and real environment. Many of the later experiments in illusion were built directly on this kind of theatrical opportunity, and on the very limitations and contradictions of the theatre. Some important work has been done in this way, but it has been possible, also, to notice a confusion of dramatic illusion with theatrical play: some recent minor work suggests, in a strange recurrence, not men trapped in a room but actors and dramatists trapped in a theatre, seeing what can be done within those accepted limits. It is often a useful exercise, but it can be an evasion, when we look at actual contemporary dramatic possibilities.

In method, film and television offer certain real solutions to many of the recurrent problems of modern dramatic form, though in practice, in ordinary use, they often simply repeat some familiar deadlocks. At the same time, these potentially liberating media, which have already released certain newly mobile forms, are often, by habit, still treated as inferior. They may get audiences, but the important work, it is felt, is still in the culturally warranted form: the theatre, where drama happens, as opposed to film and television, where entertainment happens. I do not know any real country in which this comparison can be seriously made: not only is there now a body of serious drama, in film and television, but also, in most theatres, there is work of at least no higher level than ordinary film and television production. As a cultural convention, however, the contrast persists.

I believe there can be little doubt, when the critical history of the next half-century of drama comes to be written, that the majority of its examples will be taken from these new forms. It is indeed with just this realization, and facing the acute problems of developing a critical method which would be adequate for what is in many ways a wholly new kind of analysis, that I have tried to bring together, at a decisive point of transition, the development of modern drama in its traditionally written forms. I do not of course mean that the theatre will become unimportant: for certain kinds of drama it is still essential, and it is still, in practice, inventive and innovating, so that new forms will almost certainly be developed. Again, in some kinds of work, but only some kinds, "live" performance is an advantage. But as I read the development of modern drama, and as I try to relate it to the continuing social crisis with which, throughout, it has been closely related, I see in film and television the evidence and the promise of new kinds of action, of complex seeing made actual in a directly composed performance, of new kinds of relation between action and speech, of changes in the fundamental concept of dramatic imagery, which open up not simply as techniques (as they are still, on the whole, regarded) but as responses to an altering structure of feeling, and as new and important relations with audiences. There are as many problems, in this new work, as in any of the work we have studied. The position of the writer is already quite different, and not always, in practice, to his advantage. The new relations with audiences can be exploited as often as honestly welcomed and developed. The inherited separation between "verbal" and "visual" dramatic conventions is not easily overcome, and it is possible to waste much energy in a false competition between them. But it has been a record of difficulty and struggle, throughout.

CONCLUSION

I shall try, in a later essay, to connect the history of modern drama, in its theatrical forms, with the already major achievement of modern film drama, and the already interesting achievement of television drama. But what I have defined, in the present book, is what I believe to be the meaning of the dramatic tradition of the modern theatre: a record of difficulty and struggle; but still primarily, from that first major generation to its many successors, from Ibsen to Brecht, one of the great periods of dramatic history: a major creative achievement, of our own civilization, which gives us a continuing understanding, imagination and courage.

NOTES

Page

27 "Heavy . . .": M. C. Bradbrook, *Ibsen the Norwegian*, p. 77

33 "a situation . . .": T. S. Eliot, *Hamlet, Selected Essays*, p. 145

43 "such that . . .": T. S. Eliot, *ibid.*, p. 45

43 "The illusion . . .": Henrik Ibsen, letter to Gosse, *Collected Works* (Heinemann) Vol. V, p. xiv

47 "the classic . . .": William Archer, in Ibsen: *Collected Works* (Heinemann) Vol. VI, p. xii

53 Brandes: *Ibsen and Bjornson, Dramatic Opinions*, p. 31 and p. 115
   Lee: *The Ibsen Secret*, p. 4
   Faguet: quoted in Lee, *op. cit.*, p. 116

54 Bradbrook: *Ibsen the Norwegian*, p. 98 and p. 99
   Archer: introduction to *Masterbuilder Solness*, in *Collected Works* (Heinemann), Vol. X, p. xxviii
   Sprinchorn: *The Genius of the Scandinavian Theater*, p. 81

63 Mankowitz: *The Critic*, Autumn 1947, p. 82

70 "ultimately . . .": G. Wilson Knight, *The Wheel of Fire*, p. 16

71 "drama . . .": D. H. Lawrence, *Sea and Sardinia*, p. 189

77 "In the '80s . . .": *Memorandum to the Members of the Intimate Theatre* (1908)

82 "drama . . ." Cf. note on 71

126 Peacock, *The Poet and the Theatre*

135 Freyer: in *Politics and Letters*, Spring 1948, p. 5

175 a "form . . .": T. S. Eliot, *A Dialogue on Dramatic Poetry, Selected Essays*, p. 50

176 one "character . . .": *The Use of Poetry and the Use of Criticism*, p. 153

190 ". . . network . . .": T. S. Eliot, *Ben Jonson, Selected Essays*, p. 155

194 "If one . . .": *Edinburgh Evening Dispatch*, 26 August 1953

201 "The rescue . . .": W. H. Auden in Flores: *The Kafka Problem*, p. 47

211 "The all-important . . .": *The Dark Tower*, p. 12

212 Brinnin: *Dylan Thomas in America*

236 "raid . . .": T. S. Eliot, *East Coker*, V

253 Turner: in *Scrutinies* (ed. Rickword), p. 139

297 "the secret . . .": *La Tragédie du langage*, p. 6
   "As plots . . .": *L'Invraisemblable, l'insolite, mon univers*, p. 1

299 ". . . spectacle . . .": *Discovering the Theatre*, p. 6

315 "only the victims": Introduction to translation, *Four Plays*

INDEX

Figures in *italics* indicate principal references

Abbey Theatre, *115-18*, 147, 151, 153
Adding Machine, The, 261, 267
Advent, 93
Aeschylus, 16, 176, 220, 222, 225
After the Fall, 275-6
Alfieri, 223, 226
All My Sons, 268-73
Anna Christie, 267, 293
Anniversary, The, 105-6
Anouilh, Jean, 21, 222, *227-9*, 331
Antigone (Anouilh), 222, *227-9*
Antoine, 77
Archer, William, 54, 101
Arden, John, 21, 211, *325-8*
Aristotle, 277-8
Arms and the Man, 163, 248-9, 254
Ascent of F6, The, 199, *202-5*, 261
At the Hawk's Well, 118-19, 126
Auden, W. H., *199-206*, 261, 273, 341
Audience, The, 167
Auto-da-Fé, 64
Avaries, Les, 247

Baal, 283
Babbitt, 272
Back to Methuselah, 249, 252-3
Balcony, The, 305-8
Bald Prima Donna, The, 296-7
Baudelaire, 129
Beaver Coat, The, 240
Becket, 117
Beckett, Samuel, 21, *299-305*, 323, 324,
    340, 341
Berliner Ensemble, 277
Berretto a Sonagli, Il, 163
Birthday Party, The, 322-5
Bishop's Bonfire, The, 153
Bjornson, B., 75
Blood Wedding, *167-70*, 171, 172
Bradbrook, M. C., 54
Bradley, A. C., 245
Brand, 11, 26, 33, *34-9*, 42, 43, 44,
    46, 50, 51, 58, 64, 65, 67, 70, 74,
    226
Brandes, G., 38, 53
Brecht, Bertolt, 20, 21, 220, 234, *277-90*,
    312, 313, 326, 331, 341, 344, 347
Brieux, E., 246-7
Brinnin, J. M., 212
Büchner, Georg, 21, *233-9*, 240, 289,
    331, 337

Burnt Norton, 86
Butterfly's Evil Spell, The, 167

Calderón, 167
Calvary, 126
Camus, Albert, 220
Candida, *247-51*, 254, 255
Canetti, Elias, 64
Capek, K., 261
Cat and the Moon, The, 126
Cat on a Hot Tin Roof, 267-8
Cathleen ni Houlihan, 122
Caucasian Chalk Circle, The, 277, *283-4*
Celestina, 167
Chekhov, Anton, 21, 57, *101-11*, 159,
    165, 221, 244, 257, 279, 290, 316,
    331, 335, 338, 340
Cherry Orchard, The, 101, 105, 106, *107-9*
Chiarelli, Luigi, *159-61*
Choephoroi, 176
Cock-a-doodle Dandy, 153
Cocktail Party, The, 39, *188-94*, 195, 197,
    325
Collier's Friday Night, A, 257-9
Commedia dell' arte, *160-1*
Confidential Clerk, The, *194-7*
Conrad, Joseph, 69
Convention, *12-16*, 20-1, 27-30, 49, 99,
    278-81, 288-90, 297, 312, 324, 331-2,
    334-5, 339-41, 343-6
Countess Cathleen, The, 119-21
Creditors, 77, 85
Crimes and Crimes, 93
Crucible, The, *273*, 275

Dance of Death, The, (Auden), 199
Dance of Death, The, (Strindberg), 49,
    76, *93-4*
Danton's Death, 233, *236-9*
Dark is Light Enough, The, 316
Dark Tower, The, 212
Daughter-in-Law, The, 257-8
David, 257
Dead, The, 146
Death of a Salesman, 268, *270-3*
Death of Cuchulain, The, 127-8
Deirdre, 122-3
Deirdre of the Sorrows, 129, 131, *137-40*
Desire under the Elms, 267, 293
Devil's Disciple, The, 207, 254
Doctor's Dilemma, The, 249

Dog Beneath the Skin, The, 199-204
Doll's House, A, 25, 26, 32, 47-50, 53, 54, 55, 75, 80, 94
Draw the Fires, 261
Drayman Henschel, 240
Dreaming of the Bones, The, 126
Dreamplay, 76, 83, 95-6
Dubliners, 146
Dumas fils, 240
Dürrenmatt, Friedrich, 21, *312-15*

Each in his own Way, 164
East Coker, 86
Easter, 93-5
Elder Statesman, The, 174, *197-8*
Electra (Euripides), 220-1
Electra (Sophocles), 220-1
Electre, 222-5
Eliot, George, 116
Eliot, T. S., 21, 63, 122, 135, *174-98*, 217, 228, 319, 323, 325, 331, 333, 335
Elizabethan drama, 30, 49, 289
Emperor and Galilean, 26, 43, *44-7*, 51, 65
Emperor Jones, 276, 293
Enemy of the People, An, 53, 55, 243
Epic theatre, *277-9*, 331
Eric XIV, 93
Euripides, 220-1
Exiles, 141-6
Expressionism, 11, 20, 73-4, 93, 99, 151-2, 165, 201, 234, *261-6*, 267, 271-2, 289, 302, 305, 315, 331, *338-45*

Faguet, E., 53, 66
Family Reunion, The, *183-8*, 189, 190, 191, 197
Father, The, 49, 76, 77, *78-80*, 85, 93
Fear and Misery in the Third Reich, 282
Feast at Solhoug, The, 31
Fielding, H., 244
Fight for Barbara, The, 257-8
Film, 43, 93, 336, 345-6
Finnegans Wake, 141
Fire Raisers, The, 308-12
Flies, The, 222, 225-7
Four Quartets, 87, 187-8
Freud, S., 220, 222
Freyer, G., 135, 137
Frisch, Max, 21, *308-12*, 313
From Morn till Midnight, 261
Fry, Christopher, 206-11, 217, 316, 319

Galileo Galilei, The Life of, 277, 284-5, *287-8*, 313
Galsworthy, J., 254
Genet, Jean, 21, *305-8*
Gerontion, 174, 198

Ghosts, 25,' 26, 47, *50-3*, 55, 65, 74, 75, 167, 339
Ghost Sonata, 76, 83, *96-9*
Giraudoux, Jean, 21, 222, *223-5*, 229
Giuoco delle Parti, 161
Good Woman of Sezuan, The, 277, *282-3*
Granville-Barker, H., 185
Great God Brown, The, 293
Greek drama, 27, 28, 179, 180, 220-1, 223, 277, 309
Green Helmet, The, 124-5
Greene, Graham, 221
Grein, J. T., 244
Gustavus Vasa, 93

Hairy Ape, The, 267, 293
Hamlet, 27, 223
Hardy, Thomas, 116
Hauptmann, Gerhart, 21, 228, *240-3*, 261, 337
Heartbreak House, 316
Hedda Gabler, 25, 26, 50, 53, 54, *62-4*, 65, 67, 74
Hegel, 302
Henry the Fourth, 162, *164-6*
Herne's Egg, The, 127
Hinkemann, 261, 263, 264
Hopkins, G. M., 233
Hoppla!, 261-6
Hour-Glass, The, 125
House of Bernarda Alba, The, 167, *172-3*
Huxley, Aldous, 74

Ibsen, Henrik, 11, 15, 16, 20, 21, *25-74*, 75, 80, 101, 102, 103, 106, 109, 116, 129, 130, 134, 141, 157, 167, 175, 184, 201, 220, 221, 226, 228, 240, 243, 244, 246, 247, 257, 268, 270, 277, 278, 290, 293, 294, 331, 333, 334, 335, 337, 338, 340, 341, 344, 347
If Five Years Pass, 167
Intrigue drama, *27-32*, 44, 159-60, 228, 315
Ionesco, Eugene, 21, *296-9*, 323, 324, 341
Iphigenia in Delphi, 240
Isherwood, Christopher, *199-206*, 261, 341
Ivanov, 103, 106

Jew of Malta, The, 63
John Bull's Other Island, 254
John Gabriel Borkman, 65, 67, 70, 94, 134 188
Johnston, Denis, 186
Jones, Daniel, 212
Jonson, Ben, 129, 135

Joyce, James, 21, *141-6*, 215-17, 305, 340
Jung, C. G., 220
Juno and the Paycock, *148-9*, 150, 151

Kaiser, G., 261
King's Threshold, The, 122-3

Lady from the Sea, 62, 65, 67
Lady Inger of Ostraat, 30-1
Lady Julie, 50, 55, 64, 76, 77, 78, *81-5*, 96, 167, 268
Lady's not for Burning, The, 207, 210
Land of Heart's Desire, The, 119-20
Lawrence, D. H., 21, 75, 257-60, 320, 336, 337
League of Youth, The, 26, 43, 47, 268
Leavis, F. R., 120
Lee, J., 53-4
Lesson, The, 296-9
Lillo, G., 30
Little Eyolf, 65, 67-70
London Merchant, The, 30
Long Day's Journey into Night, 223, 267, *293-6*
Look Back in Anger, 318-22
Lorca, Federico Garcia, 21, *167-73*
Love after Death, 167
Love's Comedy, 32
Lucky Peter's Travels, 76, 95

Ma non è una cosa seria, 161
Macbeth, 30
Machine Wreckers, The, 261
MacNeice, Louis, 211-12
Magic Mountain, The, 312
Mankowitz, W., 63
Mann, Thomas, 312
Mansfield, K., 258
Marching Song, 316-8
Marlowe, C., 63
Married Man, The, 257-8
Mask and the Face, The, 159-60
Masses and Man, 261
Masterbuilder, The, 26, 33, 64, 65, *66-7*, 68
Master Olof, 76
Measures Taken, The, 281
Memory of Two Mondays, A, 273-5
Merry-go-Round, The, 257-8
Michael Kramer, 240
Miller, Arthur, 21, *267-76*
Molière, 129, 135
Moon in the Yellow River, 186
Moore, George, 117
Mother Courage and her Children, 277, 284, 285-7, 288
Mourning Becomes Electra, *222-3*, 267, 293

Munro, C. K., 206
Murder in the Cathedral, 39, 174, *179-83*, 188, 193, 228
Myth, 21, *220-9*

Naturalism, 11, 13-14, 20, 47-50, 52-3, 73, 81, 85-6, 101, 111, 131, 145-6, 151, 157, 159, 165, 175, 240-3, 265-6, 270, 278, 279, 288-90, 293, 316-22, 323, 325, *331-42*, 344
Nemirovich-Danchenko, 111
Nightingale in Wittenberg, The, 95
Nōh drama, 127

O'Casey, Sean, 21, *147-53*, 241
Odets, C., 267
Odour of Chrysanthemums, 258-60
On Baile's Strand, 123-4
O'Neill, Eugene, 21, 99, *222-3*, 267, 293-6, 340
Only Jealousy of Emer, The, 126
On the Frontier, 199, *205-6*
Oresteia, 220-1
Orestes (Alfieri), 223
Orestes (Voltaire), 223
Osborne, John, 21, 202, *318-22*

Paid on Both Sides, 199
Peacock, R., 126
Peer Gynt, 11, 26, 33, *39-43*, 44, 50, 58, 64, 65, 67, 70, 74, 76, 87, 136, 169, 201
Pensaci Giacomino, 161, 163
Philanderer, The, 247-8
Physicists, The, 312-15
Piacere dell' Onestà, Il, 161
Pillars of Society, 43, 47, 51, 53, 55
Pinter, Harold, 21, 322-5, 340
Pirandello, Luigi, 21, 50, *157-66*, *244*, 290, 299, 312, 313, 331, 341
Playboy of the Western World, The, 129, 130, 131, 133, *135-7*, 147, 149
Playing with Fire, 85
Plough and the Stars, The, 150-1
Portrait of a Lady, 174, 176
Pot of Broth, The, 122
Pretenders, The, 26, *33*, 34, 64, 65
Prufrock, 174
Purgatory, 127

Quintessence of Ibsenism, The, 25, *244*, 246

Rainbow, The, 80
Red Roses for Me, 153
Renaissance drama, 27, 28, 336
Resurrection, The, 127
Rhinoceros, The, 296

Rice, E., 261, 267
Riders to the Sea, 129, 131, *133*, 149, 336
Right you are, 162-4
Rilke, R. M., 25
Road to Damascus, The, 76, *86-93*, 95, 221, 261, 339
Rock, The, 174, 178-9
Rojas, F. de, 167
Romantic literature, 13, 70, 159, 166, 233, 339
Rosmersholm, 40, 53, 54, *58-62*, 65, 74, 268
Rumour, The, 206
R.U.R., 261

Saga of the Folkungs, 93
Saint Joan, 252-6
Sartre, J.-P., 21, 222, *225-7*, 229
Scott, C., 25
Seagull, The, 57, *101-4*, 106, 111
Serjeant Musgrave's Dance, 211, 325-8
Shadow of a Gunman, The, *147-8*, 151
Shadow of the Glen, The, 129, 130, *131-2*, 133
Shadowy Waters, The, 121-2
Shakespeare, 16, 27, 135, 175, 177, 223, 237, 245-6, 251, 257, 289, 335
Shaw, G. B., 21, 25, 32, 34, 65, 163, 182, 207, 241, *244-56*, 316
Shoemaker's Prodigious Wife, The, 167
Silver Tassie, The, *151-3*, 241
Six Characters in search of an Author, 157-9, 160, 161, 162, 164
Sleep of Prisoners, A, 210-211
Sons and Lovers, 258
Sophocles, 220-1, 223
Sprinchorn, E., 54
Stanislavsky, K., 15, 16, 111, 279, 340
Star Turns Red, The, 153
Strange Interlude, 293
Strindberg, August, 21, 49, 50, 64, *75-100*, 106, 109, 159, 163, 167, 169, 175, 201, 220, 221, 228, 240, 244, 257, 261, 267, 277, 290, 293, 294, 296, 299, 305, 320, 331, 332, 333, 338, 340, 341, 342, 344
Stronger, The, 85
Structure of feeling, 12, *16-20*, 21, 99, 107, 290, 297, 331, 340, 343
Sunken Bell, The, 240
Sweeney Agonistes, 174, *176-8*, 183, 184, 323
Symbolism, 53-7, 73, 102-4, 221, 261
Synge, J. M., 21, 122, *129-40*, 244, 254, 260, 305, 336, 337

Tennyson, Alfred, 117
Thérèse Raquin, 77

Third Man, The, 221
Thomas, Dylan, 211-19
Three Sisters, The, 105-7, *109-10*
Threepenny Opera, 278, 281
Tinker's Wedding, The, 129-31, *132*, 133
Titus Andronicus, 30
Toller, Ernst, 21, *261-6*, 341
Tonight We Improvise, 160
Touch and Go, 257-8
Toumanova, N. A., 103
Transfiguration, 265
Turner, W. J., 253
Tutto per Bene, 162

Ulysses, 141, 146, 215-17
Ulysses' Bow, 240
Uncle Vanya, 105
Under Milk Wood, 212-19
Unicorn from the Stars, The, 125

Vega, Lope de, 167
Venus Observed, 207, 210
Verity, A. W., 245
Victorian theatre, 118, 248
View from the Bridge, A, 274-5
Vikings at Helgeland, The, 31-2
Vishnevsky, A. S., 101
Voltaire, 223, 226

Waiting for Godot, 299-305
Waiting for Lefty, 267
Waste, 185
Waste Land, The, 174, 176
Weavers, The, *240-3*, 261
Wedekind, F., 261
Well of the Saints, The, 129, 131, *133-5*, 162
When We Dead Awaken, 26, 33, 46, 59, 64, 65, 67, 68, *70-4*, 141, 144, 201
Where there is Nothing, 125
Whiting, John, 21, *316-18*
Widowers' Houses, 241, 247, 249
Widowing of Mrs Holroyd, The, 257-60
Wild Duck, The, 53, 54, *56-8*, 60, 65, 67, 68, 80, 94, 102, 103, 109, 134
Wilde, Oscar, 207
Williams, Tennessee, 267-8, 274
Women in Love, 258
Wood Spirit, The, 103
Wordsworth, William, 235
World of Paul Slickey, The, 202
Woyzeck, *233-6*, 238, 326
Wuthering Heights, 80, 85

Yeats, W. B., 21, *115-28*, 138
Yerma, 167, *170-2*

Zola, E., 77, 130, 240